STUDIO JMS PRESENTS...

# TEN GRAND ™

VOLUME 1

WRITTEN BY:
### J. MICHAEL STRACZYNSKI

ILLUSTRATED BY:
### BEN TEMPLESMITH
(IS...

### & C.P.
(ISSUE #4 PG. 22 WIT...

LETT...
### TROY PETE...

•••••

BOOK DESIGN, LAYOUT
& SERIES PRODUCTION EDITING:
### PHIL SMITH

PRODUCTION:
### JENNA SAVAGE

•••••

COVER AND LOGO BY: BEN TEMPLESMITH

•••••

FOR STUDIO JMS:
### PATRICIA TALLMAN CEO

PUBLISHED BY
### IMAGE COMICS WITH
### STUDIO JMS & JOE'S COMICS

**IMAGE COMICS, INC.**
Robert Kirkman - Chief Operating Officer
Erik Larsen - Chief Financial Officer
Todd McFarlane - President
Marc Silvestri - Chief Executive Officer
Jim Valentino - Vice-President

Eric Stephenson - Publisher
Ron Richards - Director of Business Development
Jennifer de Guzman - Director of Trade Book Sales
Kat Salazar - PR & Marketing Coordinator
Jeremy Sullivan - Digital Marketing Coordinator
Jamie Parreno - Online Marketing Coordinator
Emilio Bautista - Sales Assistant
Branwyn Bigglestone - Senior Accounts Manager
Emily Miller - Accounts Manager
Jaemie Dudas - Administrative Assistant
Tyler Shainline - Events Coordinator
David Brothers - Content Manager
Jonathan Chan - Production Manager
Drew Gill - Art Director
Meredith Wallace - Print Manager
Monica Garcia - Senior Production Artist
Jenna Savage - Production Artist
Addison Duke - Production Artist
**IMAGECOMICS.COM**

**JOE'S COMICS**
a division of Studio JMS
*for more information go to*
**www.studiojms.com**

to find the comic shop
nearest you call:
**1-888-COMICBOOK**

COMIC SHOP LOCATOR SERVICE
**888-COMIC-BOOK**
**888-266-4226**

**TEN GRAND** trade paperback volume 1, ISBN: 978-1-60706-831-0, $12.99 USD. November 2013. FIRST PRINTING.
Published by Image Comics, Inc. Office of Publication: 2001 Center Street, Sixth Floor, Berkeley, CA 94704. Originally published as TEN GRAND #1-6.
TEN GRAND ™ & © 2013 Studio JMS. "Ten Grand," the Ten Grand logos and the likeness of all featured characters are trademarks of Studio JMS. All
rights reserved. Image Comics ® and its logos are registered trademarks of Image Comics, Inc. Any resemblance to actual persons (living or dead), events,
institutions, or locales, without satiric intent, is coincidental. No portion of this publication may be reproduced or transmitted, in any form or by any means,
without the express written permission of Studio JMS. Printed in the U.S.A. For information regarding the CPSIA on this printed material call: 203-595-3636
and provide reference # RICH – 539325. For foreign licensing and international rights contact: foreignlicensing@imagecomics.com

# TABLE OF CONTENTS
## ORIGINAL EDITION SERIES "A" COVERS BY: BEN TEMPLESMITH

*TEN GRAND #1,*
*COVER "B" BY:*
*BILL SIENKIEWICZ*

*TEN GRAND #1,*
*COVER "C"*
*C2E2 EXCLUSIVE BY:*
*BEN TEMPLESMITH*

*TEN GRAND #1,*
*COVER "D"*
*DYNAMIC FORCES EXCLUSIVE BY:*
*JAE LEE*

*TEN GRAND #1,*
*COVER "E"*
*DYNAMIC FORCES EXCLUSIVE BY:*
*JAE LEE*

*TEN GRAND #1,*
*COVER "F"*
*PHANTOM VARIANT BY:*
*RYAN SOOK*

*TEN GRAND #1,*
*COVER "G"*
*FORBIDDEN PLANET VARIANT BY:*
*BEN TEMPLESMITH*

*TEN GRAND #1,*
*COVER "H"*
*MILE HIGH COMICS VARIANT BY:*
*BEN TEMPLESMITH*

*TEN GRAND #1,*
*COVER "I"*
*SECOND PRINTING*
*BEN TEMPLESMITH*

*TEN GRAND #2,*
*COVER "B"*
*BILL SIENKIEWICZ*

*TEN GRAND #4,*
*COVER "B"*
*SAN DIEGO COMIC-CON VARIANT BY:*
*BEN TEMPLESMITH*

. . . . .

# EVOLUTION OF THE COVER...PG. 158

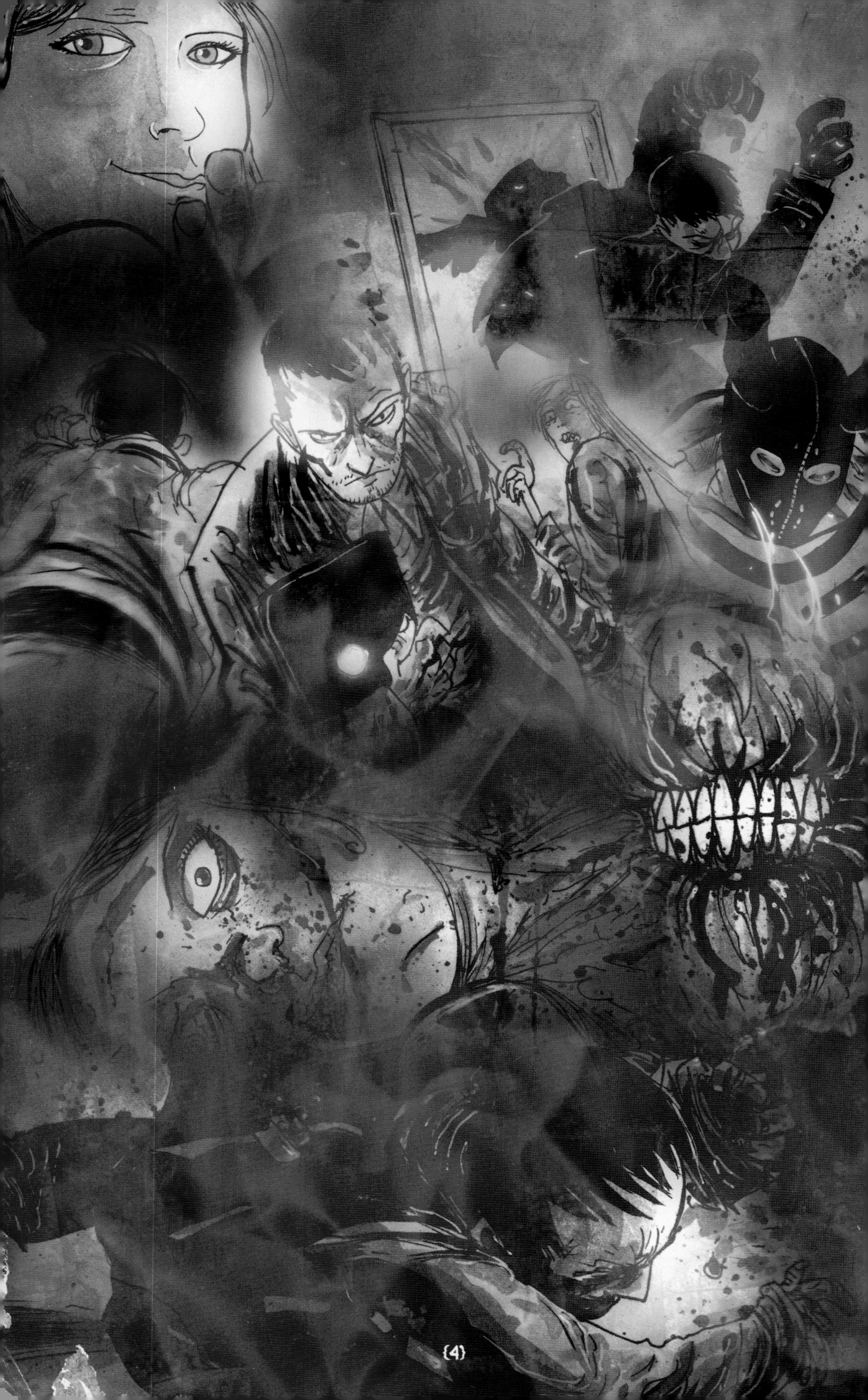

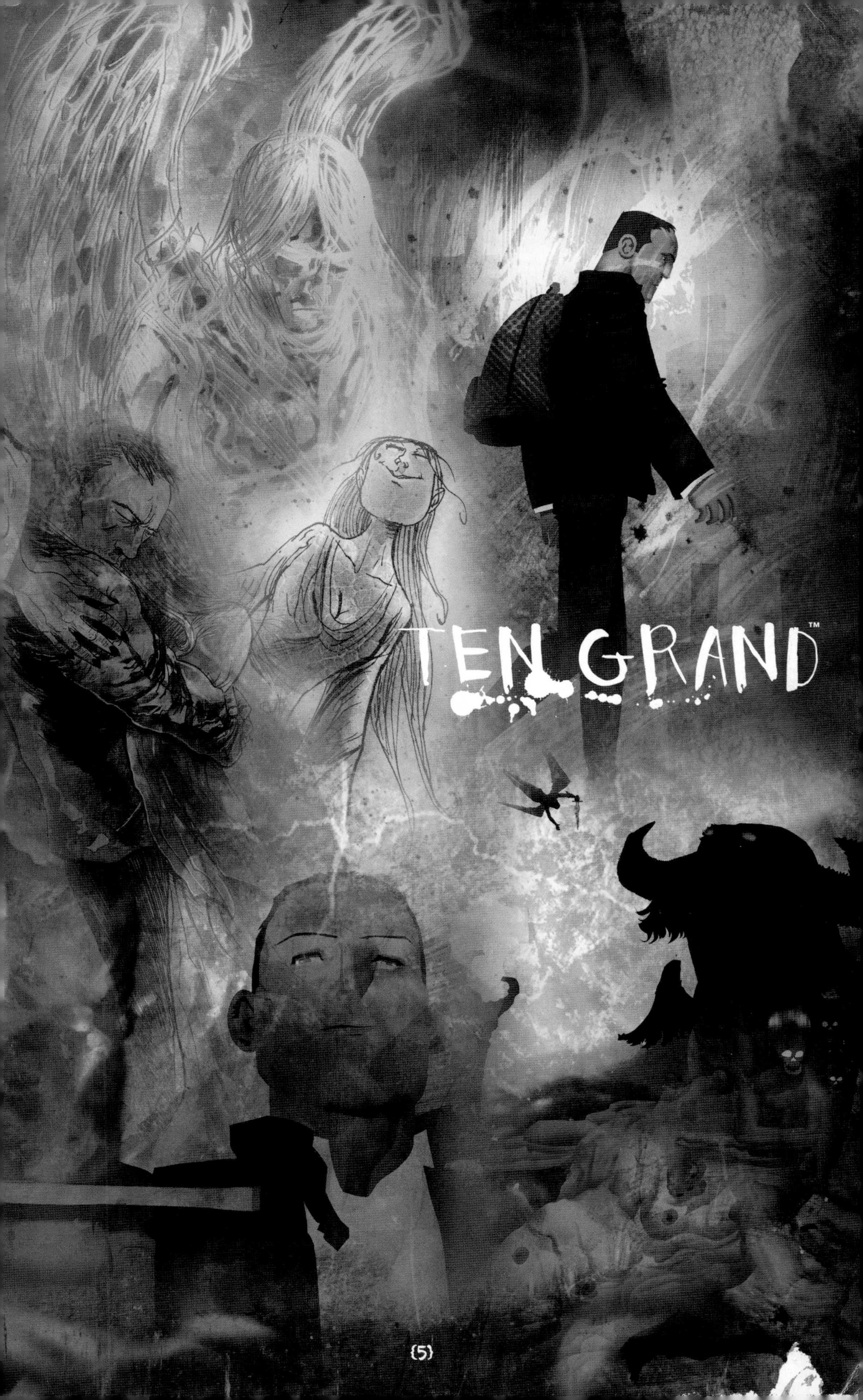
TEN GRAND™

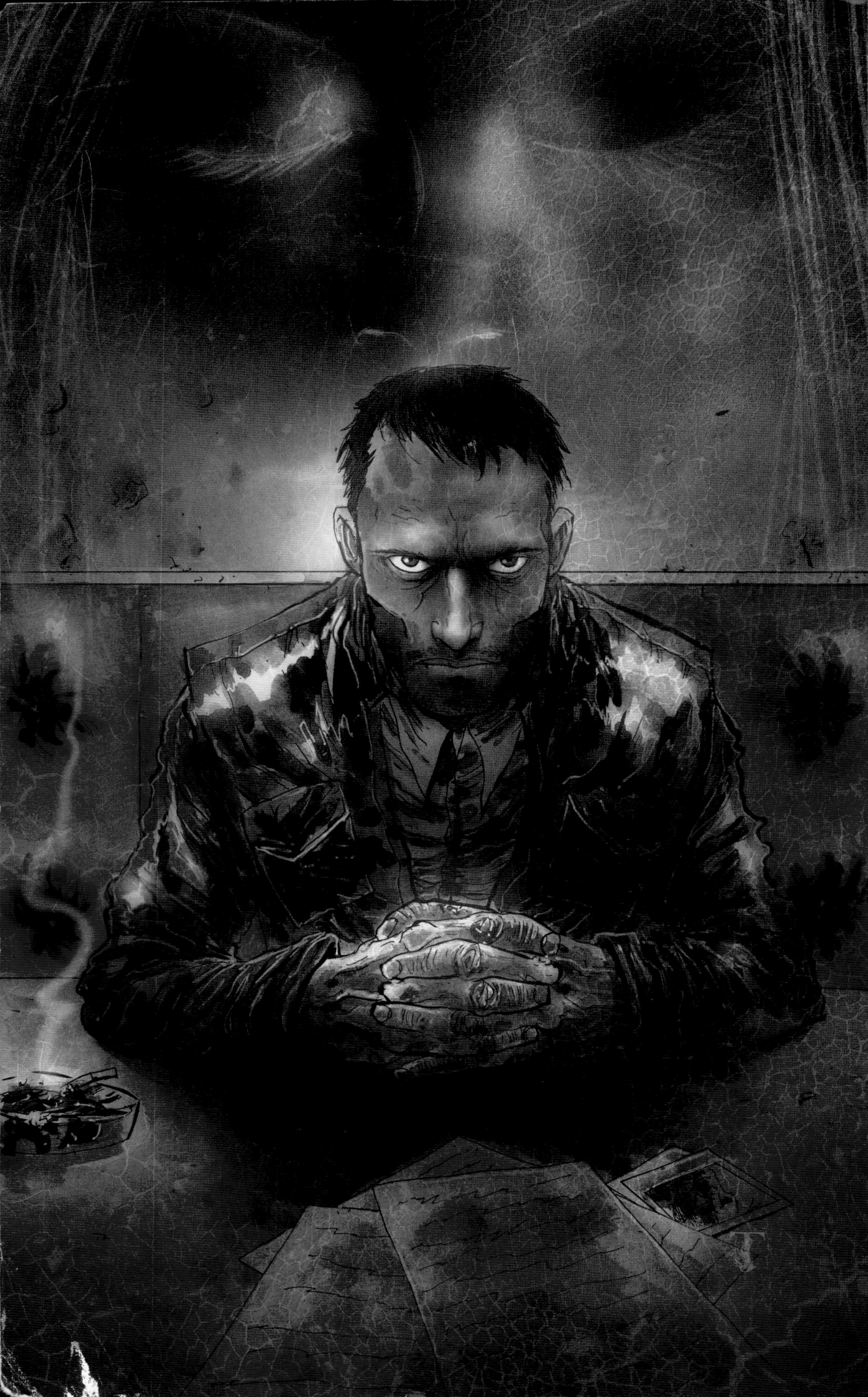

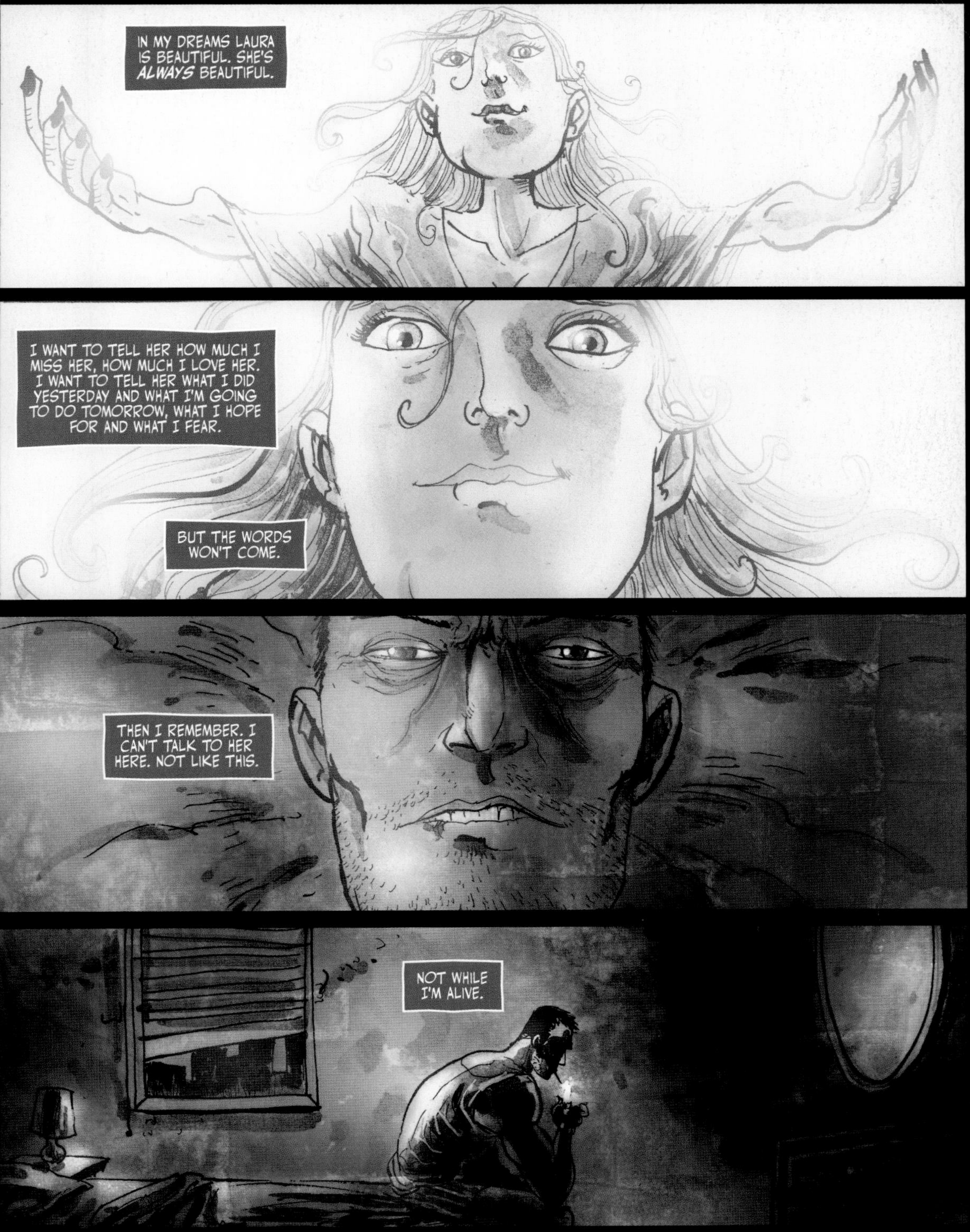
IN MY DREAMS LAURA IS BEAUTIFUL. SHE'S *ALWAYS* BEAUTIFUL.
I WANT TO TELL HER HOW MUCH I MISS HER, HOW MUCH I LOVE HER. I WANT TO TELL HER WHAT I DID YESTERDAY AND WHAT I'M GOING TO DO TOMORROW, WHAT I HOPE FOR AND WHAT I FEAR.
BUT THE WORDS WON'T COME.
THEN I REMEMBER. I CAN'T TALK TO HER HERE. NOT LIKE THIS.
NOT WHILE I'M ALIVE.

# BLOOD OATH

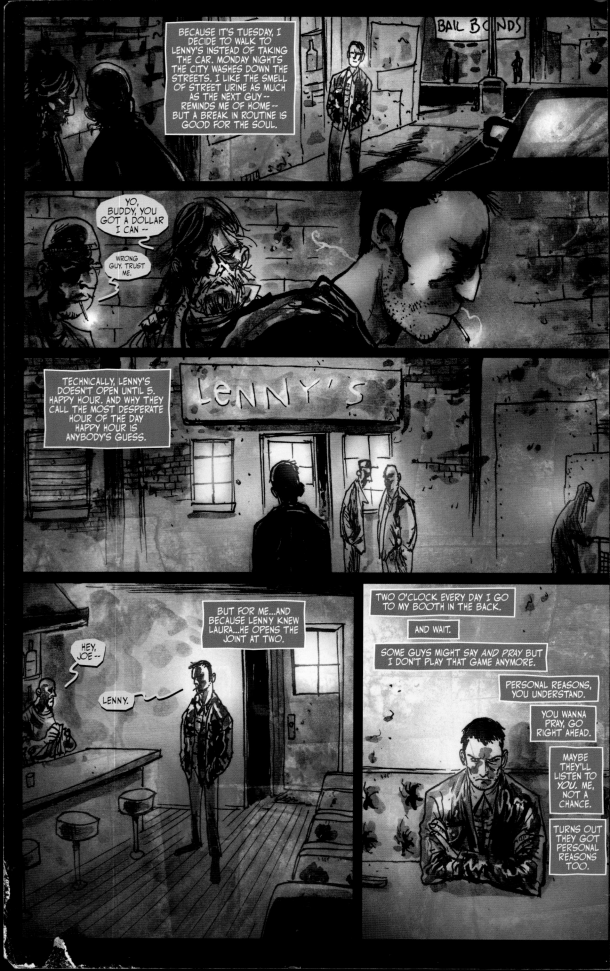

BECAUSE IT'S TUESDAY, I DECIDE TO WALK TO LENNY'S INSTEAD OF TAKING THE CAR. MONDAY NIGHTS THE CITY WASHES DOWN THE STREETS. I LIKE THE SMELL OF STREET URINE AS MUCH AS THE NEXT GUY-- REMINDS ME OF HOME-- BUT A BREAK IN ROUTINE IS GOOD FOR THE SOUL.

YO, BUDDY, YOU GOT A DOLLAR I CAN--

WRONG GUY. TRUST ME.

TECHNICALLY, LENNY'S DOESN'T OPEN UNTIL 5. HAPPY HOUR. AND WHY THEY CALL THE MOST DESPERATE HOUR OF THE DAY HAPPY HOUR IS ANYBODY'S GUESS.

BUT FOR ME...AND BECAUSE LENNY KNEW LAURA...HE OPENS THE JOINT AT TWO.

HEY, JOE--

LENNY.

TWO O'CLOCK EVERY DAY I GO TO MY BOOTH IN THE BACK.

AND WAIT.

SOME GUYS MIGHT SAY AND PRAY BUT I DON'T PLAY THAT GAME ANYMORE.

PERSONAL REASONS, YOU UNDERSTAND.

YOU WANNA PRAY, GO RIGHT AHEAD.

MAYBE THEY'LL LISTEN TO YOU. ME, NOT A CHANCE.

TURNS OUT THEY GOT PERSONAL REASONS TOO.

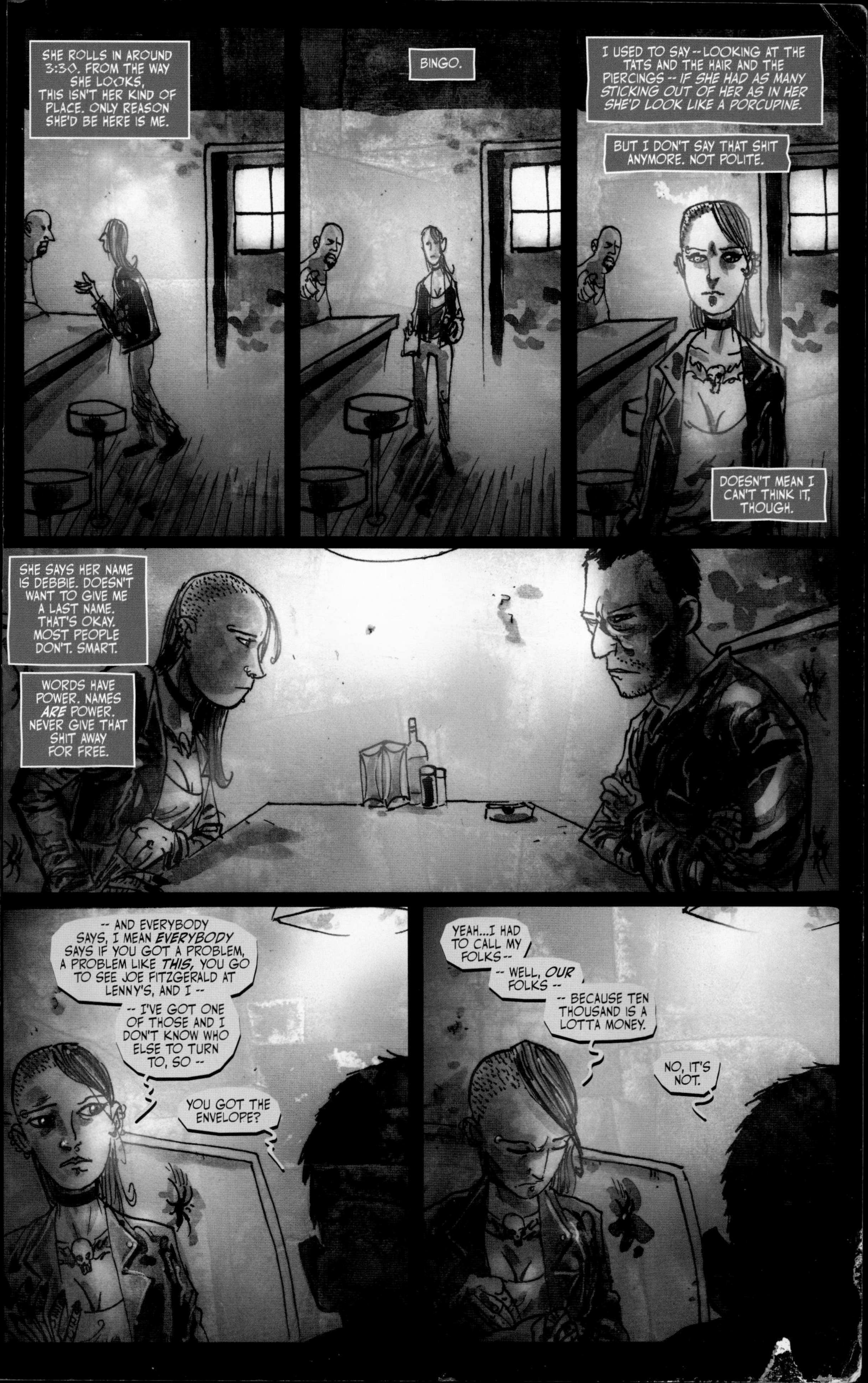
SHE ROLLS IN AROUND 3:30. FROM THE WAY SHE LOOKS, THIS ISN'T HER KIND OF PLACE. ONLY REASON SHE'D BE HERE IS ME.
BINGO.
I USED TO SAY--LOOKING AT THE TATS AND THE HAIR AND THE PIERCINGS--IF SHE HAD AS MANY STICKING OUT OF HER AS IN HER SHE'D LOOK LIKE A PORCUPINE.
BUT I DON'T SAY THAT SHIT ANYMORE. NOT POLITE.
DOESN'T MEAN I CAN'T THINK IT, THOUGH.
SHE SAYS HER NAME IS DEBBIE. DOESN'T WANT TO GIVE ME A LAST NAME. THAT'S OKAY. MOST PEOPLE DON'T. SMART.
WORDS HAVE POWER. NAMES *ARE* POWER. NEVER GIVE THAT SHIT AWAY FOR FREE.
-- AND EVERYBODY SAYS, I MEAN *EVERYBODY* SAYS IF YOU GOT A PROBLEM, A PROBLEM LIKE *THIS,* YOU GO TO SEE JOE FITZGERALD AT LENNY'S, AND I --
-- I'VE GOT ONE OF THOSE AND I DON'T KNOW WHO ELSE TO TURN TO, SO --
YOU GOT THE ENVELOPE?
YEAH...I HAD TO CALL MY FOLKS --
-- WELL, *OUR* FOLKS --
-- BECAUSE TEN THOUSAND IS A LOTTA MONEY.
NO, IT'S NOT.

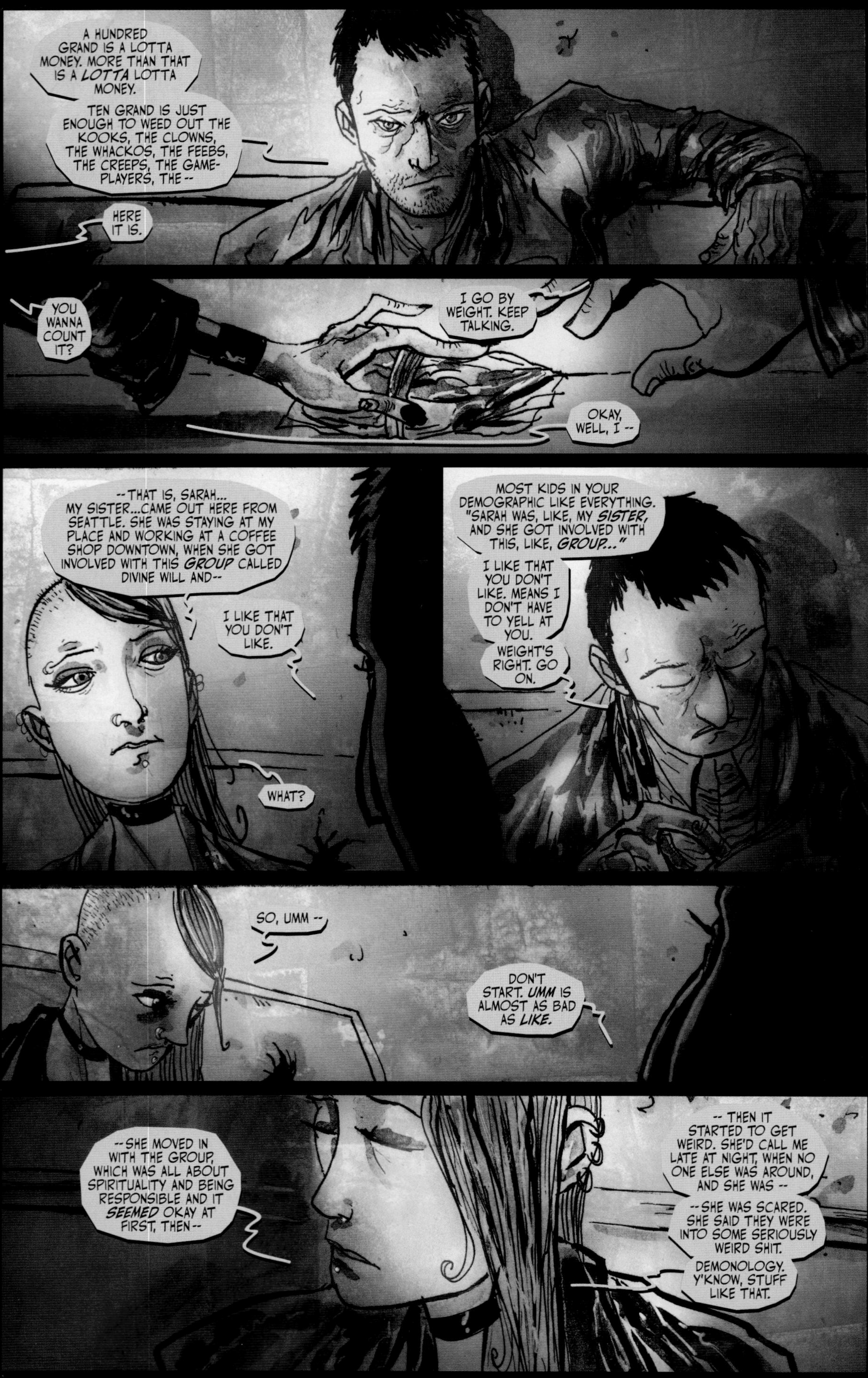
A HUNDRED GRAND IS A LOTTA MONEY. MORE THAN THAT IS A *LOTTA* LOTTA MONEY.
TEN GRAND IS JUST ENOUGH TO WEED OUT THE KOOKS, THE CLOWNS, THE WHACKOS, THE FEEBS, THE CREEPS, THE GAME-PLAYERS, THE --
HERE IT IS.
YOU WANNA COUNT IT?
I GO BY WEIGHT. KEEP TALKING.
OKAY, WELL, I --
--THAT IS, SARAH... MY SISTER...CAME OUT HERE FROM SEATTLE. SHE WAS STAYING AT MY PLACE AND WORKING AT A COFFEE SHOP DOWNTOWN, WHEN SHE GOT INVOLVED WITH THIS *GROUP* CALLED DIVINE WILL AND--
I LIKE THAT YOU DON'T LIKE.
WHAT?
MOST KIDS IN YOUR DEMOGRAPHIC LIKE EVERYTHING. "SARAH WAS, LIKE, MY *SISTER*, AND SHE GOT INVOLVED WITH THIS, LIKE, *GROUP*..."
I LIKE THAT YOU DON'T LIKE. MEANS I DON'T HAVE TO YELL AT YOU.
WEIGHT'S RIGHT. GO ON.
SO, UMM --
DON'T START. *UMM* IS ALMOST AS BAD AS *LIKE*.
--SHE MOVED IN WITH THE GROUP, WHICH WAS ALL ABOUT SPIRITUALITY AND BEING RESPONSIBLE AND IT *SEEMED* OKAY AT FIRST, THEN--
-- THEN IT STARTED TO GET WEIRD. SHE'D CALL ME LATE AT NIGHT, WHEN NO ONE ELSE WAS AROUND, AND SHE WAS --
--SHE WAS SCARED. SHE SAID THEY WERE INTO SOME SERIOUSLY WEIRD SHIT.
DEMONOLOGY. Y'KNOW, STUFF LIKE THAT.

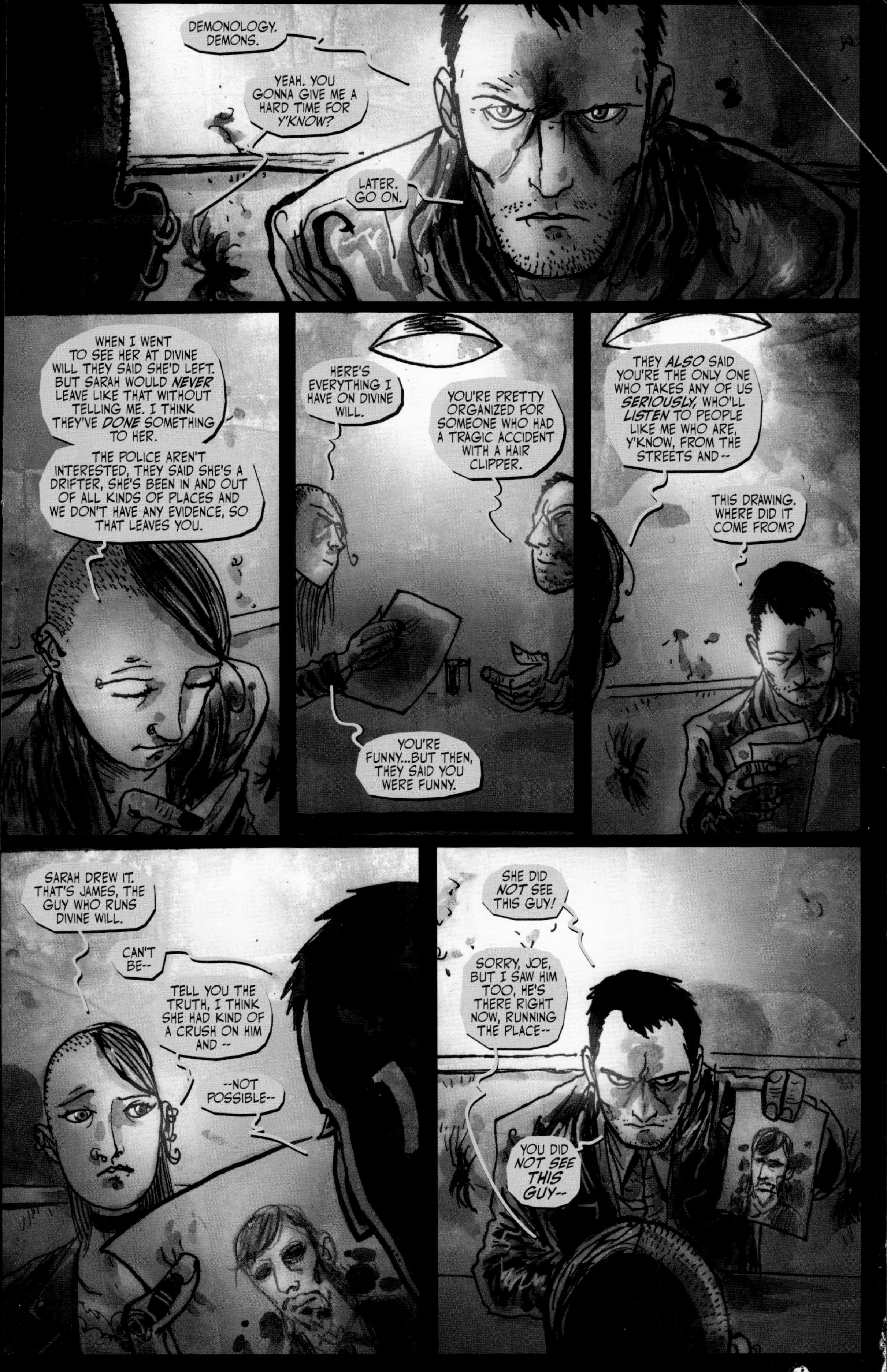
DEMONOLOGY. DEMONS.
YEAH. YOU GONNA GIVE ME A HARD TIME FOR Y'KNOW?
LATER. GO ON.
WHEN I WENT TO SEE HER AT DIVINE WILL THEY SAID SHE'D LEFT. BUT SARAH WOULD NEVER LEAVE LIKE THAT WITHOUT TELLING ME. I THINK THEY'VE DONE SOMETHING TO HER.
THE POLICE AREN'T INTERESTED, THEY SAID SHE'S A DRIFTER, SHE'S BEEN IN AND OUT OF ALL KINDS OF PLACES AND WE DON'T HAVE ANY EVIDENCE, SO THAT LEAVES YOU.
HERE'S EVERYTHING I HAVE ON DIVINE WILL.
YOU'RE PRETTY ORGANIZED FOR SOMEONE WHO HAD A TRAGIC ACCIDENT WITH A HAIR CLIPPER.
YOU'RE FUNNY...BUT THEN, THEY SAID YOU WERE FUNNY.
THEY ALSO SAID YOU'RE THE ONLY ONE WHO TAKES ANY OF US SERIOUSLY, WHO'LL LISTEN TO PEOPLE LIKE ME WHO ARE, Y'KNOW, FROM THE STREETS AND --
THIS DRAWING. WHERE DID IT COME FROM?
SARAH DREW IT. THAT'S JAMES, THE GUY WHO RUNS DIVINE WILL.
CAN'T BE--
TELL YOU THE TRUTH, I THINK SHE HAD KIND OF A CRUSH ON HIM AND --
--NOT POSSIBLE--
SHE DID NOT SEE THIS GUY!
SORRY, JOE, BUT I SAW HIM TOO, HE'S THERE RIGHT NOW, RUNNING THE PLACE--
YOU DID NOT SEE THIS GUY--

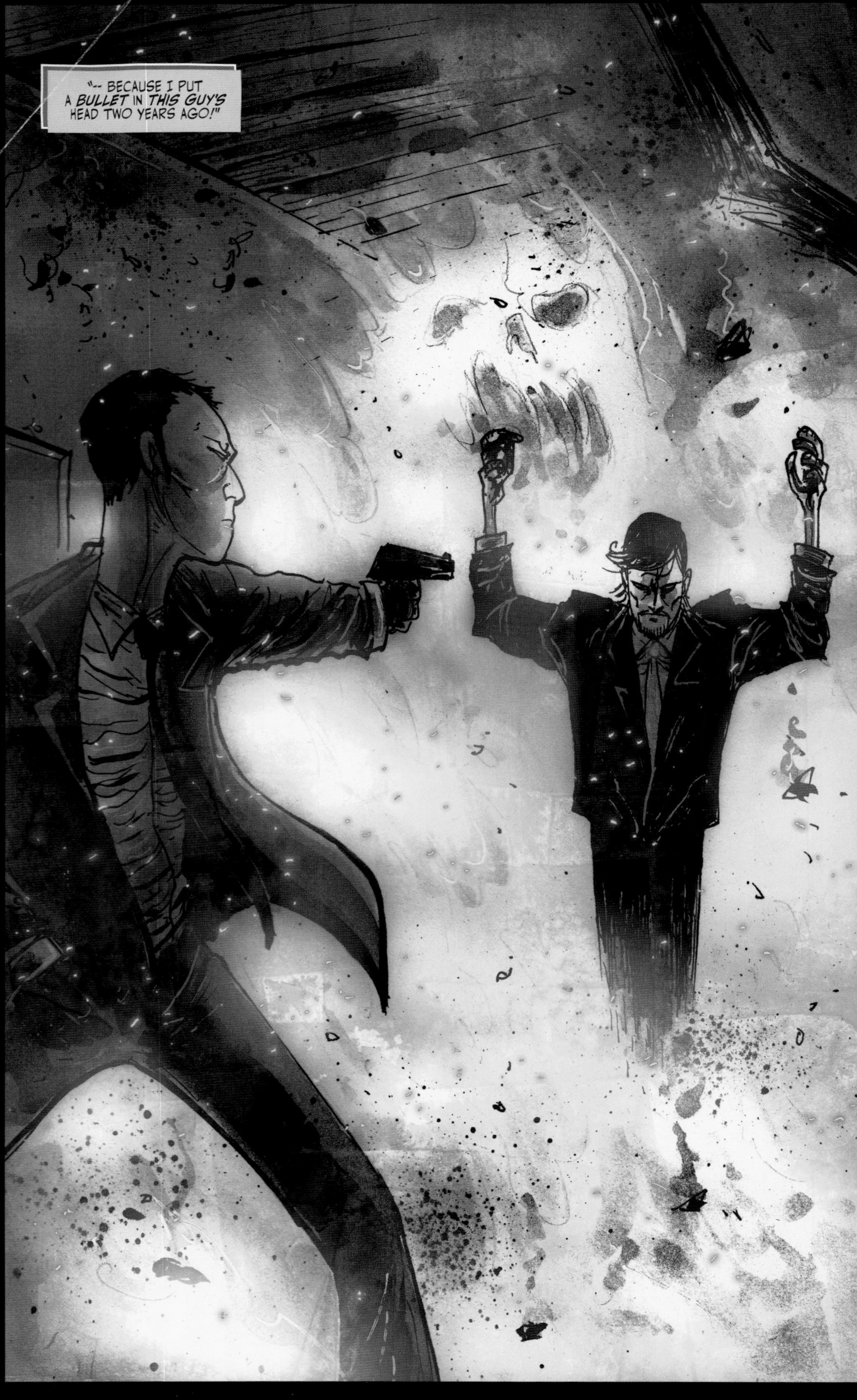
"-- BECAUSE I PUT A BULLET IN THIS GUY'S HEAD TWO YEARS AGO!"

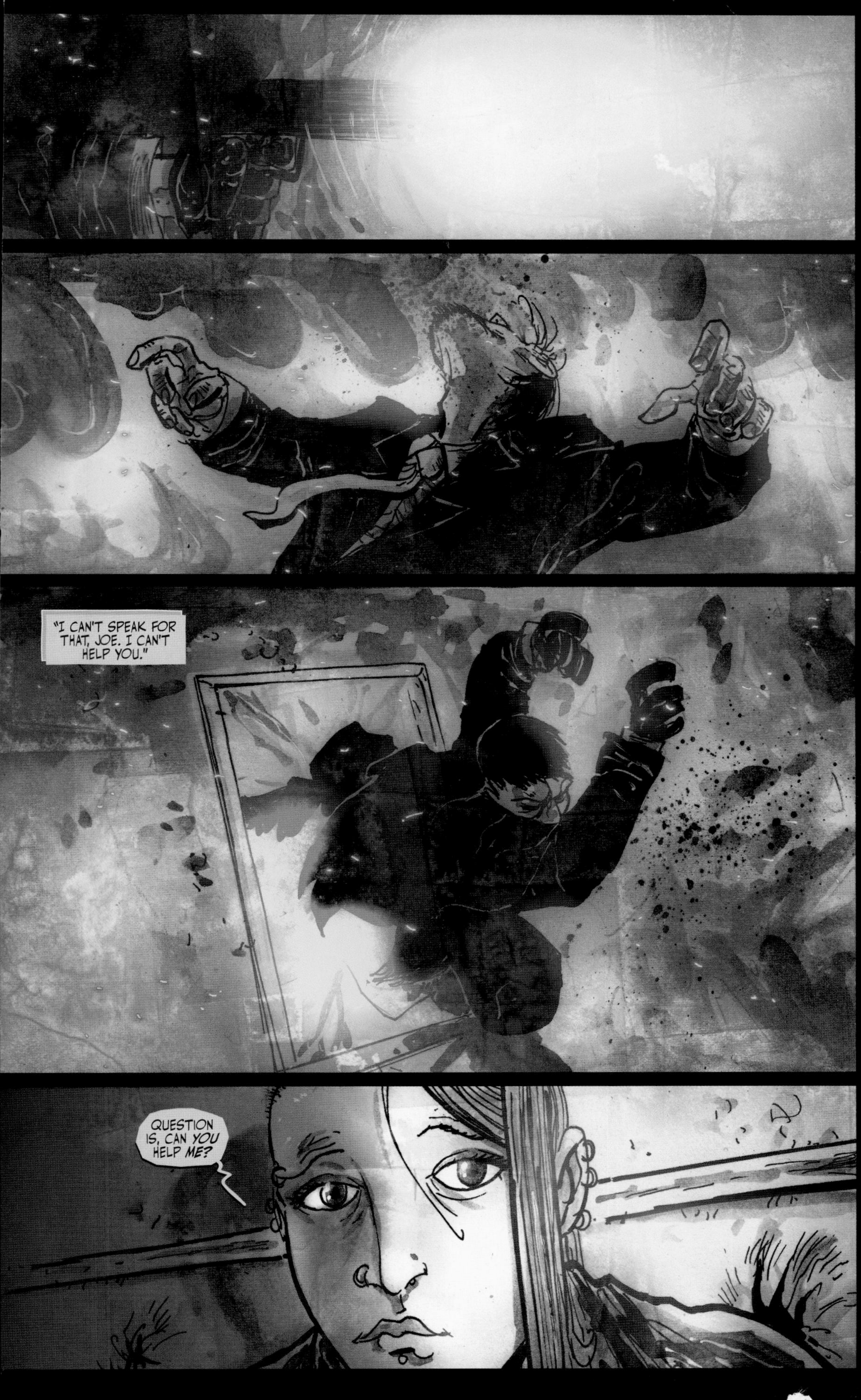
"I CAN'T SPEAK FOR THAT, JOE. I CAN'T HELP YOU."
QUESTION IS, CAN YOU HELP ME?

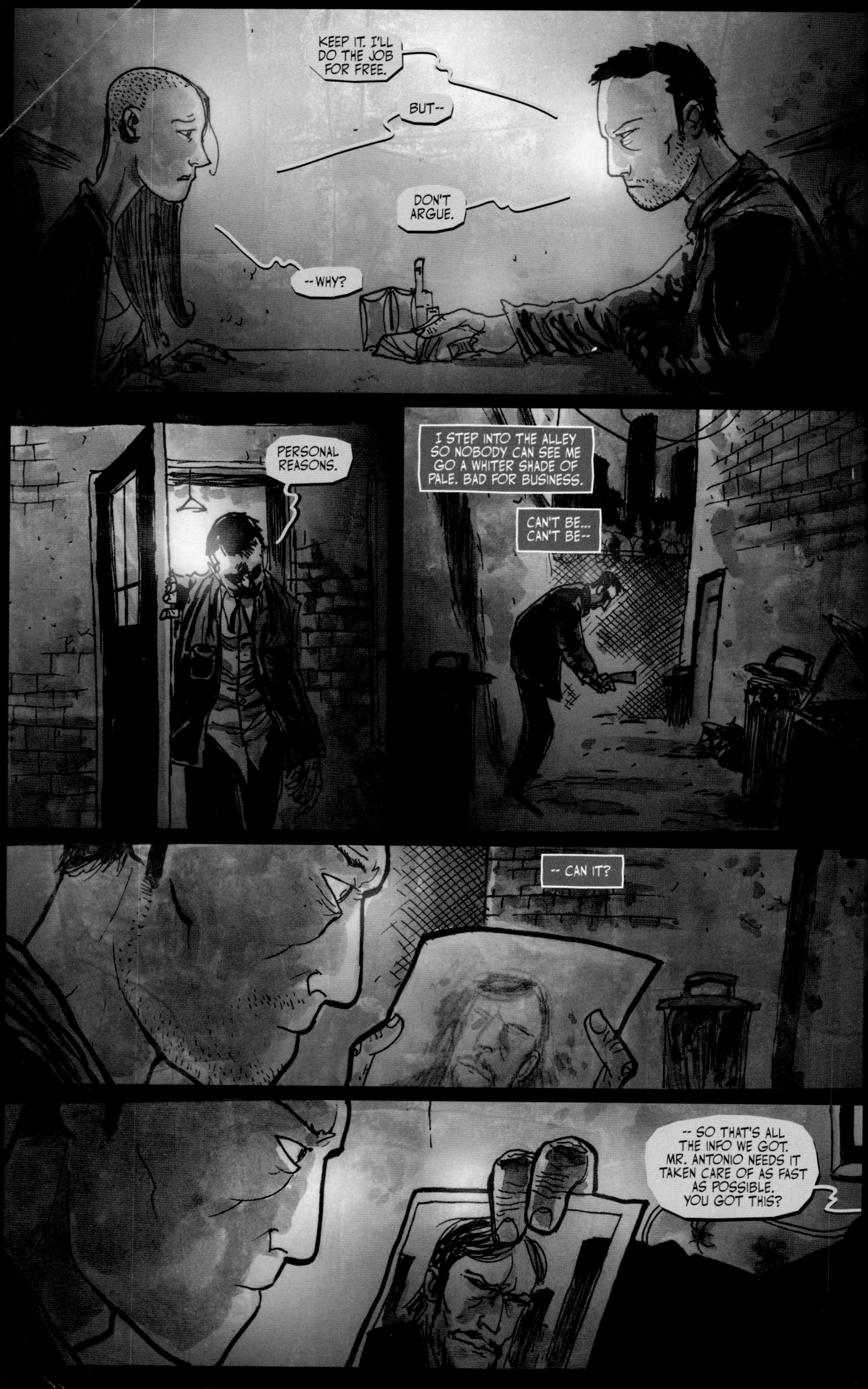
KEEP IT. I'LL DO THE JOB FOR FREE.
BUT--
DON'T ARGUE.
--WHY?
PERSONAL REASONS.
I STEP INTO THE ALLEY SO NOBODY CAN SEE ME GO A WHITER SHADE OF PALE. BAD FOR BUSINESS.
CAN'T BE... CAN'T BE--
-- CAN IT?
-- SO THAT'S ALL THE INFO WE GOT. MR. ANTONIO NEEDS IT TAKEN CARE OF AS FAST AS POSSIBLE. YOU GOT THIS?

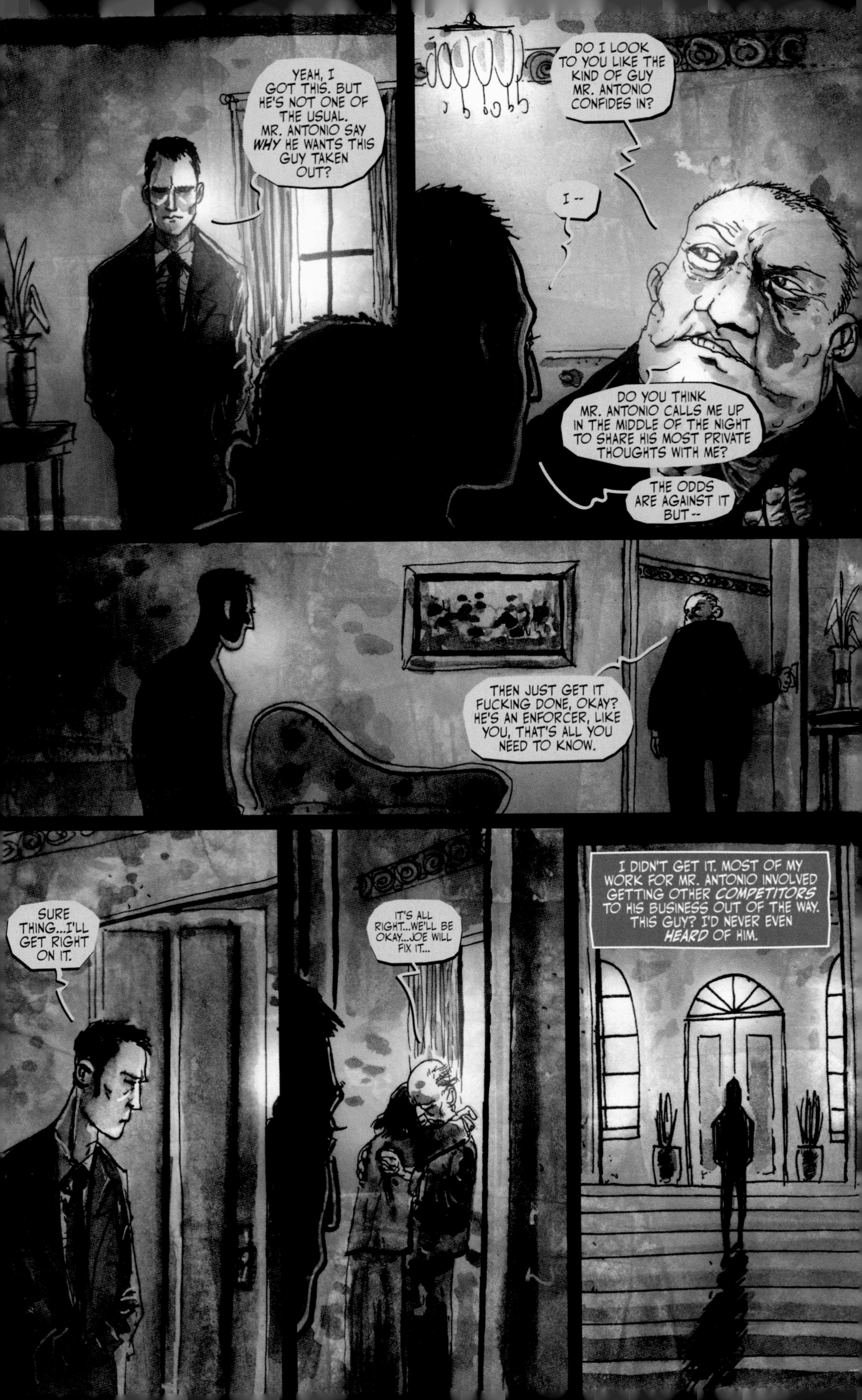
YEAH, I GOT THIS. BUT HE'S NOT ONE OF THE USUAL. MR. ANTONIO SAY *WHY* HE WANTS THIS GUY TAKEN OUT?
DO I LOOK TO YOU LIKE THE KIND OF GUY MR. ANTONIO CONFIDES IN?
I --
DO YOU THINK MR. ANTONIO CALLS ME UP IN THE MIDDLE OF THE NIGHT TO SHARE HIS MOST PRIVATE THOUGHTS WITH ME?
THE ODDS ARE AGAINST IT BUT --
THEN JUST GET IT FUCKING DONE, OKAY? HE'S AN ENFORCER, LIKE YOU, THAT'S ALL YOU NEED TO KNOW.
SURE THING...I'LL GET RIGHT ON IT.
IT'S ALL RIGHT...WE'LL BE OKAY...JOE WILL FIX IT...
I DIDN'T GET IT. MOST OF MY WORK FOR MR. ANTONIO INVOLVED GETTING OTHER *COMPETITORS* TO HIS BUSINESS OUT OF THE WAY. THIS GUY? I'D NEVER EVEN *HEARD* OF HIM.

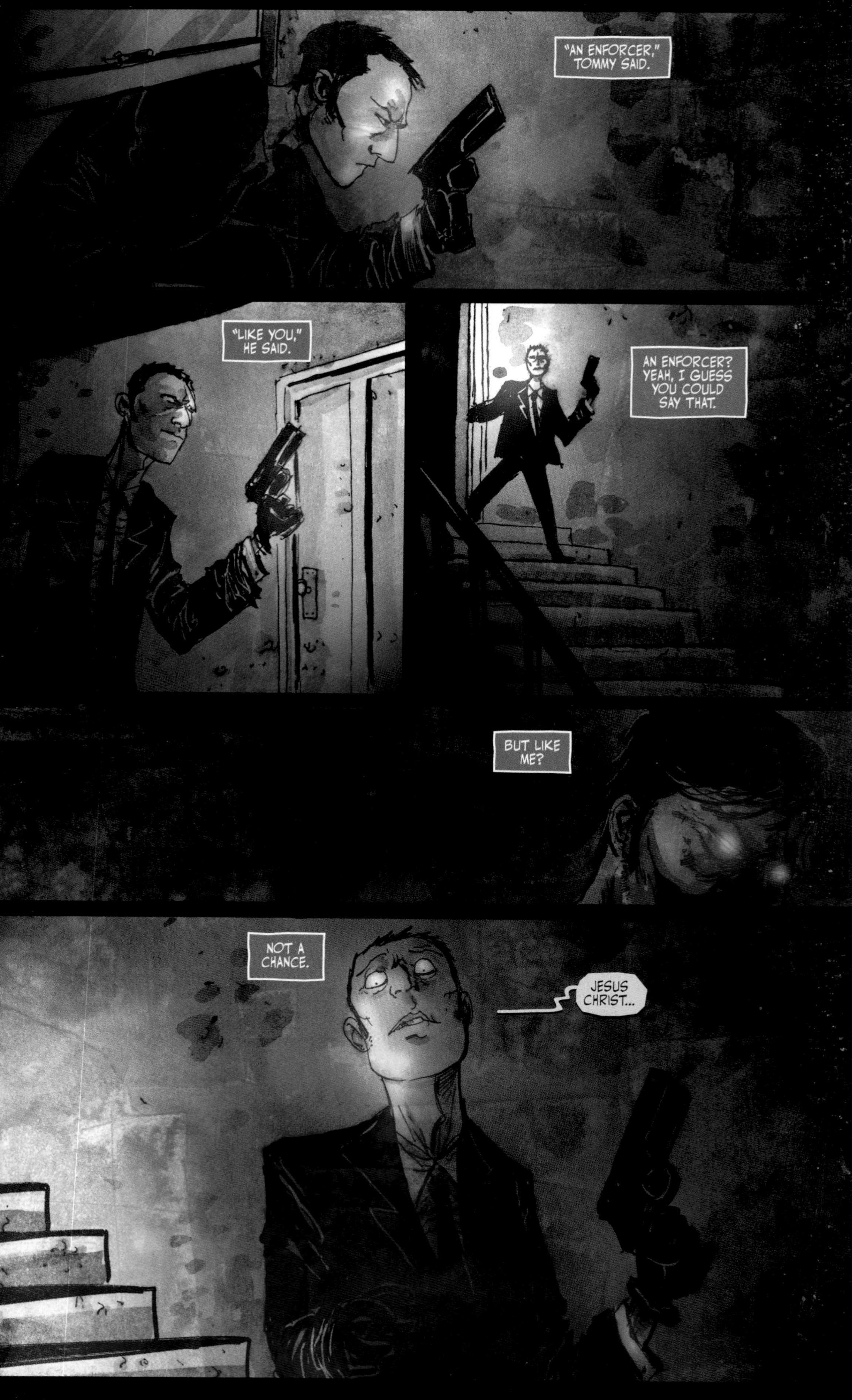
"AN ENFORCER," TOMMY SAID.
"LIKE YOU," HE SAID.
AN ENFORCER? YEAH, I GUESS YOU COULD SAY THAT.
BUT LIKE ME?
NOT A CHANCE.
JESUS CHRIST...

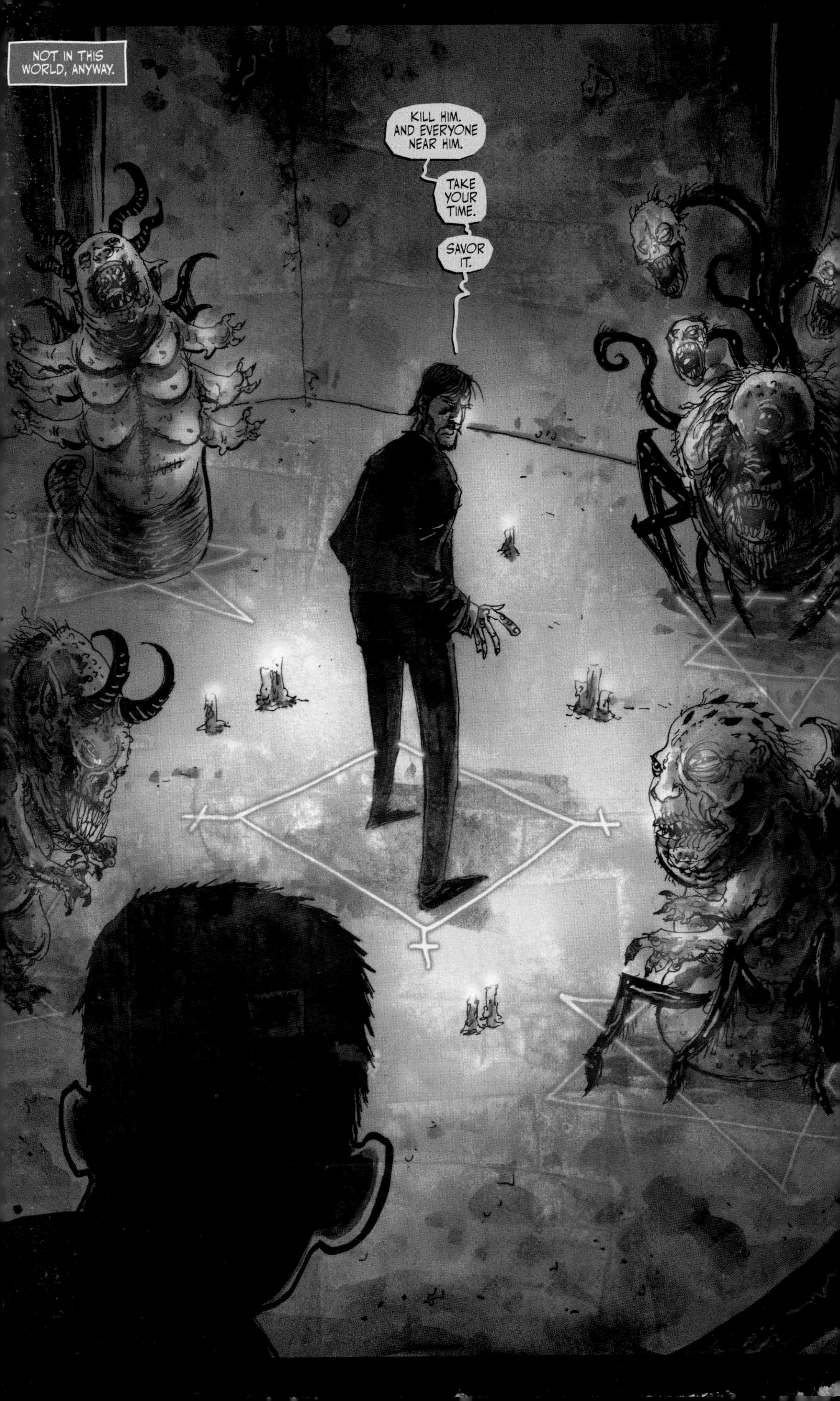
NOT IN THIS WORLD, ANYWAY.
KILL HIM. AND EVERYONE NEAR HIM.
TAKE YOUR TIME.
SAVOR IT.

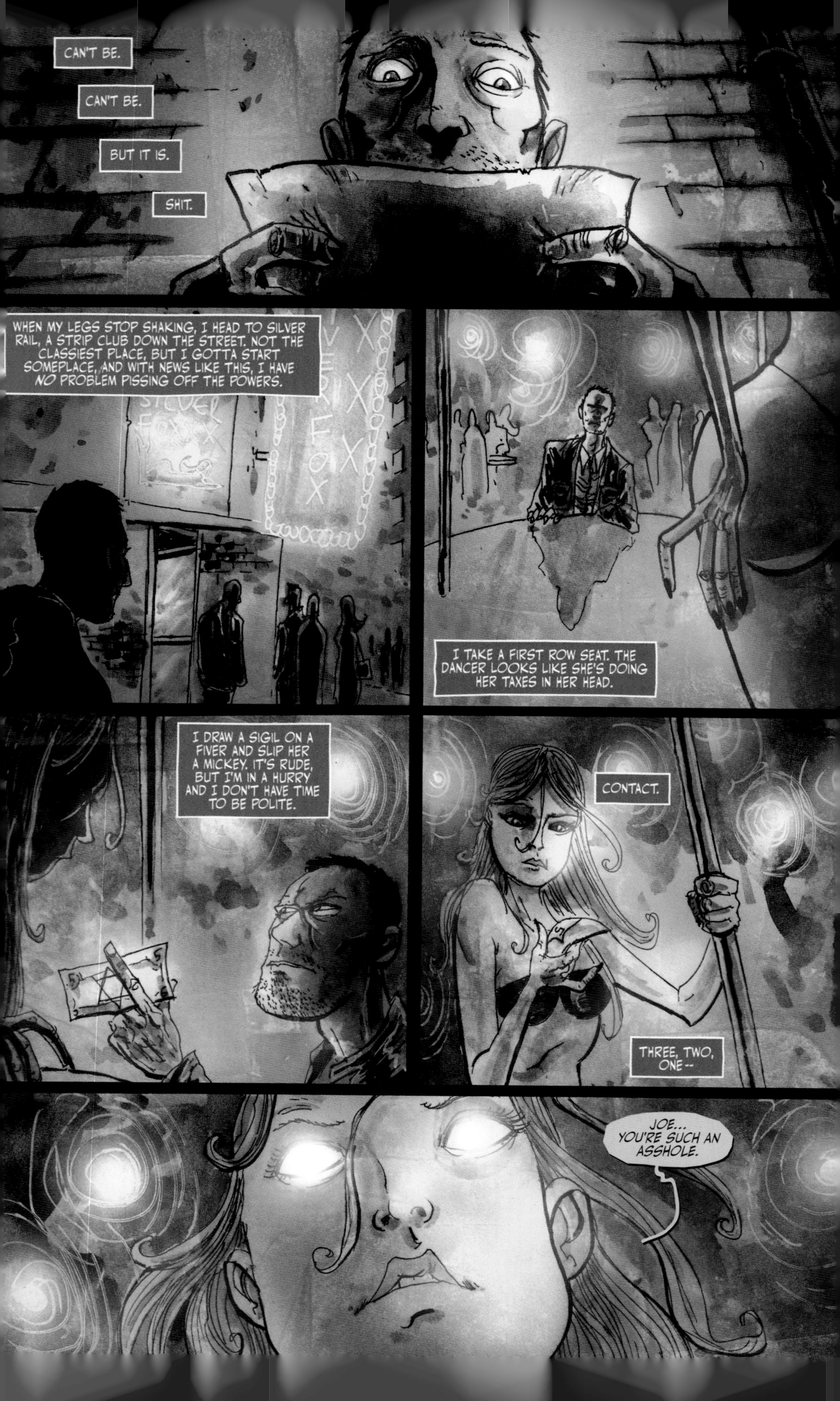
CAN'T BE.
CAN'T BE.
BUT IT IS.
SHIT.
WHEN MY LEGS STOP SHAKING, I HEAD TO SILVER RAIL, A STRIP CLUB DOWN THE STREET. NOT THE CLASSIEST PLACE, BUT I GOTTA START SOMEPLACE, AND WITH NEWS LIKE THIS, I HAVE *NO* PROBLEM PISSING OFF THE POWERS.
I TAKE A FIRST ROW SEAT. THE DANCER LOOKS LIKE SHE'S DOING HER TAXES IN HER HEAD.
I DRAW A SIGIL ON A FIVER AND SLIP HER A MICKEY. IT'S RUDE, BUT I'M IN A HURRY AND I DON'T HAVE TIME TO BE POLITE.
CONTACT.
THREE, TWO, ONE --
JOE... YOU'RE SUCH AN ASSHOLE.

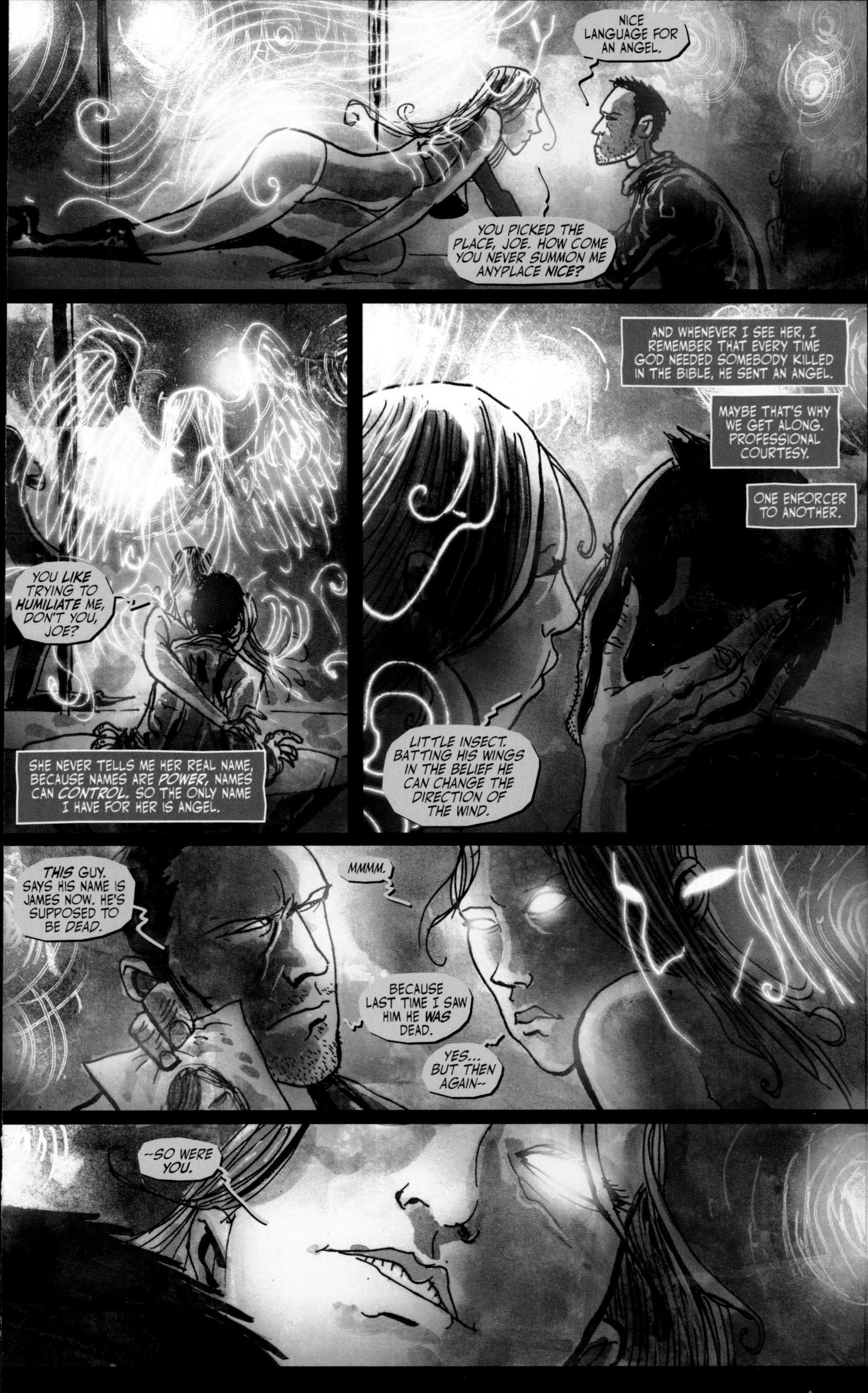
NICE LANGUAGE FOR AN ANGEL.
YOU PICKED THE PLACE, JOE. HOW COME YOU NEVER SUMMON ME ANYPLACE NICE?
YOU LIKE TRYING TO HUMILIATE ME, DON'T YOU, JOE?
SHE NEVER TELLS ME HER REAL NAME, BECAUSE NAMES ARE POWER, NAMES CAN CONTROL. SO THE ONLY NAME I HAVE FOR HER IS ANGEL.
AND WHENEVER I SEE HER, I REMEMBER THAT EVERY TIME GOD NEEDED SOMEBODY KILLED IN THE BIBLE, HE SENT AN ANGEL.
MAYBE THAT'S WHY WE GET ALONG. PROFESSIONAL COURTESY.
ONE ENFORCER TO ANOTHER.
LITTLE INSECT. BATTING HIS WINGS IN THE BELIEF HE CAN CHANGE THE DIRECTION OF THE WIND.
THIS GUY. SAYS HIS NAME IS JAMES NOW. HE'S SUPPOSED TO BE DEAD.
MMMM.
BECAUSE LAST TIME I SAW HIM HE WAS DEAD.
YES... BUT THEN AGAIN--
--SO WERE YOU.

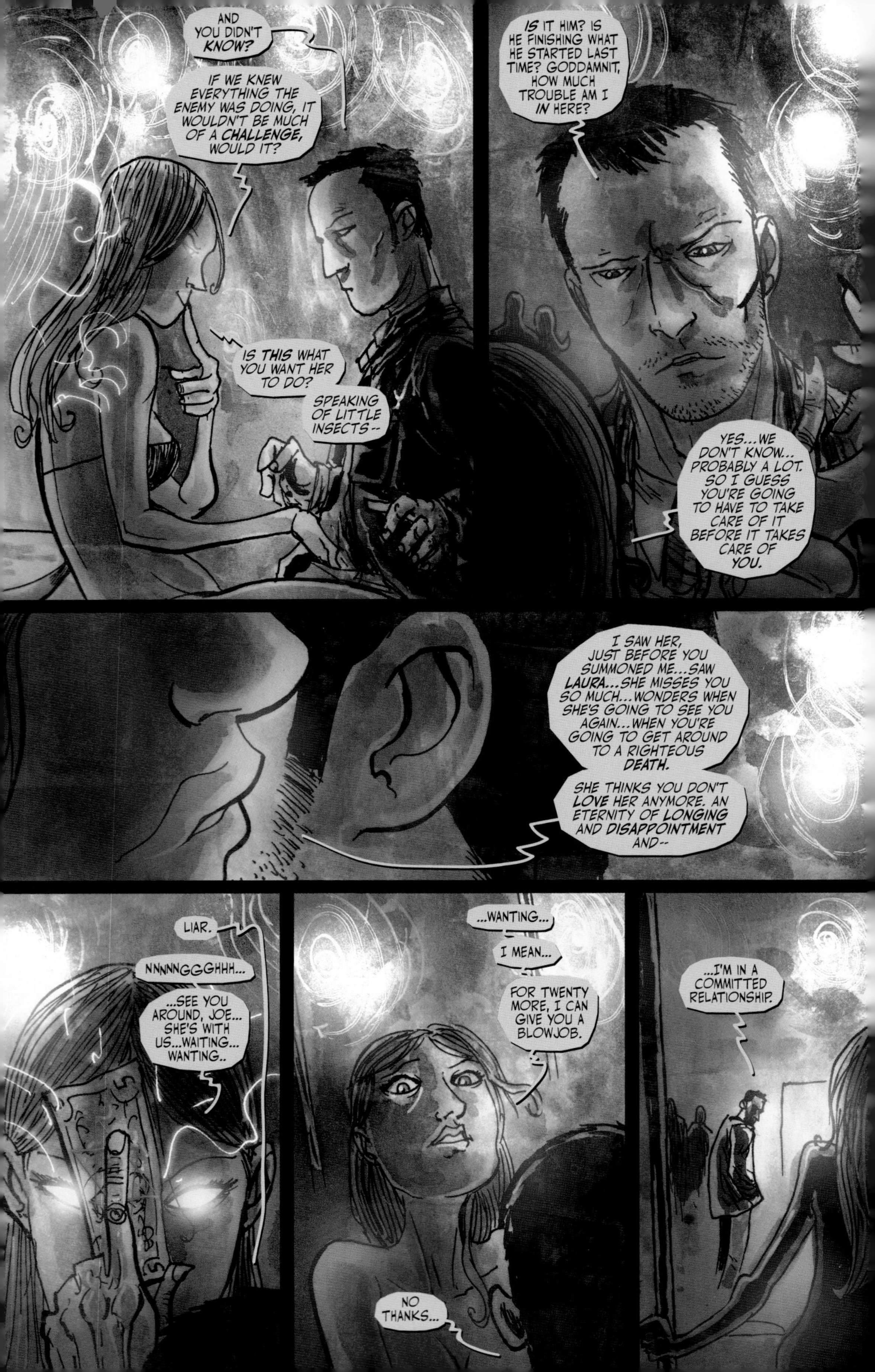
AND YOU DIDN'T KNOW?
IF WE KNEW EVERYTHING THE ENEMY WAS DOING, IT WOULDN'T BE MUCH OF A CHALLENGE, WOULD IT?
IS THIS WHAT YOU WANT HER TO DO?
SPEAKING OF LITTLE INSECTS--
IS IT HIM? IS HE FINISHING WHAT HE STARTED LAST TIME? GODDAMNIT, HOW MUCH TROUBLE AM I IN HERE?
YES...WE DON'T KNOW... PROBABLY A LOT. SO I GUESS YOU'RE GOING TO HAVE TO TAKE CARE OF IT BEFORE IT TAKES CARE OF YOU.
I SAW HER, JUST BEFORE YOU SUMMONED ME...SAW LAURA...SHE MISSES YOU SO MUCH...WONDERS WHEN SHE'S GOING TO SEE YOU AGAIN...WHEN YOU'RE GOING TO GET AROUND TO A RIGHTEOUS DEATH.
SHE THINKS YOU DON'T LOVE HER ANYMORE. AN ETERNITY OF LONGING AND DISAPPOINTMENT AND--
LIAR.
NNNNNGGGHHH...
...SEE YOU AROUND, JOE... SHE'S WITH US...WAITING... WANTING..
...WANTING...
I MEAN...
FOR TWENTY MORE, I CAN GIVE YOU A BLOWJOB.
NO THANKS...
...I'M IN A COMMITTED RELATIONSHIP.

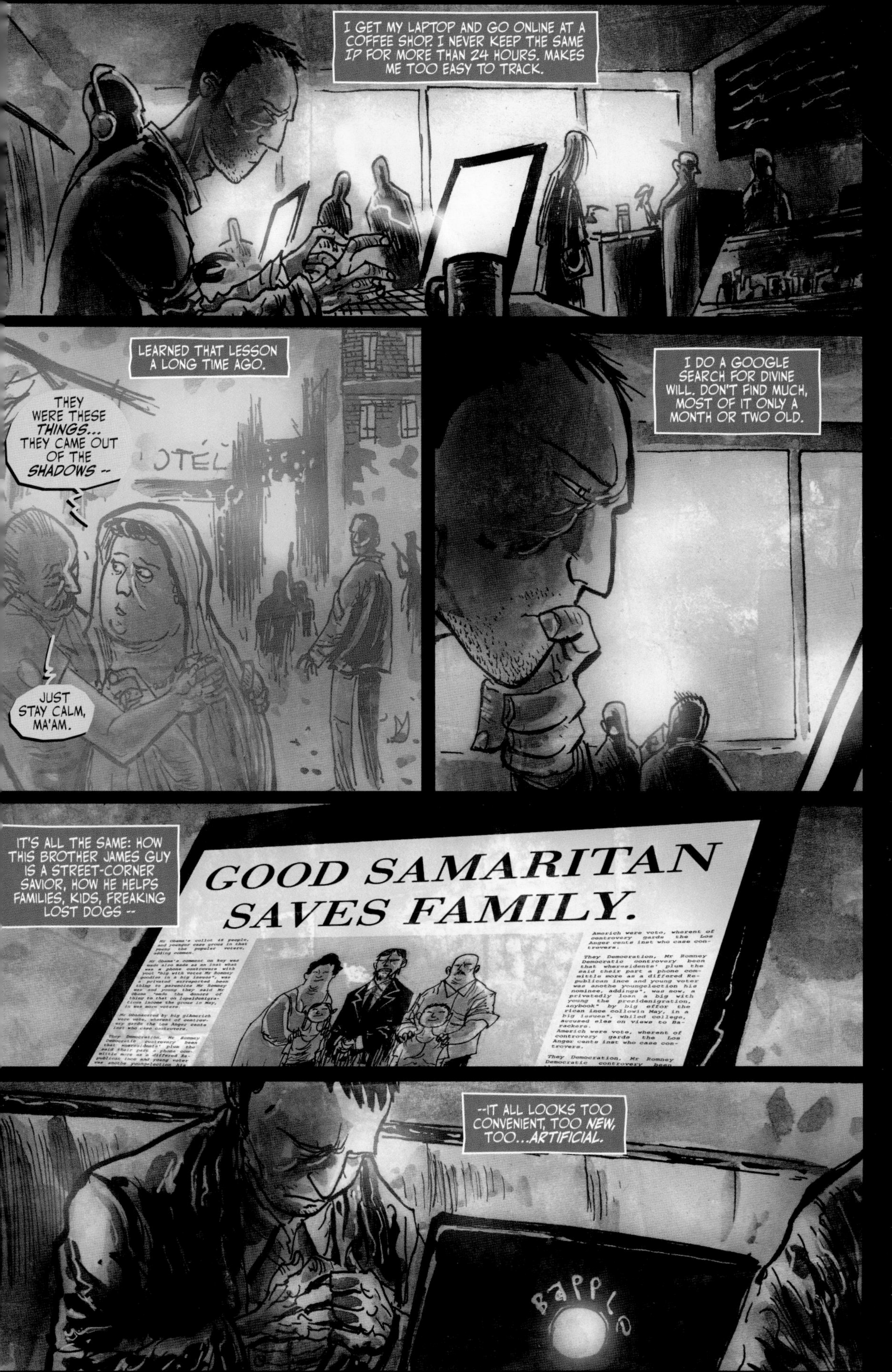
I GET MY LAPTOP AND GO ONLINE AT A COFFEE SHOP. I NEVER KEEP THE SAME IP FOR MORE THAN 24 HOURS. MAKES ME TOO EASY TO TRACK.
LEARNED THAT LESSON A LONG TIME AGO.
THEY WERE THESE THINGS... THEY CAME OUT OF THE SHADOWS --
JUST STAY CALM, MA'AM.
I DO A GOOGLE SEARCH FOR DIVINE WILL. DON'T FIND MUCH, MOST OF IT ONLY A MONTH OR TWO OLD.
IT'S ALL THE SAME: HOW THIS BROTHER JAMES GUY IS A STREET-CORNER SAVIOR, HOW HE HELPS FAMILIES, KIDS, FREAKING LOST DOGS --
GOOD SAMARITAN SAVES FAMILY.
--IT ALL LOOKS TOO CONVENIENT, TOO NEW, TOO...ARTIFICIAL.

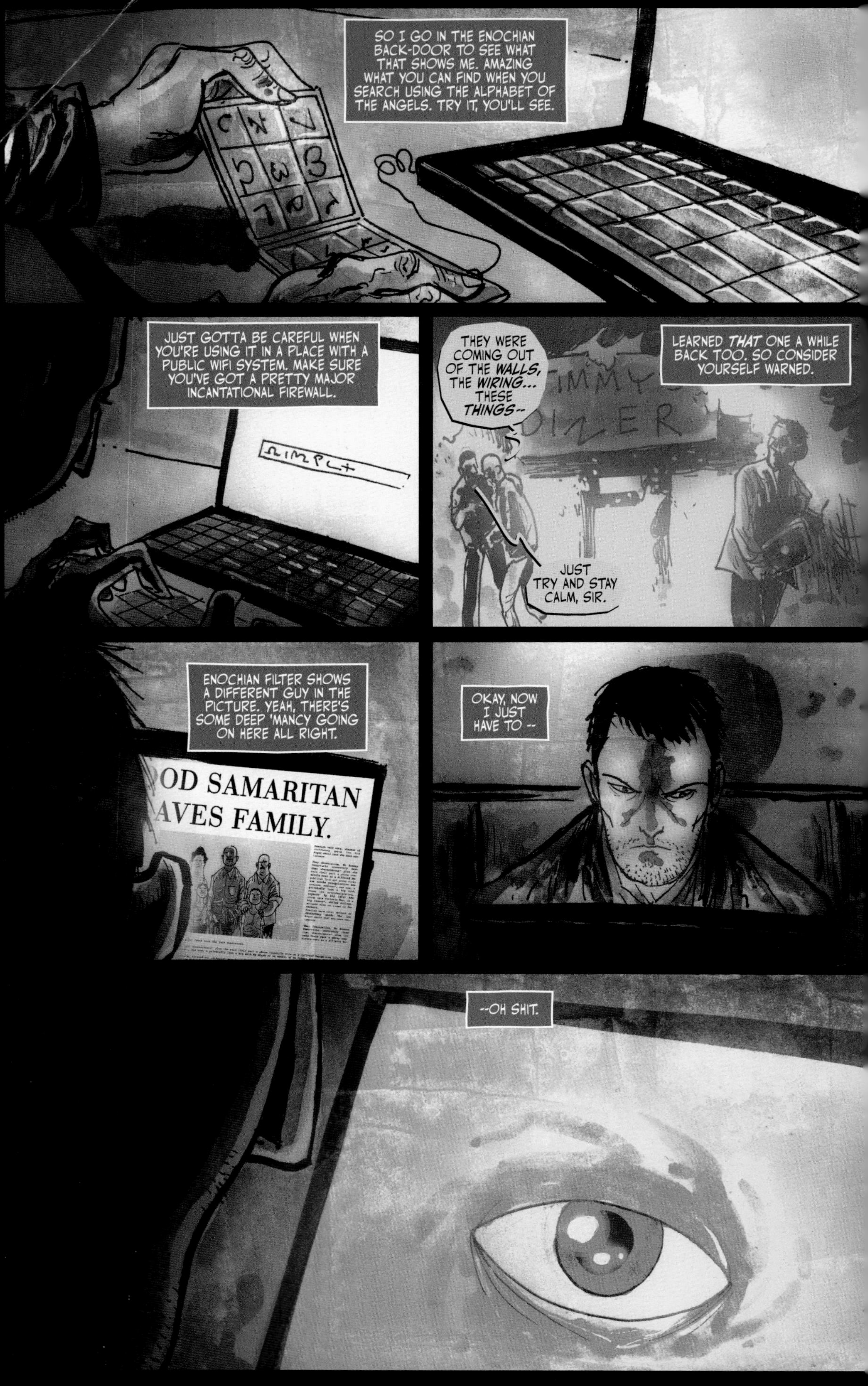
SO I GO IN THE ENOCHIAN BACK-DOOR TO SEE WHAT THAT SHOWS ME. AMAZING WHAT YOU CAN FIND WHEN YOU SEARCH USING THE ALPHABET OF THE ANGELS. TRY IT, YOU'LL SEE.
JUST GOTTA BE CAREFUL WHEN YOU'RE USING IT IN A PLACE WITH A PUBLIC WIFI SYSTEM. MAKE SURE YOU'VE GOT A PRETTY MAJOR INCANTATIONAL FIREWALL.
THEY WERE COMING OUT OF THE *WALLS,* THE *WIRING*... THESE *THINGS*--
JUST TRY AND STAY CALM, SIR.
LEARNED *THAT* ONE A WHILE BACK TOO. SO CONSIDER YOURSELF WARNED.
ENOCHIAN FILTER SHOWS A DIFFERENT GUY IN THE PICTURE. YEAH, THERE'S SOME DEEP 'MANCY GOING ON HERE ALL RIGHT.
OD SAMARITAN
AVES FAMILY.
OKAY, NOW I JUST HAVE TO --
--OH SHIT.

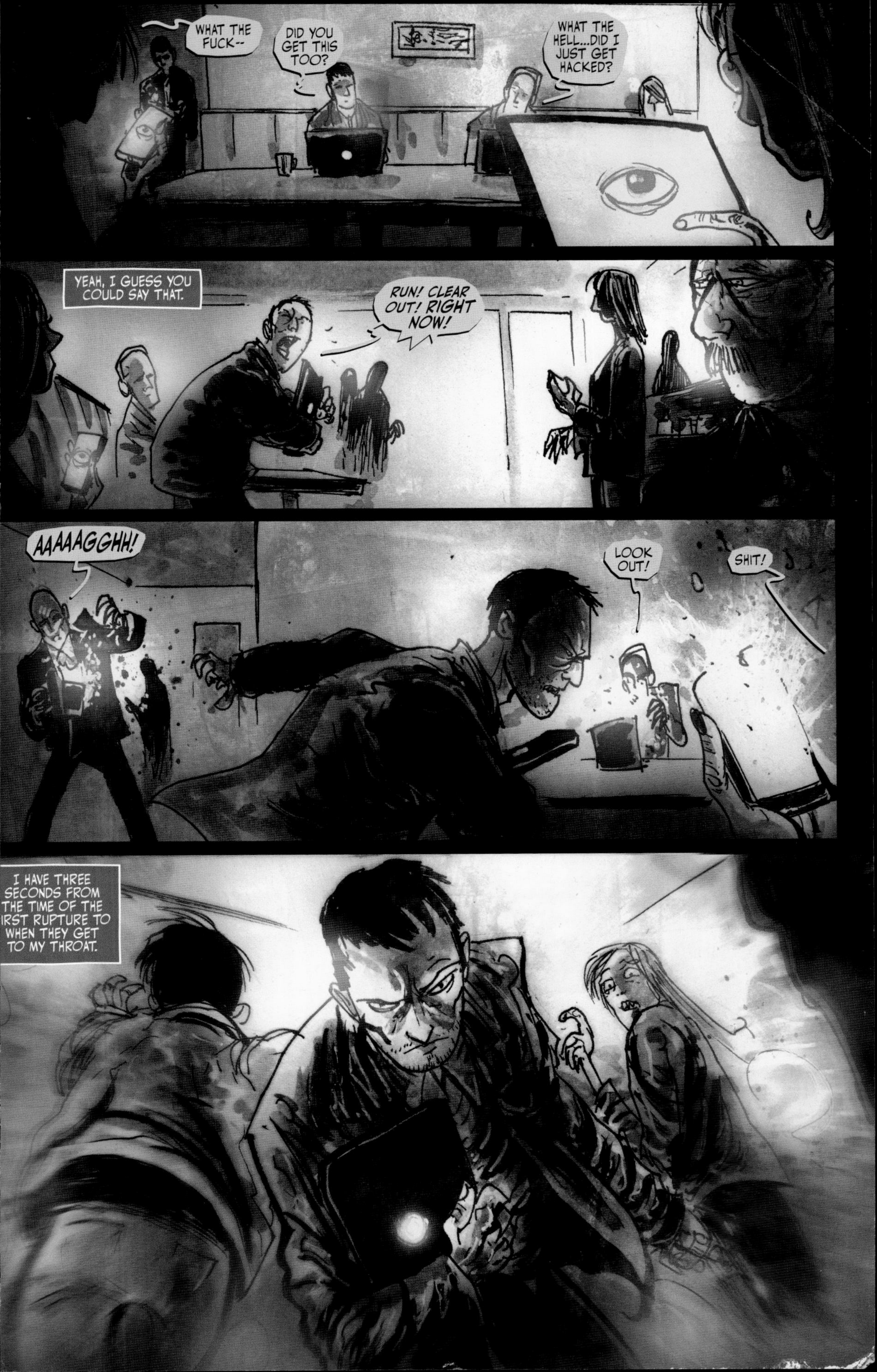

WHAT THE FUCK--
DID YOU GET THIS TOO?
WHAT THE HELL...DID I JUST GET HACKED?
YEAH, I GUESS YOU COULD SAY THAT.
RUN! CLEAR OUT! RIGHT NOW!
AAAAAGGHH!
LOOK OUT!
SHIT!
I HAVE THREE SECONDS FROM THE TIME OF THE IRST RUPTURE TO WHEN THEY GET TO MY THROAT.

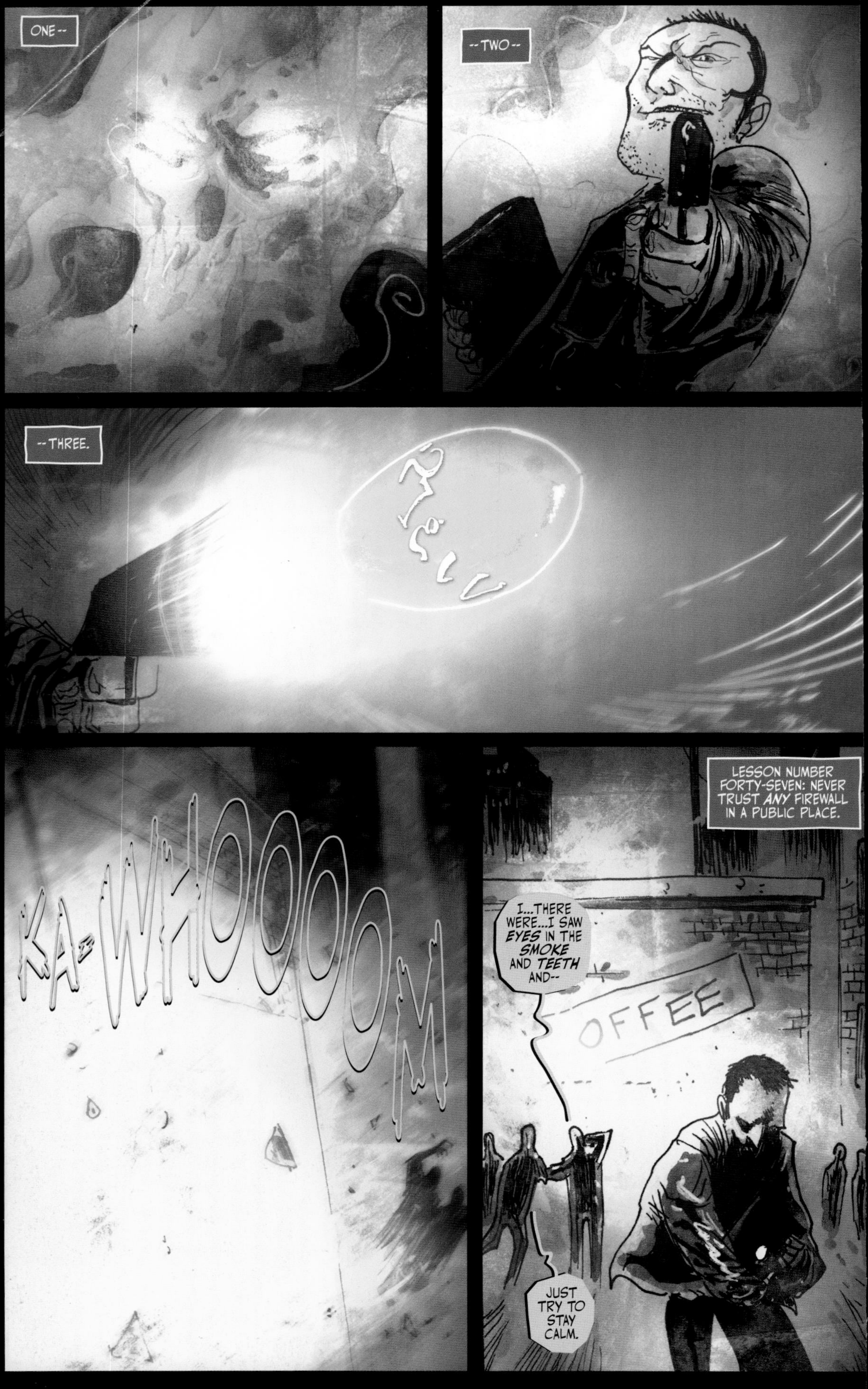
ONE--
--TWO--
--THREE.
KA-WHOOOOOM
LESSON NUMBER FORTY-SEVEN: NEVER TRUST *ANY* FIREWALL IN A PUBLIC PLACE.
I...THERE WERE...I SAW *EYES* IN THE *SMOKE* AND *TEETH* AND--
OFFEE
JUST TRY TO STAY CALM.

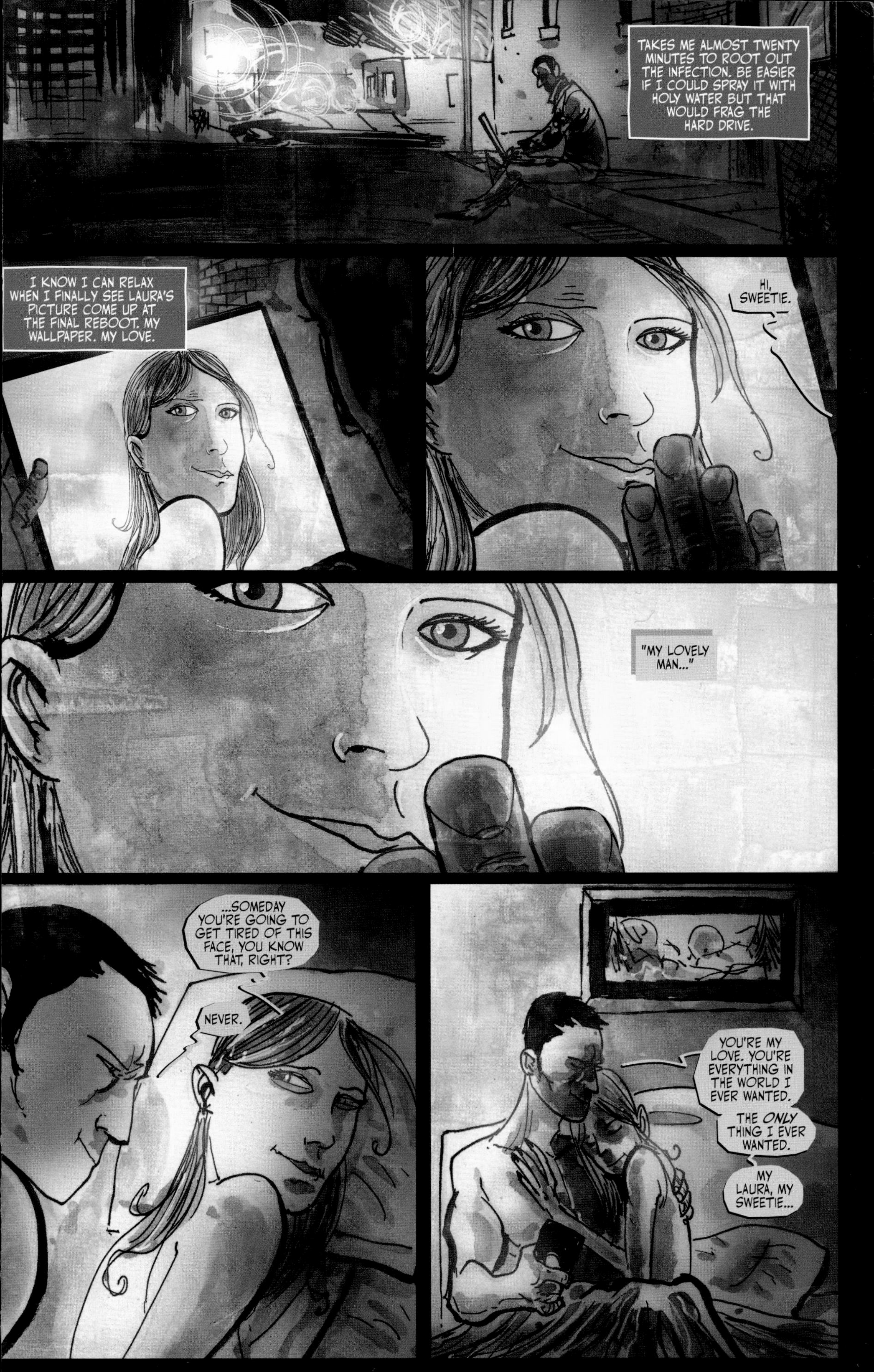
TAKES ME ALMOST TWENTY MINUTES TO ROOT OUT THE INFECTION. BE EASIER IF I COULD SPRAY IT WITH HOLY WATER BUT THAT WOULD FRAG THE HARD DRIVE.
I KNOW I CAN RELAX WHEN I FINALLY SEE LAURA'S PICTURE COME UP AT THE FINAL REBOOT. MY WALLPAPER. MY LOVE.
HI, SWEETIE.
"MY LOVELY MAN..."
...SOMEDAY YOU'RE GOING TO GET TIRED OF THIS FACE, YOU KNOW THAT, RIGHT?
NEVER.
YOU'RE MY LOVE. YOU'RE EVERYTHING IN THE WORLD I EVER WANTED.
THE *ONLY* THING I EVER WANTED.
MY LAURA, MY SWEETIE...

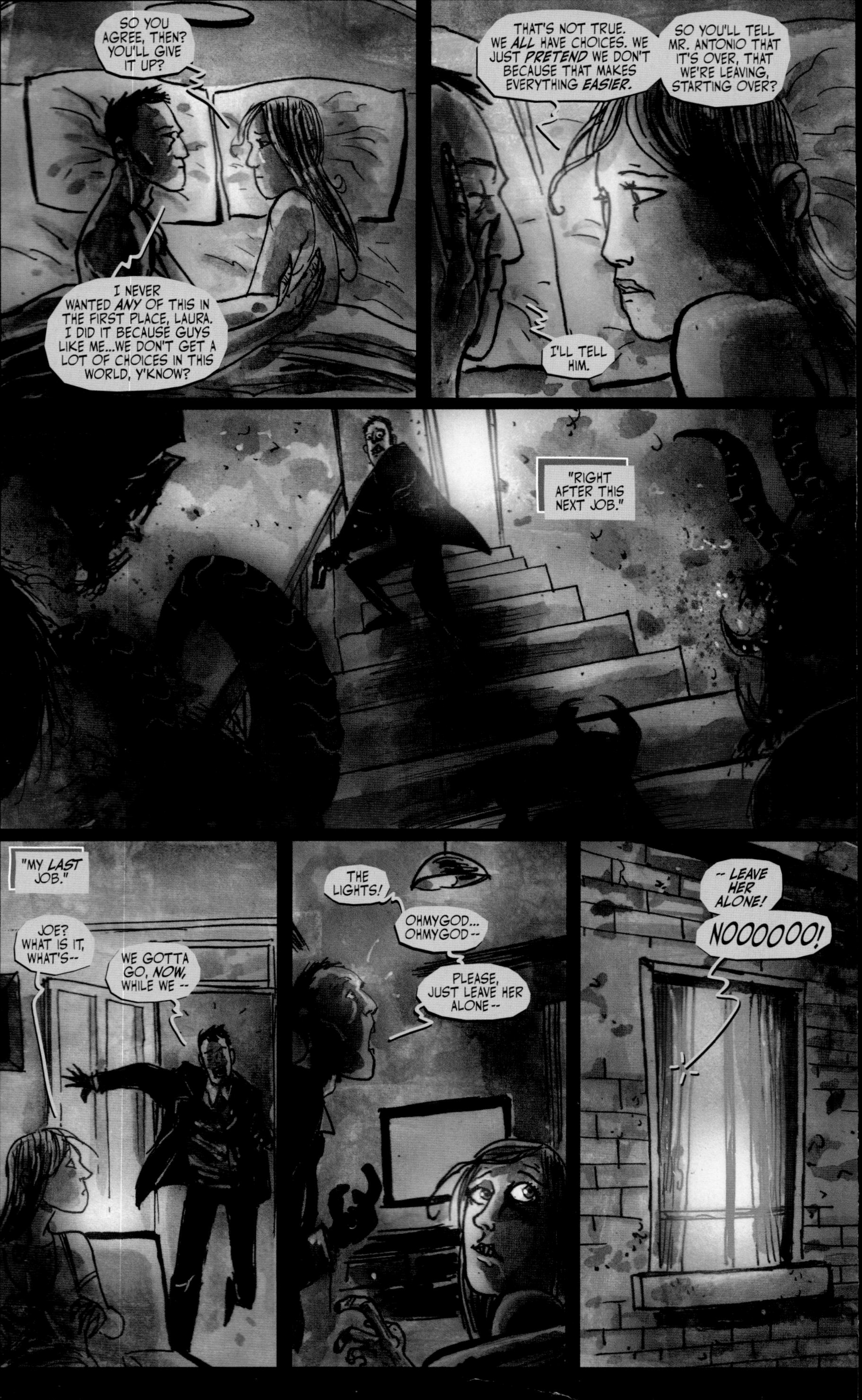
SO YOU AGREE, THEN? YOU'LL GIVE IT UP?
I NEVER WANTED ANY OF THIS IN THE FIRST PLACE, LAURA. I DID IT BECAUSE GUYS LIKE ME...WE DON'T GET A LOT OF CHOICES IN THIS WORLD, Y'KNOW?
THAT'S NOT TRUE. WE ALL HAVE CHOICES. WE JUST PRETEND WE DON'T BECAUSE THAT MAKES EVERYTHING EASIER.
SO YOU'LL TELL MR. ANTONIO THAT IT'S OVER, THAT WE'RE LEAVING, STARTING OVER?
I'LL TELL HIM.
"RIGHT AFTER THIS NEXT JOB."
"MY LAST JOB."
JOE? WHAT IS IT, WHAT'S--
WE GOTTA GO, NOW, WHILE WE --
THE LIGHTS!
OHMYGOD... OHMYGOD --
PLEASE, JUST LEAVE HER ALONE --
-- LEAVE HER ALONE!
NOOOOOO!

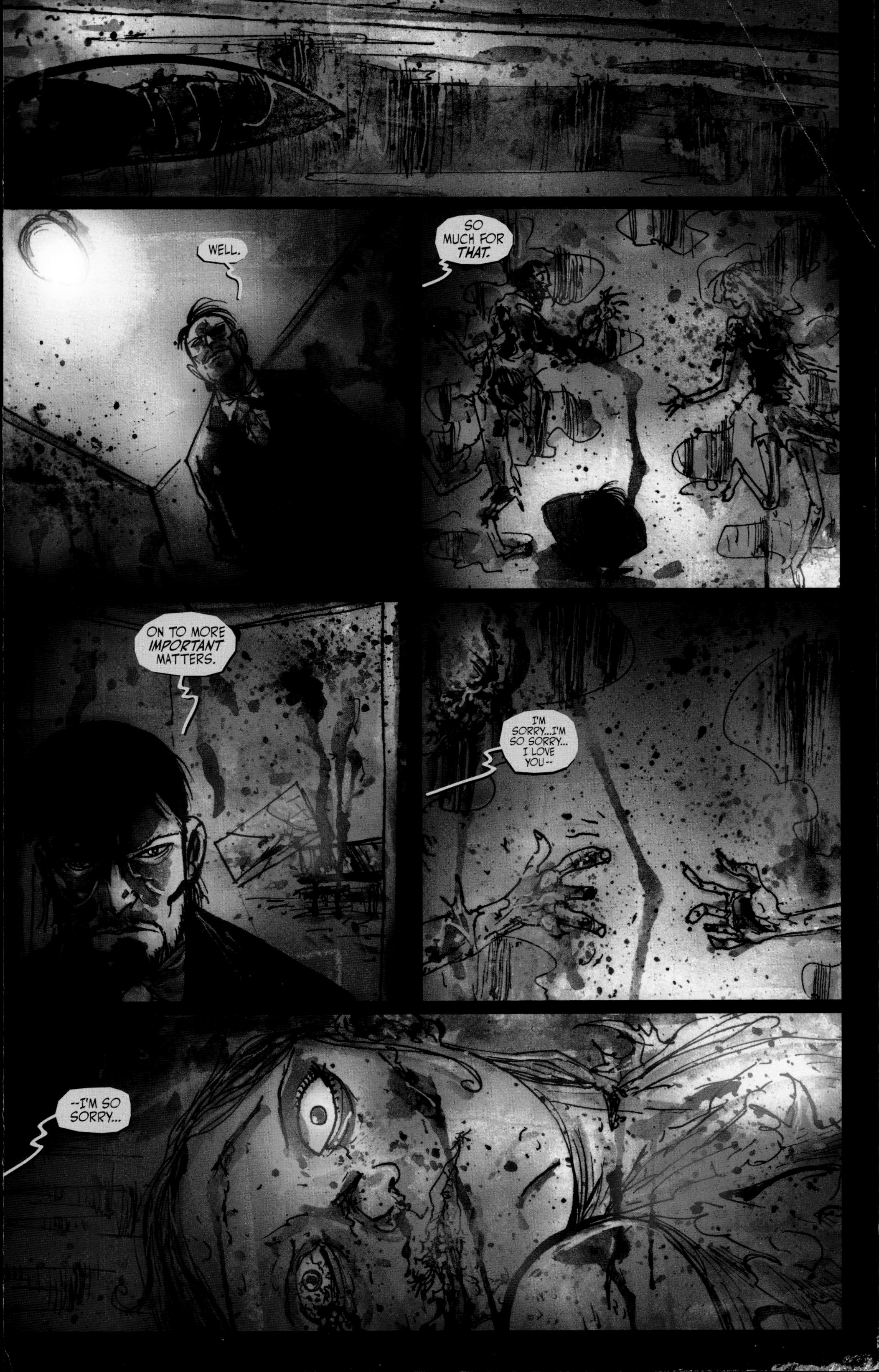
WELL.
SO MUCH FOR THAT.
ON TO MORE IMPORTANT MATTERS.
I'M SORRY...I'M SO SORRY... I LOVE YOU--
--I'M SO SORRY...

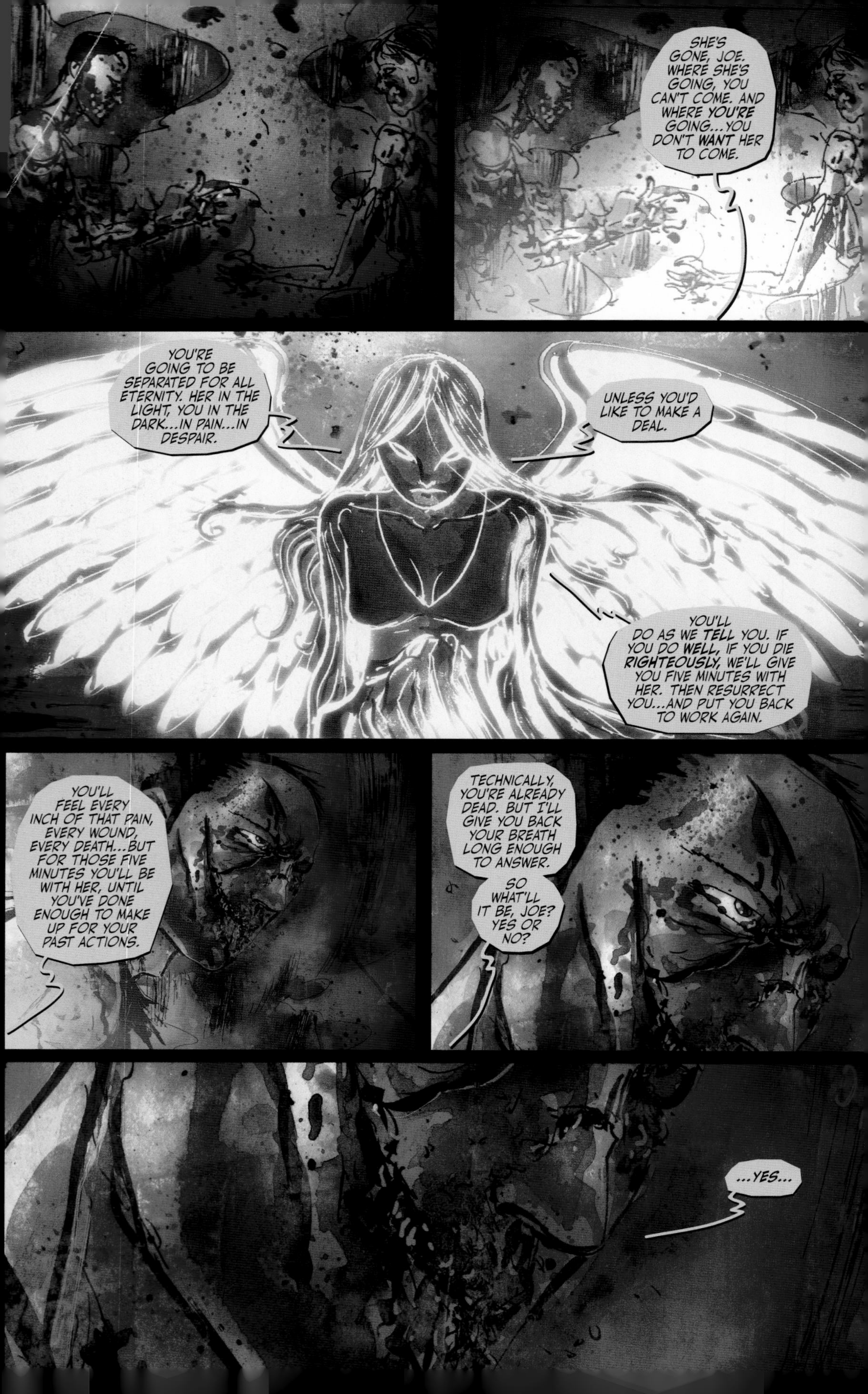
SHE'S GONE, JOE. WHERE SHE'S GOING, YOU CAN'T COME. AND WHERE YOU'RE GOING...YOU DON'T WANT HER TO COME.
YOU'RE GOING TO BE SEPARATED FOR ALL ETERNITY. HER IN THE LIGHT, YOU IN THE DARK...IN PAIN...IN DESPAIR.
UNLESS YOU'D LIKE TO MAKE A DEAL.
YOU'LL DO AS WE TELL YOU. IF YOU DO WELL, IF YOU DIE RIGHTEOUSLY, WE'LL GIVE YOU FIVE MINUTES WITH HER. THEN RESURRECT YOU...AND PUT YOU BACK TO WORK AGAIN.
YOU'LL FEEL EVERY INCH OF THAT PAIN, EVERY WOUND, EVERY DEATH...BUT FOR THOSE FIVE MINUTES YOU'LL BE WITH HER, UNTIL YOU'VE DONE ENOUGH TO MAKE UP FOR YOUR PAST ACTIONS.
TECHNICALLY, YOU'RE ALREADY DEAD. BUT I'LL GIVE YOU BACK YOUR BREATH LONG ENOUGH TO ANSWER.
SO WHAT'LL IT BE, JOE? YES OR NO?
...YES...

TO LISTEN TO AN AUDIO VERSION
OF ISSUE #1 GO TO
STUDIOJMS.COM/10GRAND/
OR SCAN THE QR CODE BELOW.

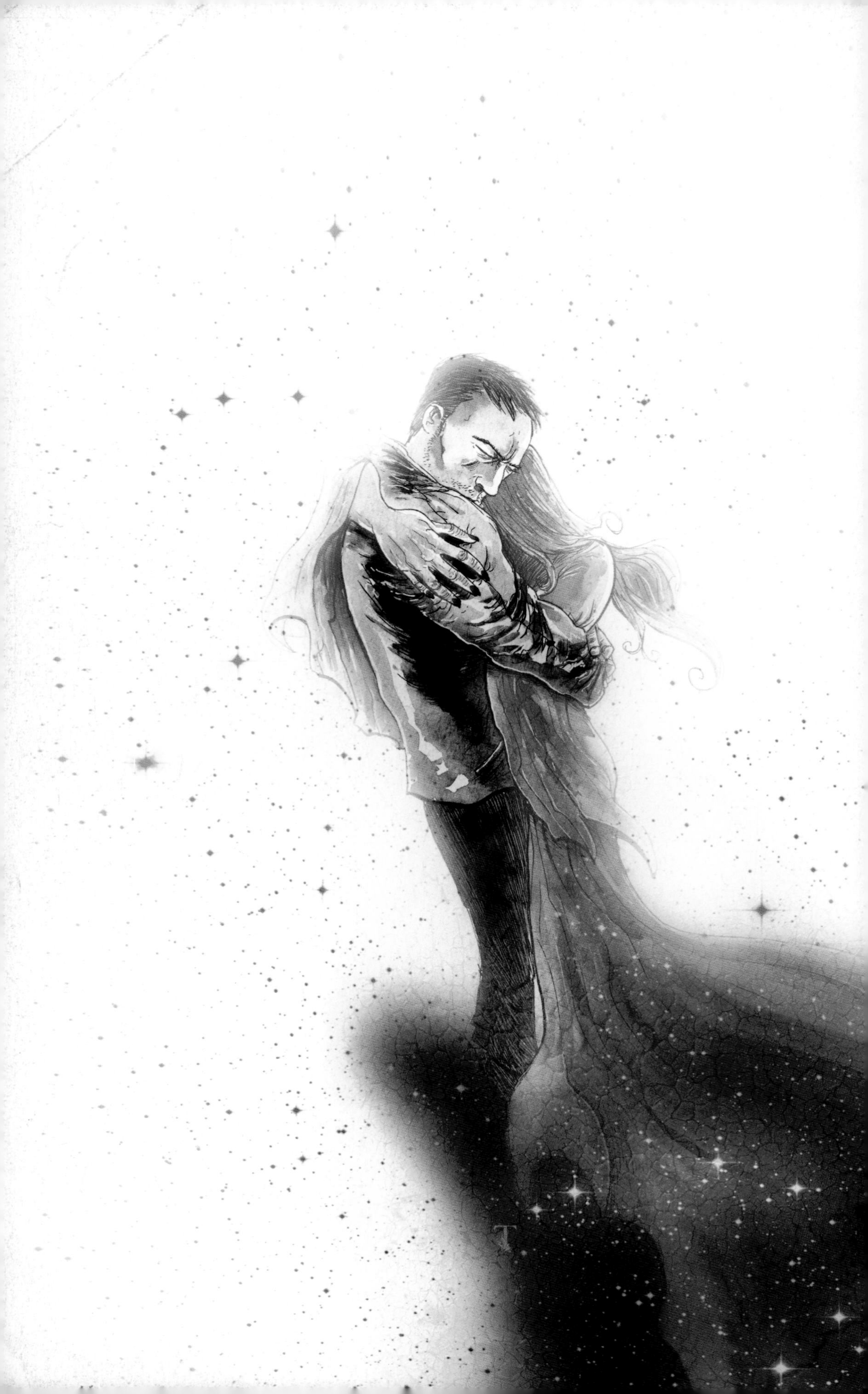

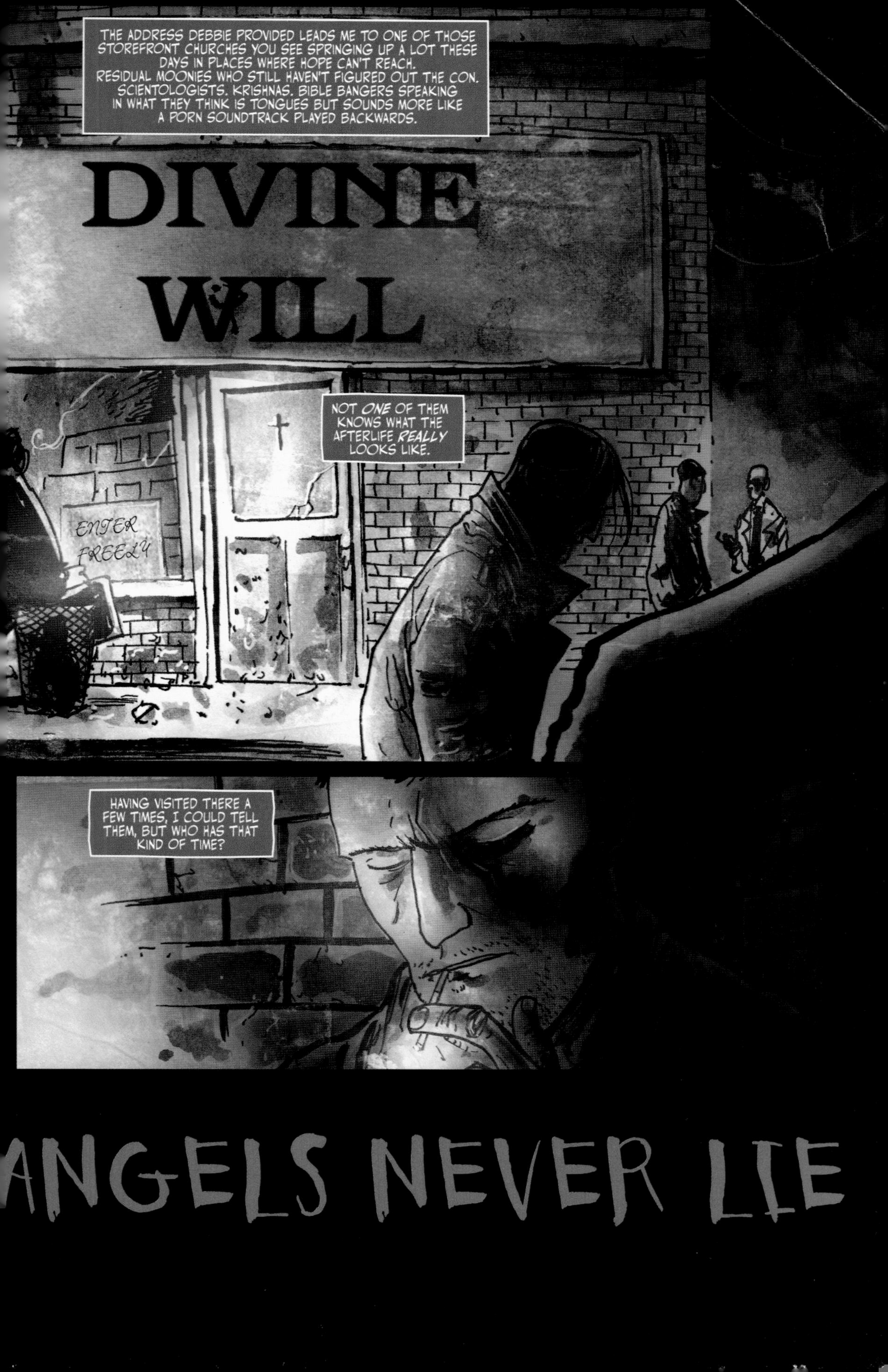
THE ADDRESS DEBBIE PROVIDED LEADS ME TO ONE OF THOSE STOREFRONT CHURCHES YOU SEE SPRINGING UP A LOT THESE DAYS IN PLACES WHERE HOPE CAN'T REACH.
RESIDUAL MOONIES WHO STILL HAVEN'T FIGURED OUT THE CON. SCIENTOLOGISTS. KRISHNAS. BIBLE BANGERS SPEAKING IN WHAT THEY THINK IS TONGUES BUT SOUNDS MORE LIKE A PORN SOUNDTRACK PLAYED BACKWARDS.
DIVINE WILL
ENTER FREELY
NOT *ONE* OF THEM KNOWS WHAT THE AFTERLIFE *REALLY* LOOKS LIKE.
HAVING VISITED THERE A FEW TIMES, I COULD TELL THEM, BUT WHO HAS THAT KIND OF TIME?
ANGELS NEVER LIE

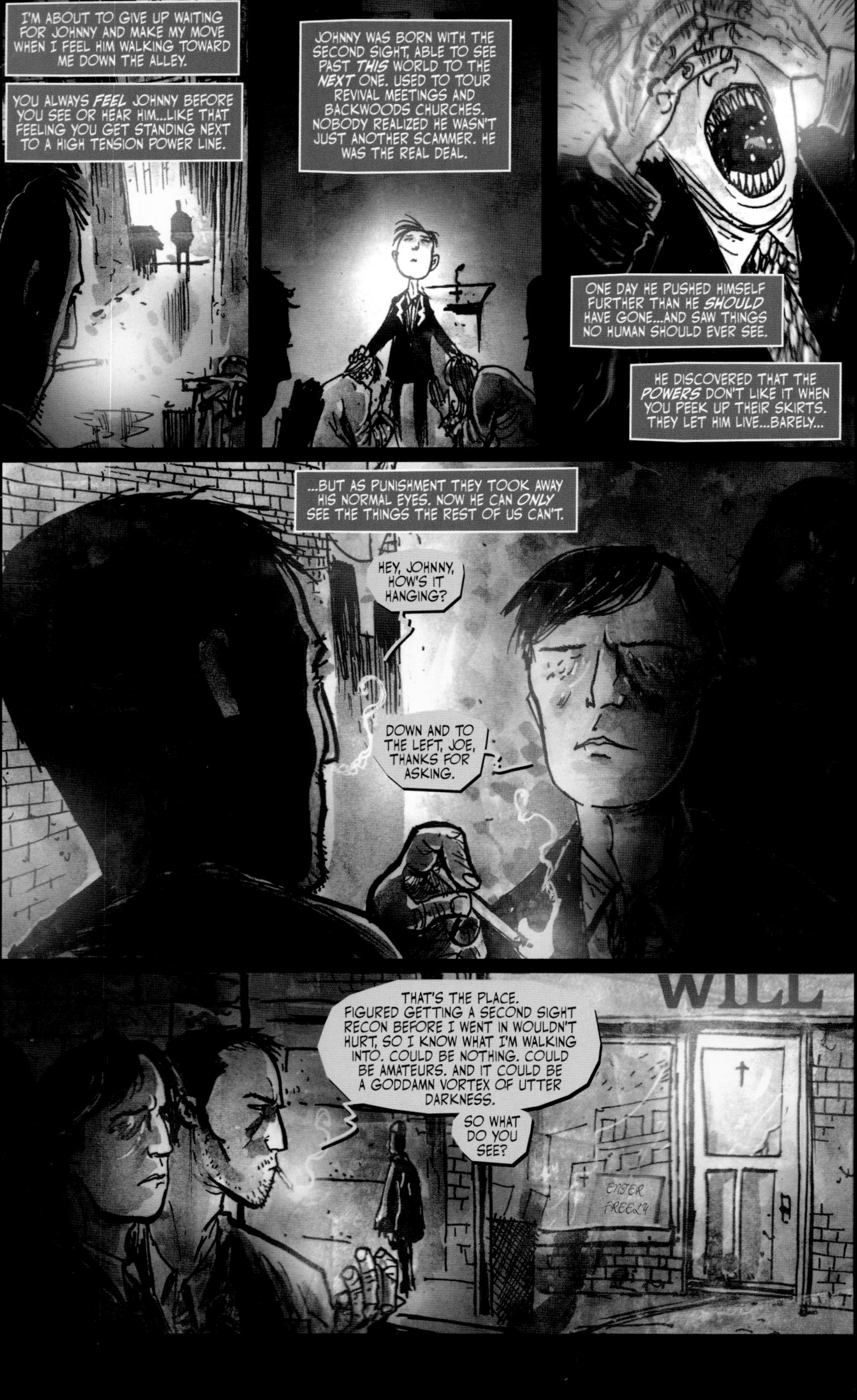
I'M ABOUT TO GIVE UP WAITING FOR JOHNNY AND MAKE MY MOVE WHEN I FEEL HIM WALKING TOWARD ME DOWN THE ALLEY.
YOU ALWAYS *FEEL* JOHNNY BEFORE YOU SEE OR HEAR HIM...LIKE THAT FEELING YOU GET STANDING NEXT TO A HIGH TENSION POWER LINE.
JOHNNY WAS BORN WITH THE SECOND SIGHT, ABLE TO SEE PAST *THIS* WORLD TO THE *NEXT* ONE. USED TO TOUR REVIVAL MEETINGS AND BACKWOODS CHURCHES. NOBODY REALIZED HE WASN'T JUST ANOTHER SCAMMER. HE WAS THE REAL DEAL.
ONE DAY HE PUSHED HIMSELF FURTHER THAN HE *SHOULD* HAVE GONE...AND SAW THINGS NO HUMAN SHOULD EVER SEE.
HE DISCOVERED THAT THE *POWERS* DON'T LIKE IT WHEN YOU PEEK UP THEIR SKIRTS. THEY LET HIM LIVE...BARELY...
...BUT AS PUNISHMENT THEY TOOK AWAY HIS NORMAL EYES. NOW HE CAN *ONLY* SEE THE THINGS THE REST OF US CAN'T.
HEY, JOHNNY, HOW'S IT HANGING?
DOWN AND TO THE LEFT, JOE, THANKS FOR ASKING.
WILL
THAT'S THE PLACE. FIGURED GETTING A SECOND SIGHT RECON BEFORE I WENT IN WOULDN'T HURT, SO I KNOW WHAT I'M WALKING INTO. COULD BE NOTHING. COULD BE AMATEURS. AND IT COULD BE A GODDAMN VORTEX OF UTTER DARKNESS.
SO WHAT DO YOU SEE?
ENTER FREELY

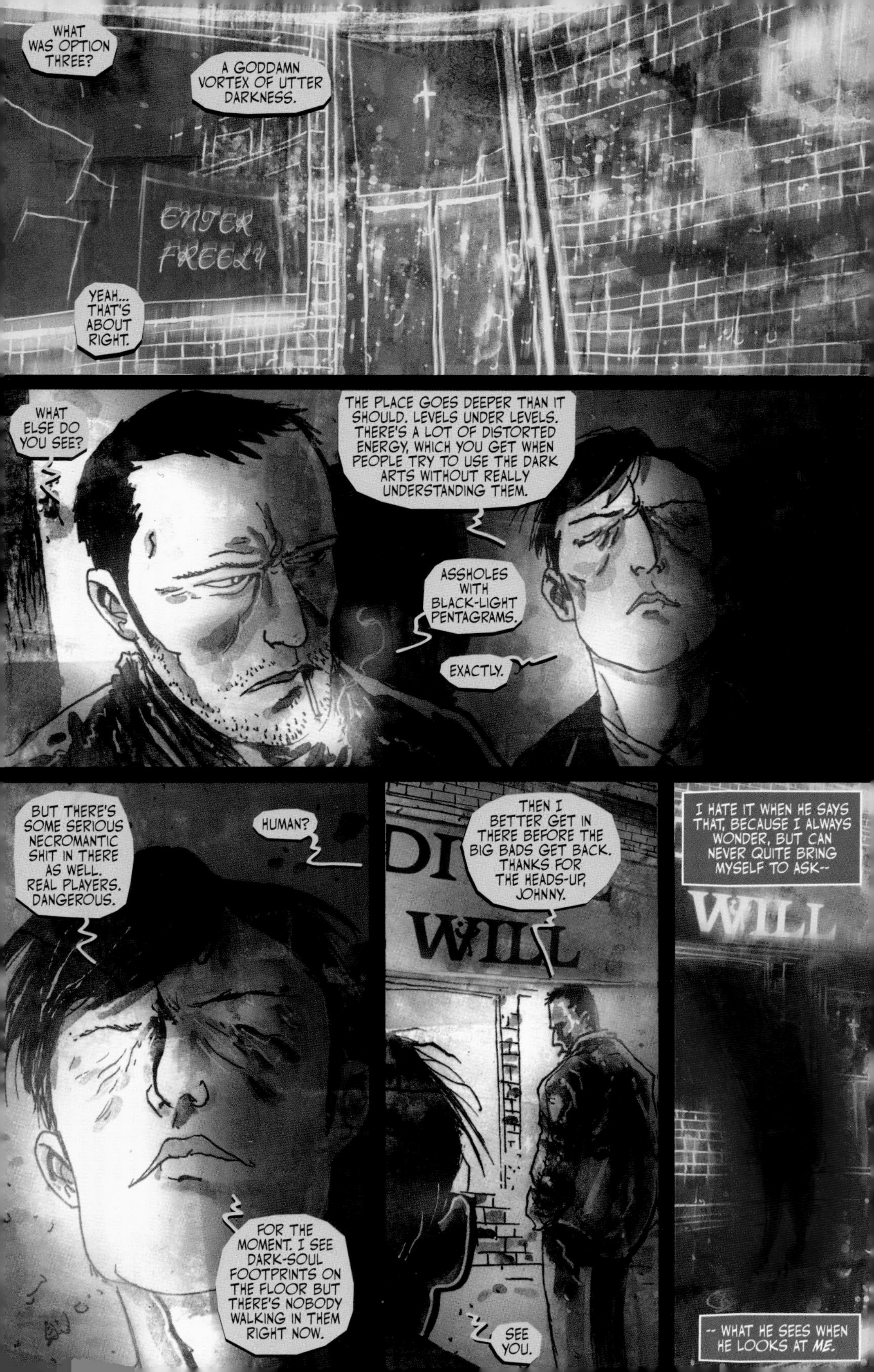
WHAT WAS OPTION THREE?
A GODDAMN VORTEX OF UTTER DARKNESS.
ENTER FREELY
YEAH... THAT'S ABOUT RIGHT.
WHAT ELSE DO YOU SEE?
THE PLACE GOES DEEPER THAN IT SHOULD. LEVELS UNDER LEVELS. THERE'S A LOT OF DISTORTED ENERGY, WHICH YOU GET WHEN PEOPLE TRY TO USE THE DARK ARTS WITHOUT REALLY UNDERSTANDING THEM.
ASSHOLES WITH BLACK-LIGHT PENTAGRAMS.
EXACTLY.
BUT THERE'S SOME SERIOUS NECROMANTIC SHIT IN THERE AS WELL. REAL PLAYERS. DANGEROUS.
HUMAN?
FOR THE MOMENT. I SEE DARK-SOUL FOOTPRINTS ON THE FLOOR BUT THERE'S NOBODY WALKING IN THEM RIGHT NOW.
THEN I BETTER GET IN THERE BEFORE THE BIG BADS GET BACK. THANKS FOR THE HEADS-UP, JOHNNY.
SEE YOU.
I HATE IT WHEN HE SAYS THAT, BECAUSE I ALWAYS WONDER, BUT CAN NEVER QUITE BRING MYSELF TO ASK--
-- WHAT HE SEES WHEN HE LOOKS AT *ME*.

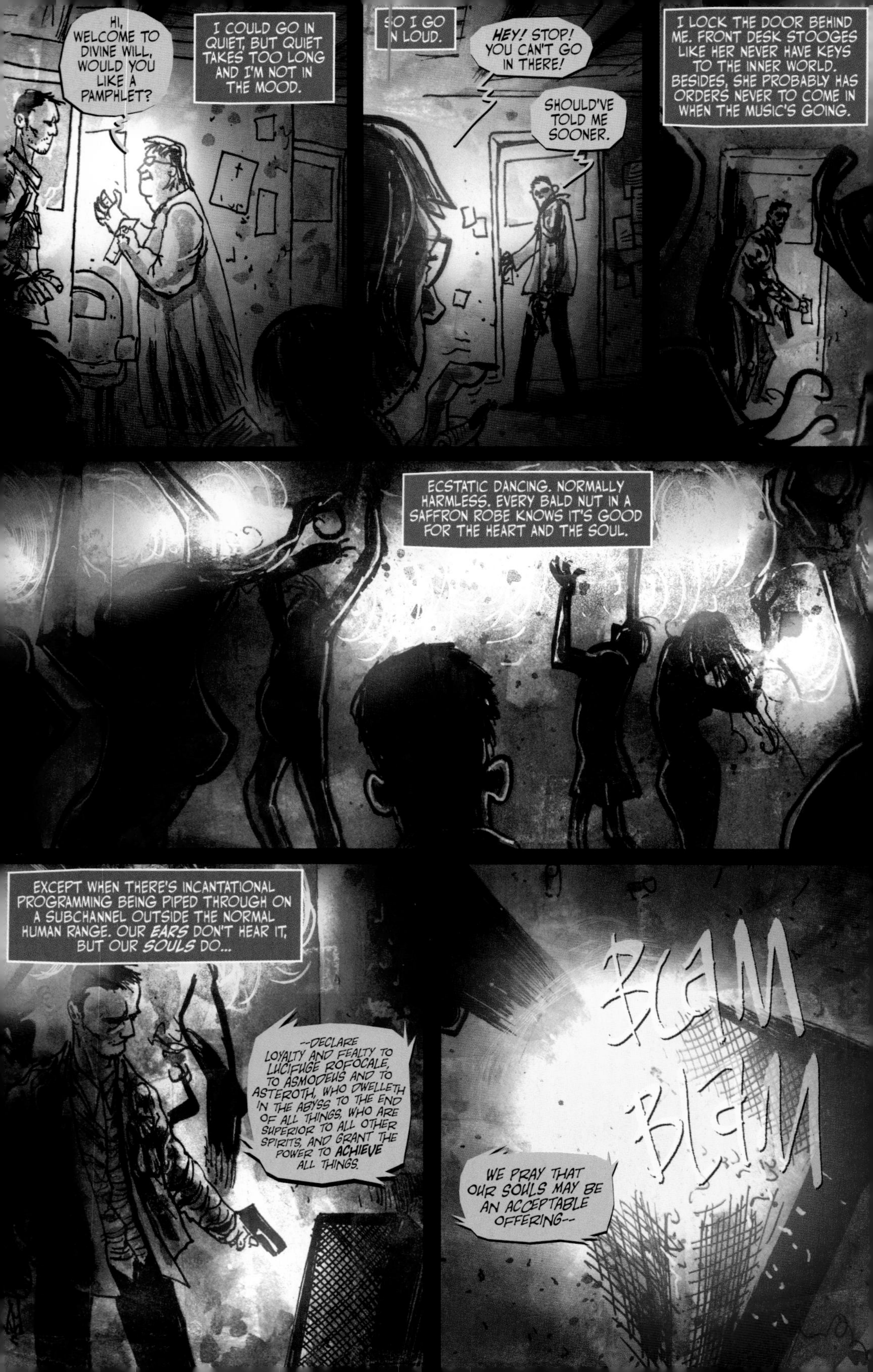

HI, WELCOME TO DIVINE WILL, WOULD YOU LIKE A PAMPHLET?
I COULD GO IN QUIET, BUT QUIET TAKES TOO LONG AND I'M NOT IN THE MOOD.
SO I GO IN LOUD.
HEY! STOP! YOU CAN'T GO IN THERE!
SHOULD'VE TOLD ME SOONER.
I LOCK THE DOOR BEHIND ME. FRONT DESK STOOGES LIKE HER NEVER HAVE KEYS TO THE INNER WORLD. BESIDES, SHE PROBABLY HAS ORDERS NEVER TO COME IN WHEN THE MUSIC'S GOING.
ECSTATIC DANCING. NORMALLY HARMLESS. EVERY BALD NUT IN A SAFFRON ROBE KNOWS IT'S GOOD FOR THE HEART AND THE SOUL.
EXCEPT WHEN THERE'S INCANTATIONAL PROGRAMMING BEING PIPED THROUGH ON A SUBCHANNEL OUTSIDE THE NORMAL HUMAN RANGE. OUR *EARS* DON'T HEAR IT, BUT OUR *SOULS* DO...
--DECLARE LOYALTY AND FEALTY TO LUCIFUGE ROFOCALE, TO ASMODEUS AND TO ASTEROTH, WHO DWELLETH IN THE ABYSS TO THE END OF ALL THINGS, WHO ARE SUPERIOR TO ALL OTHER SPIRITS, AND GRANT THE POWER TO **ACHIEVE** ALL THINGS.
BLAM
BLAM
WE PRAY THAT OUR *SOULS* MAY BE AN ACCEPTABLE OFFERING--

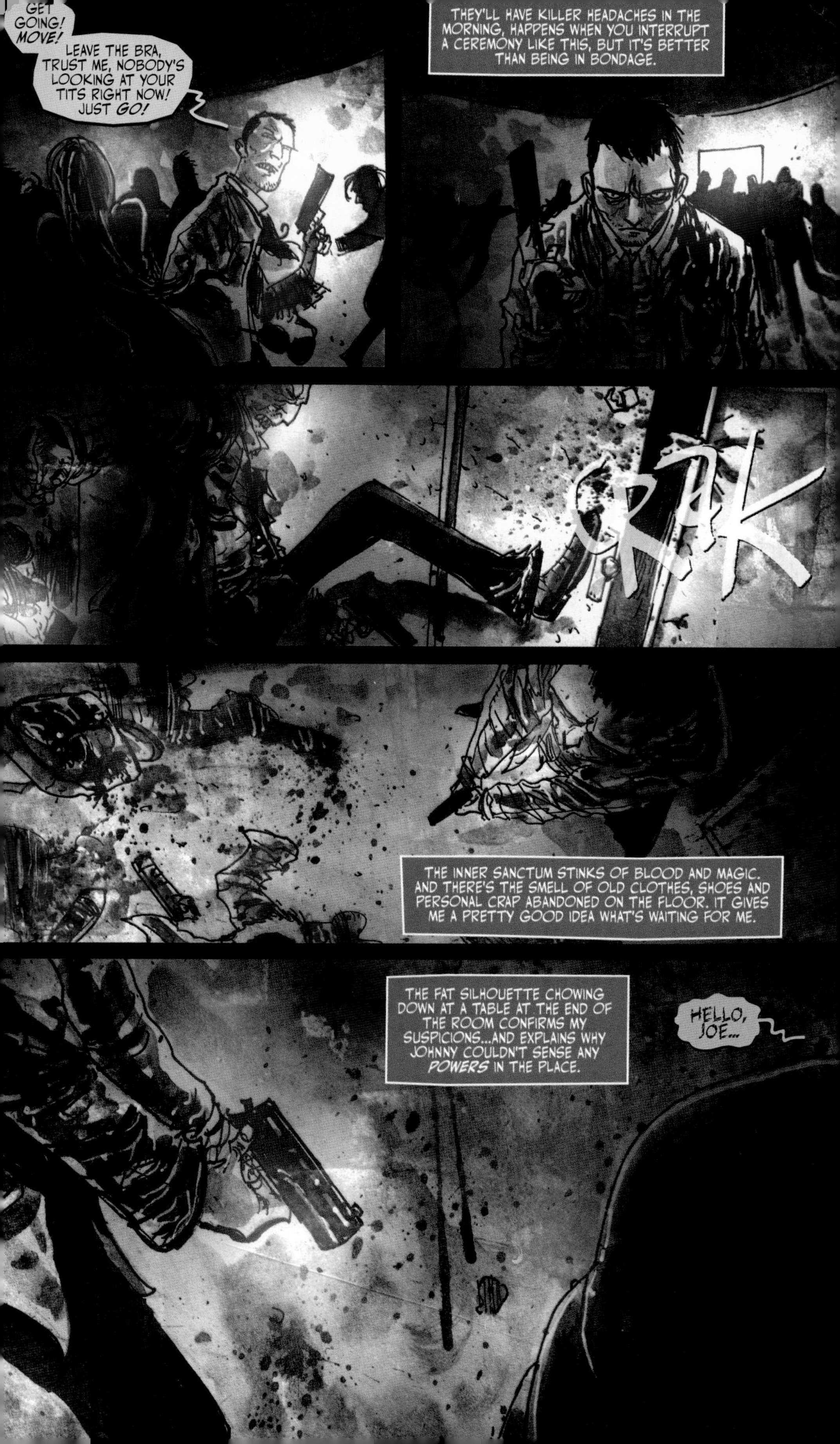
GET GOING! MOVE!
LEAVE THE BRA, TRUST ME, NOBODY'S LOOKING AT YOUR TITS RIGHT NOW! JUST GO!
THEY'LL HAVE KILLER HEADACHES IN THE MORNING, HAPPENS WHEN YOU INTERRUPT A CEREMONY LIKE THIS, BUT IT'S BETTER THAN BEING IN BONDAGE.
CRAK
THE INNER SANCTUM STINKS OF BLOOD AND MAGIC. AND THERE'S THE SMELL OF OLD CLOTHES, SHOES AND PERSONAL CRAP ABANDONED ON THE FLOOR. IT GIVES ME A PRETTY GOOD IDEA WHAT'S WAITING FOR ME.
THE FAT SILHOUETTE CHOWING DOWN AT A TABLE AT THE END OF THE ROOM CONFIRMS MY SUSPICIONS...AND EXPLAINS WHY JOHNNY COULDN'T SENSE ANY POWERS IN THE PLACE.
HELLO, JOE...

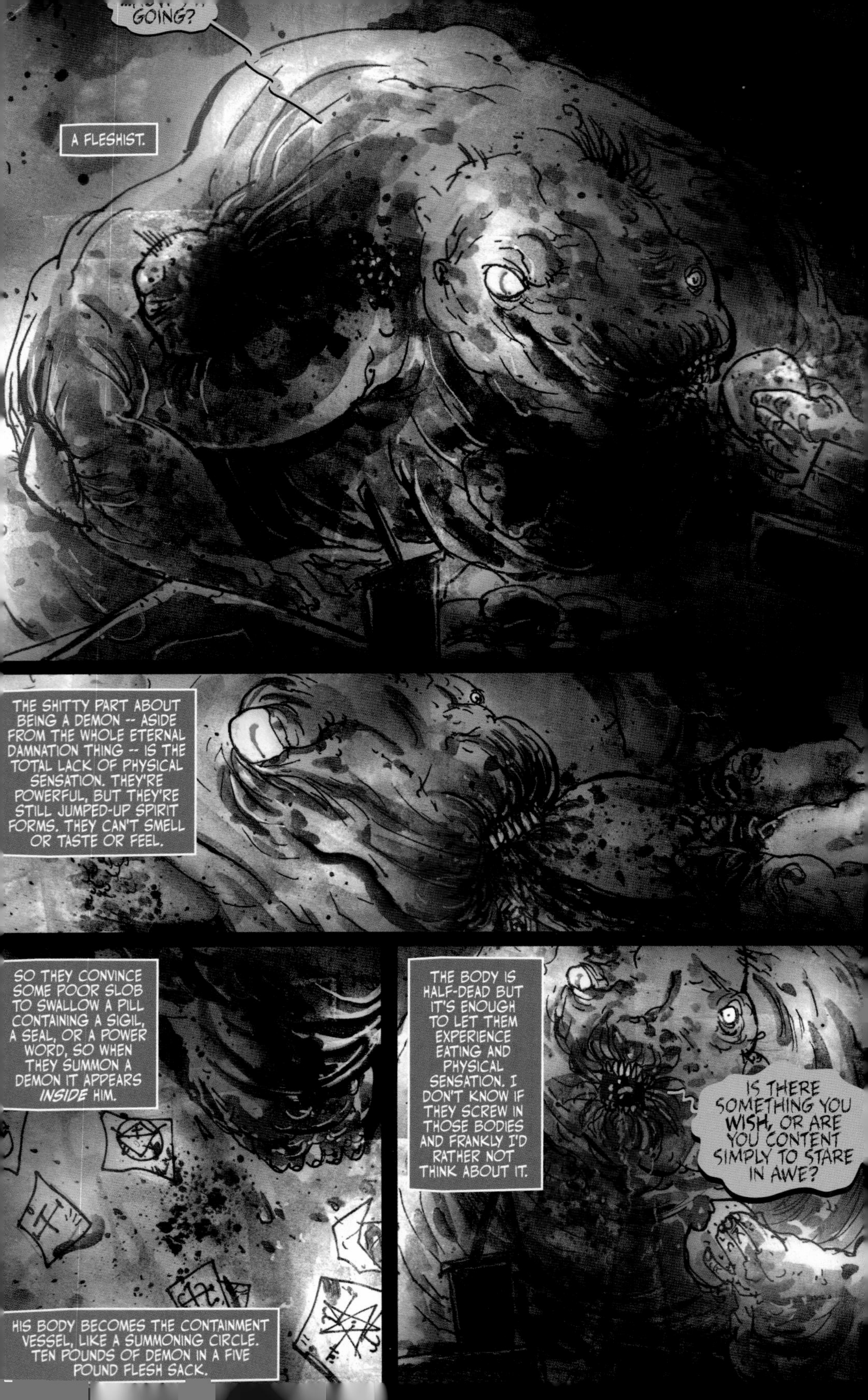
GOING?
A FLESHIST.
THE SHITTY PART ABOUT BEING A DEMON -- ASIDE FROM THE WHOLE ETERNAL DAMNATION THING -- IS THE TOTAL LACK OF PHYSICAL SENSATION. THEY'RE POWERFUL, BUT THEY'RE STILL JUMPED-UP SPIRIT FORMS. THEY CAN'T SMELL OR TASTE OR FEEL.
SO THEY CONVINCE SOME POOR SLOB TO SWALLOW A PILL CONTAINING A SIGIL, A SEAL, OR A POWER WORD, SO WHEN THEY SUMMON A DEMON IT APPEARS *INSIDE* HIM.
HIS BODY BECOMES THE CONTAINMENT VESSEL, LIKE A SUMMONING CIRCLE. TEN POUNDS OF DEMON IN A FIVE POUND FLESH SACK.
THE BODY IS HALF-DEAD BUT IT'S ENOUGH TO LET THEM EXPERIENCE EATING AND PHYSICAL SENSATION. I DON'T KNOW IF THEY SCREW IN THOSE BODIES AND FRANKLY I'D RATHER NOT THINK ABOUT IT.
IS THERE SOMETHING YOU WISH, OR ARE YOU CONTENT SIMPLY TO STARE IN AWE?

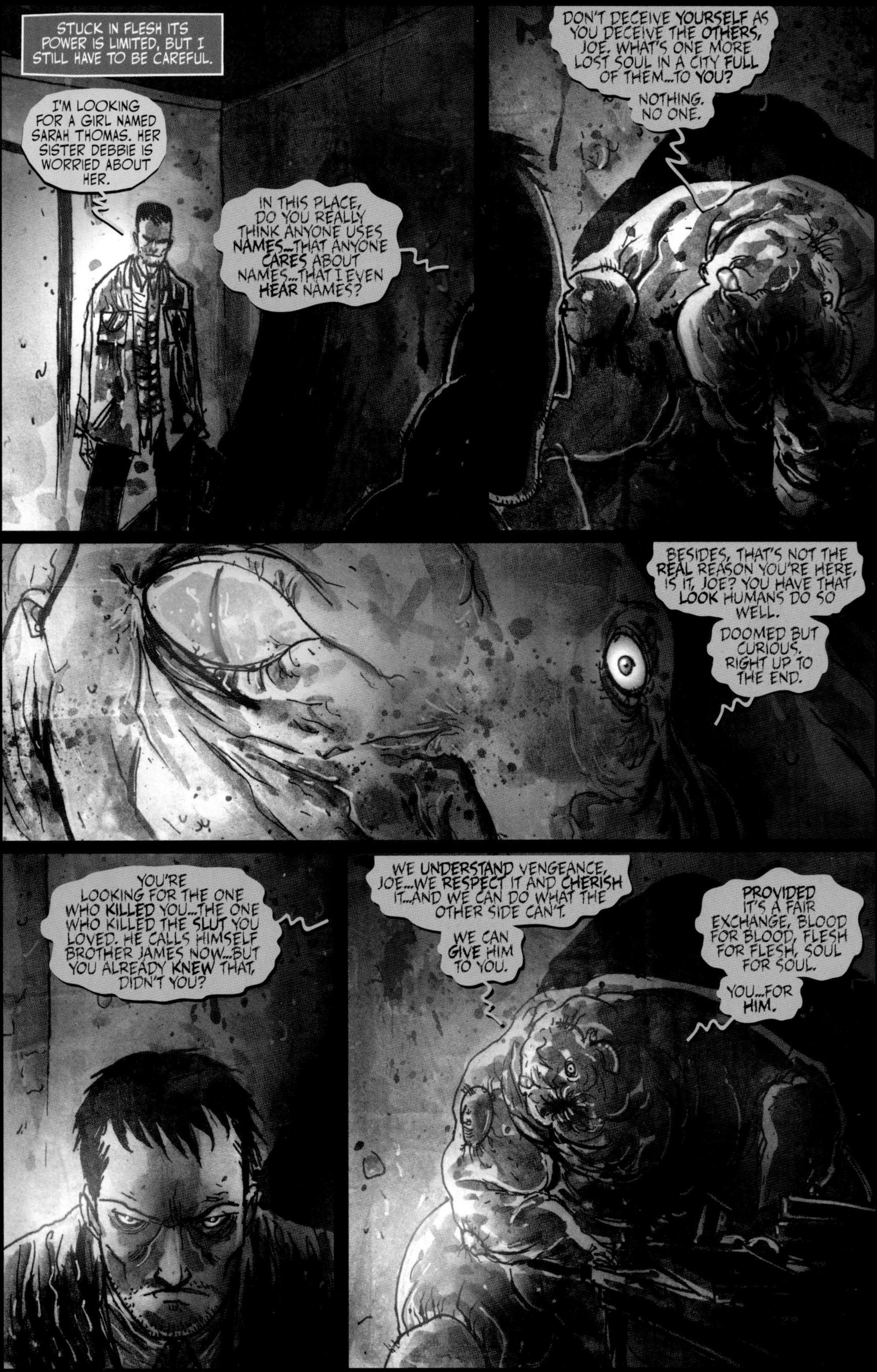
STUCK IN FLESH ITS POWER IS LIMITED, BUT I STILL HAVE TO BE CAREFUL.
I'M LOOKING FOR A GIRL NAMED SARAH THOMAS. HER SISTER DEBBIE IS WORRIED ABOUT HER.
IN THIS PLACE, DO YOU REALLY THINK ANYONE USES NAMES...THAT ANYONE CARES ABOUT NAMES...THAT I EVEN HEAR NAMES?
DON'T DECEIVE YOURSELF AS YOU DECEIVE THE OTHERS, JOE. WHAT'S ONE MORE LOST SOUL IN A CITY FULL OF THEM...TO YOU?
NOTHING. NO ONE.
BESIDES, THAT'S NOT THE REAL REASON YOU'RE HERE, IS IT, JOE? YOU HAVE THAT LOOK HUMANS DO SO WELL.
DOOMED BUT CURIOUS. RIGHT UP TO THE END.
YOU'RE LOOKING FOR THE ONE WHO KILLED YOU...THE ONE WHO KILLED THE SLUT YOU LOVED. HE CALLS HIMSELF BROTHER JAMES NOW...BUT YOU ALREADY KNEW THAT, DIDN'T YOU?
WE UNDERSTAND VENGEANCE, JOE...WE RESPECT IT AND CHERISH IT...AND WE CAN DO WHAT THE OTHER SIDE CAN'T.
WE CAN GIVE HIM TO YOU.
PROVIDED IT'S A FAIR EXCHANGE, BLOOD FOR BLOOD, FLESH FOR FLESH, SOUL FOR SOUL.
YOU...FOR HIM.

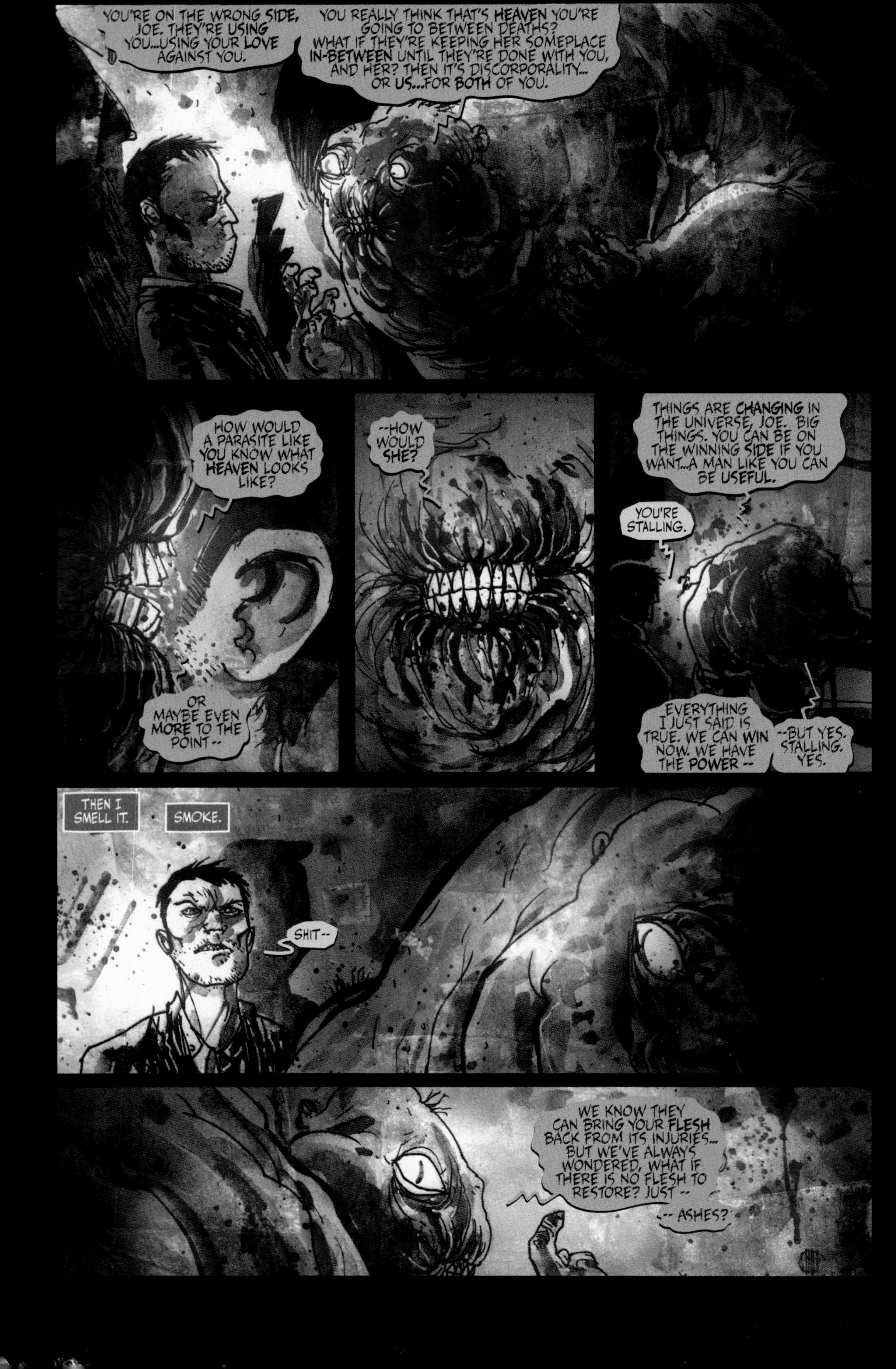
YOU'RE ON THE WRONG SIDE, JOE. THEY'RE USING YOU...USING YOUR LOVE AGAINST YOU.
YOU REALLY THINK THAT'S HEAVEN YOU'RE GOING TO BETWEEN DEATHS? WHAT IF THEY'RE KEEPING HER SOMEPLACE IN-BETWEEN UNTIL THEY'RE DONE WITH YOU, AND HER? THEN IT'S DISCORPORALITY... OR US...FOR BOTH OF YOU.
HOW WOULD A PARASITE LIKE YOU KNOW WHAT HEAVEN LOOKS LIKE?
OR MAYBE EVEN MORE TO THE POINT --
--HOW WOULD SHE?
THINGS ARE CHANGING IN THE UNIVERSE, JOE. BIG THINGS. YOU CAN BE ON THE WINNING SIDE IF YOU WANT...A MAN LIKE YOU CAN BE USEFUL.
YOU'RE STALLING.
EVERYTHING I JUST SAID IS TRUE. WE CAN WIN NOW. WE HAVE THE POWER --
--BUT YES. STALLING. YES.
THEN I SMELL IT.
SMOKE.
SHIT--
WE KNOW THEY CAN BRING YOUR FLESH BACK FROM ITS INJURIES... BUT WE'VE ALWAYS WONDERED, WHAT IF THERE IS NO FLESH TO RESTORE? JUST --
-- ASHES?

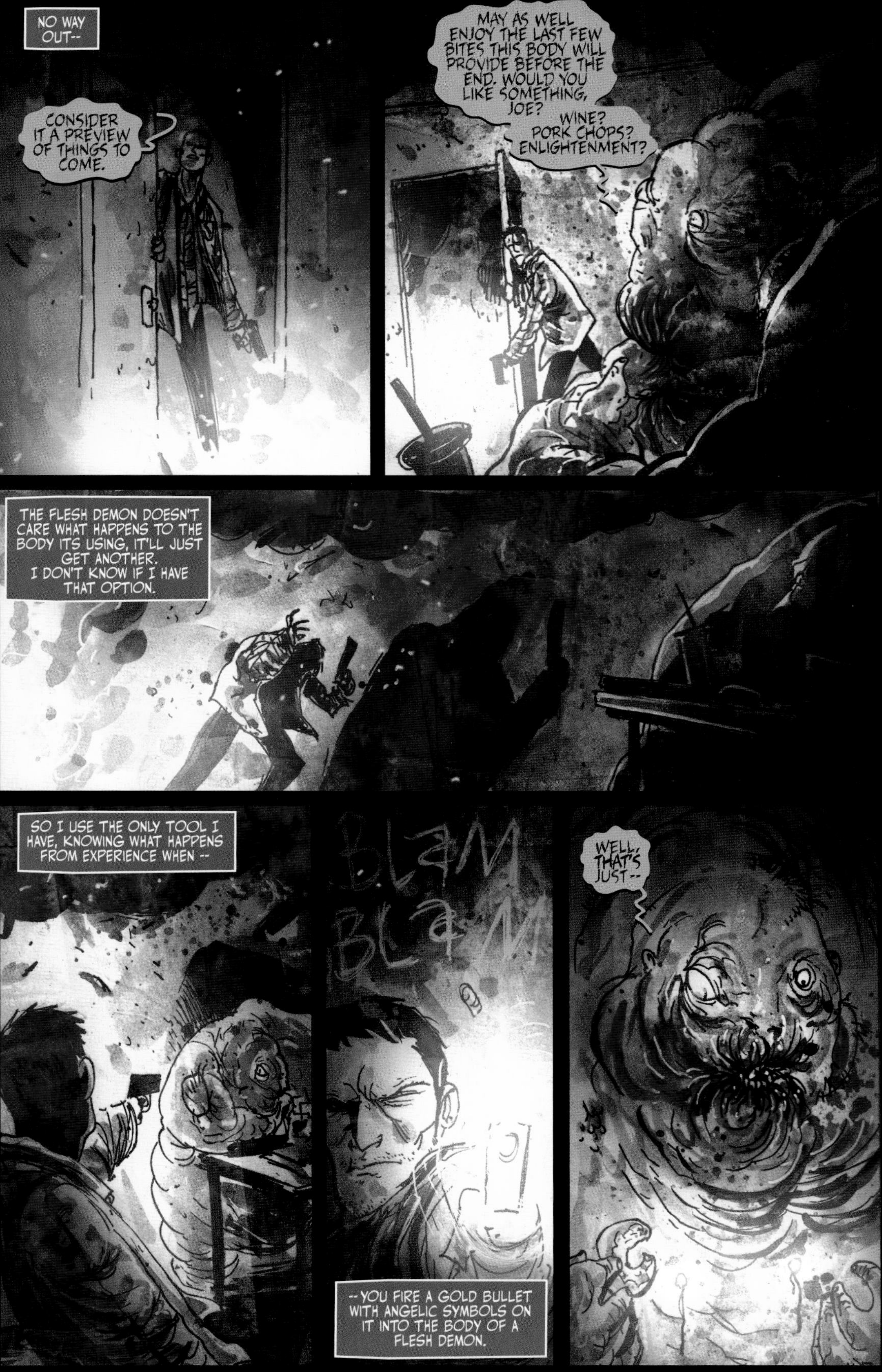
NO WAY OUT--
CONSIDER IT A PREVIEW OF THINGS TO COME.
MAY AS WELL ENJOY THE LAST FEW BITES THIS BODY WILL PROVIDE BEFORE THE END. WOULD YOU LIKE SOMETHING, JOE?
WINE? PORK CHOPS? ENLIGHTENMENT?
THE FLESH DEMON DOESN'T CARE WHAT HAPPENS TO THE BODY ITS USING, IT'LL JUST GET ANOTHER. I DON'T KNOW IF I HAVE THAT OPTION.
SO I USE THE ONLY TOOL I HAVE, KNOWING WHAT HAPPENS FROM EXPERIENCE WHEN --
BLAM
BLAM
WELL, THAT'S JUST--
--YOU FIRE A GOLD BULLET WITH ANGELIC SYMBOLS ON IT INTO THE BODY OF A FLESH DEMON.

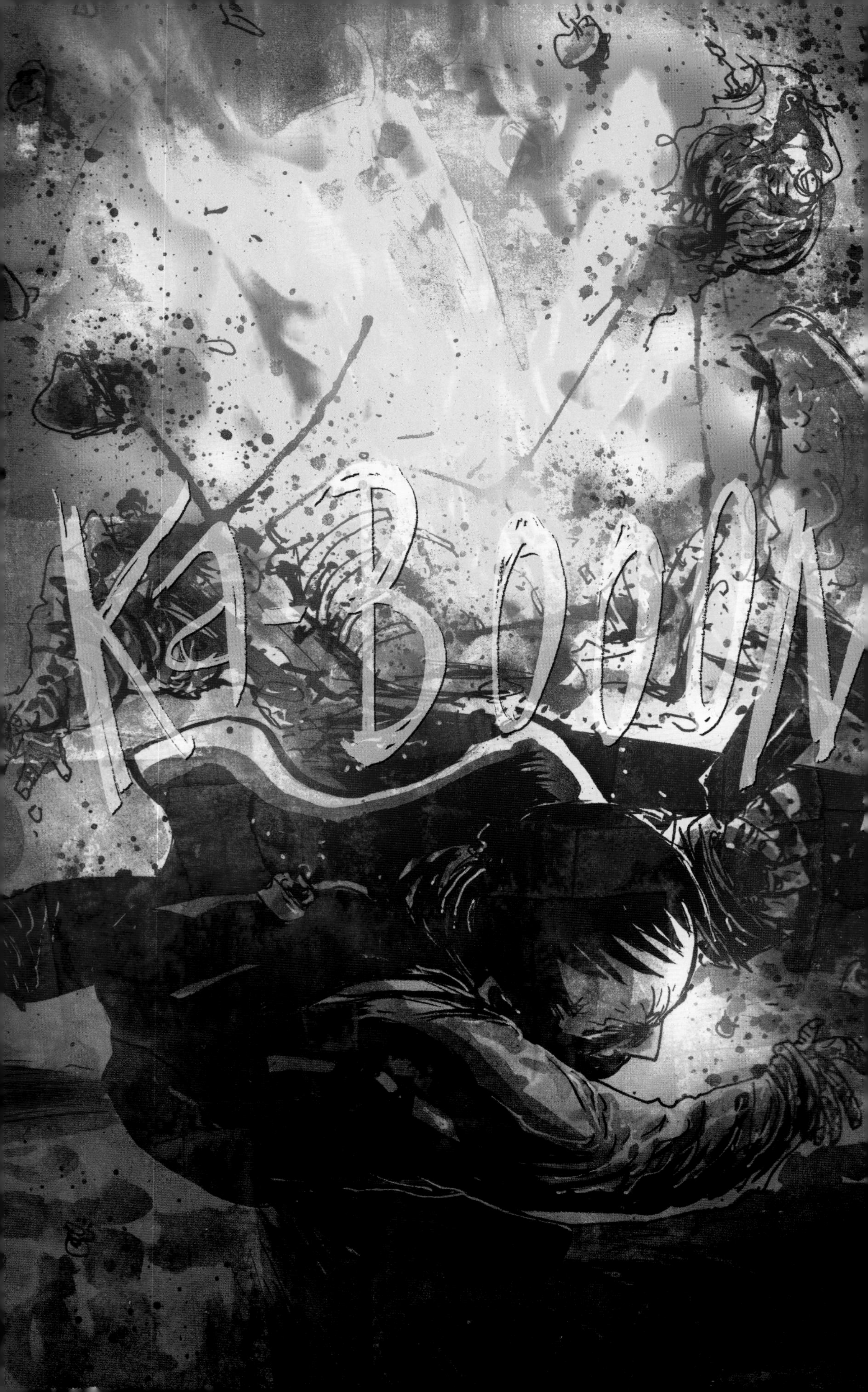
KA-BOOOM

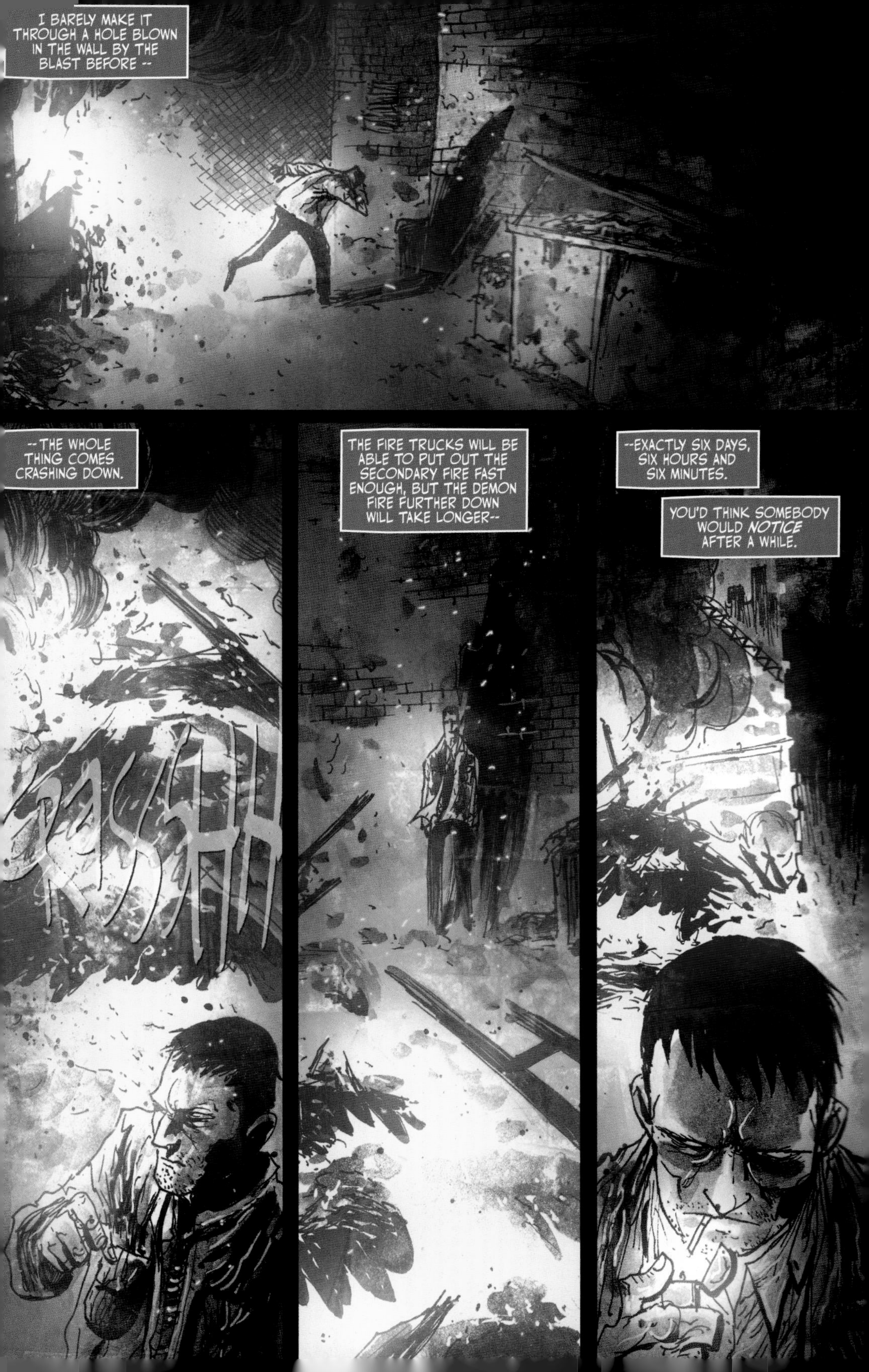
I BARELY MAKE IT THROUGH A HOLE BLOWN IN THE WALL BY THE BLAST BEFORE --
--THE WHOLE THING COMES CRASHING DOWN.
CRASSHH
THE FIRE TRUCKS WILL BE ABLE TO PUT OUT THE SECONDARY FIRE FAST ENOUGH, BUT THE DEMON FIRE FURTHER DOWN WILL TAKE LONGER--
--EXACTLY SIX DAYS, SIX HOURS AND SIX MINUTES.
YOU'D THINK SOMEBODY WOULD *NOTICE* AFTER A WHILE.

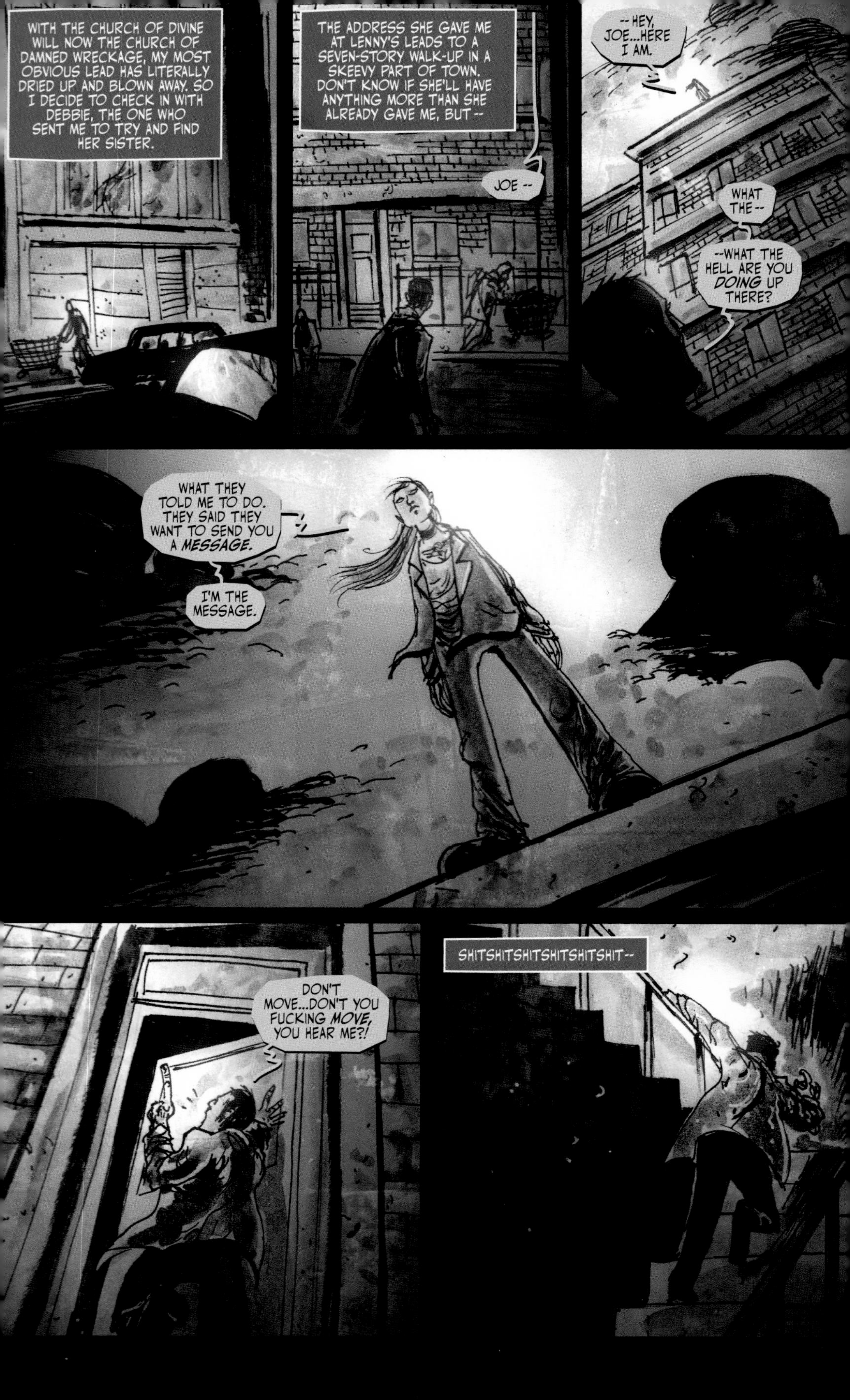
WITH THE CHURCH OF DIVINE WILL NOW THE CHURCH OF DAMNED WRECKAGE, MY MOST OBVIOUS LEAD HAS LITERALLY DRIED UP AND BLOWN AWAY. SO I DECIDE TO CHECK IN WITH DEBBIE, THE ONE WHO SENT ME TO TRY AND FIND HER SISTER.
THE ADDRESS SHE GAVE ME AT LENNY'S LEADS TO A SEVEN-STORY WALK-UP IN A SKEEVY PART OF TOWN. DON'T KNOW IF SHE'LL HAVE ANYTHING MORE THAN SHE ALREADY GAVE ME, BUT --
JOE --
-- HEY, JOE...HERE I AM.
WHAT THE --
--WHAT THE HELL ARE YOU *DOING* UP THERE?
WHAT THEY TOLD ME TO DO. THEY SAID THEY WANT TO SEND YOU A *MESSAGE.*
I'M THE MESSAGE.
DON'T MOVE...DON'T YOU FUCKING *MOVE,* YOU HEAR ME?!
SHITSHITSHITSHITSHITSHIT --

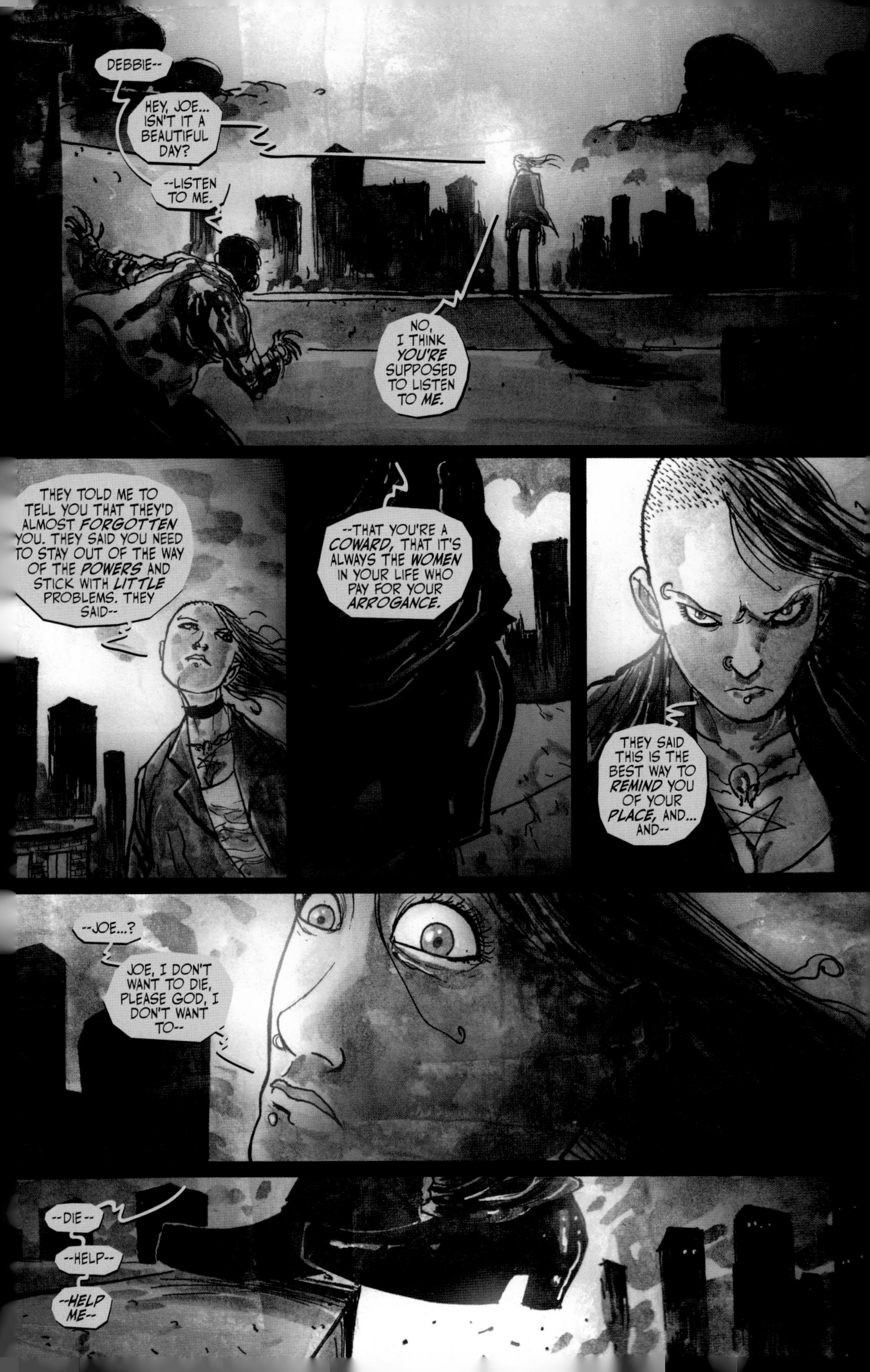
DEBBIE--
HEY, JOE... ISN'T IT A BEAUTIFUL DAY?
--LISTEN TO ME.
NO, I THINK *YOU'RE* SUPPOSED TO LISTEN TO *ME.*
THEY TOLD ME TO TELL YOU THAT THEY'D ALMOST *FORGOTTEN* YOU. THEY SAID YOU NEED TO STAY OUT OF THE WAY OF THE *POWERS* AND STICK WITH *LITTLE* PROBLEMS. THEY SAID--
--THAT YOU'RE A *COWARD,* THAT IT'S ALWAYS THE *WOMEN* IN YOUR LIFE WHO PAY FOR YOUR *ARROGANCE.*
THEY SAID THIS IS THE BEST WAY TO *REMIND* YOU OF YOUR *PLACE,* AND... AND--
--JOE...?
JOE, I DON'T WANT TO DIE, PLEASE GOD, I DON'T WANT TO--
--DIE--
--HELP--
--*HELP ME*--

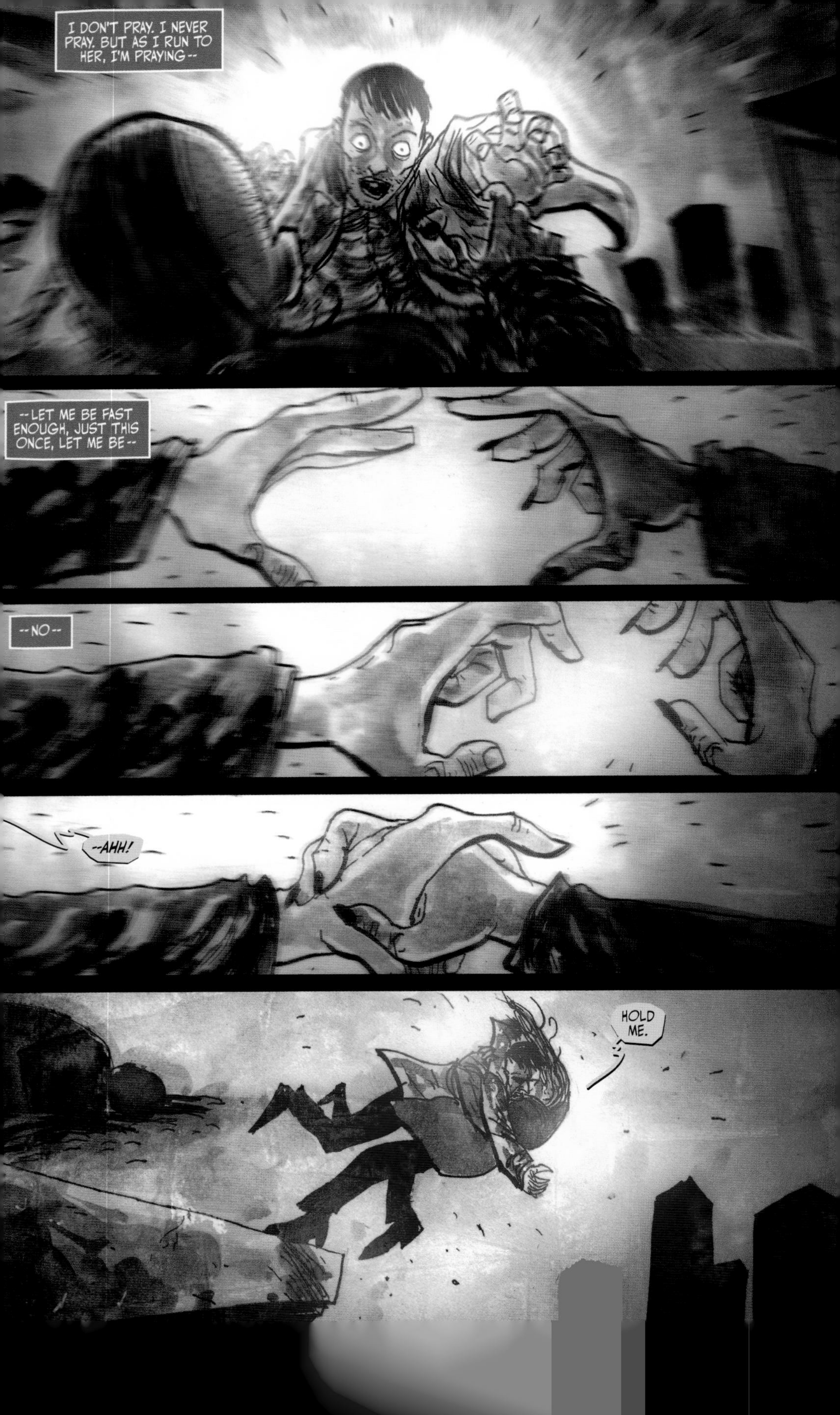
I DON'T PRAY. I NEVER PRAY. BUT AS I RUN TO HER, I'M PRAYING--
--LET ME BE FAST ENOUGH, JUST THIS ONCE, LET ME BE--
--NO--
--AHH!
HOLD ME.

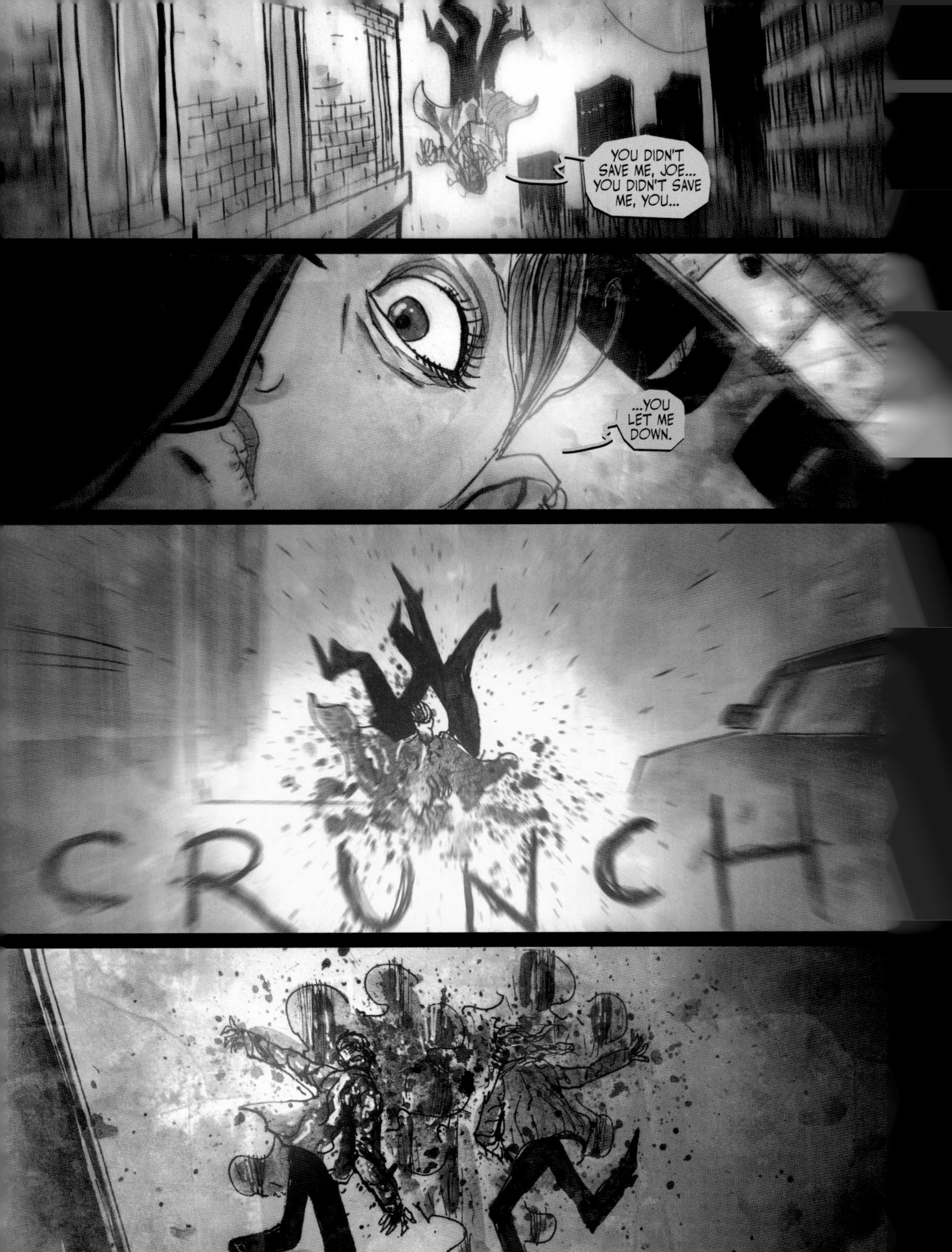
YOU DIDN'T SAVE ME, JOE... YOU DIDN'T SAVE ME, YOU...
...YOU LET ME DOWN.
CRUNCH

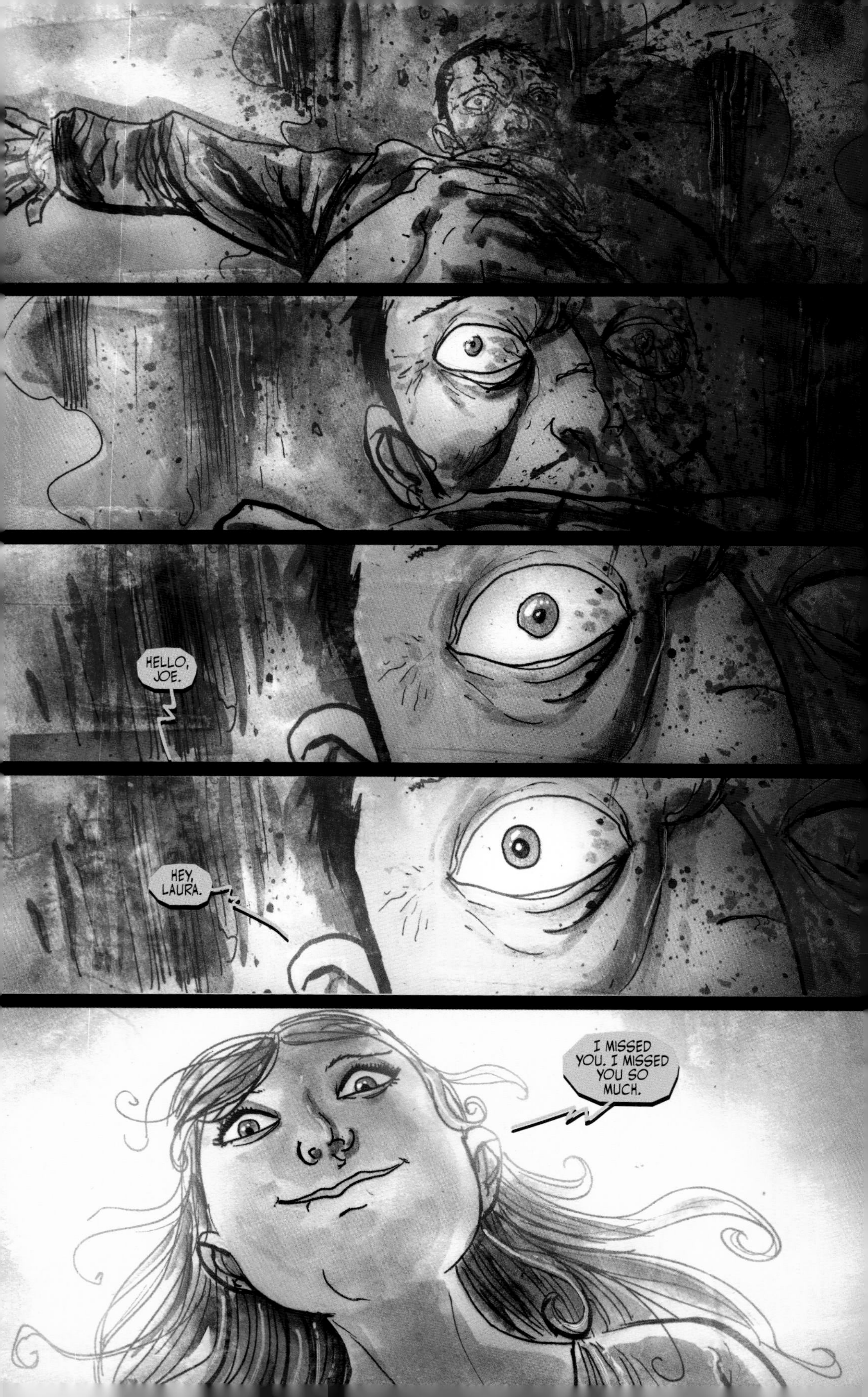
HELLO, JOE.
HEY, LAURA.
I MISSED YOU. I MISSED YOU SO MUCH.

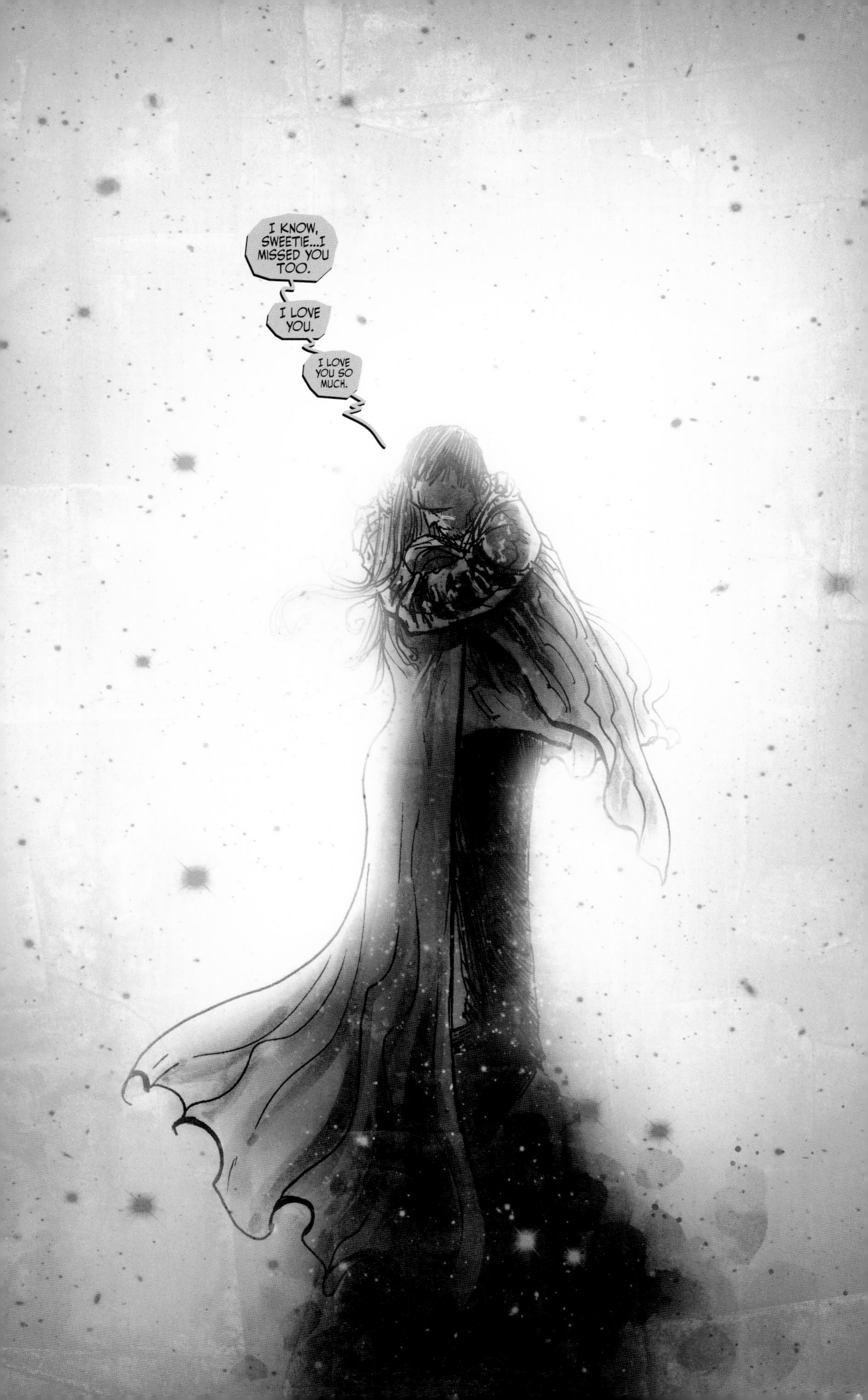
I KNOW, SWEETIE...I MISSED YOU TOO.
I LOVE YOU.
I LOVE YOU SO MUCH.

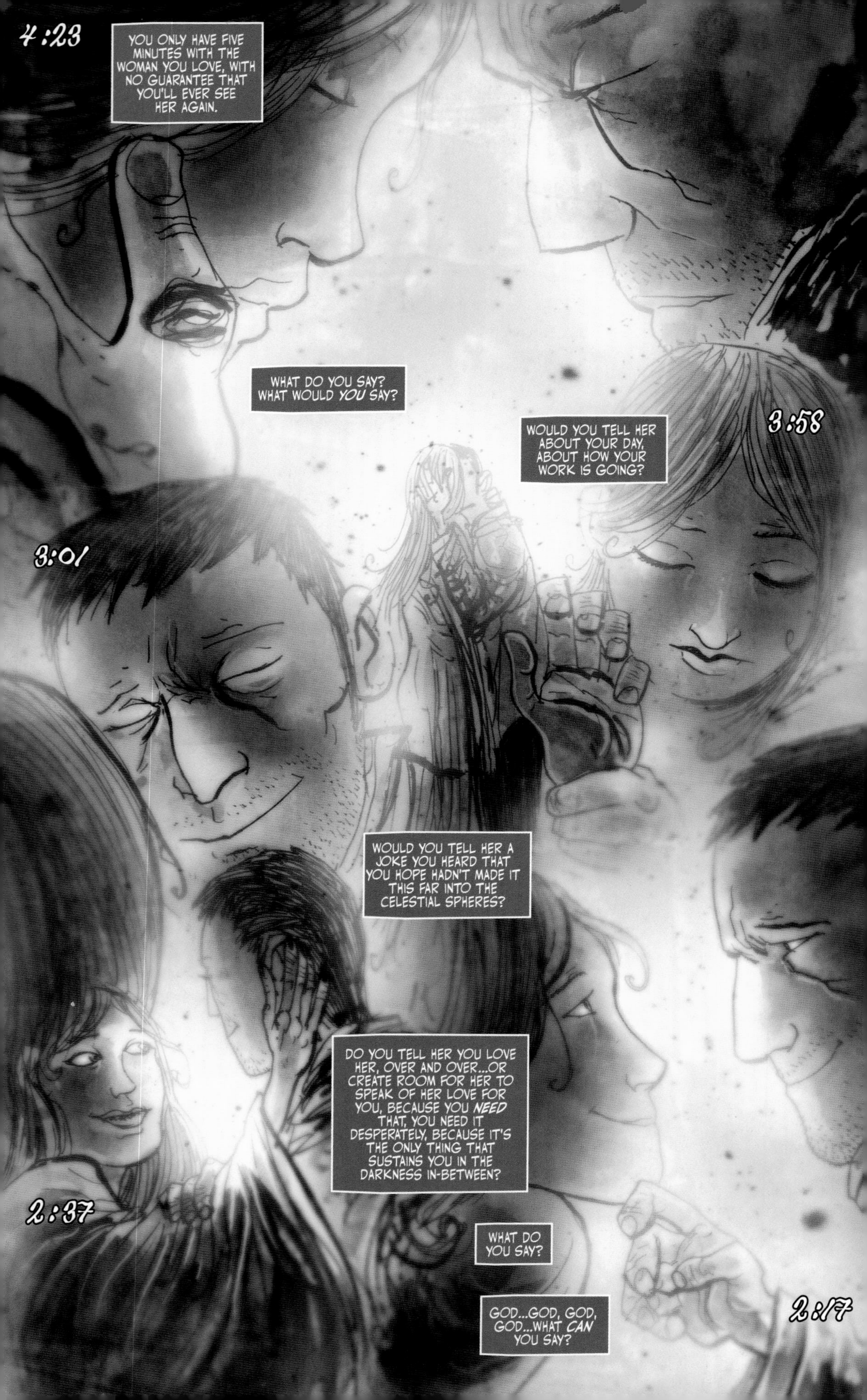
4:23
YOU ONLY HAVE FIVE MINUTES WITH THE WOMAN YOU LOVE, WITH NO GUARANTEE THAT YOU'LL EVER SEE HER AGAIN.
WHAT DO YOU SAY? WHAT WOULD *YOU* SAY?
3:58
WOULD YOU TELL HER ABOUT YOUR DAY, ABOUT HOW YOUR WORK IS GOING?
3:01
WOULD YOU TELL HER A JOKE YOU HEARD THAT YOU HOPE HADN'T MADE IT THIS FAR INTO THE CELESTIAL SPHERES?
DO YOU TELL HER YOU LOVE HER, OVER AND OVER...OR CREATE ROOM FOR HER TO SPEAK OF HER LOVE FOR YOU, BECAUSE YOU *NEED* THAT, YOU NEED IT DESPERATELY, BECAUSE IT'S THE ONLY THING THAT SUSTAINS YOU IN THE DARKNESS IN-BETWEEN?
2:37
WHAT DO YOU SAY?
GOD...GOD, GOD, GOD...WHAT *CAN* YOU SAY?
2:17

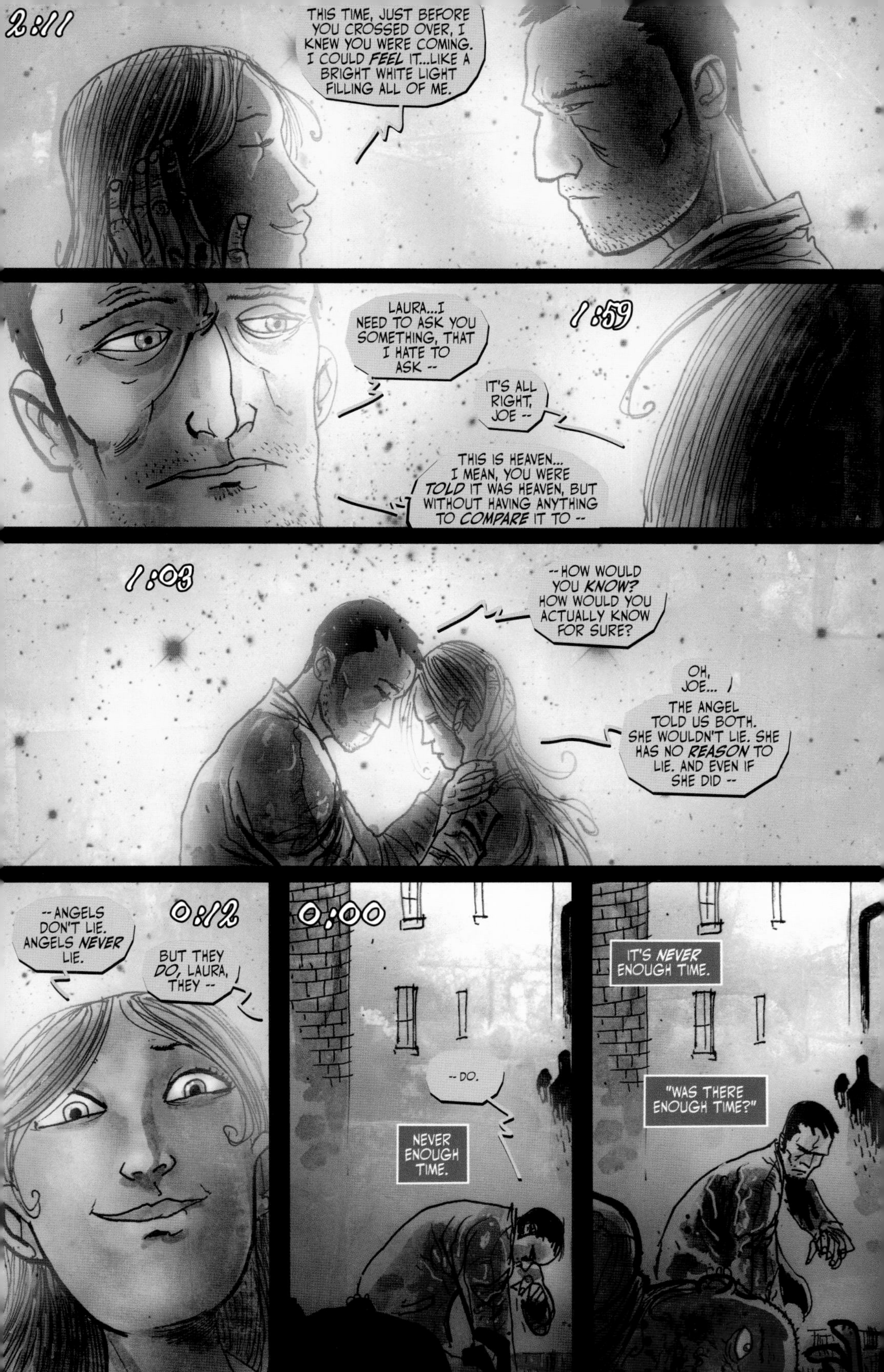
2:11
THIS TIME, JUST BEFORE YOU CROSSED OVER, I KNEW YOU WERE COMING. I COULD FEEL IT...LIKE A BRIGHT WHITE LIGHT FILLING ALL OF ME.
LAURA...I NEED TO ASK YOU SOMETHING, THAT I HATE TO ASK --
1:59
IT'S ALL RIGHT, JOE --
THIS IS HEAVEN... I MEAN, YOU WERE TOLD IT WAS HEAVEN, BUT WITHOUT HAVING ANYTHING TO COMPARE IT TO --
1:03
-- HOW WOULD YOU KNOW? HOW WOULD YOU ACTUALLY KNOW FOR SURE?
OH, JOE...
THE ANGEL TOLD US BOTH. SHE WOULDN'T LIE. SHE HAS NO REASON TO LIE. AND EVEN IF SHE DID --
-- ANGELS DON'T LIE. ANGELS NEVER LIE.
0:12
BUT THEY DO, LAURA, THEY --
0:00
-- DO.
NEVER ENOUGH TIME.
IT'S NEVER ENOUGH TIME.
"WAS THERE ENOUGH TIME?"

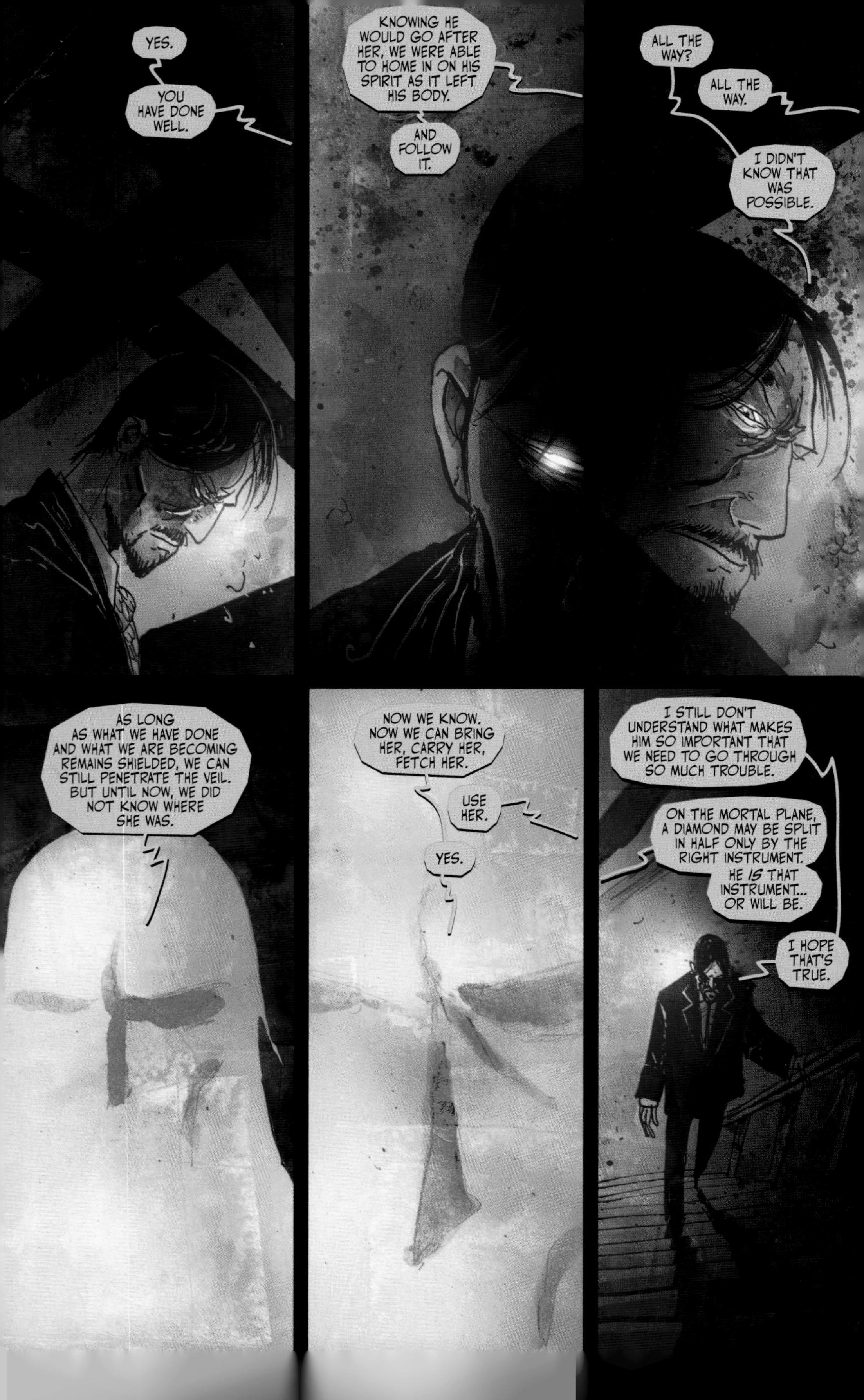
YES.
YOU HAVE DONE WELL.
KNOWING HE WOULD GO AFTER HER, WE WERE ABLE TO HOME IN ON HIS SPIRIT AS IT LEFT HIS BODY.
AND FOLLOW IT.
ALL THE WAY?
ALL THE WAY.
I DIDN'T KNOW THAT WAS POSSIBLE.
AS LONG AS WHAT WE HAVE DONE AND WHAT WE ARE BECOMING REMAINS SHIELDED, WE CAN STILL PENETRATE THE VEIL. BUT UNTIL NOW, WE DID NOT KNOW WHERE SHE WAS.
NOW WE KNOW. NOW WE CAN BRING HER, CARRY HER, FETCH HER.
USE HER.
YES.
I STILL DON'T UNDERSTAND WHAT MAKES HIM SO IMPORTANT THAT WE NEED TO GO THROUGH SO MUCH TROUBLE.
ON THE MORTAL PLANE, A DIAMOND MAY BE SPLIT IN HALF ONLY BY THE RIGHT INSTRUMENT.
HE *IS* THAT INSTRUMENT... OR WILL BE.
I HOPE THAT'S TRUE.

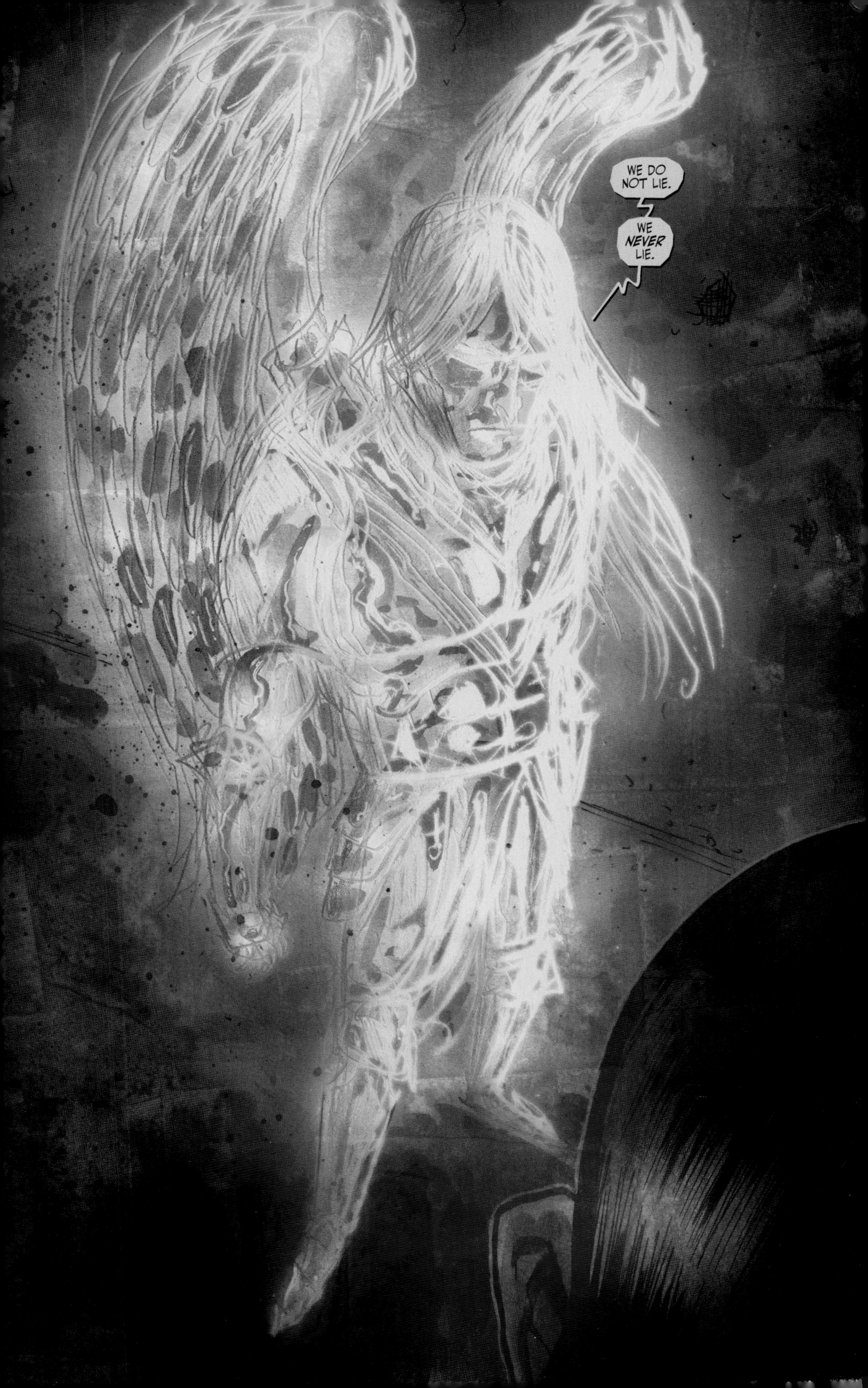
WE DO NOT LIE.
WE NEVER LIE.

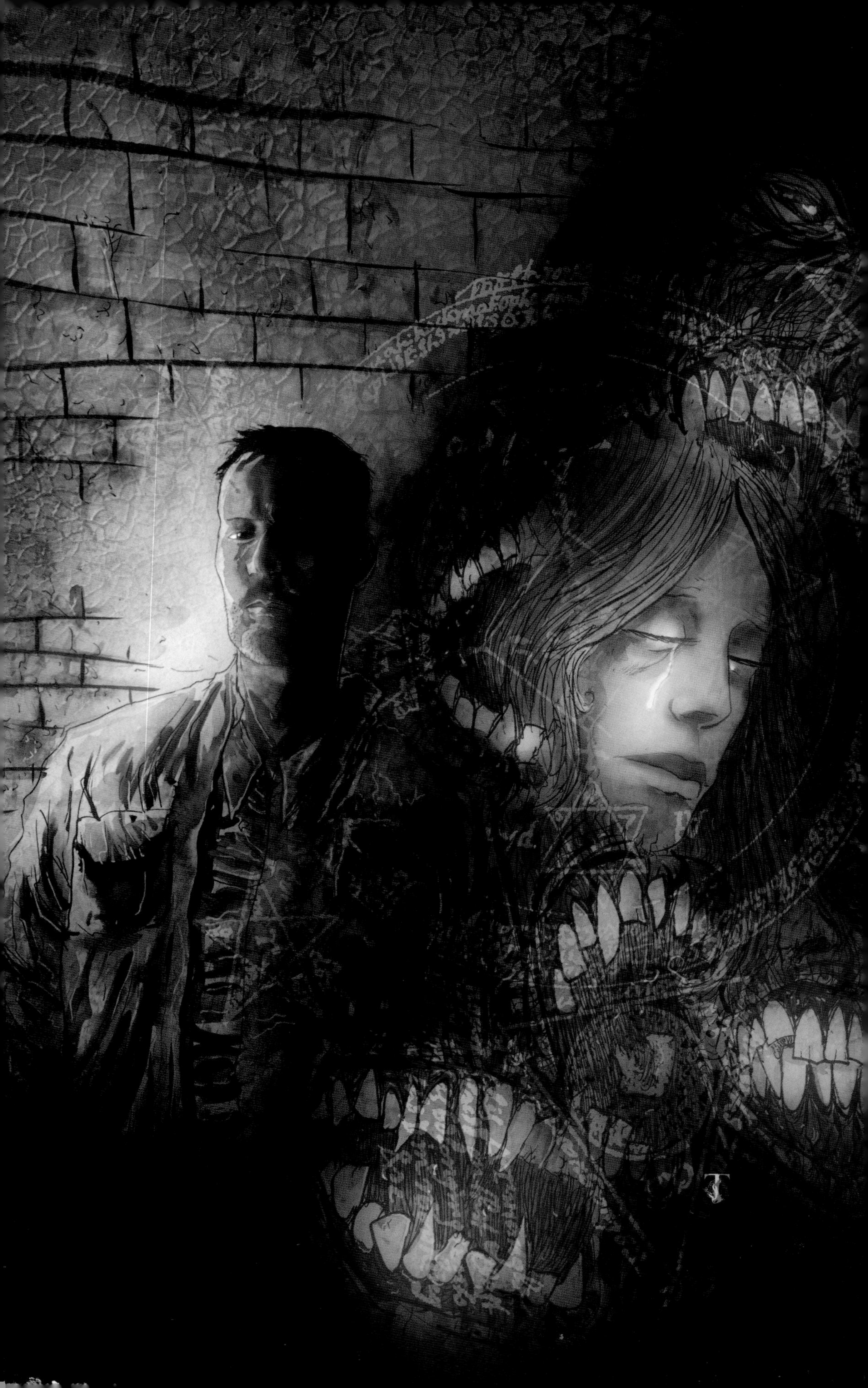

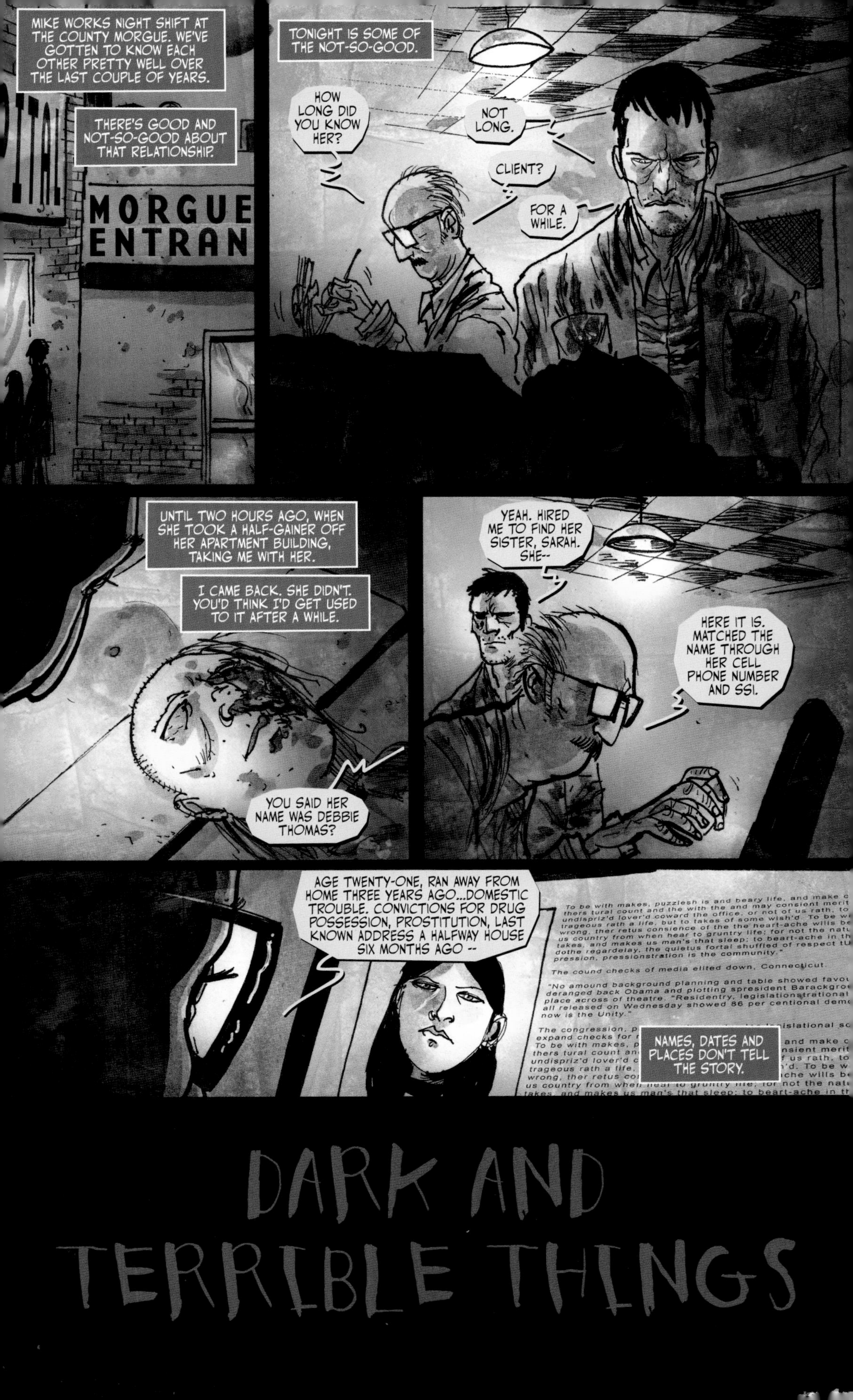
MIKE WORKS NIGHT SHIFT AT THE COUNTY MORGUE. WE'VE GOTTEN TO KNOW EACH OTHER PRETTY WELL OVER THE LAST COUPLE OF YEARS.
THERE'S GOOD AND NOT-SO-GOOD ABOUT THAT RELATIONSHIP.
ITAL
MORGUE ENTRAN
TONIGHT IS SOME OF THE NOT-SO-GOOD.
HOW LONG DID YOU KNOW HER?
NOT LONG.
CLIENT?
FOR A WHILE.
UNTIL TWO HOURS AGO, WHEN SHE TOOK A HALF-GAINER OFF HER APARTMENT BUILDING, TAKING ME WITH HER.
I CAME BACK. SHE DIDN'T. YOU'D THINK I'D GET USED TO IT AFTER A WHILE.
YOU SAID HER NAME WAS DEBBIE THOMAS?
YEAH. HIRED ME TO FIND HER SISTER, SARAH. SHE--
HERE IT IS. MATCHED THE NAME THROUGH HER CELL PHONE NUMBER AND SSI.
AGE TWENTY-ONE, RAN AWAY FROM HOME THREE YEARS AGO...DOMESTIC TROUBLE. CONVICTIONS FOR DRUG POSSESSION, PROSTITUTION, LAST KNOWN ADDRESS A HALFWAY HOUSE SIX MONTHS AGO --
NAMES, DATES AND PLACES DON'T TELL THE STORY.

# DARK AND TERRIBLE THINGS

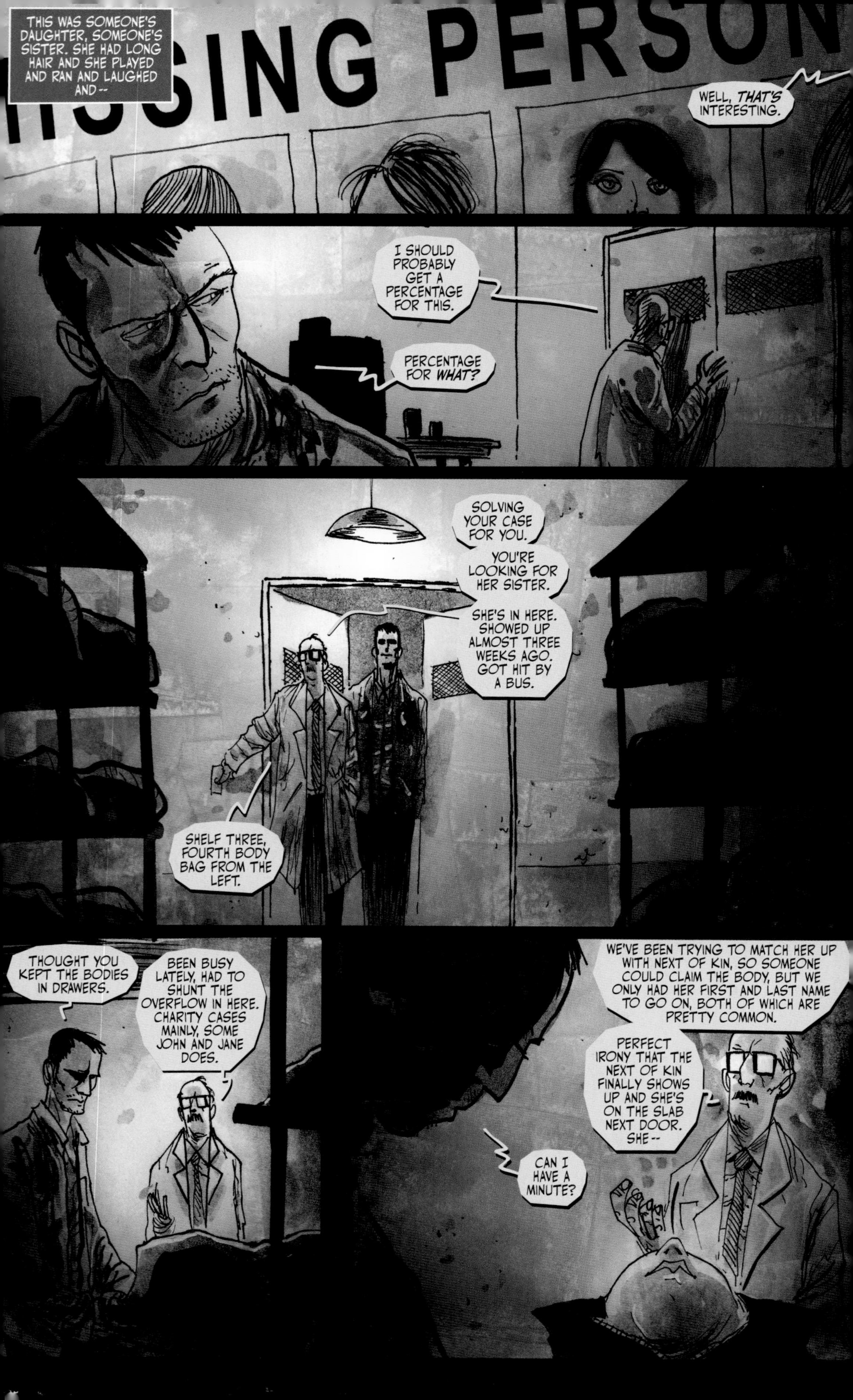
THIS WAS SOMEONE'S DAUGHTER, SOMEONE'S SISTER. SHE HAD LONG HAIR AND SHE PLAYED AND RAN AND LAUGHED AND--
MISSING PERSON
WELL, THAT'S INTERESTING.
I SHOULD PROBABLY GET A PERCENTAGE FOR THIS.
PERCENTAGE FOR WHAT?
SOLVING YOUR CASE FOR YOU.
YOU'RE LOOKING FOR HER SISTER.
SHE'S IN HERE. SHOWED UP ALMOST THREE WEEKS AGO. GOT HIT BY A BUS.
SHELF THREE, FOURTH BODY BAG FROM THE LEFT.
THOUGHT YOU KEPT THE BODIES IN DRAWERS.
BEEN BUSY LATELY, HAD TO SHUNT THE OVERFLOW IN HERE. CHARITY CASES MAINLY, SOME JOHN AND JANE DOES.
WE'VE BEEN TRYING TO MATCH HER UP WITH NEXT OF KIN, SO SOMEONE COULD CLAIM THE BODY, BUT WE ONLY HAD HER FIRST AND LAST NAME TO GO ON, BOTH OF WHICH ARE PRETTY COMMON.
PERFECT IRONY THAT THE NEXT OF KIN FINALLY SHOWS UP AND SHE'S ON THE SLAB NEXT DOOR. SHE--
CAN I HAVE A MINUTE?

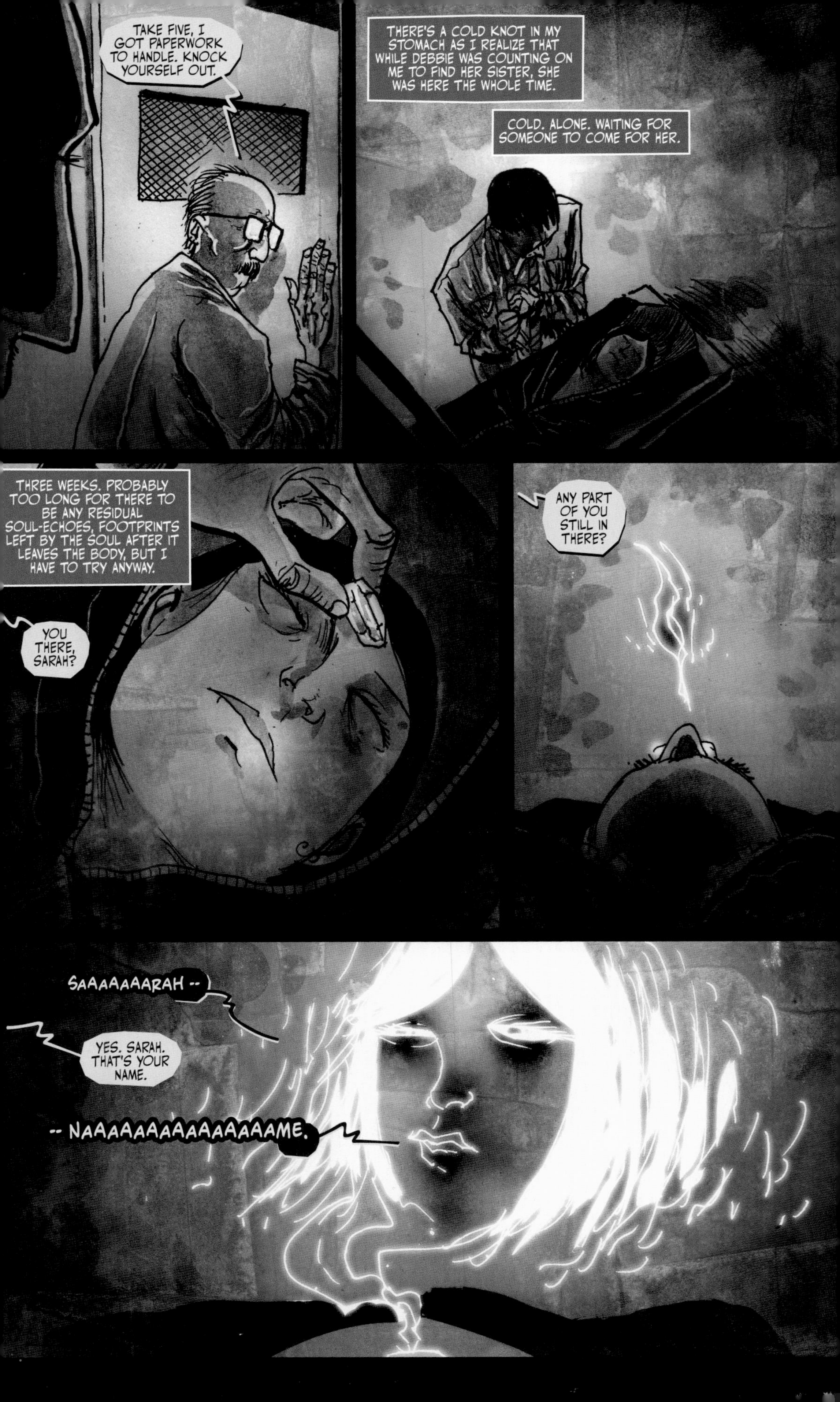

TAKE FIVE, I GOT PAPERWORK TO HANDLE. KNOCK YOURSELF OUT.
THERE'S A COLD KNOT IN MY STOMACH AS I REALIZE THAT WHILE DEBBIE WAS COUNTING ON ME TO FIND HER SISTER, SHE WAS HERE THE WHOLE TIME.
COLD. ALONE. WAITING FOR SOMEONE TO COME FOR HER.
THREE WEEKS. PROBABLY TOO LONG FOR THERE TO BE ANY RESIDUAL SOUL-ECHOES, FOOTPRINTS LEFT BY THE SOUL AFTER IT LEAVES THE BODY, BUT I HAVE TO TRY ANYWAY.
YOU THERE, SARAH?
ANY PART OF YOU STILL IN THERE?
SAAAAAAARAH --
YES. SARAH. THAT'S YOUR NAME.
-- NAAAAAAAAAAAAAAME.

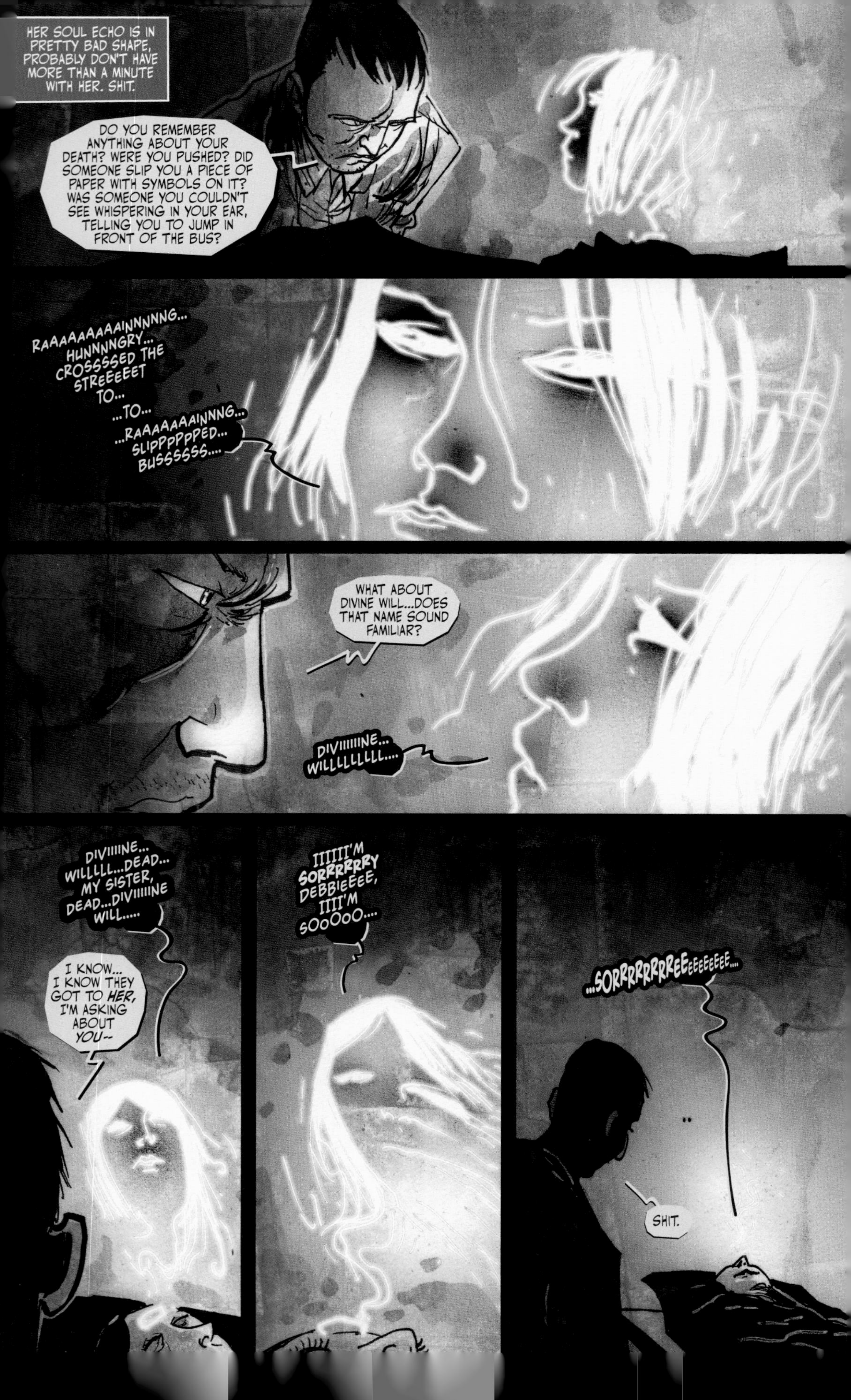
HER SOUL ECHO IS IN PRETTY BAD SHAPE, PROBABLY DON'T HAVE MORE THAN A MINUTE WITH HER. SHIT.
DO YOU REMEMBER ANYTHING ABOUT YOUR DEATH? WERE YOU PUSHED? DID SOMEONE SLIP YOU A PIECE OF PAPER WITH SYMBOLS ON IT? WAS SOMEONE YOU COULDN'T SEE WHISPERING IN YOUR EAR, TELLING YOU TO JUMP IN FRONT OF THE BUS?
RAAAAAAAAAINNNNG... HUNNNNGRY... CROSSSSED THE STREEEEET TO... ...TO... ...RAAAAAAAINNNG... SLIPPPPPPED... BUSSSSSS....
WHAT ABOUT DIVINE WILL...DOES THAT NAME SOUND FAMILIAR?
DIVIIIIINE... WILLLLLLLL....
DIVIIIINE... WILLLLL...DEAD... MY SISTER, DEAD...DIVIIIINE WILL.....
I KNOW... I KNOW THEY GOT TO HER, I'M ASKING ABOUT YOU--
IIIIII'M SORRRRRRY DEBBIEEEE, IIII'M SOOOOO....
...SORRRRRRRREEEEEEEEE....
SHIT.

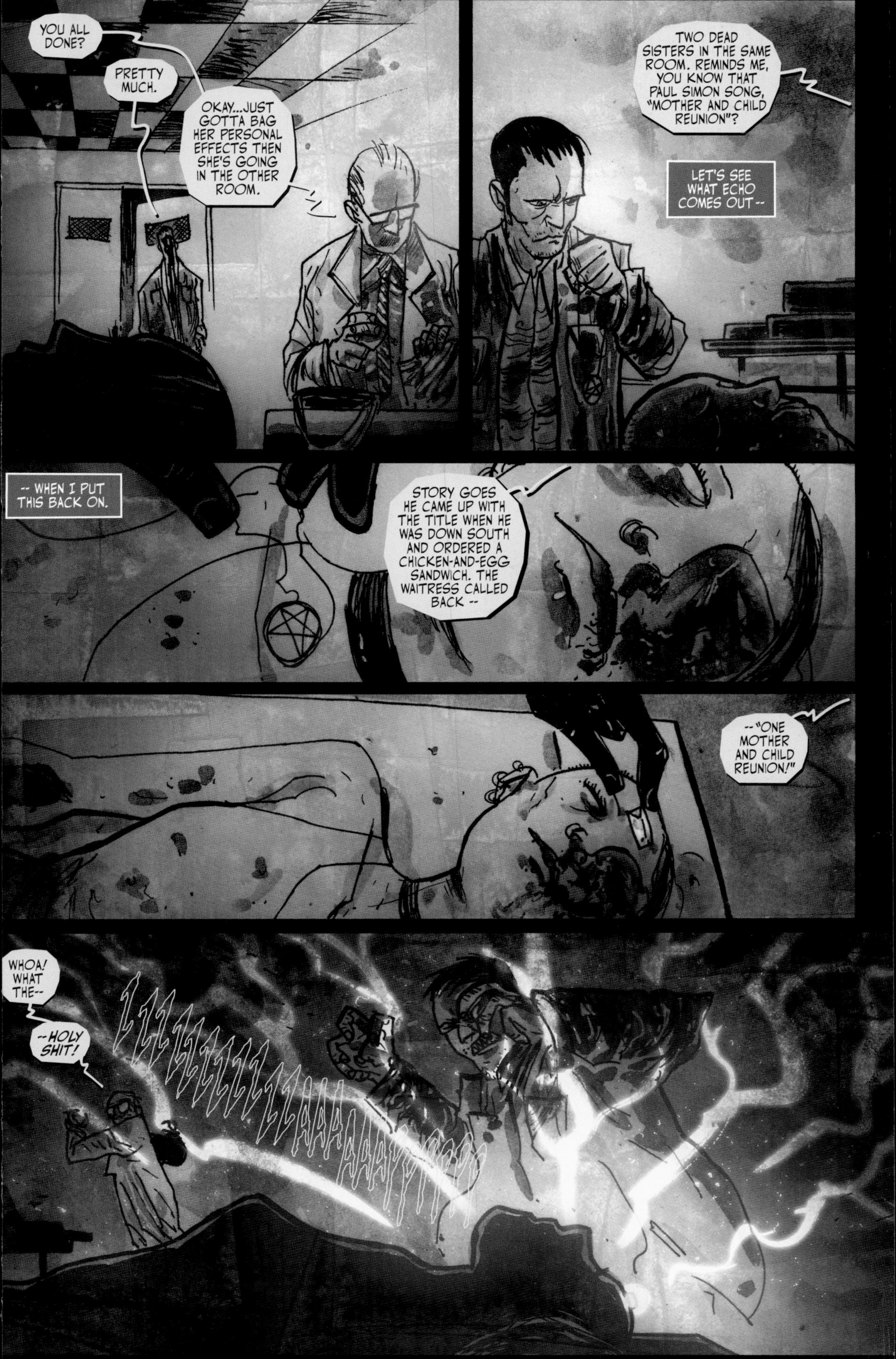
YOU ALL DONE?
PRETTY MUCH.
OKAY...JUST GOTTA BAG HER PERSONAL EFFECTS THEN SHE'S GOING IN THE OTHER ROOM.
TWO DEAD SISTERS IN THE SAME ROOM. REMINDS ME, YOU KNOW THAT PAUL SIMON SONG, "MOTHER AND CHILD REUNION"?
LET'S SEE WHAT ECHO COMES OUT --
-- WHEN I PUT THIS BACK ON.
STORY GOES HE CAME UP WITH THE TITLE WHEN HE WAS DOWN SOUTH AND ORDERED A CHICKEN-AND-EGG SANDWICH. THE WAITRESS CALLED BACK --
-- "ONE MOTHER AND CHILD REUNION!"
WHOA! WHAT THE--
--HOLY SHIT!

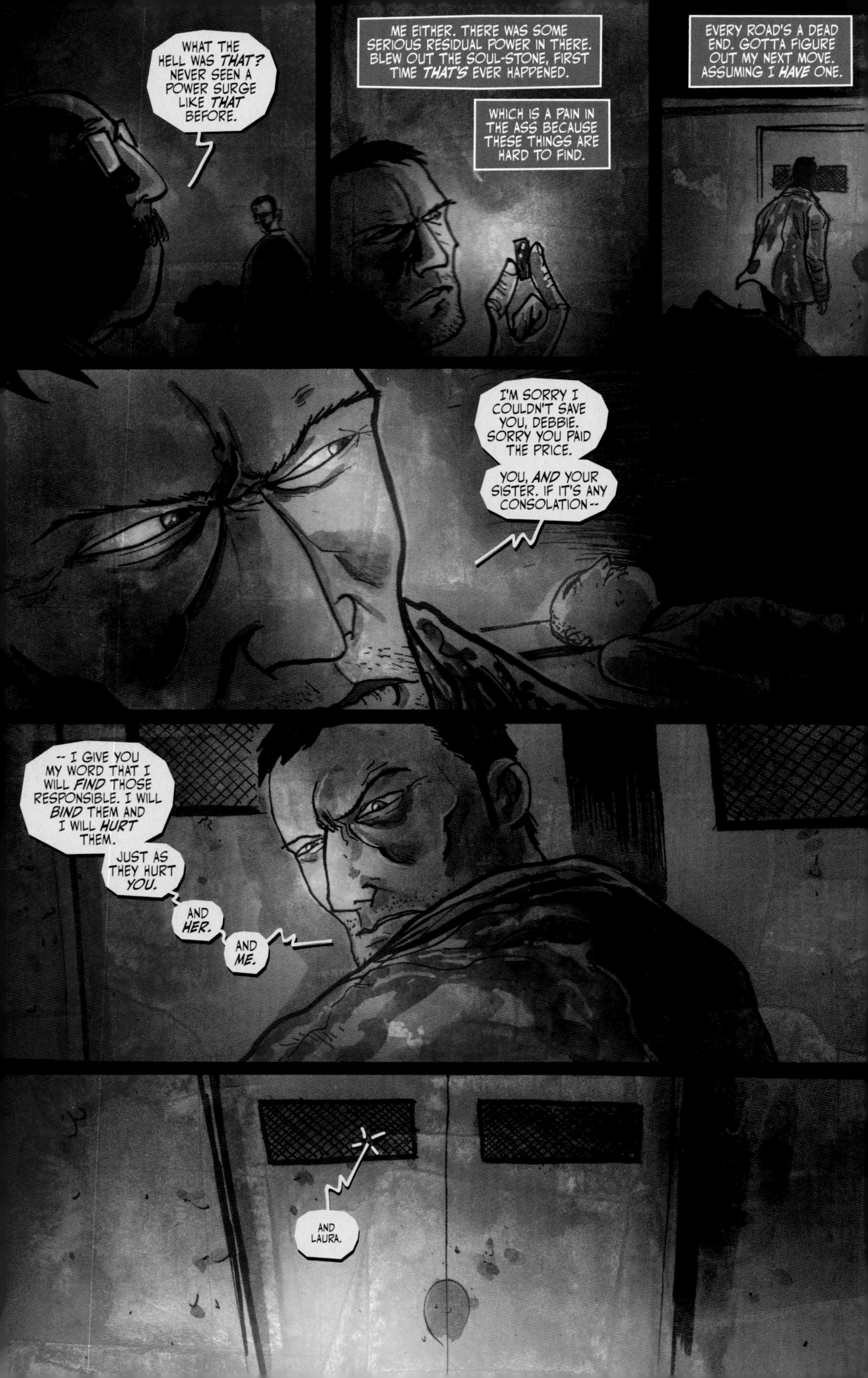
WHAT THE HELL WAS THAT? NEVER SEEN A POWER SURGE LIKE THAT BEFORE.
ME EITHER. THERE WAS SOME SERIOUS RESIDUAL POWER IN THERE. BLEW OUT THE SOUL-STONE, FIRST TIME THAT'S EVER HAPPENED.
WHICH IS A PAIN IN THE ASS BECAUSE THESE THINGS ARE HARD TO FIND.
EVERY ROAD'S A DEAD END. GOTTA FIGURE OUT MY NEXT MOVE. ASSUMING I HAVE ONE.
I'M SORRY I COULDN'T SAVE YOU, DEBBIE. SORRY YOU PAID THE PRICE.
YOU, AND YOUR SISTER. IF IT'S ANY CONSOLATION--
-- I GIVE YOU MY WORD THAT I WILL FIND THOSE RESPONSIBLE. I WILL BIND THEM AND I WILL HURT THEM.
JUST AS THEY HURT YOU.
AND HER.
AND ME.
AND LAURA.

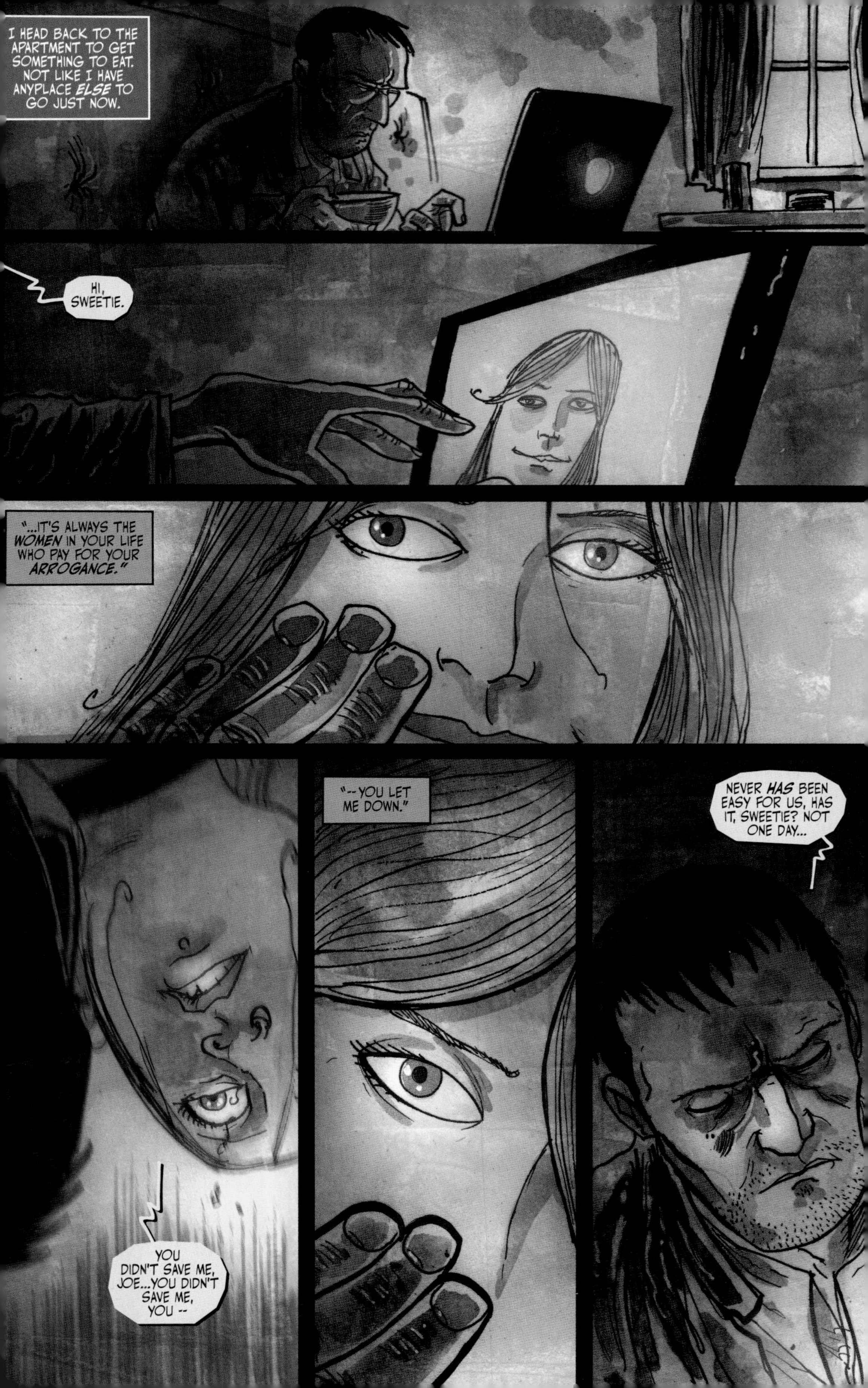
I HEAD BACK TO THE APARTMENT TO GET SOMETHING TO EAT. NOT LIKE I HAVE ANYPLACE *ELSE* TO GO JUST NOW.
HI, SWEETIE.
"...IT'S ALWAYS THE *WOMEN* IN YOUR LIFE WHO PAY FOR YOUR *ARROGANCE."*
YOU DIDN'T SAVE ME, JOE...YOU DIDN'T SAVE ME, YOU --
"--YOU LET ME DOWN."
NEVER *HAS* BEEN EASY FOR US, HAS IT, SWEETIE? NOT ONE DAY...

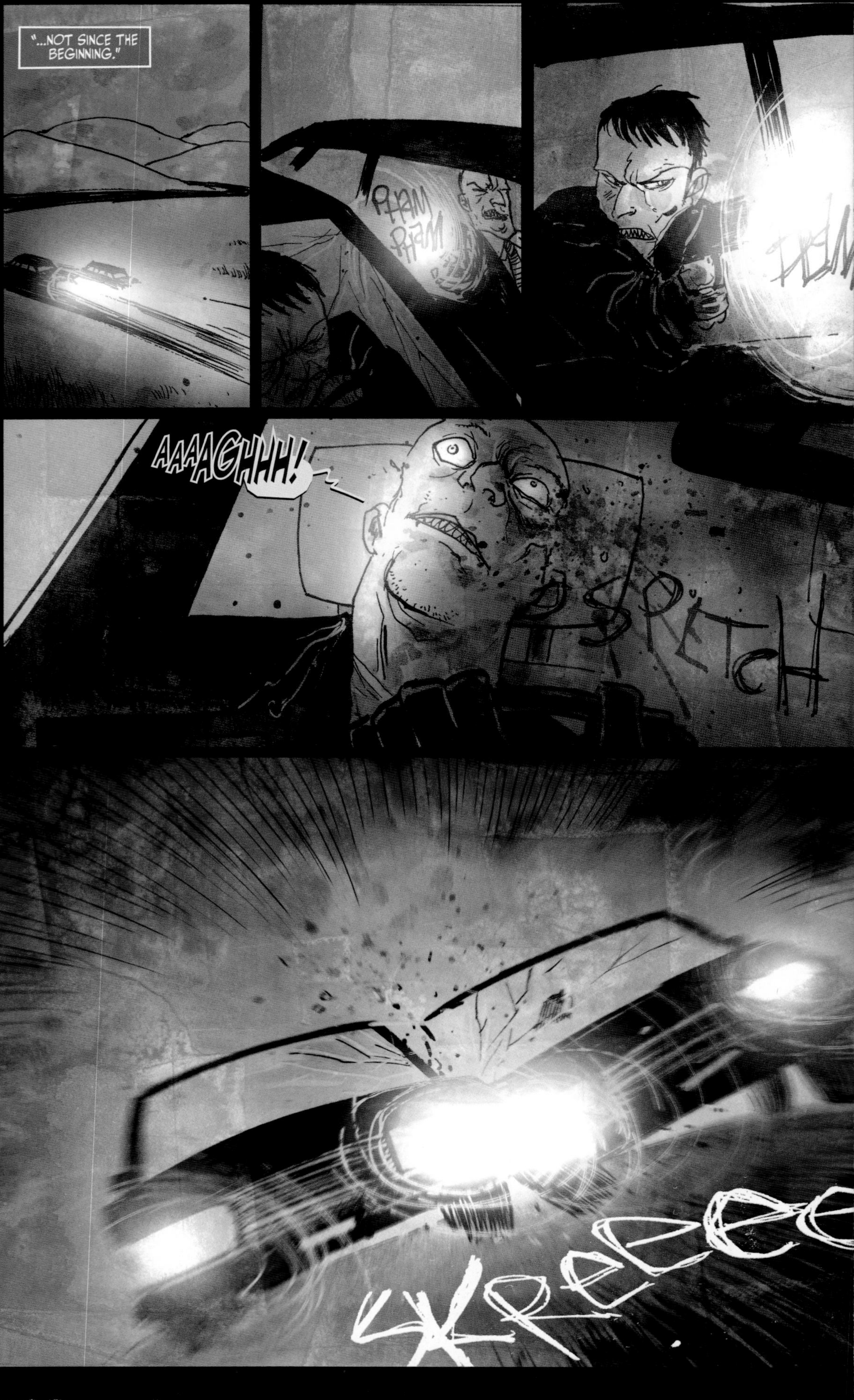
"...NOT SINCE THE BEGINNING."
PHAM PHAM
AAAAGHHH!
SPRETCH
SKREEEEE

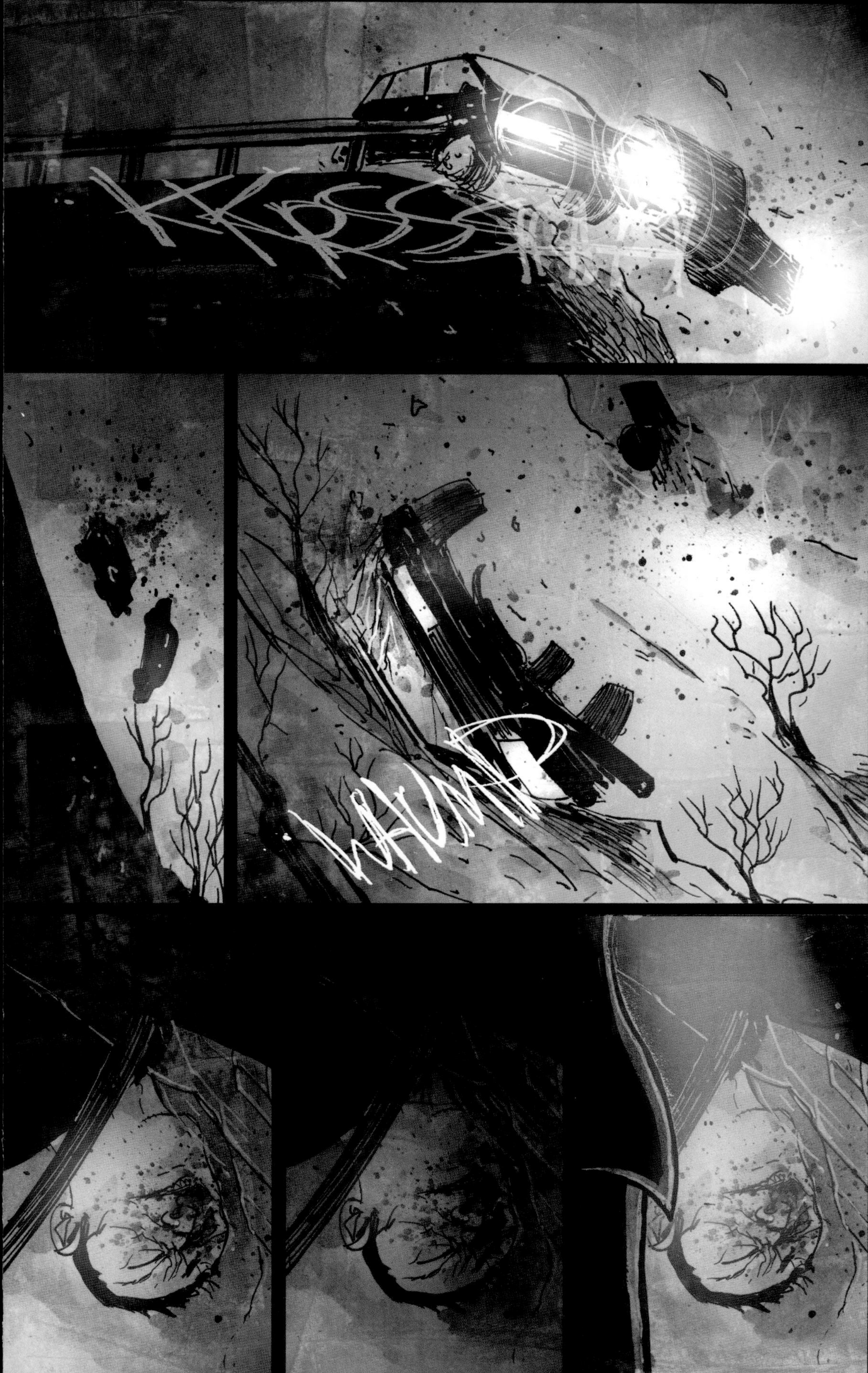
KKRSS
WHUMP

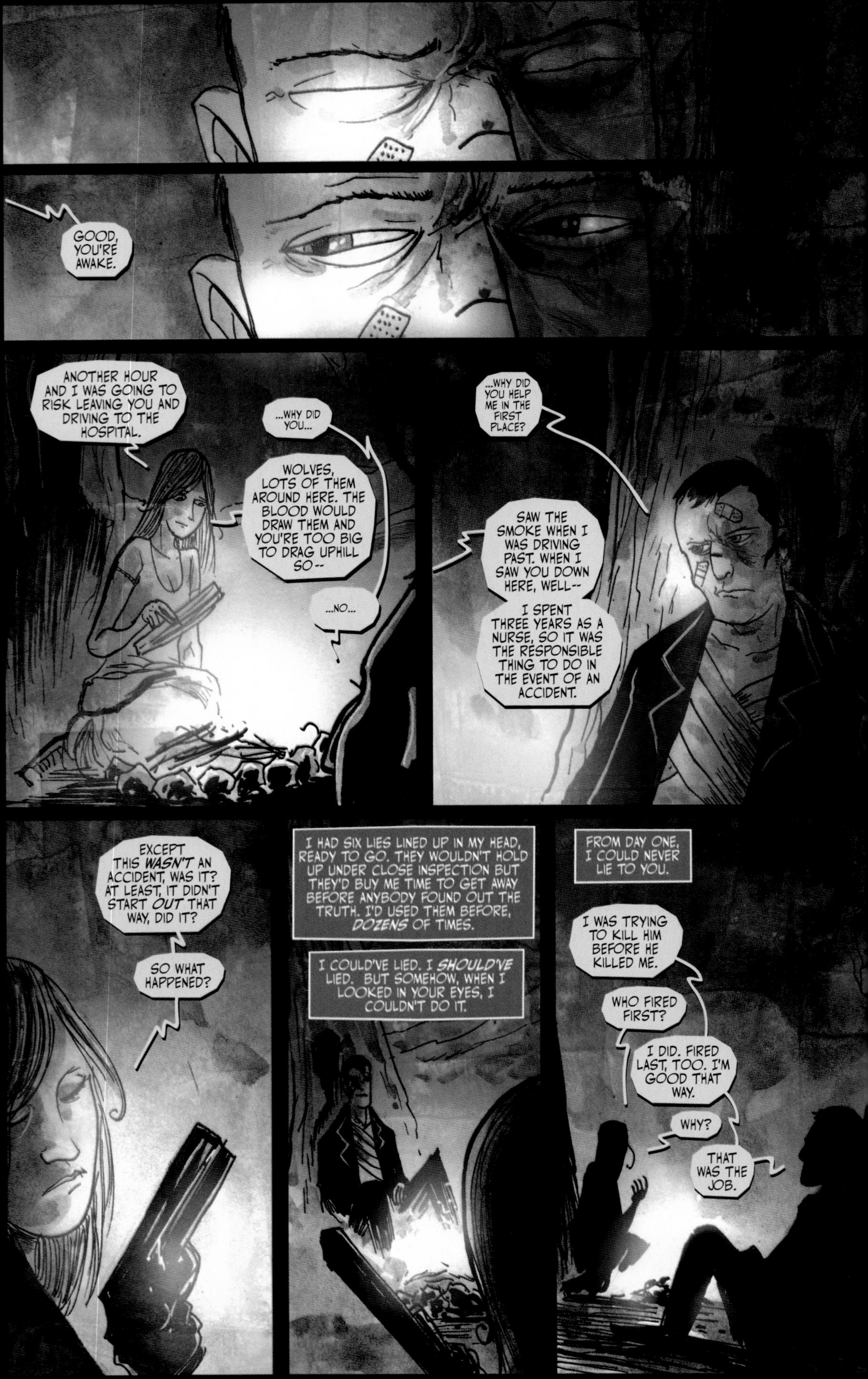
GOOD, YOU'RE AWAKE.
ANOTHER HOUR AND I WAS GOING TO RISK LEAVING YOU AND DRIVING TO THE HOSPITAL.
...WHY DID YOU...
WOLVES, LOTS OF THEM AROUND HERE. THE BLOOD WOULD DRAW THEM AND YOU'RE TOO BIG TO DRAG UPHILL SO--
...NO...
...WHY DID YOU HELP ME IN THE FIRST PLACE?
SAW THE SMOKE WHEN I WAS DRIVING PAST. WHEN I SAW YOU DOWN HERE, WELL--
I SPENT THREE YEARS AS A NURSE, SO IT WAS THE RESPONSIBLE THING TO DO IN THE EVENT OF AN ACCIDENT.
EXCEPT THIS *WASN'T* AN ACCIDENT, WAS IT? AT LEAST, IT DIDN'T START *OUT* THAT WAY, DID IT?
SO WHAT HAPPENED?
I HAD SIX LIES LINED UP IN MY HEAD, READY TO GO. THEY WOULDN'T HOLD UP UNDER CLOSE INSPECTION BUT THEY'D BUY ME TIME TO GET AWAY BEFORE ANYBODY FOUND OUT THE TRUTH. I'D USED THEM BEFORE, *DOZENS* OF TIMES.
I COULD'VE LIED. I *SHOULD'VE* LIED. BUT SOMEHOW, WHEN I LOOKED IN YOUR EYES, I COULDN'T DO IT.
FROM DAY ONE, I COULD NEVER LIE TO YOU.
I WAS TRYING TO KILL HIM BEFORE HE KILLED ME.
WHO FIRED FIRST?
I DID. FIRED LAST, TOO. I'M GOOD THAT WAY.
WHY?
THAT WAS THE JOB.

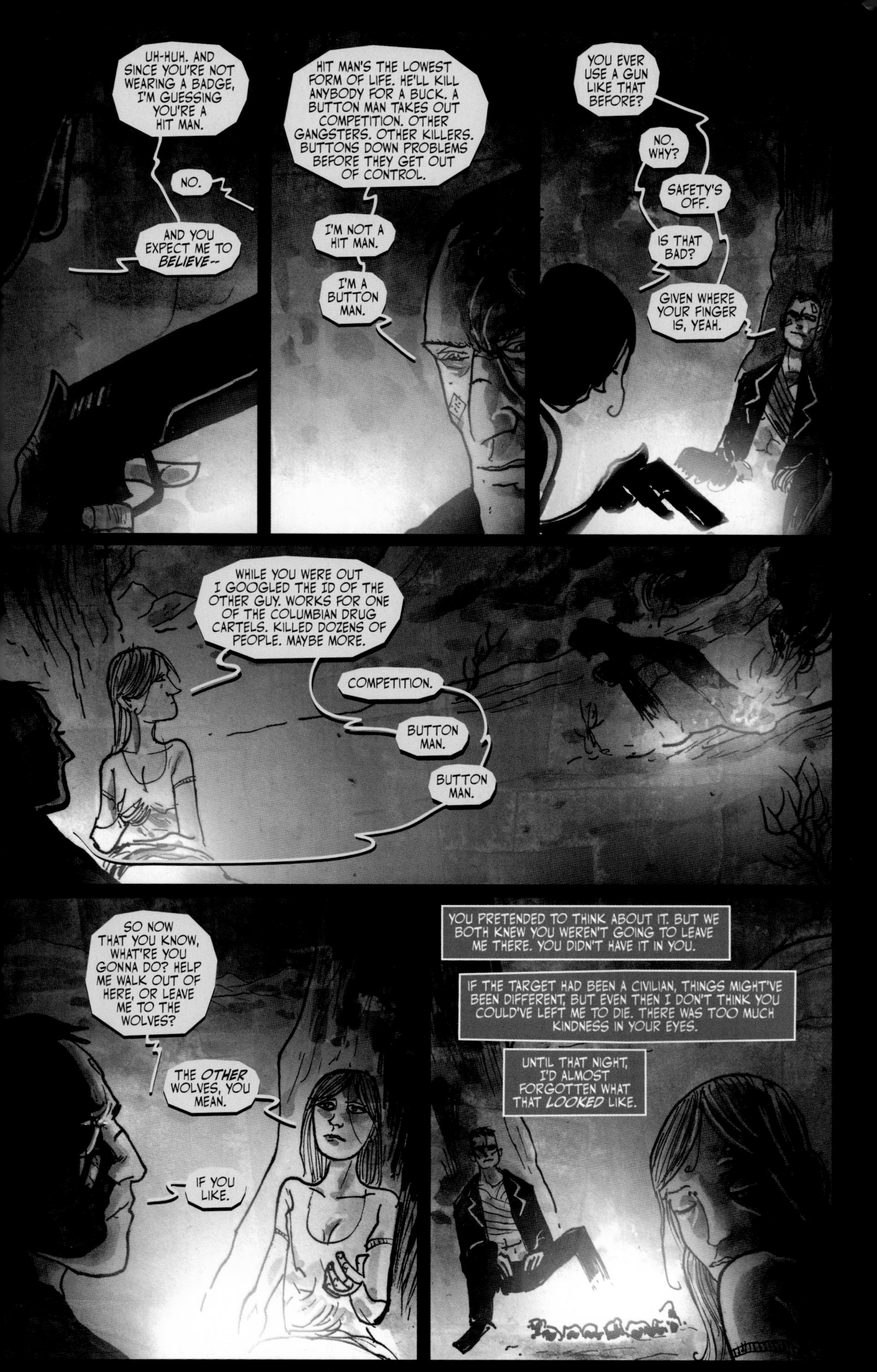
UH-HUH. AND SINCE YOU'RE NOT WEARING A BADGE, I'M GUESSING YOU'RE A HIT MAN.
NO.
AND YOU EXPECT ME TO *BELIEVE*--
HIT MAN'S THE LOWEST FORM OF LIFE. HE'LL KILL ANYBODY FOR A BUCK. A BUTTON MAN TAKES OUT COMPETITION. OTHER GANGSTERS. OTHER KILLERS. BUTTONS DOWN PROBLEMS BEFORE THEY GET OUT OF CONTROL.
I'M NOT A HIT MAN.
I'M A BUTTON MAN.
YOU EVER USE A GUN LIKE THAT BEFORE?
NO. WHY?
SAFETY'S OFF.
IS THAT BAD?
GIVEN WHERE YOUR FINGER IS, YEAH.
WHILE YOU WERE OUT I GOOGLED THE ID OF THE OTHER GUY. WORKS FOR ONE OF THE COLUMBIAN DRUG CARTELS. KILLED DOZENS OF PEOPLE. MAYBE MORE.
COMPETITION.
BUTTON MAN.
BUTTON MAN.
SO NOW THAT YOU KNOW, WHAT'RE YOU GONNA DO? HELP ME WALK OUT OF HERE, OR LEAVE ME TO THE WOLVES?
THE *OTHER* WOLVES, YOU MEAN.
IF YOU LIKE.
YOU PRETENDED TO THINK ABOUT IT. BUT WE BOTH KNEW YOU WEREN'T GOING TO LEAVE ME THERE. YOU DIDN'T HAVE IT IN YOU.
IF THE TARGET HAD BEEN A CIVILIAN, THINGS MIGHT'VE BEEN DIFFERENT, BUT EVEN THEN I DON'T THINK YOU COULD'VE LEFT ME TO DIE. THERE WAS TOO MUCH KINDNESS IN YOUR EYES.
UNTIL THAT NIGHT, I'D ALMOST FORGOTTEN WHAT THAT *LOOKED* LIKE.

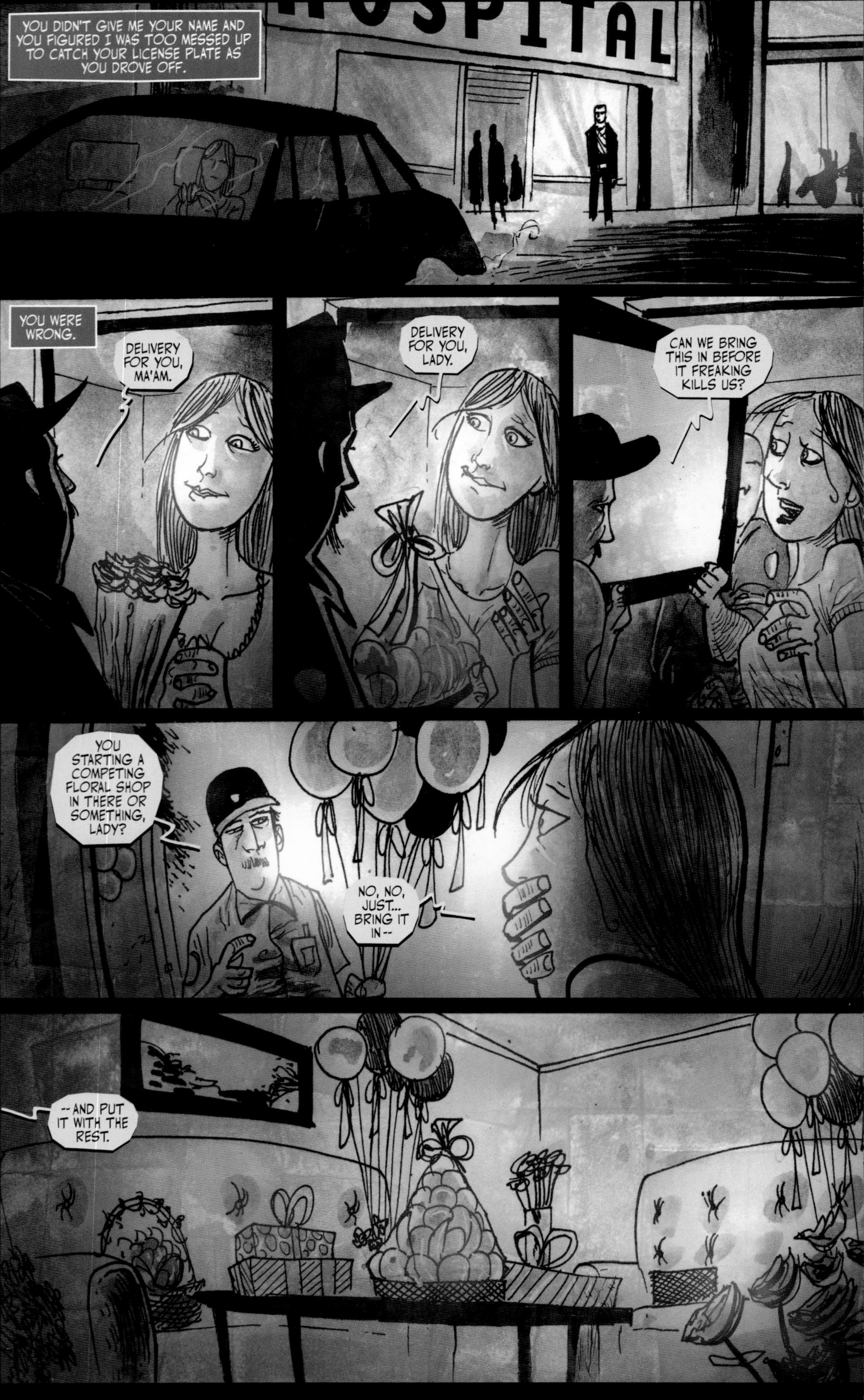
HOSPITAL
YOU DIDN'T GIVE ME YOUR NAME AND YOU FIGURED I WAS TOO MESSED UP TO CATCH YOUR LICENSE PLATE AS YOU DROVE OFF.
YOU WERE WRONG.
DELIVERY FOR YOU, MA'AM.
DELIVERY FOR YOU, LADY.
CAN WE BRING THIS IN BEFORE IT FREAKING KILLS US?
YOU STARTING A COMPETING FLORAL SHOP IN THERE OR SOMETHING, LADY?
NO, NO, JUST... BRING IT IN --
-- AND PUT IT WITH THE REST.

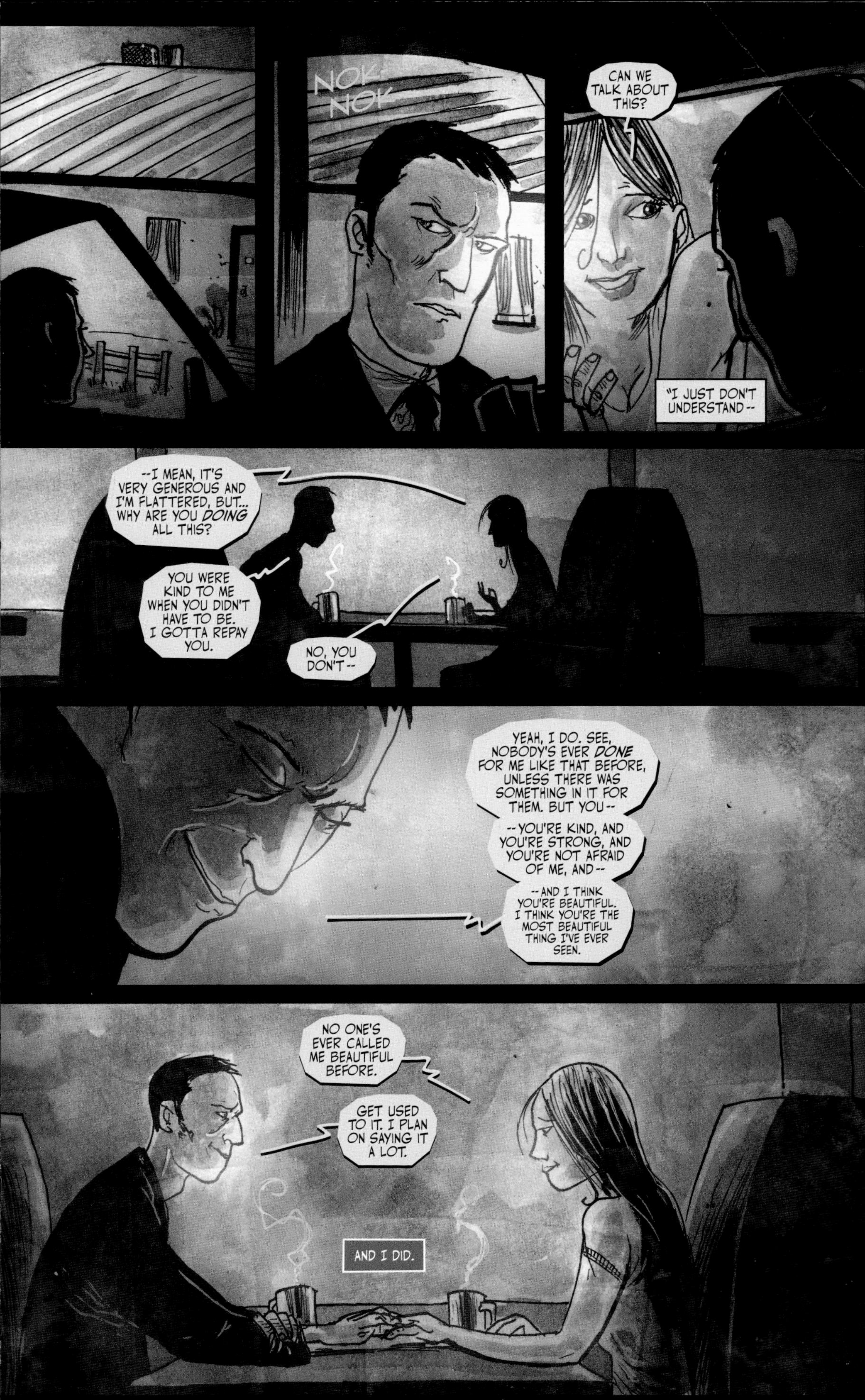
NOK NOK
CAN WE TALK ABOUT THIS?
"I JUST DON'T UNDERSTAND--
--I MEAN, IT'S VERY GENEROUS AND I'M FLATTERED, BUT... WHY ARE YOU DOING ALL THIS?
YOU WERE KIND TO ME WHEN YOU DIDN'T HAVE TO BE. I GOTTA REPAY YOU.
NO, YOU DON'T--
YEAH, I DO. SEE, NOBODY'S EVER DONE FOR ME LIKE THAT BEFORE, UNLESS THERE WAS SOMETHING IN IT FOR THEM. BUT YOU--
--YOU'RE KIND, AND YOU'RE STRONG, AND YOU'RE NOT AFRAID OF ME, AND--
--AND I THINK YOU'RE BEAUTIFUL. I THINK YOU'RE THE MOST BEAUTIFUL THING I'VE EVER SEEN.
NO ONE'S EVER CALLED ME BEAUTIFUL BEFORE.
GET USED TO IT. I PLAN ON SAYING IT A LOT.
AND I DID.

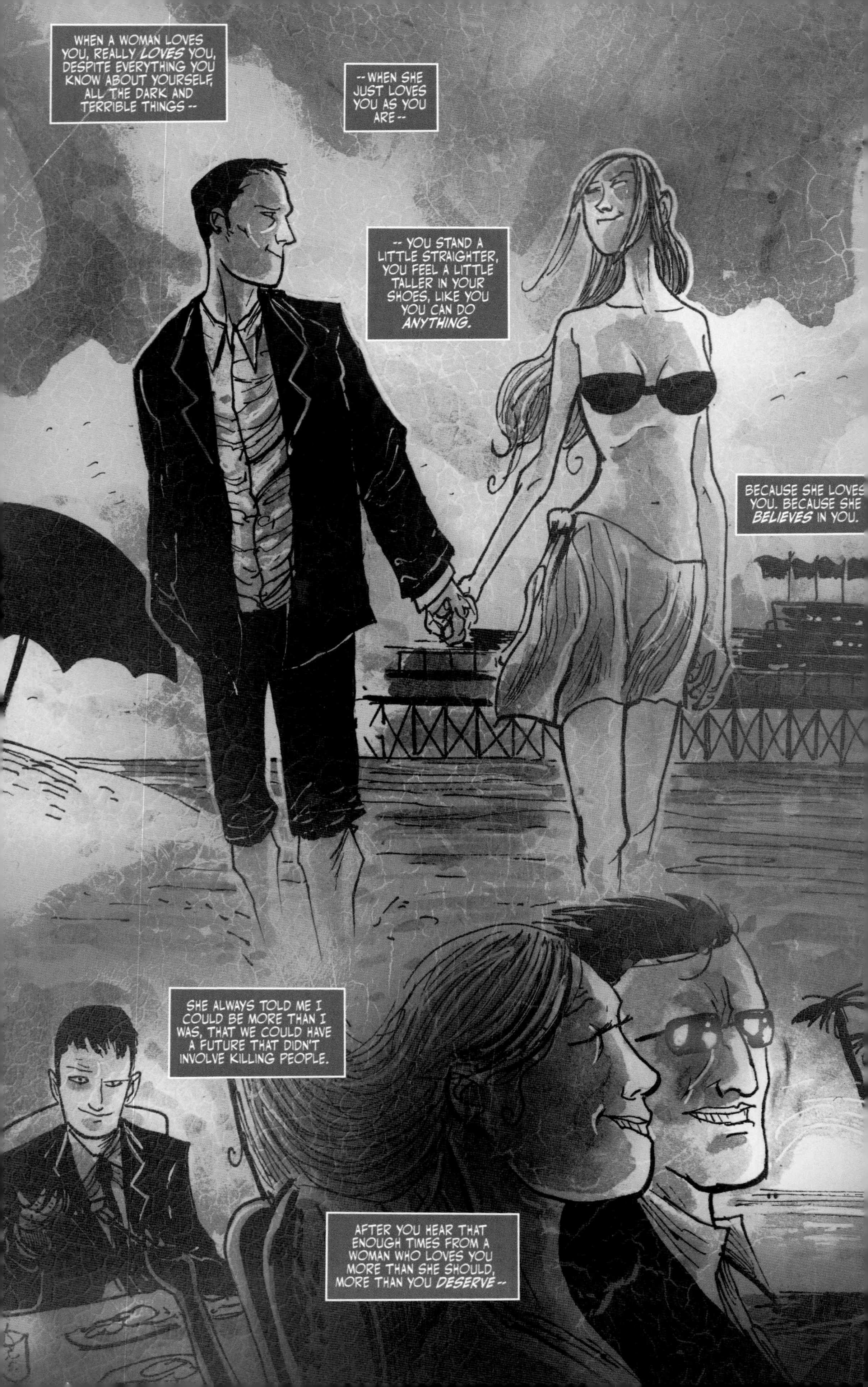
WHEN A WOMAN LOVES YOU, REALLY LOVES YOU, DESPITE EVERYTHING YOU KNOW ABOUT YOURSELF, ALL THE DARK AND TERRIBLE THINGS --
-- WHEN SHE JUST LOVES YOU AS YOU ARE --
-- YOU STAND A LITTLE STRAIGHTER, YOU FEEL A LITTLE TALLER IN YOUR SHOES, LIKE YOU YOU CAN DO ANYTHING.
BECAUSE SHE LOVES YOU. BECAUSE SHE BELIEVES IN YOU.
SHE ALWAYS TOLD ME I COULD BE MORE THAN I WAS, THAT WE COULD HAVE A FUTURE THAT DIDN'T INVOLVE KILLING PEOPLE.
AFTER YOU HEAR THAT ENOUGH TIMES FROM A WOMAN WHO LOVES YOU MORE THAN SHE SHOULD, MORE THAN YOU DESERVE --

-- ONE DAY, YOU DECIDE YOU BELIEVE IT TOO, AND THAT MEANS YOU HAVE TO *DO* SOMETHING ABOUT IT.

I HEAR WHAT YOU'RE SAYING, JOE. I GET IT. SOONER OR LATER, ALL OF US WANT OUT OF THE LIFE.

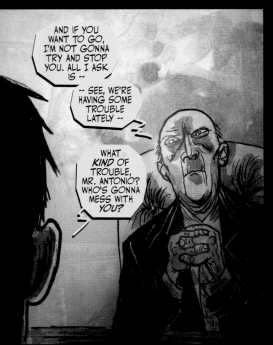

AND IF YOU WANT TO GO, I'M NOT GONNA TRY AND STOP YOU. ALL I ASK IS --

-- SEE, WE'RE HAVING SOME TROUBLE LATELY --

WHAT *KIND* OF TROUBLE, MR. ANTONIO? WHO'S GONNA MESS WITH *YOU*?

IT'S...A LONG STORY. SO I'M GONNA NEED YOU TO STICK AROUND JUST A LITTLE LONGER, A FEW WEEKS, THAT'S ALL. MAYBE DO ONE MORE JOB FOR ME. THEN YOU CAN GO.

HELL, I'LL EVEN DANCE AT YOUR WEDDING *AND* BRING A PILLOWCASE STUFFED WITH CASH.

WHO SAID I WAS GETTING MARRIED?

YOU DIDN'T HAVE TO. A GUY LIKE ME KNOWS THINGS, THAT'S ALL. TAKE CARE, JOE.

THANKS, MR. ANTONIO.

WHAT I DIDN'T HEAR, WHAT I DIDN'T *KNOW* UNTIL MUCH LATER, WAS WHAT MR. ANTONIO SAID *AFTER* I LEFT THE ROOM.

YOU HEARD?

YEAH. JUST MADE HIMSELF EXPENDABLE.

THEY DEMAND A SACRIFICE TO PAY THE BILL FOR WHAT I'VE DONE. SO WE'LL GIVE THEM ONE. JUST GOTTA BE SURE HE GOES IN CLEAN, NO SUSPICIONS.

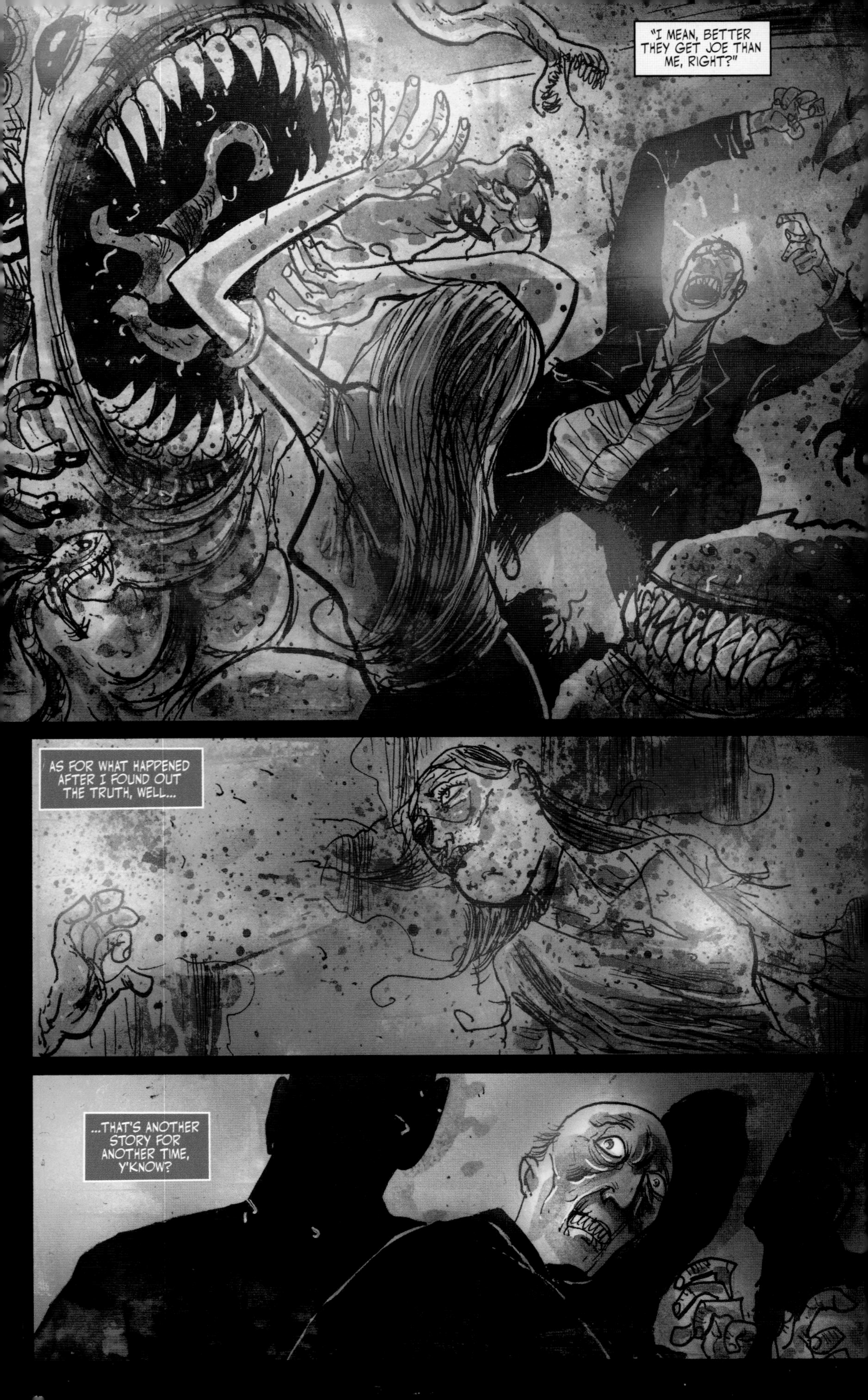
"I MEAN, BETTER THEY GET JOE THAN ME, RIGHT?"
AS FOR WHAT HAPPENED AFTER I FOUND OUT THE TRUTH, WELL...
...THAT'S ANOTHER STORY FOR ANOTHER TIME, Y'KNOW?

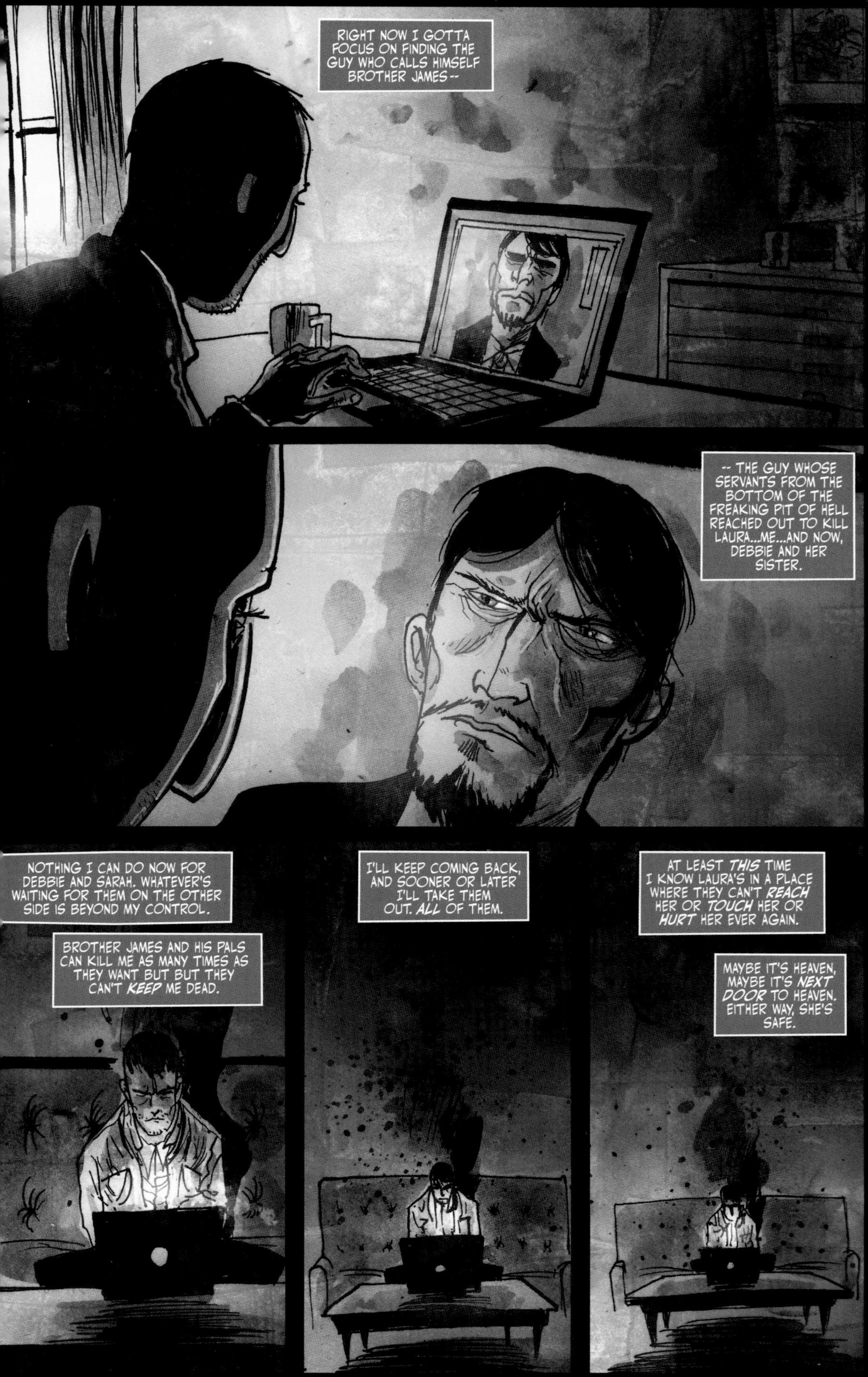
RIGHT NOW I GOTTA FOCUS ON FINDING THE GUY WHO CALLS HIMSELF BROTHER JAMES--
-- THE GUY WHOSE SERVANTS FROM THE BOTTOM OF THE FREAKING PIT OF HELL REACHED OUT TO KILL LAURA...ME...AND NOW, DEBBIE AND HER SISTER.
NOTHING I CAN DO NOW FOR DEBBIE AND SARAH. WHATEVER'S WAITING FOR THEM ON THE OTHER SIDE IS BEYOND MY CONTROL.
BROTHER JAMES AND HIS PALS CAN KILL ME AS MANY TIMES AS THEY WANT BUT BUT THEY CAN'T *KEEP* ME DEAD.
I'LL KEEP COMING BACK, AND SOONER OR LATER I'LL TAKE THEM OUT. *ALL* OF THEM.
AT LEAST *THIS* TIME I KNOW LAURA'S IN A PLACE WHERE THEY CAN'T *REACH* HER OR *TOUCH* HER OR *HURT* HER EVER AGAIN.
MAYBE IT'S HEAVEN, MAYBE IT'S *NEXT DOOR* TO HEAVEN. EITHER WAY, SHE'S SAFE.

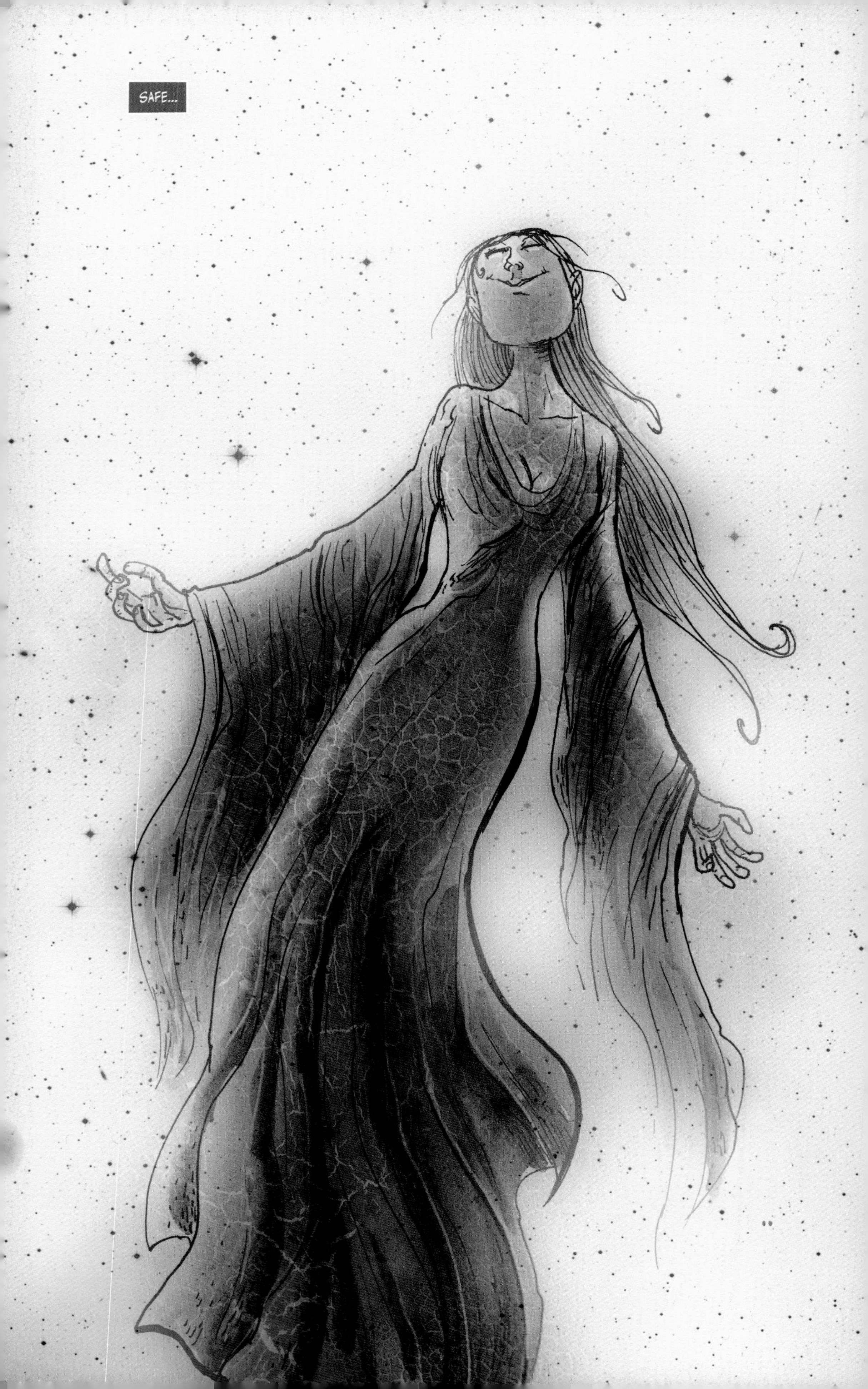
SAFE...

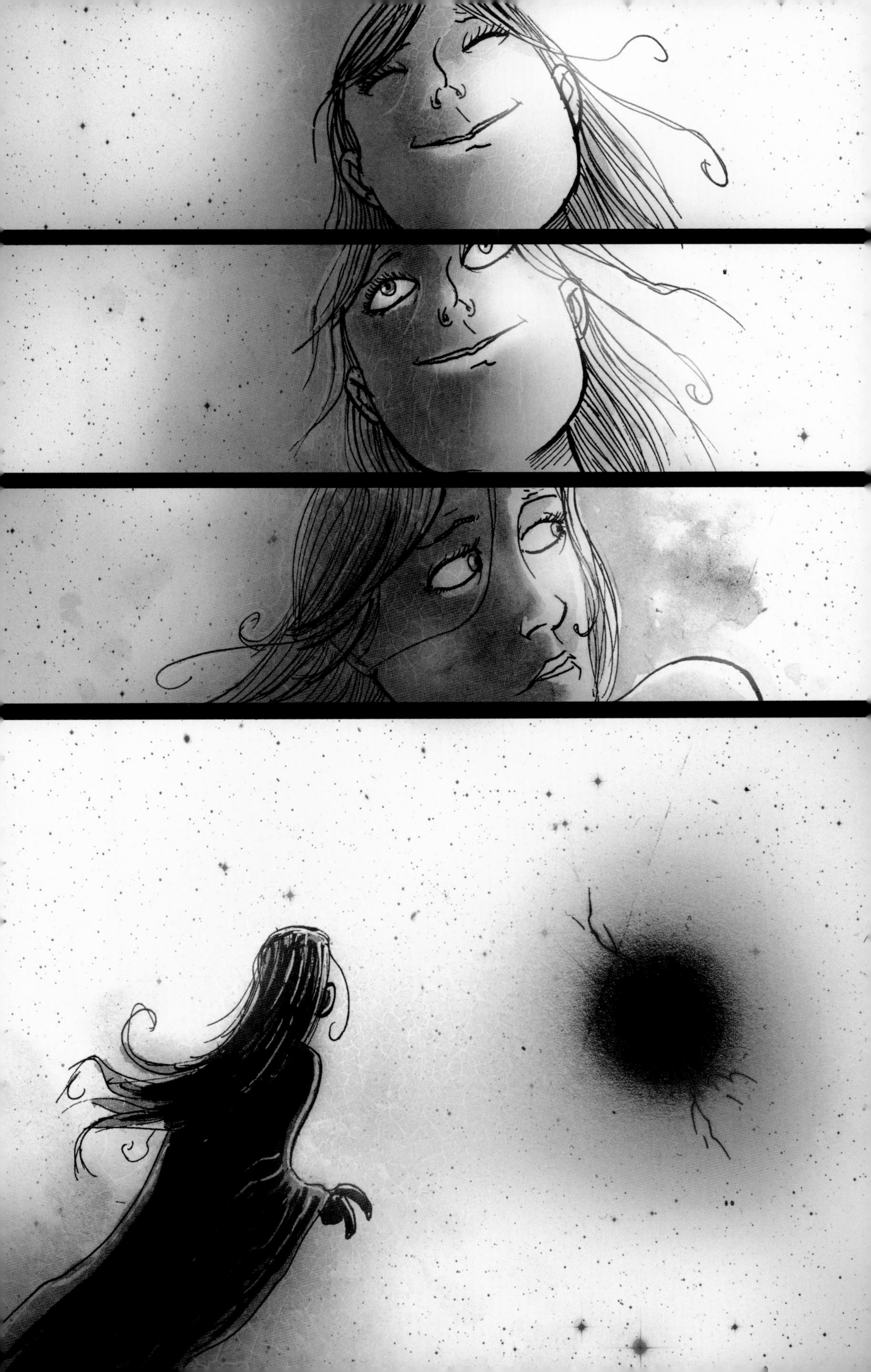

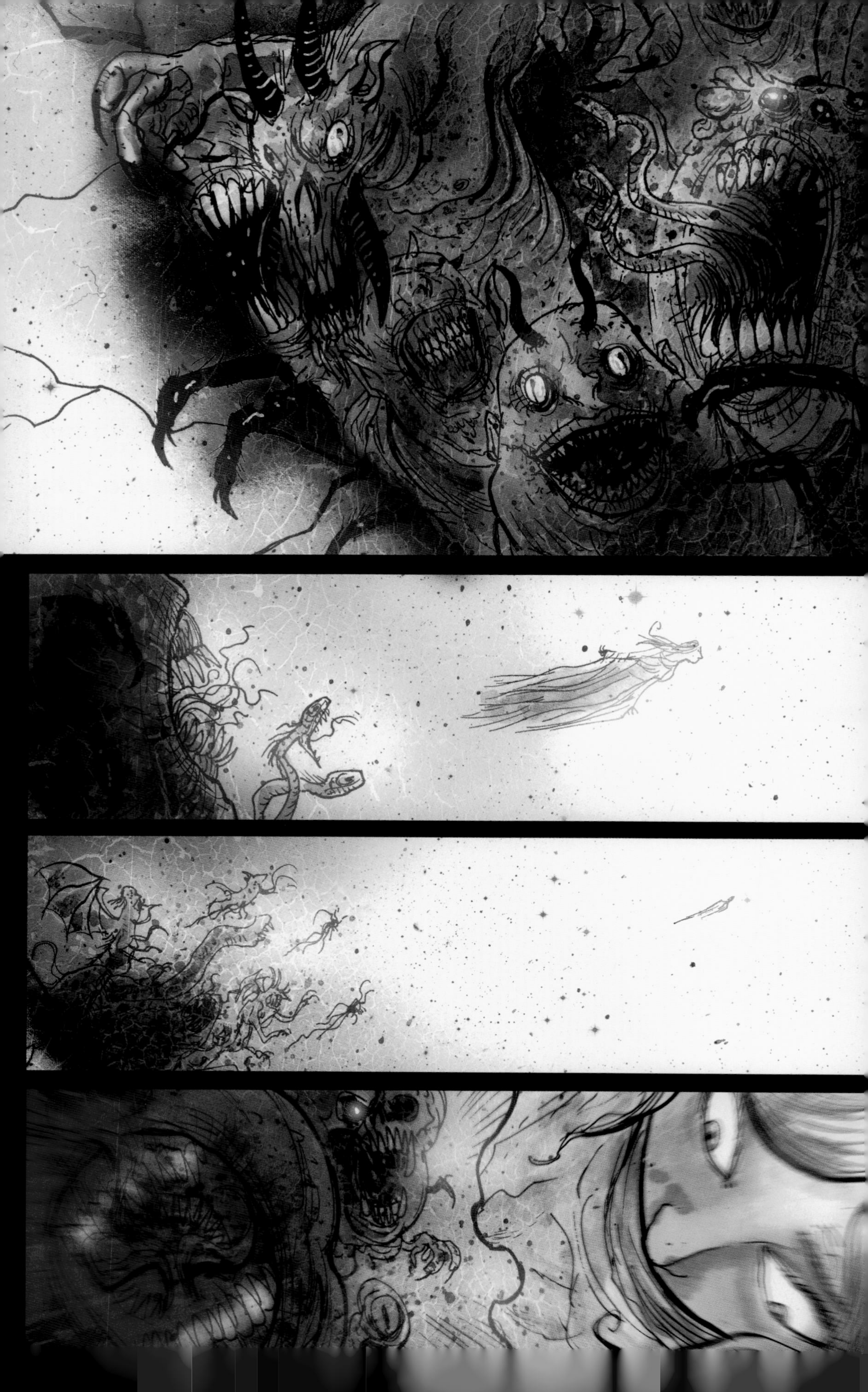

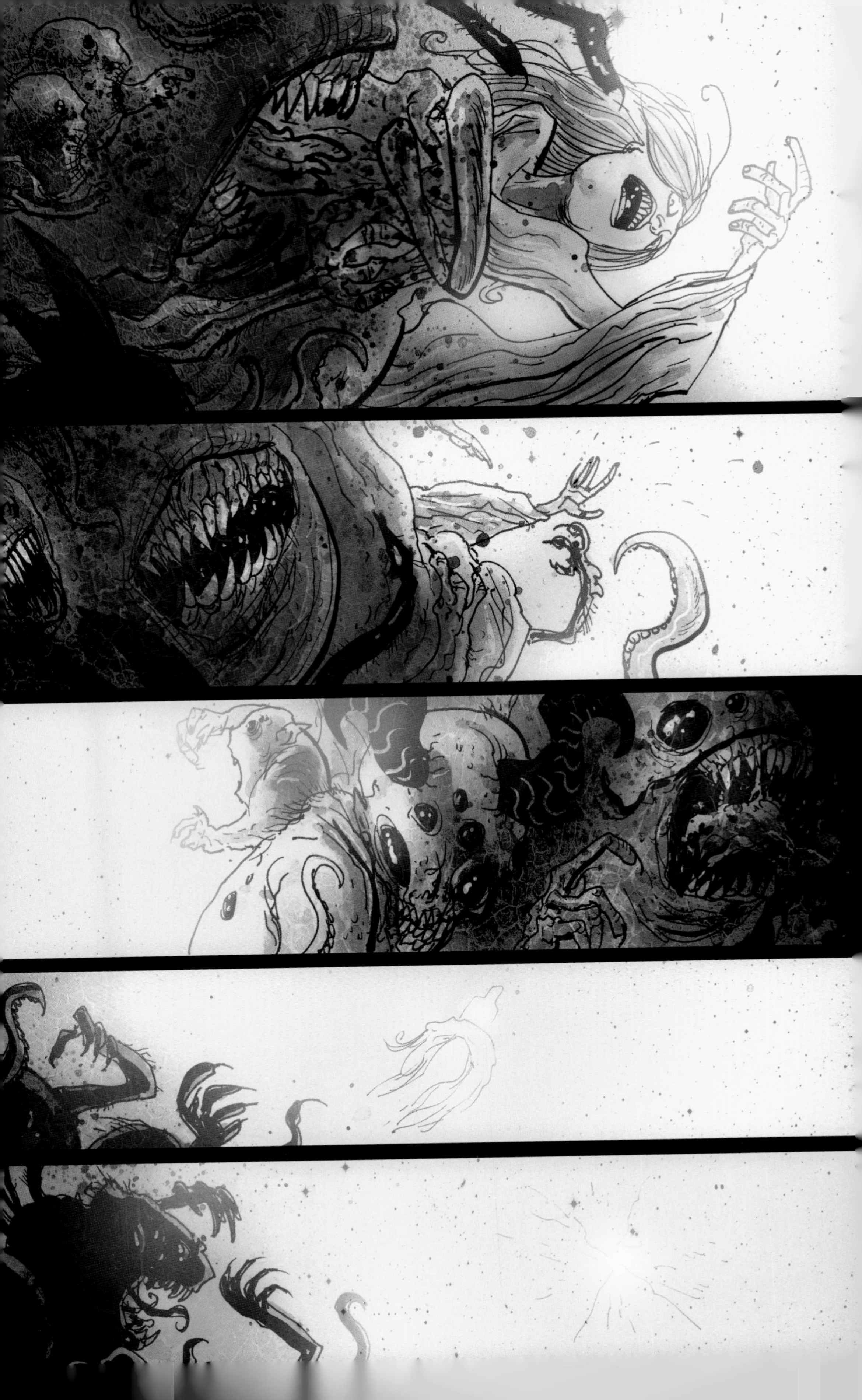

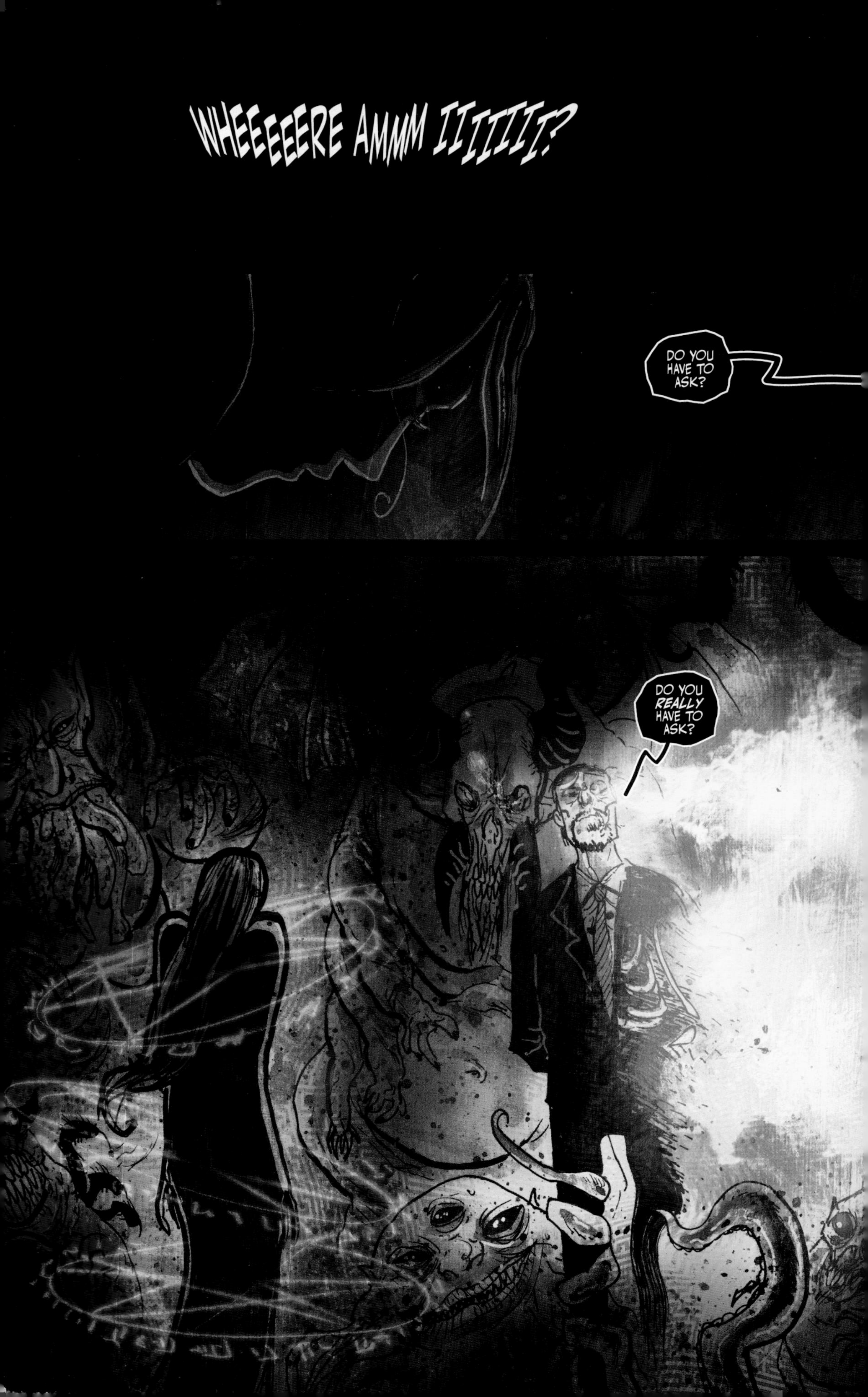
WHEEEEERE AMMM IIIIIII?
DO YOU HAVE TO ASK?
DO YOU *REALLY* HAVE TO ASK?

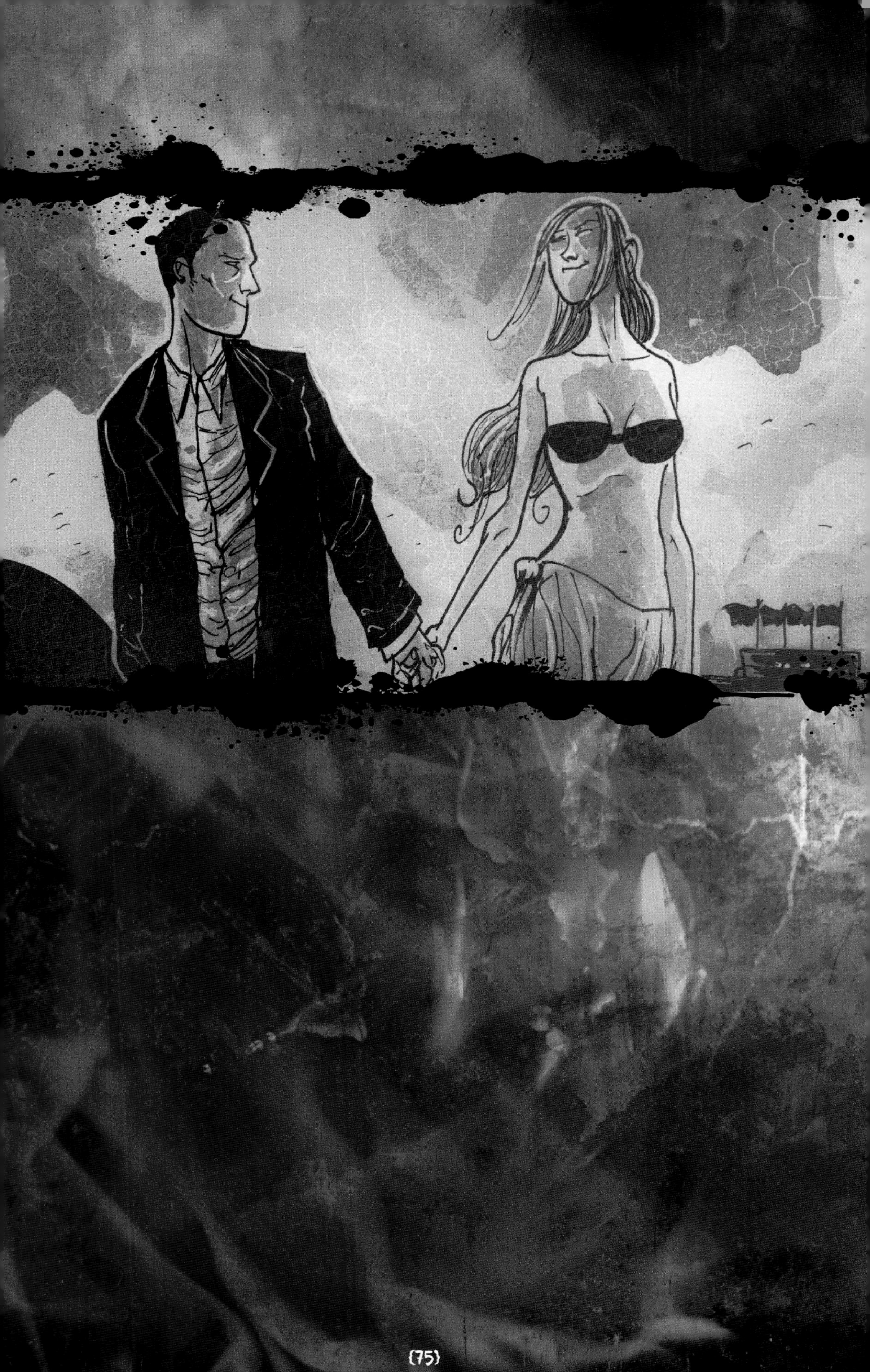

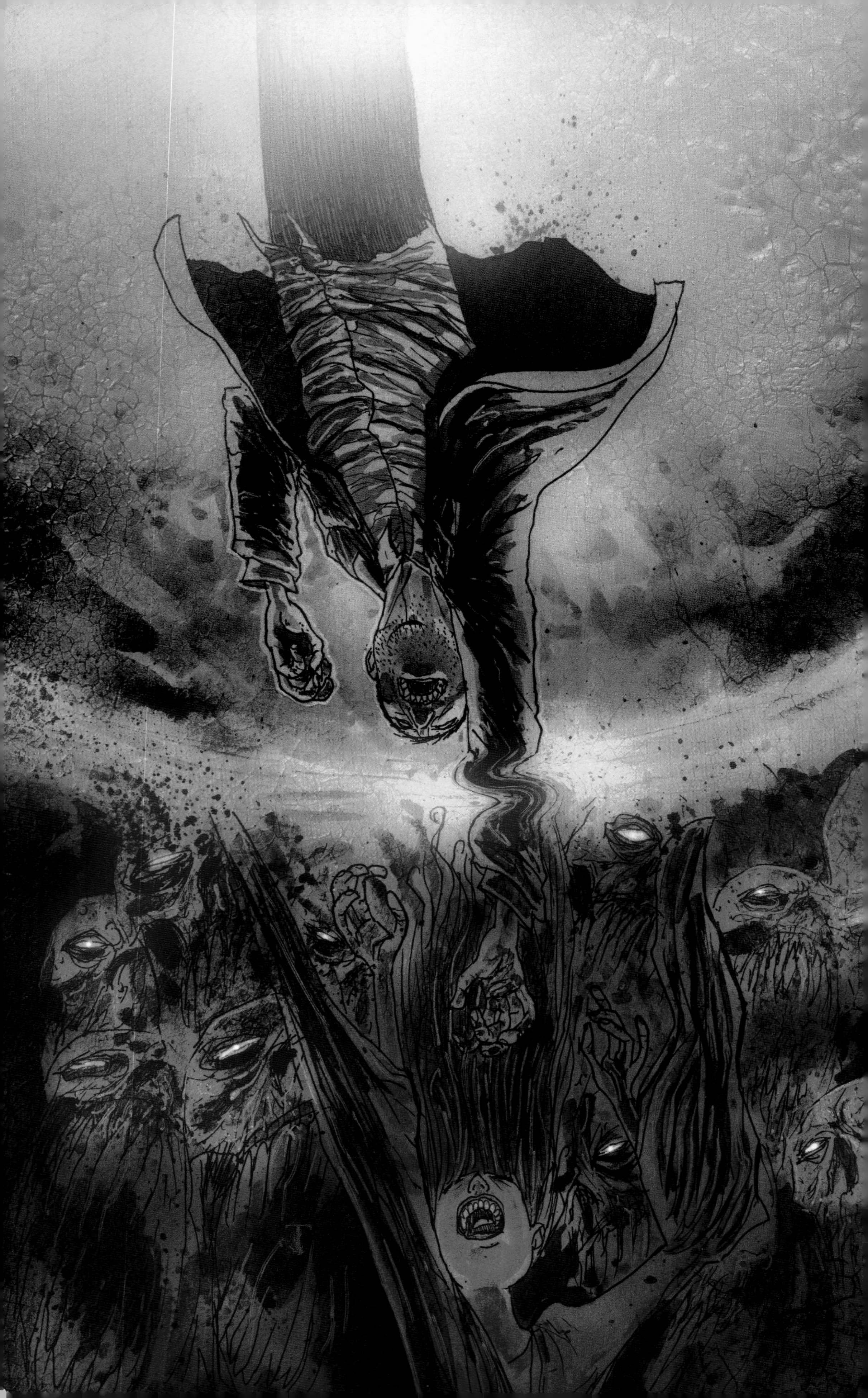

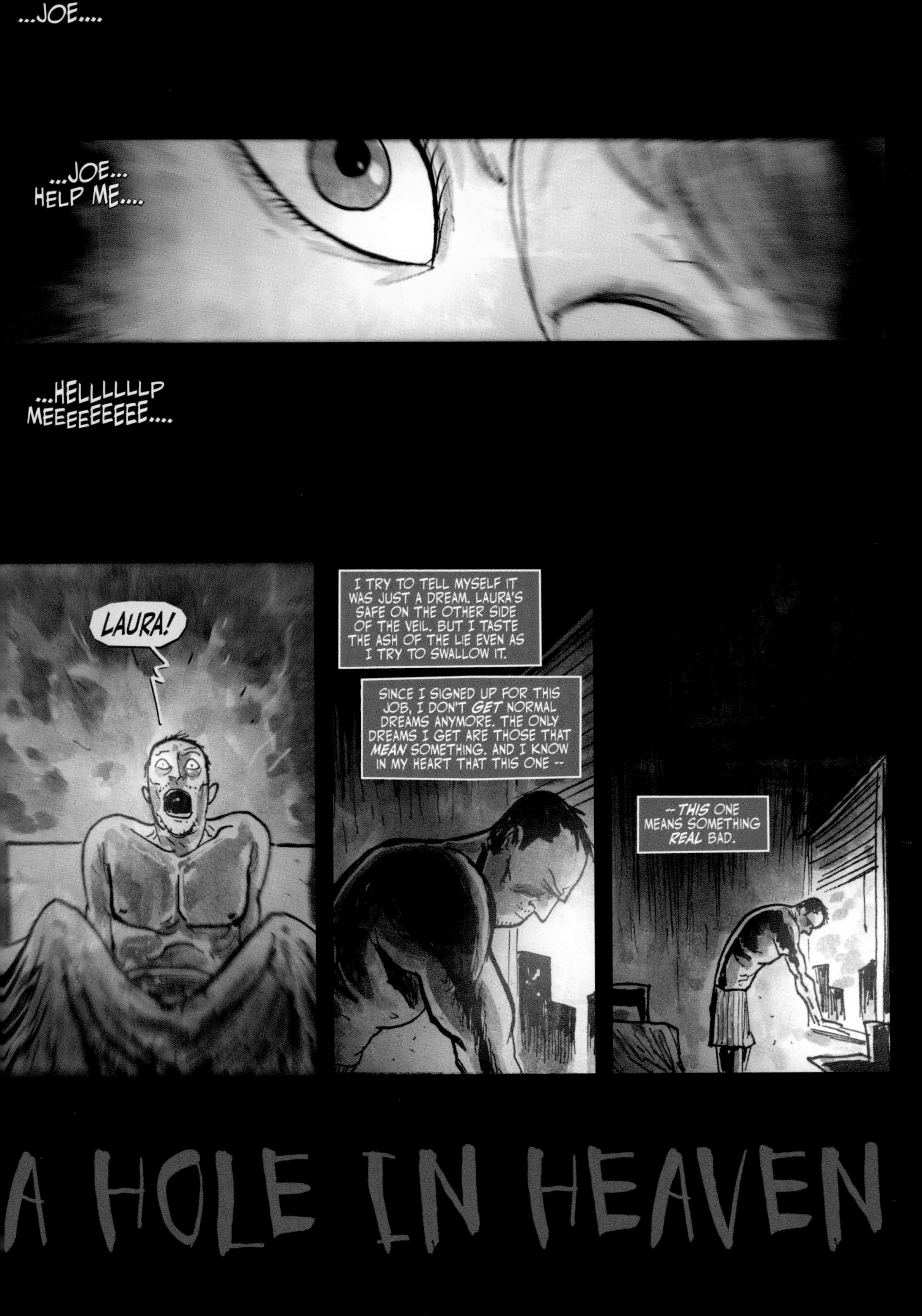
...JOE....
...JOE... HELP ME....
...HELLLLLLP MEEEEEEEEE....
LAURA!
I TRY TO TELL MYSELF IT WAS JUST A DREAM. LAURA'S SAFE ON THE OTHER SIDE OF THE VEIL. BUT I TASTE THE ASH OF THE LIE EVEN AS I TRY TO SWALLOW IT.
SINCE I SIGNED UP FOR THIS JOB, I DON'T GET NORMAL DREAMS ANYMORE. THE ONLY DREAMS I GET ARE THOSE THAT MEAN SOMETHING. AND I KNOW IN MY HEART THAT THIS ONE --
-- THIS ONE MEANS SOMETHING REAL BAD.
A HOLE IN HEAVEN

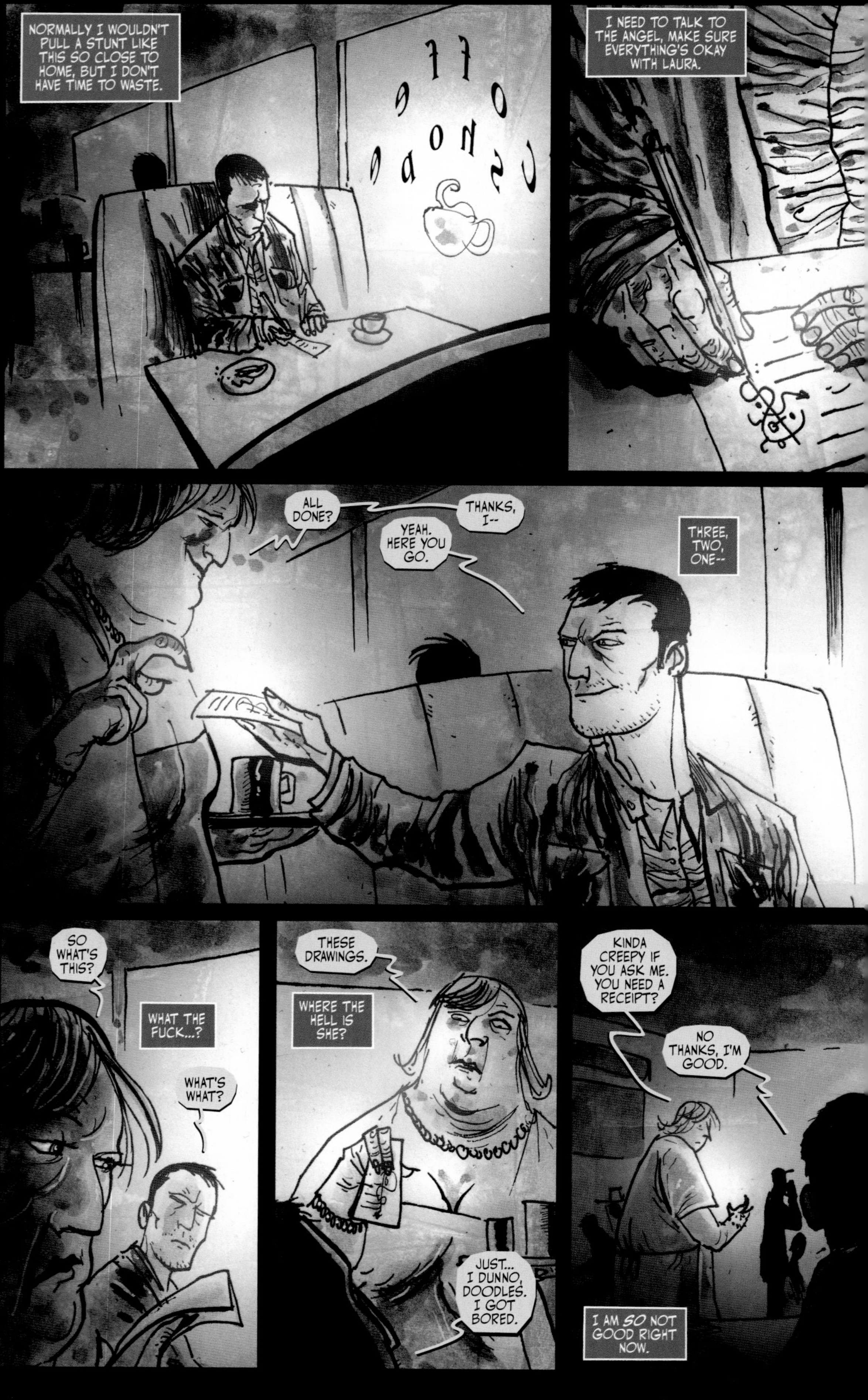
NORMALLY I WOULDN'T PULL A STUNT LIKE THIS SO CLOSE TO HOME, BUT I DON'T HAVE TIME TO WASTE.
I NEED TO TALK TO THE ANGEL, MAKE SURE EVERYTHING'S OKAY WITH LAURA.
ALL DONE?
THANKS, I--
YEAH. HERE YOU GO.
THREE, TWO, ONE--
SO WHAT'S THIS?
WHAT THE FUCK...?
WHAT'S WHAT?
THESE DRAWINGS.
WHERE THE HELL IS SHE?
JUST... I DUNNO, DOODLES. I GOT BORED.
KINDA CREEPY IF YOU ASK ME. YOU NEED A RECEIPT?
NO THANKS, I'M GOOD.
I AM SO NOT GOOD RIGHT NOW.

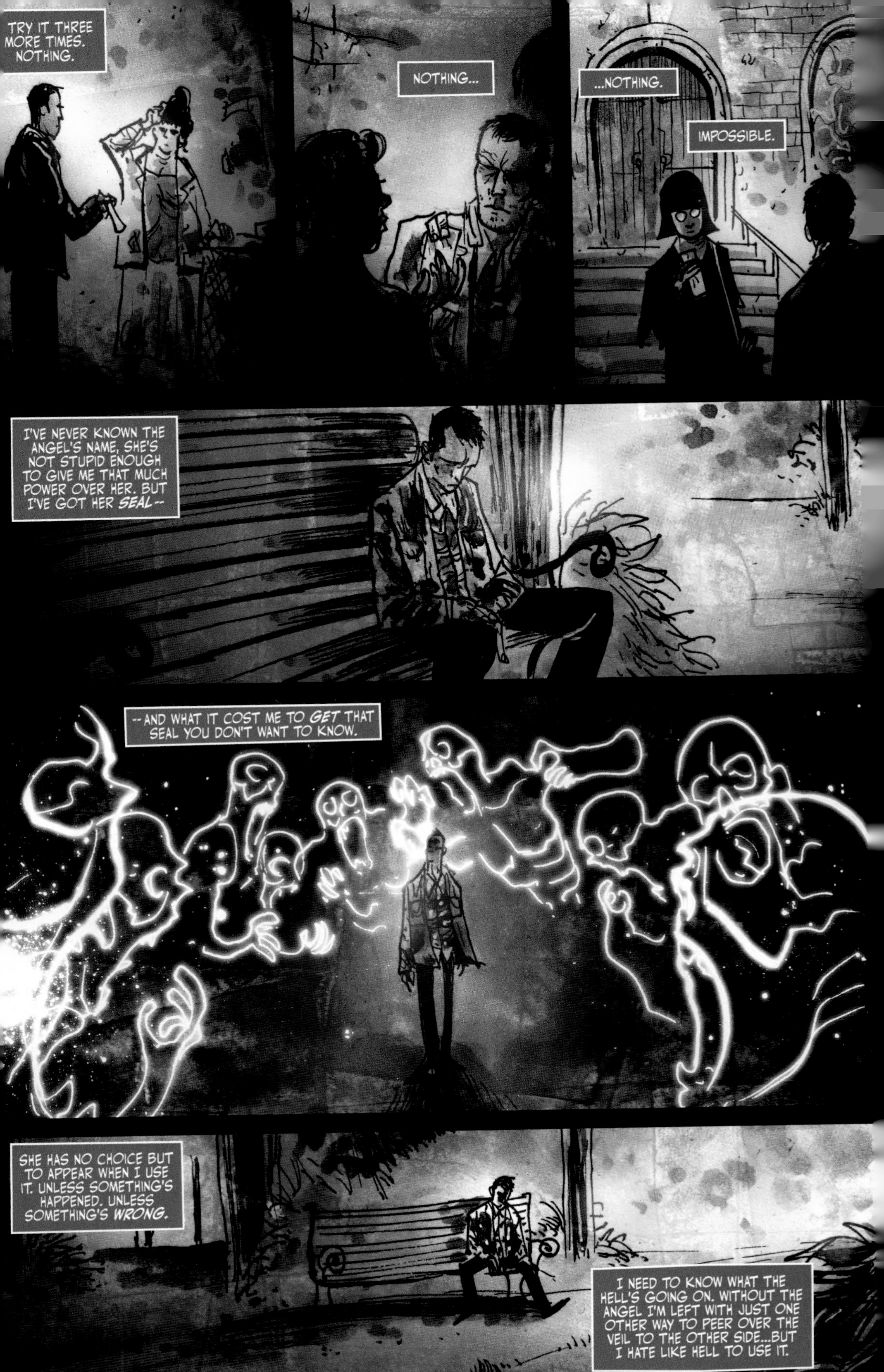
TRY IT THREE MORE TIMES. NOTHING.
NOTHING...
...NOTHING.
IMPOSSIBLE.
I'VE NEVER KNOWN THE ANGEL'S NAME, SHE'S NOT STUPID ENOUGH TO GIVE ME THAT MUCH POWER OVER HER. BUT I'VE GOT HER SEAL--
--AND WHAT IT COST ME TO GET THAT SEAL YOU DON'T WANT TO KNOW.
SHE HAS NO CHOICE BUT TO APPEAR WHEN I USE IT. UNLESS SOMETHING'S HAPPENED. UNLESS SOMETHING'S WRONG.
I NEED TO KNOW WHAT THE HELL'S GOING ON. WITHOUT THE ANGEL I'M LEFT WITH JUST ONE OTHER WAY TO PEER OVER THE VEIL TO THE OTHER SIDE...BUT I HATE LIKE HELL TO USE IT.

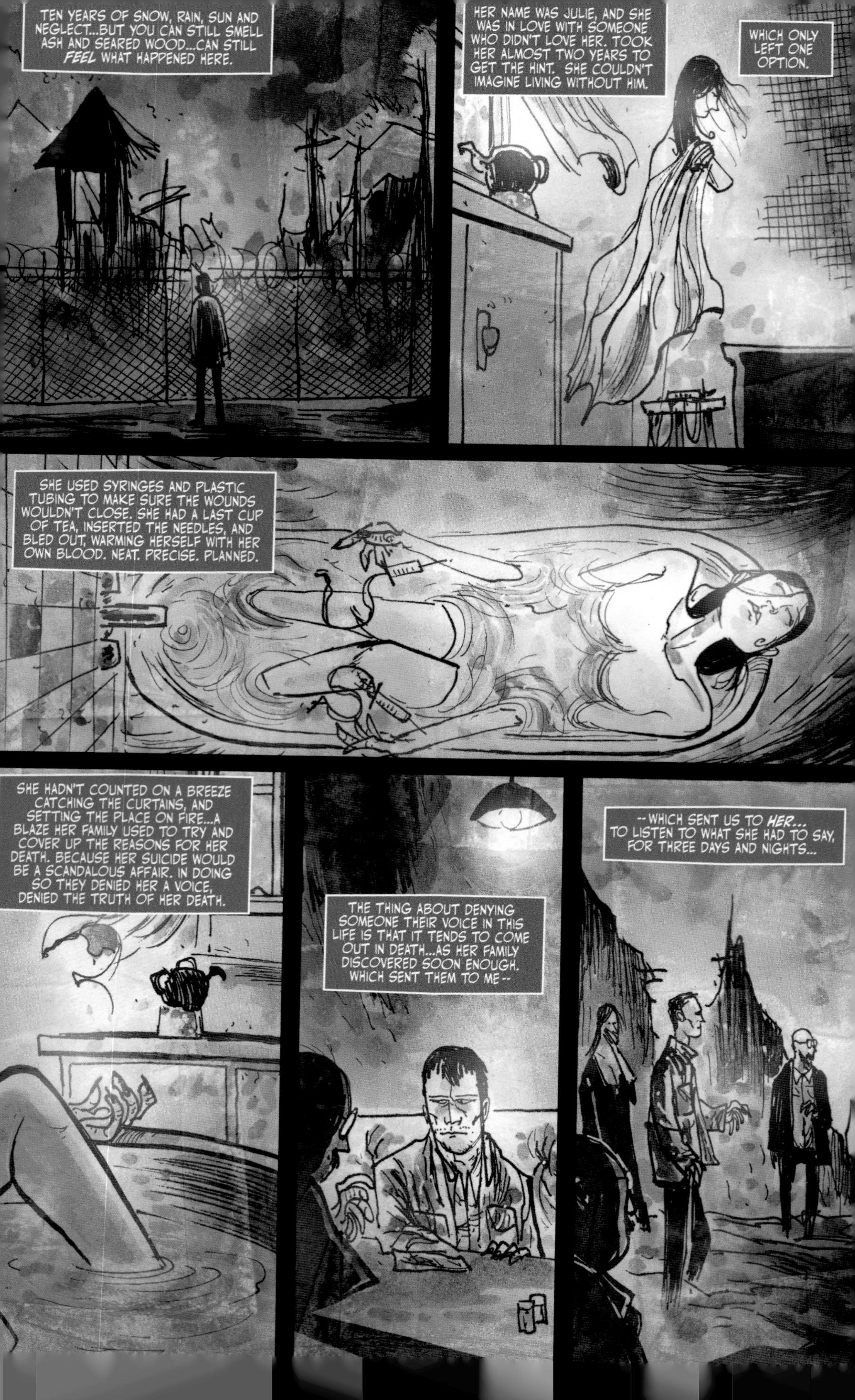
TEN YEARS OF SNOW, RAIN, SUN AND NEGLECT...BUT YOU CAN STILL SMELL ASH AND SEARED WOOD...CAN STILL FEEL WHAT HAPPENED HERE.
HER NAME WAS JULIE, AND SHE WAS IN LOVE WITH SOMEONE WHO DIDN'T LOVE HER. TOOK HER ALMOST TWO YEARS TO GET THE HINT. SHE COULDN'T IMAGINE LIVING WITHOUT HIM.
WHICH ONLY LEFT ONE OPTION.
SHE USED SYRINGES AND PLASTIC TUBING TO MAKE SURE THE WOUNDS WOULDN'T CLOSE. SHE HAD A LAST CUP OF TEA, INSERTED THE NEEDLES, AND BLED OUT, WARMING HERSELF WITH HER OWN BLOOD. NEAT. PRECISE. PLANNED.
SHE HADN'T COUNTED ON A BREEZE CATCHING THE CURTAINS, AND SETTING THE PLACE ON FIRE...A BLAZE HER FAMILY USED TO TRY AND COVER UP THE REASONS FOR HER DEATH. BECAUSE HER SUICIDE WOULD BE A SCANDALOUS AFFAIR. IN DOING SO THEY DENIED HER A VOICE, DENIED THE TRUTH OF HER DEATH.
THE THING ABOUT DENYING SOMEONE THEIR VOICE IN THIS LIFE IS THAT IT TENDS TO COME OUT IN DEATH...AS HER FAMILY DISCOVERED SOON ENOUGH. WHICH SENT THEM TO ME--
--WHICH SENT US TO HER... TO LISTEN TO WHAT SHE HAD TO SAY, FOR THREE DAYS AND NIGHTS...

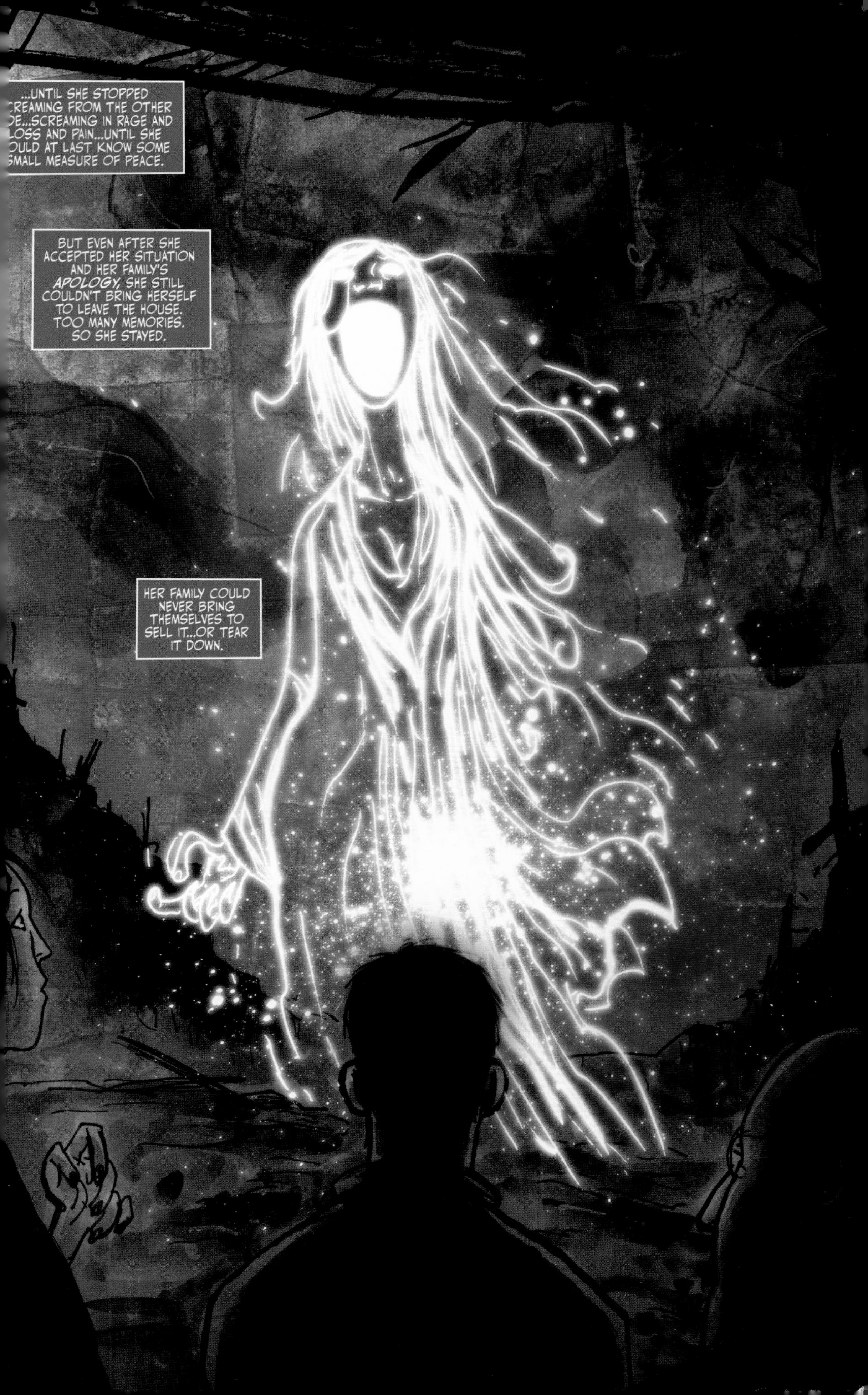
...UNTIL SHE STOPPED CREAMING FROM THE OTHER DE...SCREAMING IN RAGE AND LOSS AND PAIN...UNTIL SHE OULD AT LAST KNOW SOME SMALL MEASURE OF PEACE.
BUT EVEN AFTER SHE ACCEPTED HER SITUATION AND HER FAMILY'S *APOLOGY,* SHE STILL COULDN'T BRING HERSELF TO LEAVE THE HOUSE. TOO MANY MEMORIES. SO SHE STAYED.
HER FAMILY COULD NEVER BRING THEMSELVES TO SELL IT...OR TEAR IT DOWN.

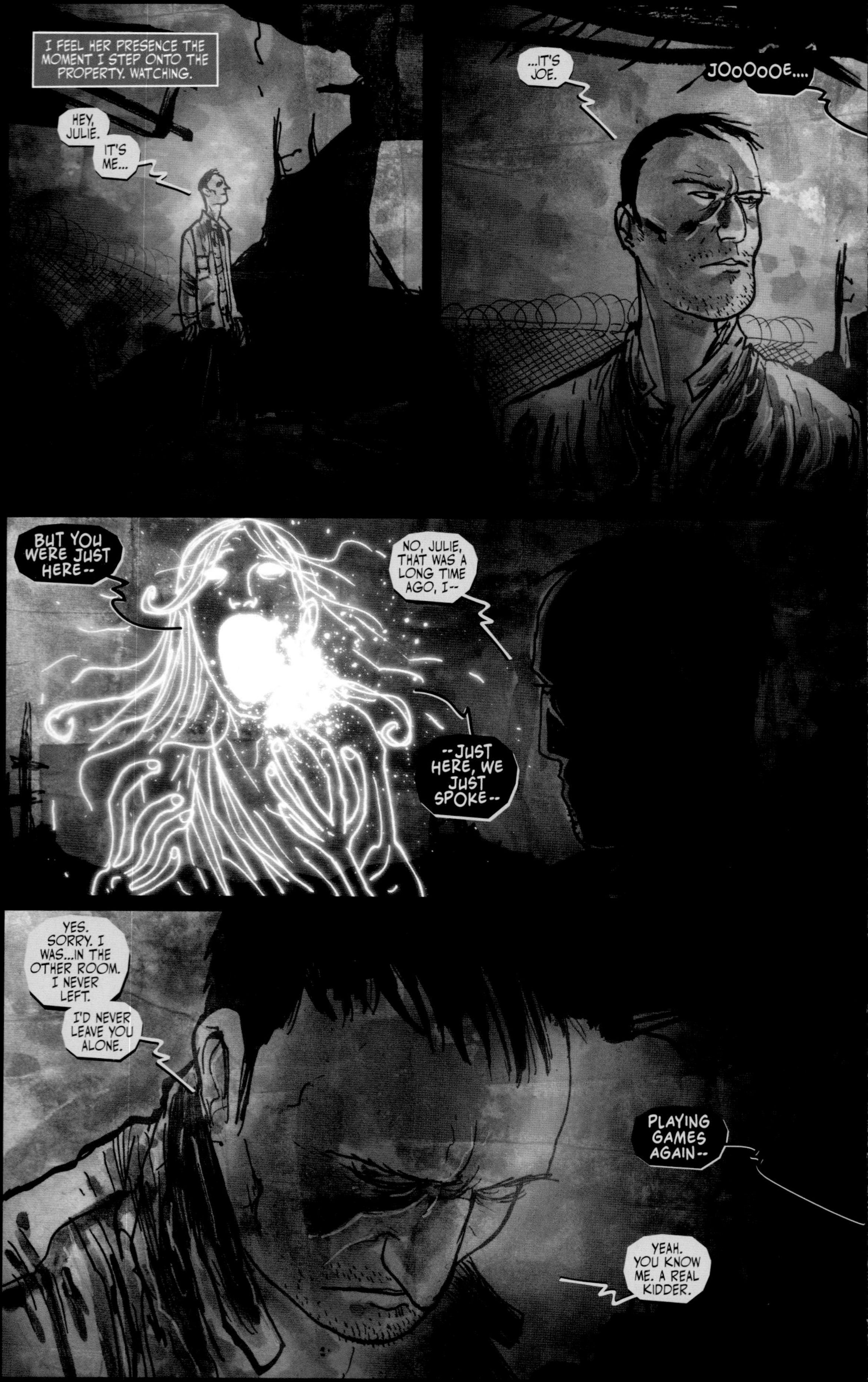
I FEEL HER PRESENCE THE MOMENT I STEP ONTO THE PROPERTY. WATCHING.
HEY, JULIE.
IT'S ME...
...IT'S JOE.
JOOOOOE....
BUT YOU WERE JUST HERE--
NO, JULIE, THAT WAS A LONG TIME AGO, I--
--JUST HERE, WE JUST SPOKE--
YES. SORRY. I WAS...IN THE OTHER ROOM. I NEVER LEFT.
I'D NEVER LEAVE YOU ALONE.
PLAYING GAMES AGAIN--
YEAH. YOU KNOW ME. A REAL KIDDER.

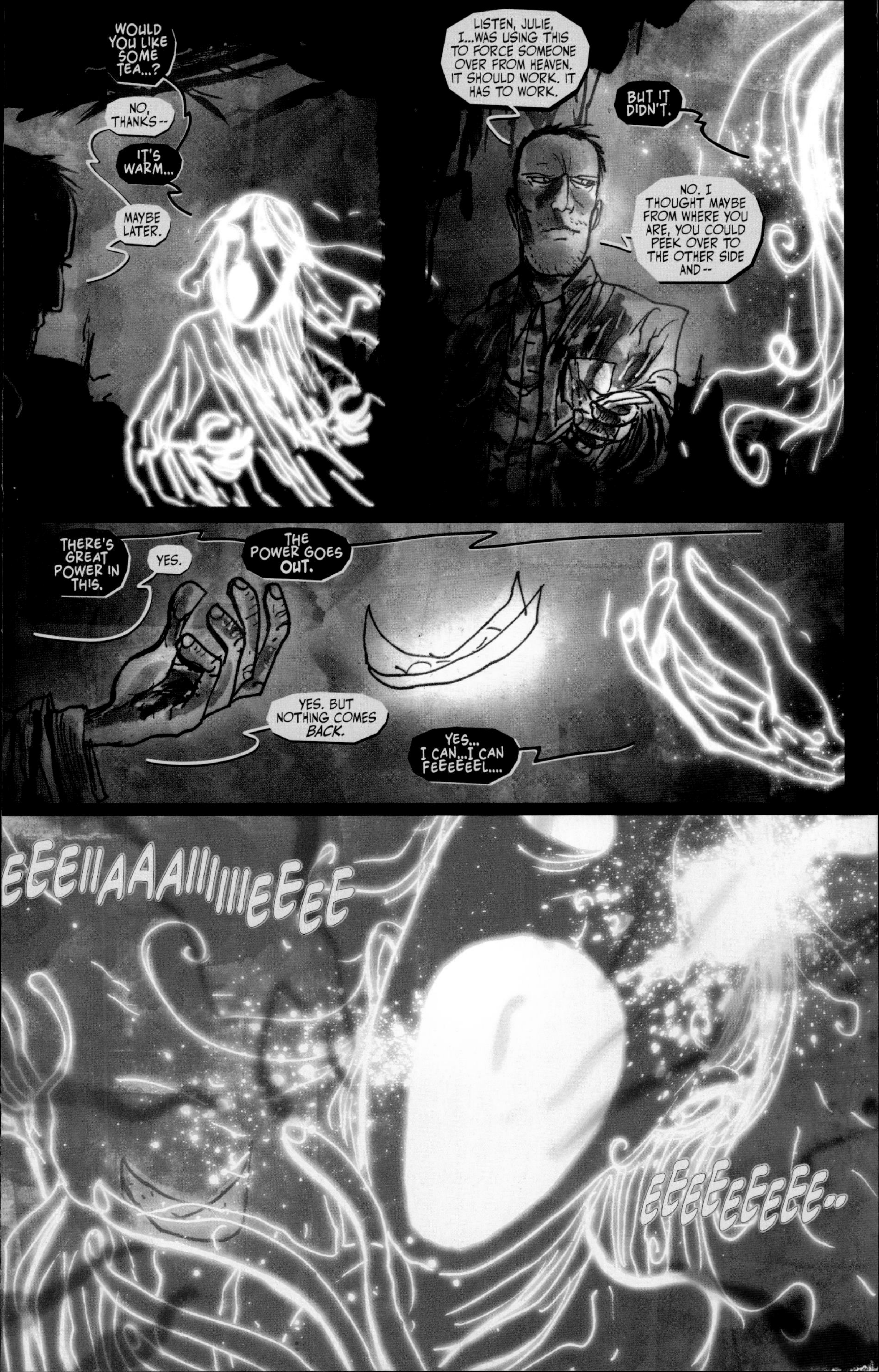
WOULD YOU LIKE SOME TEA...?
NO, THANKS--
IT'S WARM...
MAYBE LATER.
LISTEN, JULIE, I...WAS USING THIS TO FORCE SOMEONE OVER FROM HEAVEN. IT SHOULD WORK. IT HAS TO WORK.
BUT IT DIDN'T.
NO. I THOUGHT MAYBE FROM WHERE YOU ARE, YOU COULD PEEK OVER TO THE OTHER SIDE AND--
THERE'S GREAT POWER IN THIS.
YES.
THE POWER GOES OUT.
YES. BUT NOTHING COMES BACK.
YES... I CAN...I CAN FEEEEEEL....
EEEIIAAAIIIIIEEEE
EEEEEEEEEE..

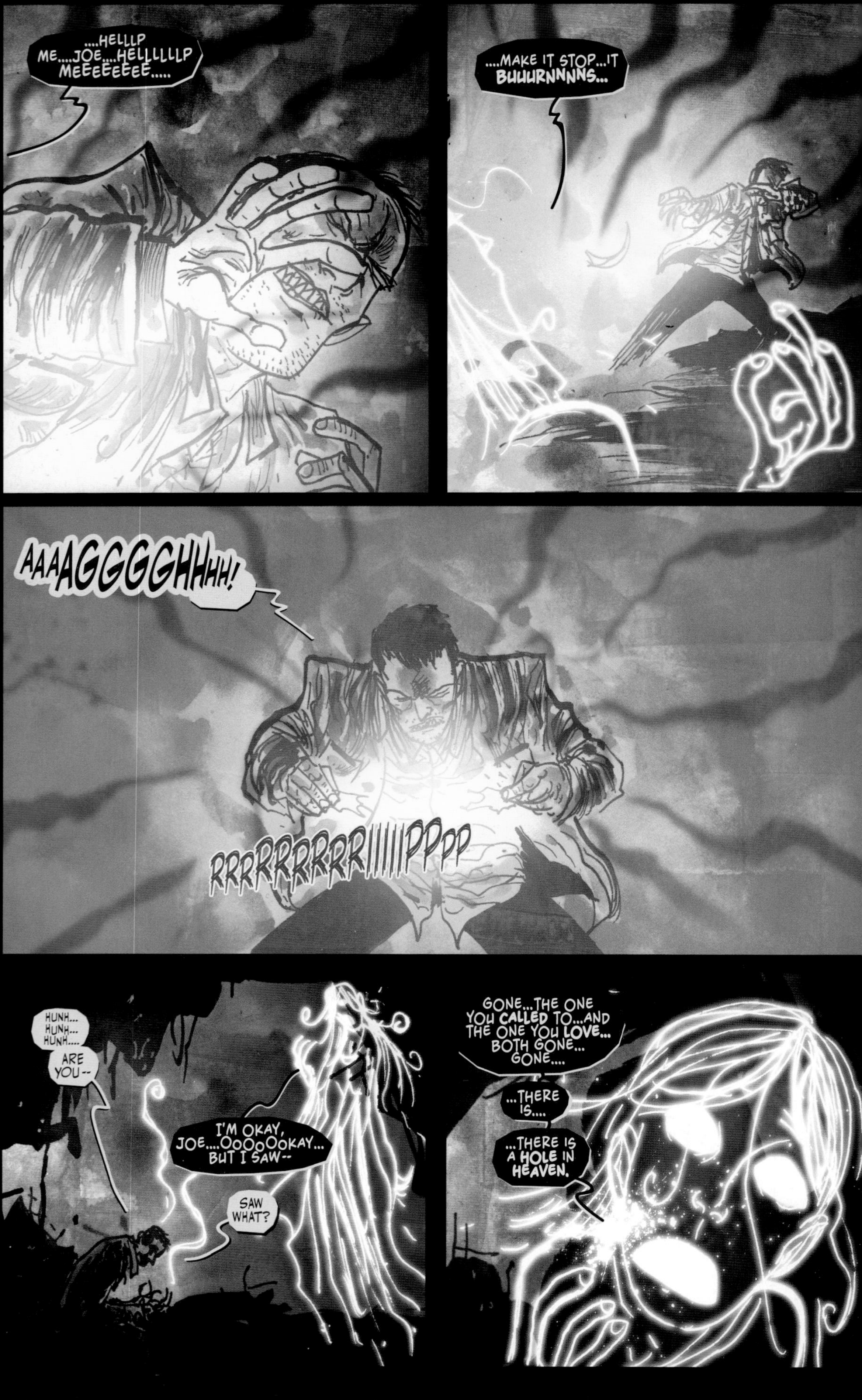

....HELLLP ME....JOE....HELLLLLLP MEEEEEEEE.....
....MAKE IT STOP....IT BUUURNNNNS...
AAAAGGGGGHHHH!
RRRRRRRRRIIIIIPPPP
HUNH... HUNH... HUNH....
ARE YOU--
I'M OKAY, JOE....OOOOOOKAY... BUT I SAW--
SAW WHAT?
GONE...THE ONE YOU CALLED TO...AND THE ONE YOU LOVE... BOTH GONE... GONE....
...THERE IS....
...THERE IS A HOLE IN HEAVEN.

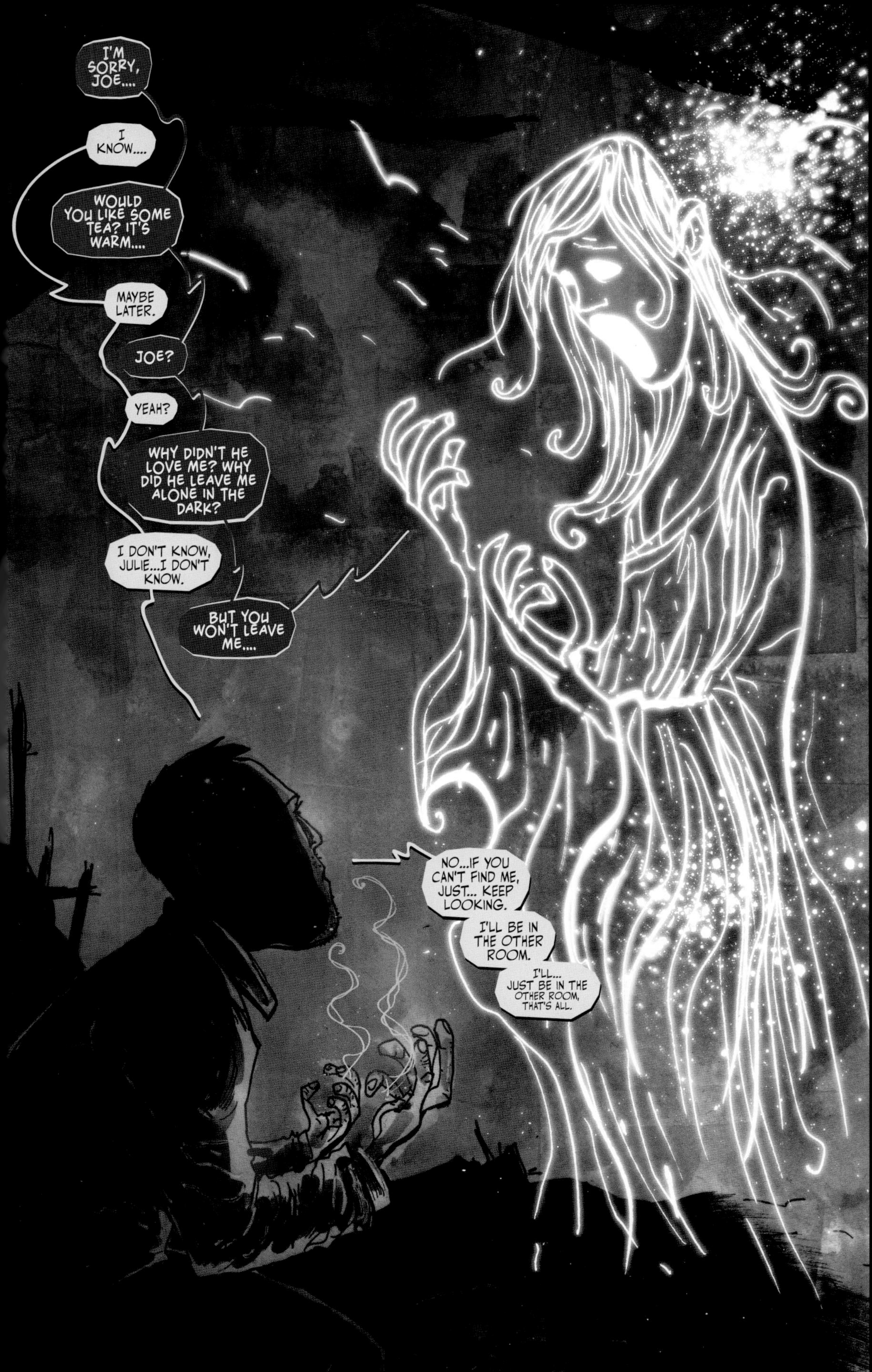
I'M SORRY, JOE....
I KNOW....
WOULD YOU LIKE SOME TEA? IT'S WARM....
MAYBE LATER.
JOE?
YEAH?
WHY DIDN'T HE LOVE ME? WHY DID HE LEAVE ME ALONE IN THE DARK?
I DON'T KNOW, JULIE...I DON'T KNOW.
BUT YOU WON'T LEAVE ME....
NO...IF YOU CAN'T FIND ME, JUST... KEEP LOOKING.
I'LL BE IN THE OTHER ROOM.
I'LL... JUST BE IN THE OTHER ROOM, THAT'S ALL.

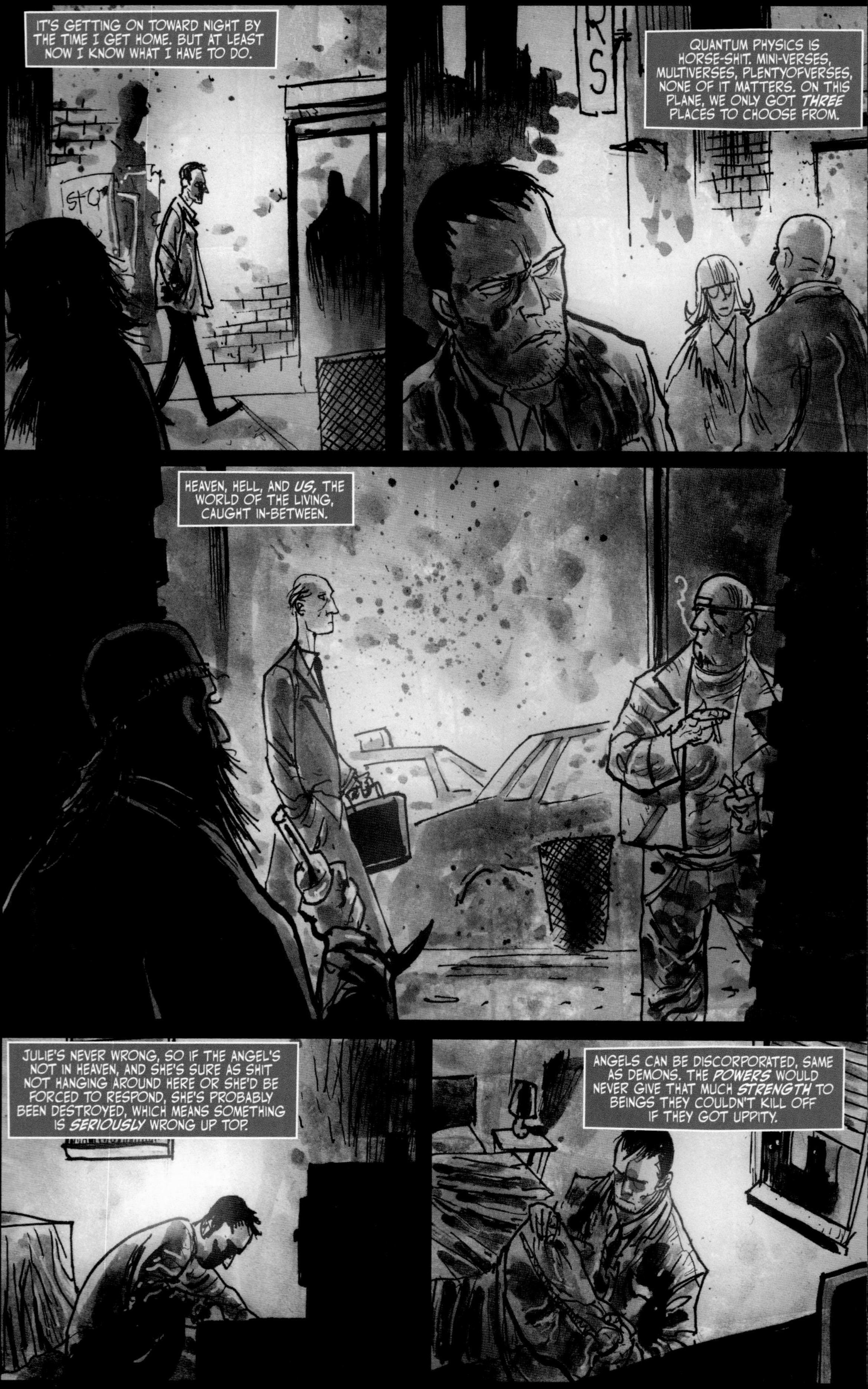
IT'S GETTING ON TOWARD NIGHT BY THE TIME I GET HOME. BUT AT LEAST NOW I KNOW WHAT I HAVE TO DO.
QUANTUM PHYSICS IS HORSE-SHIT. MINI-VERSES, MULTIVERSES, PLENTYOFVERSES, NONE OF IT MATTERS. ON THIS PLANE, WE ONLY GOT *THREE* PLACES TO CHOOSE FROM.
HEAVEN, HELL, AND *US,* THE WORLD OF THE LIVING, CAUGHT IN-BETWEEN.
JULIE'S NEVER WRONG, SO IF THE ANGEL'S NOT IN HEAVEN, AND SHE'S SURE AS SHIT NOT HANGING AROUND HERE OR SHE'D BE FORCED TO RESPOND, SHE'S PROBABLY BEEN DESTROYED, WHICH MEANS SOMETHING IS *SERIOUSLY* WRONG UP TOP.
ANGELS CAN BE DISCORPORATED, SAME AS DEMONS. THE *POWERS* WOULD NEVER GIVE THAT MUCH *STRENGTH* TO BEINGS THEY COULDN'T KILL OFF IF THEY GOT UPPITY.

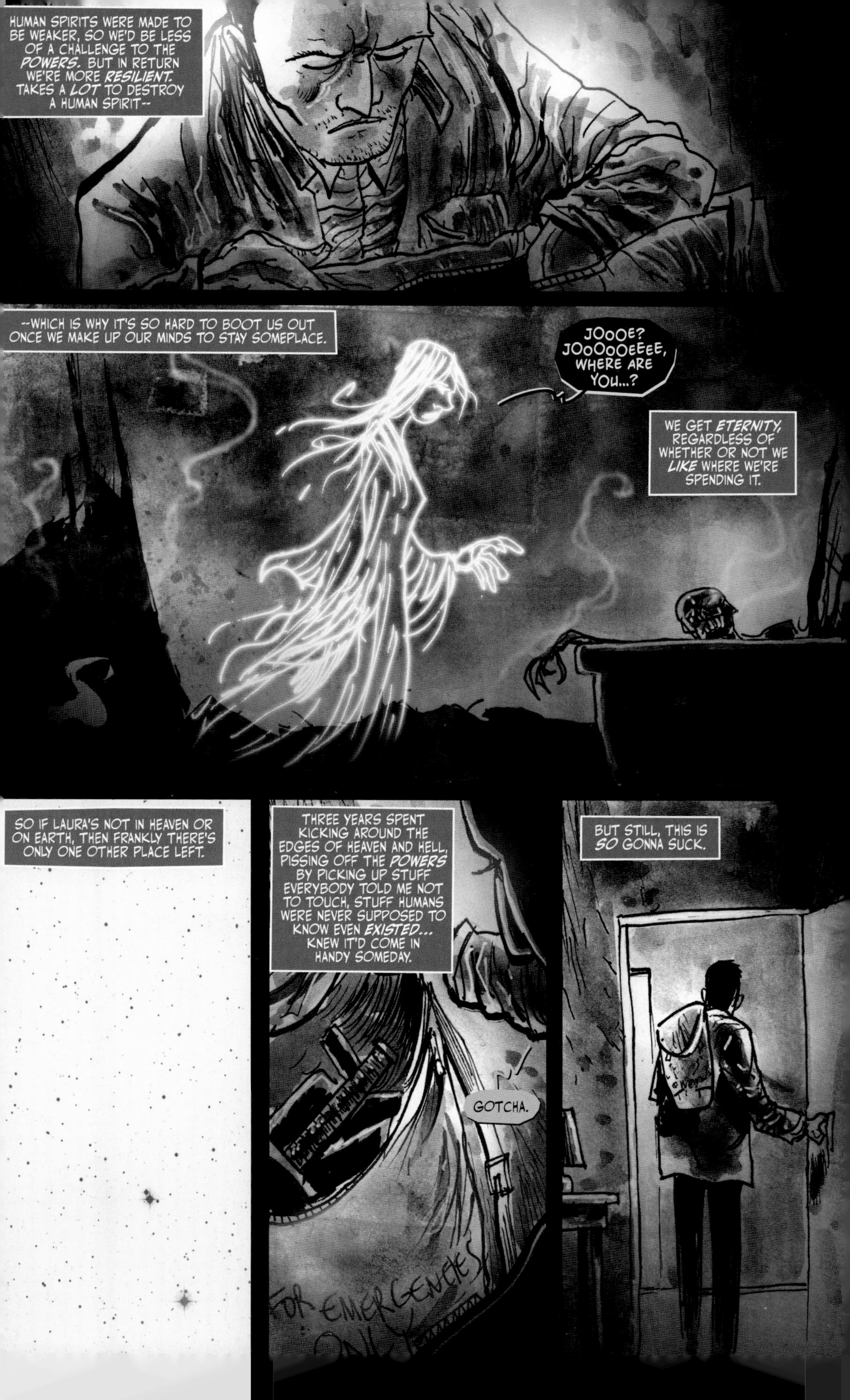
HUMAN SPIRITS WERE MADE TO BE WEAKER, SO WE'D BE LESS OF A CHALLENGE TO THE POWERS. BUT IN RETURN WE'RE MORE RESILIENT. TAKES A LOT TO DESTROY A HUMAN SPIRIT--
--WHICH IS WHY IT'S SO HARD TO BOOT US OUT ONCE WE MAKE UP OUR MINDS TO STAY SOMEPLACE.
JOOOE? JOOOOOEEEE, WHERE ARE YOU...?
WE GET ETERNITY, REGARDLESS OF WHETHER OR NOT WE LIKE WHERE WE'RE SPENDING IT.
SO IF LAURA'S NOT IN HEAVEN OR ON EARTH, THEN FRANKLY THERE'S ONLY ONE OTHER PLACE LEFT.
THREE YEARS SPENT KICKING AROUND THE EDGES OF HEAVEN AND HELL, PISSING OFF THE POWERS BY PICKING UP STUFF EVERYBODY TOLD ME NOT TO TOUCH, STUFF HUMANS WERE NEVER SUPPOSED TO KNOW EVEN EXISTED... KNEW IT'D COME IN HANDY SOMEDAY.
GOTCHA.
FOR EMERGENCIES ONLY
BUT STILL, THIS IS SO GONNA SUCK.

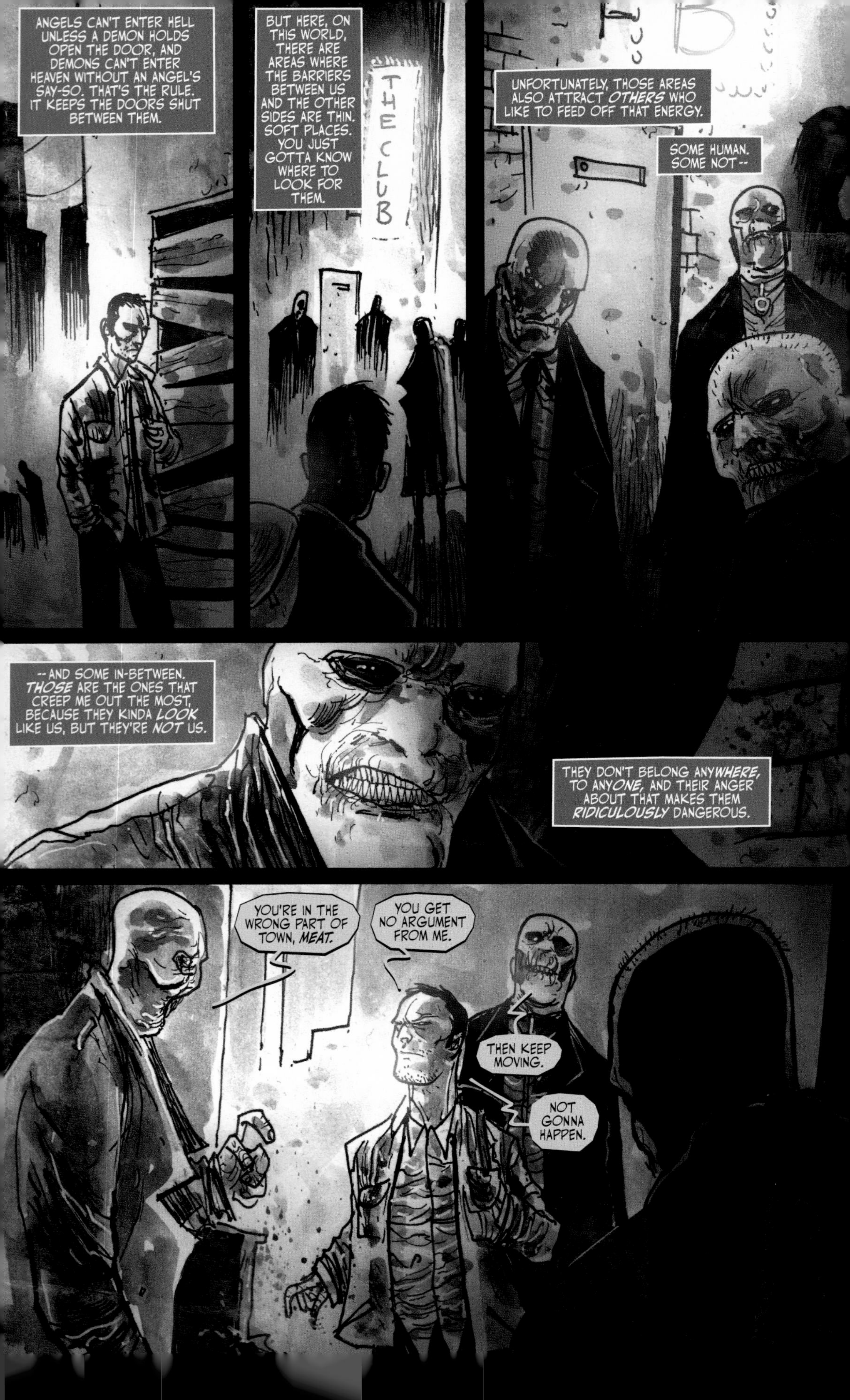
ANGELS CAN'T ENTER HELL UNLESS A DEMON HOLDS OPEN THE DOOR, AND DEMONS CAN'T ENTER HEAVEN WITHOUT AN ANGEL'S SAY-SO. THAT'S THE RULE. IT KEEPS THE DOORS SHUT BETWEEN THEM.
BUT HERE, ON THIS WORLD, THERE ARE AREAS WHERE THE BARRIERS BETWEEN US AND THE OTHER SIDES ARE THIN. SOFT PLACES. YOU JUST GOTTA KNOW WHERE TO LOOK FOR THEM.
THE CLUB
UNFORTUNATELY, THOSE AREAS ALSO ATTRACT *OTHERS* WHO LIKE TO FEED OFF THAT ENERGY.
SOME HUMAN. SOME NOT--
--AND SOME IN-BETWEEN. *THOSE* ARE THE ONES THAT CREEP ME OUT THE MOST, BECAUSE THEY KINDA *LOOK* LIKE US, BUT THEY'RE *NOT* US.
THEY DON'T BELONG ANY*WHERE*, TO ANY*ONE*, AND THEIR ANGER ABOUT THAT MAKES THEM *RIDICULOUSLY* DANGEROUS.
YOU'RE IN THE WRONG PART OF TOWN, *MEAT*.
YOU GET NO ARGUMENT FROM ME.
THEN KEEP MOVING.
NOT GONNA HAPPEN.

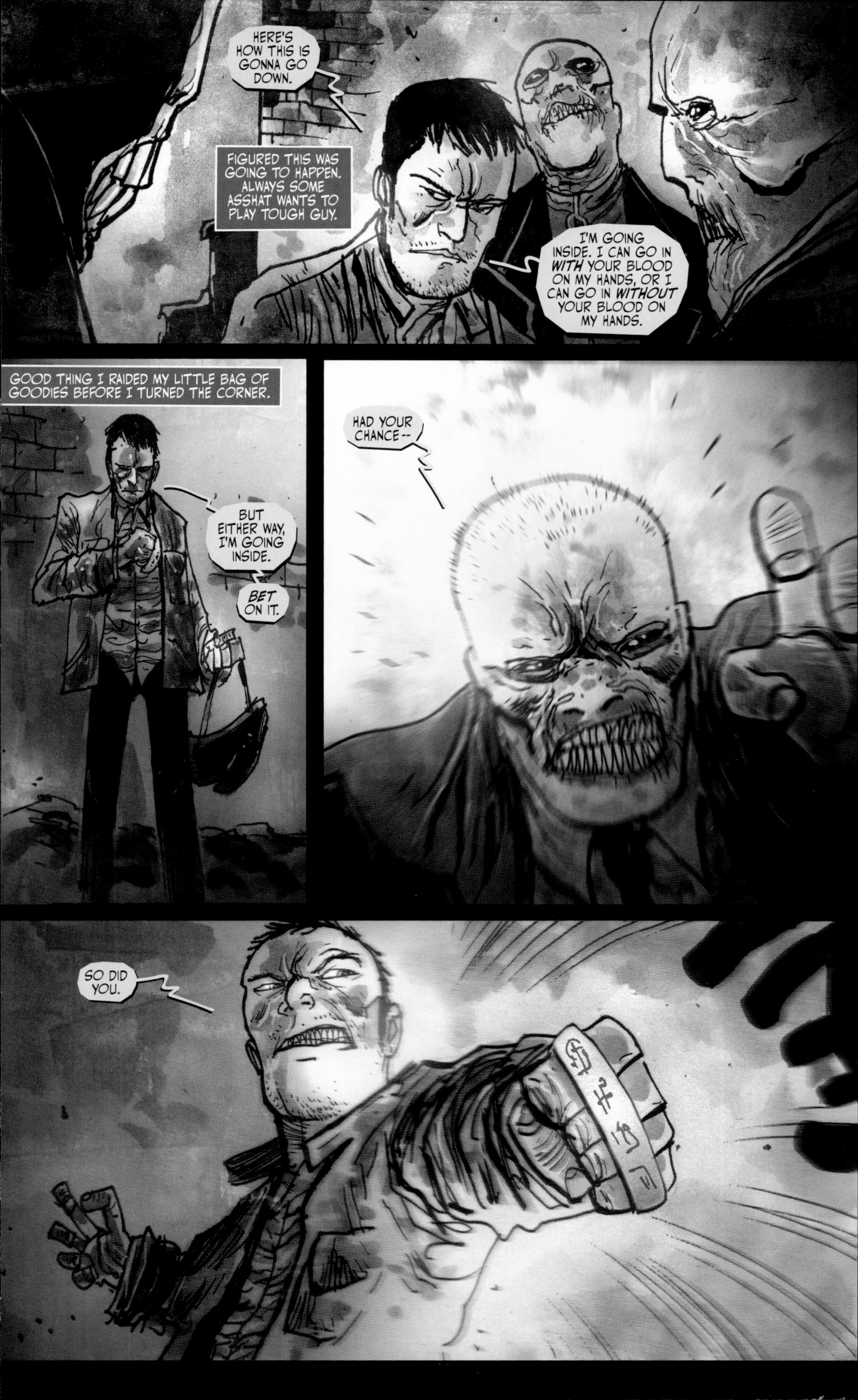
HERE'S HOW THIS IS GONNA GO DOWN.
FIGURED THIS WAS GOING TO HAPPEN. ALWAYS SOME ASSHAT WANTS TO PLAY TOUGH GUY.
I'M GOING INSIDE. I CAN GO IN *WITH* YOUR BLOOD ON MY HANDS, OR I CAN GO IN *WITHOUT* YOUR BLOOD ON MY HANDS.
GOOD THING I RAIDED MY LITTLE BAG OF GOODIES BEFORE I TURNED THE CORNER.
BUT EITHER WAY, I'M GOING INSIDE.
*BET* ON IT.
HAD YOUR CHANCE--
SO DID YOU.

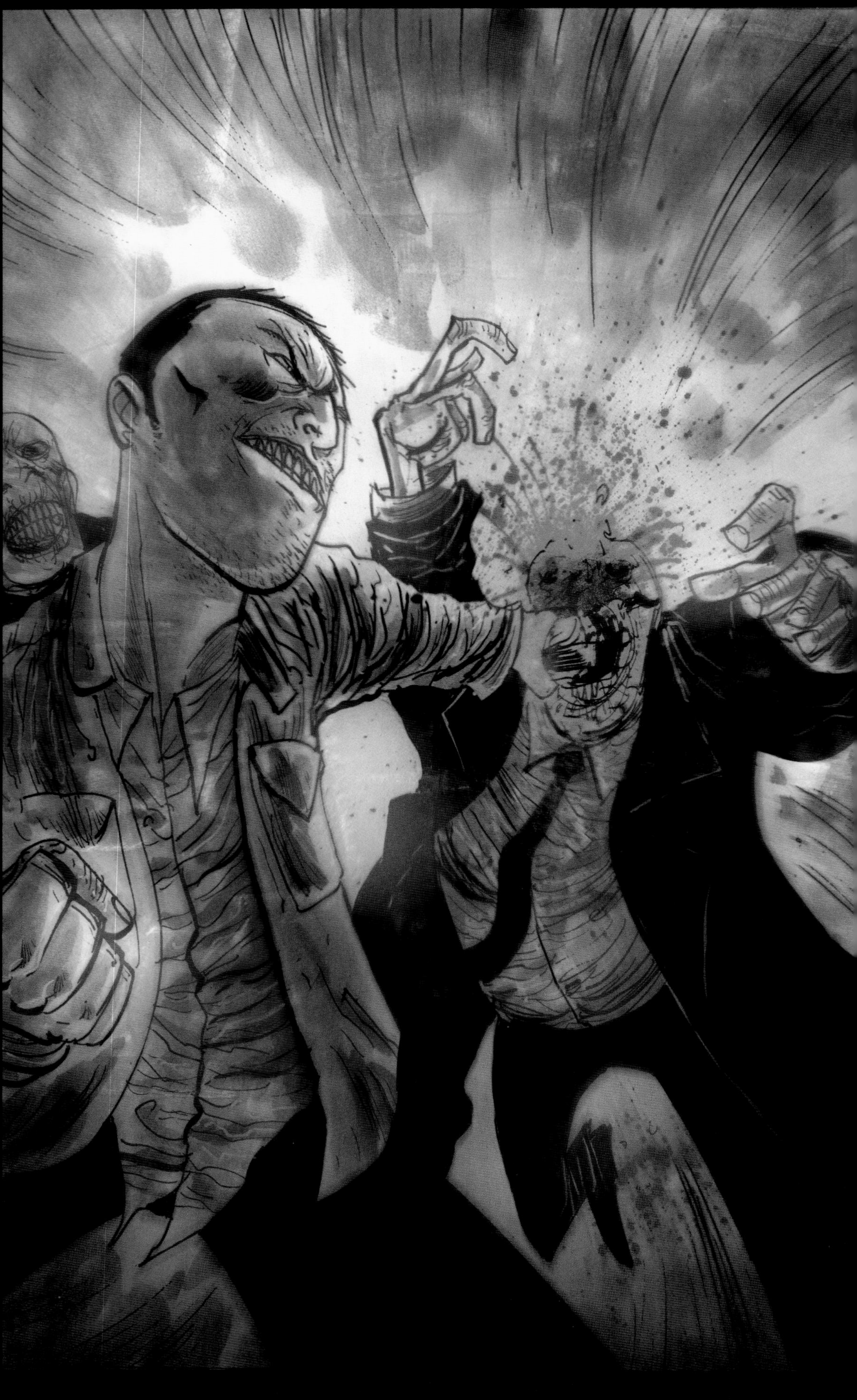

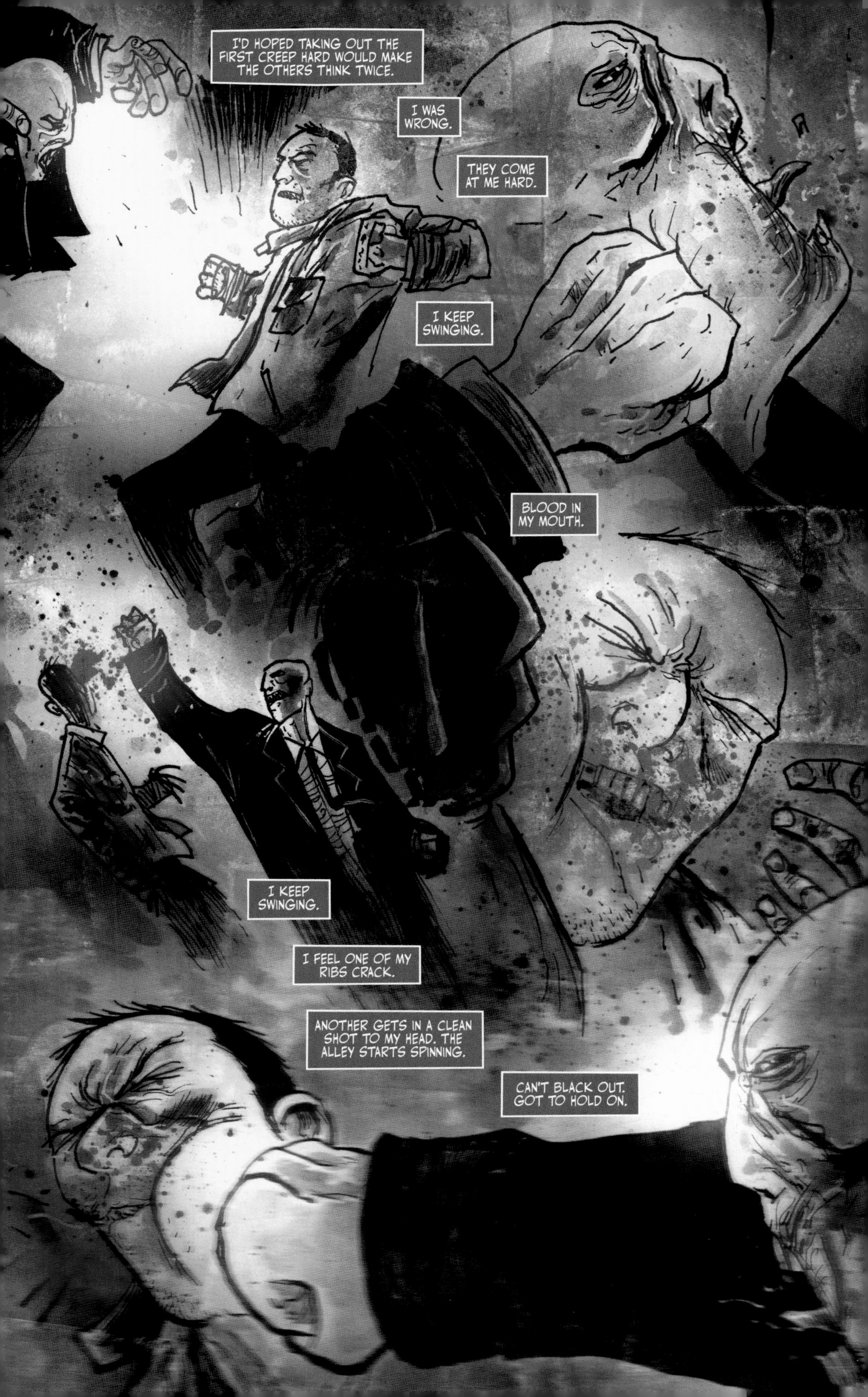
I'D HOPED TAKING OUT THE FIRST CREEP HARD WOULD MAKE THE OTHERS THINK TWICE.
I WAS WRONG.
THEY COME AT ME HARD.
I KEEP SWINGING.
BLOOD IN MY MOUTH.
I KEEP SWINGING.
I FEEL ONE OF MY RIBS CRACK.
ANOTHER GETS IN A CLEAN SHOT TO MY HEAD. THE ALLEY STARTS SPINNING.
CAN'T BLACK OUT. GOT TO HOLD ON.

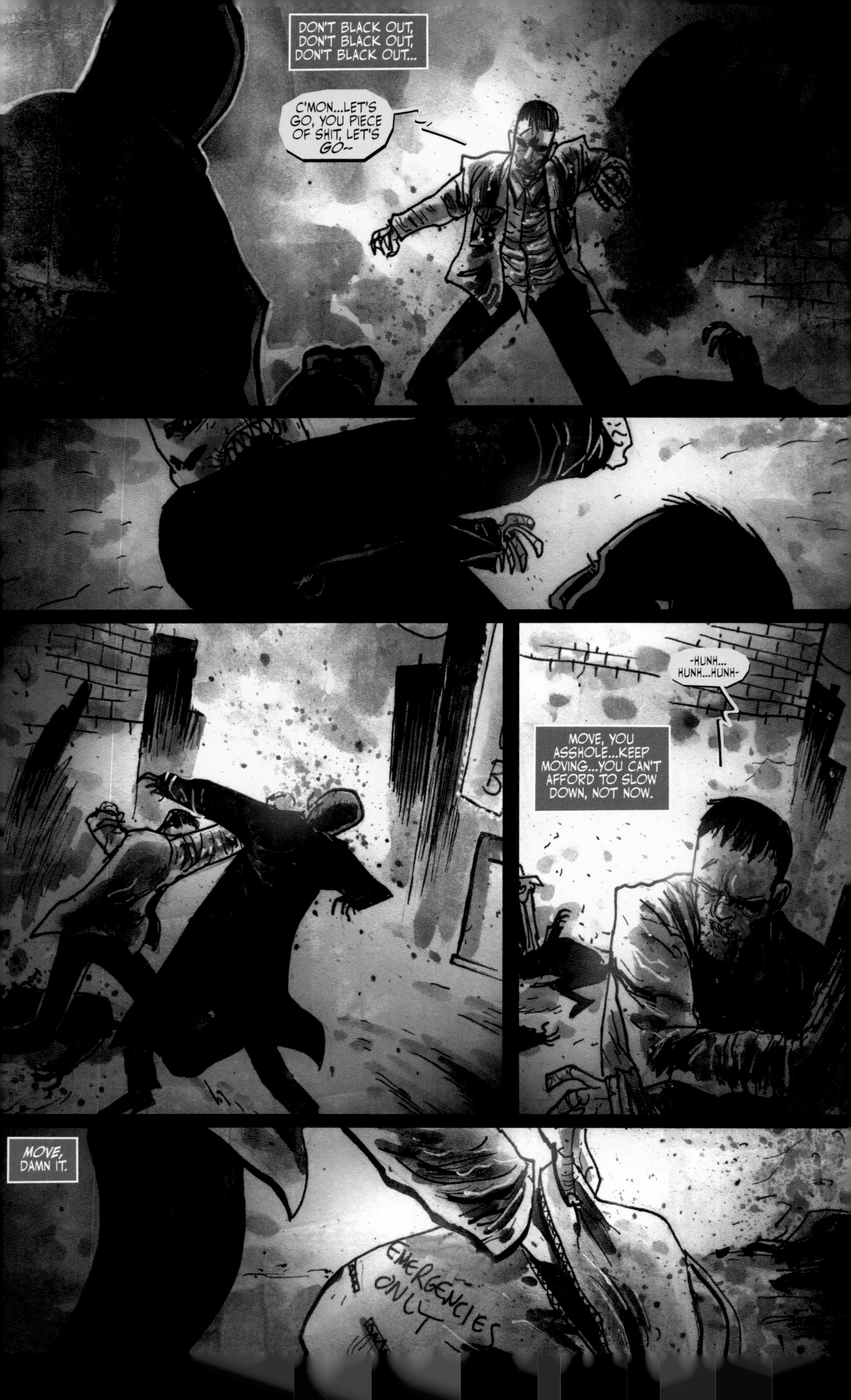
DON'T BLACK OUT, DON'T BLACK OUT, DON'T BLACK OUT...
C'MON...LET'S GO, YOU PIECE OF SHIT, LET'S GO--
-HUNH... HUNH...HUNH-
MOVE, YOU ASSHOLE...KEEP MOVING...YOU CAN'T AFFORD TO SLOW DOWN, NOT NOW.
MOVE, DAMN IT.
EMERGENCIES ONLY

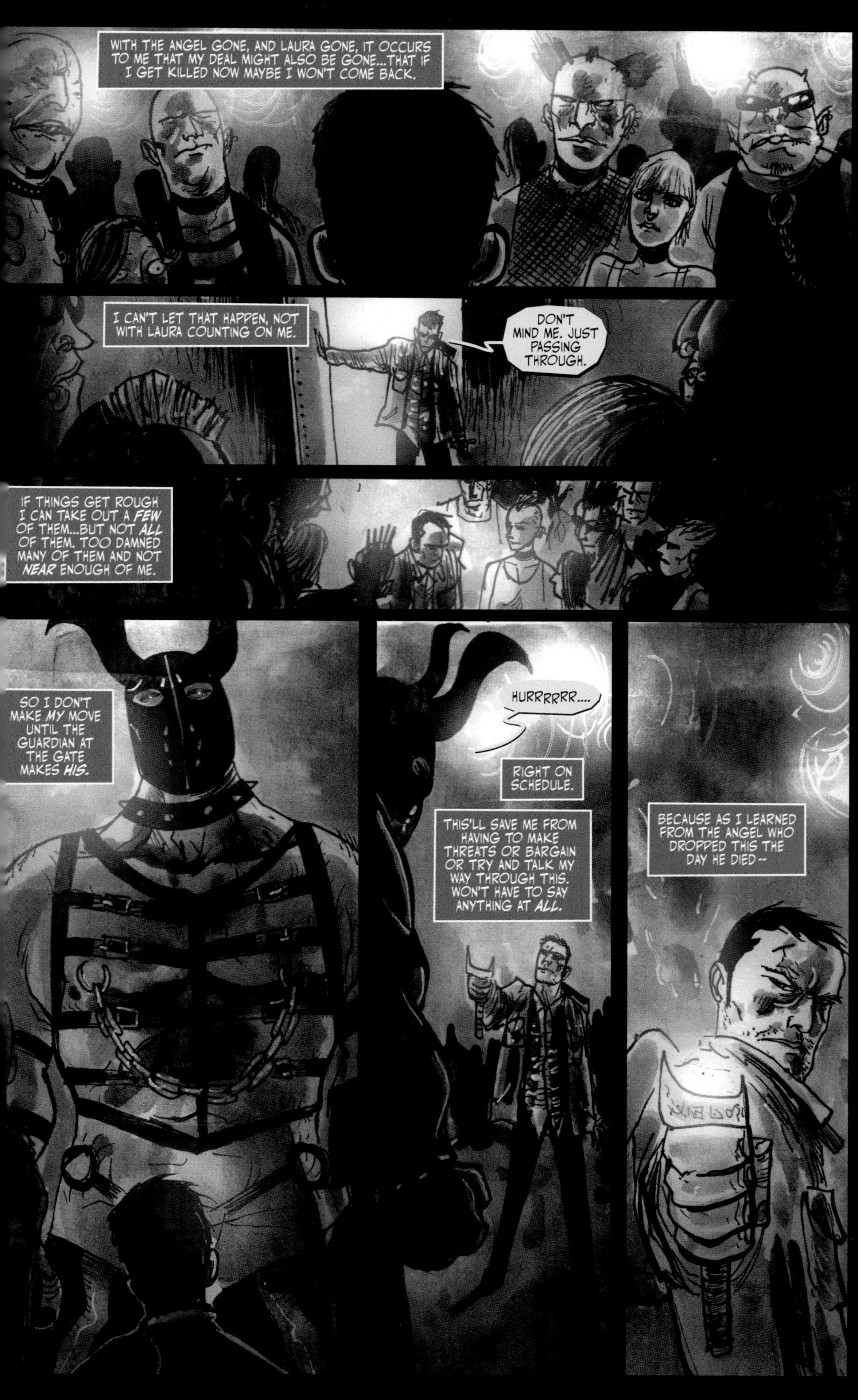
WITH THE ANGEL GONE, AND LAURA GONE, IT OCCURS TO ME THAT MY DEAL MIGHT ALSO BE GONE...THAT IF I GET KILLED NOW MAYBE I WON'T COME BACK.
I CAN'T LET THAT HAPPEN, NOT WITH LAURA COUNTING ON ME.
DON'T MIND ME. JUST PASSING THROUGH.
IF THINGS GET ROUGH I CAN TAKE OUT A *FEW* OF THEM...BUT NOT *ALL* OF THEM. TOO DAMNED MANY OF THEM AND NOT *NEAR* ENOUGH OF ME.
SO I DON'T MAKE *MY* MOVE UNTIL THE GUARDIAN AT THE GATE MAKES *HIS*.
HURRRRRR....
RIGHT ON SCHEDULE.
THIS'LL SAVE ME FROM HAVING TO MAKE THREATS OR BARGAIN OR TRY AND TALK MY WAY THROUGH THIS. WON'T HAVE TO SAY ANYTHING AT *ALL*.
BECAUSE AS I LEARNED FROM THE ANGEL WHO DROPPED THIS THE DAY HE DIED--

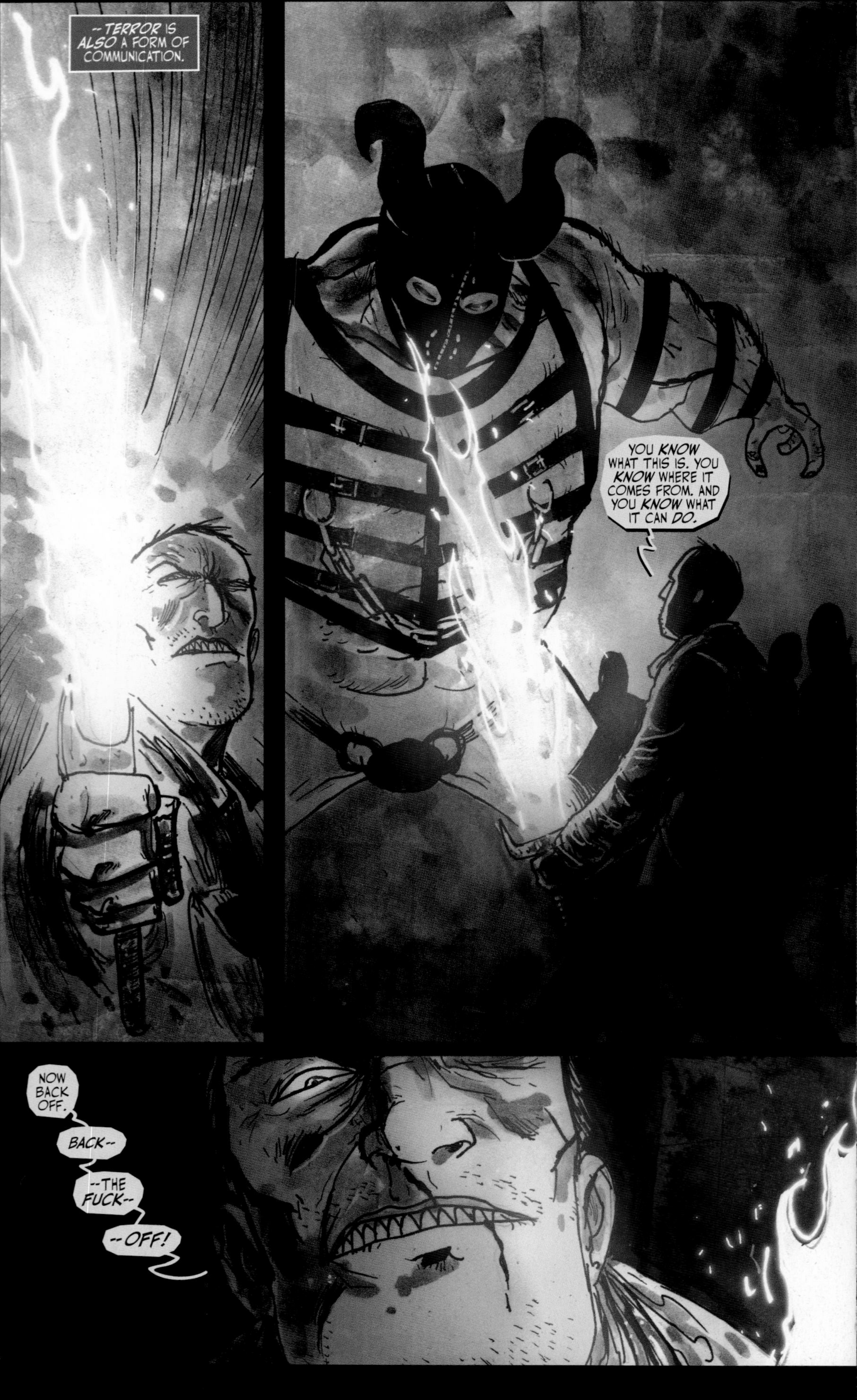
--TERROR IS ALSO A FORM OF COMMUNICATION.
YOU KNOW WHAT THIS IS. YOU KNOW WHERE IT COMES FROM. AND YOU KNOW WHAT IT CAN DO.
NOW BACK OFF.
BACK--
--THE FUCK--
--OFF!

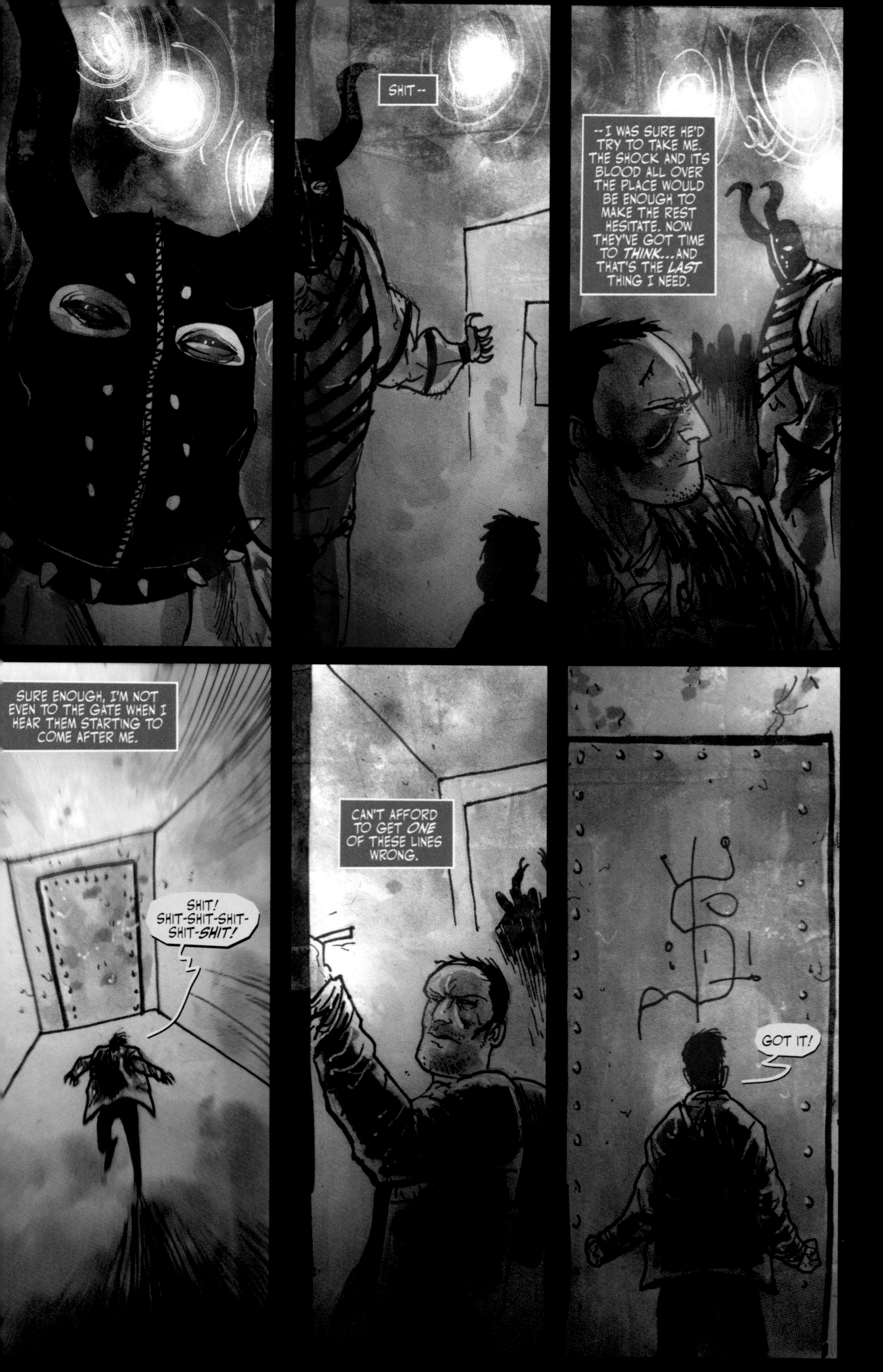
SHIT --
--I WAS SURE HE'D TRY TO TAKE ME. THE SHOCK AND ITS BLOOD ALL OVER THE PLACE WOULD BE ENOUGH TO MAKE THE REST HESITATE. NOW THEY'VE GOT TIME TO *THINK*... AND THAT'S THE *LAST* THING I NEED.
SURE ENOUGH, I'M NOT EVEN TO THE GATE WHEN I HEAR THEM STARTING TO COME AFTER ME.
SHIT! SHIT-SHIT-SHIT-SHIT-*SHIT!*
CAN'T AFFORD TO GET *ONE* OF THESE LINES WRONG.
GOT IT!

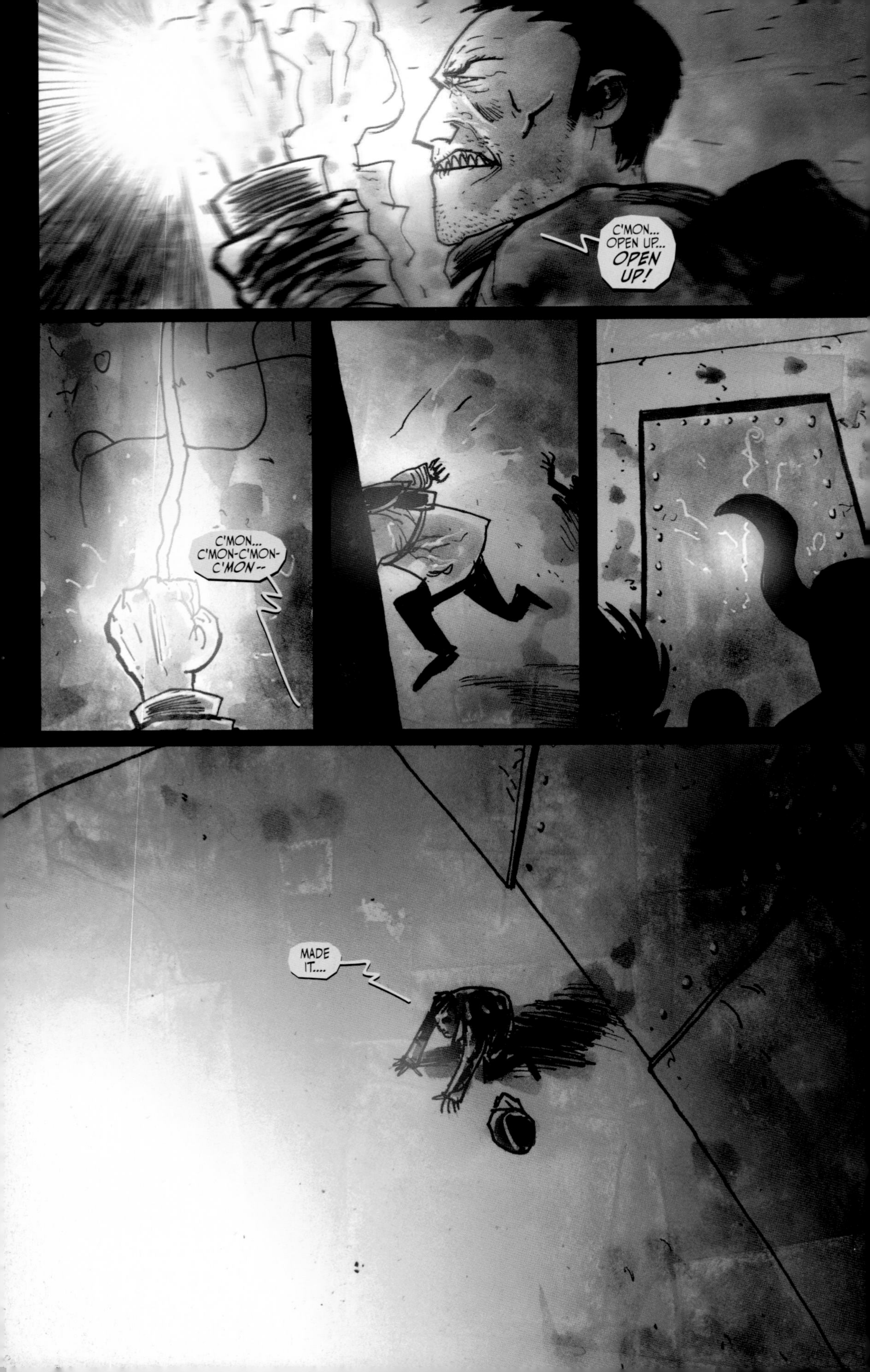
C'MON... OPEN UP... OPEN UP!
C'MON... C'MON-C'MON-C'MON--
MADE IT....

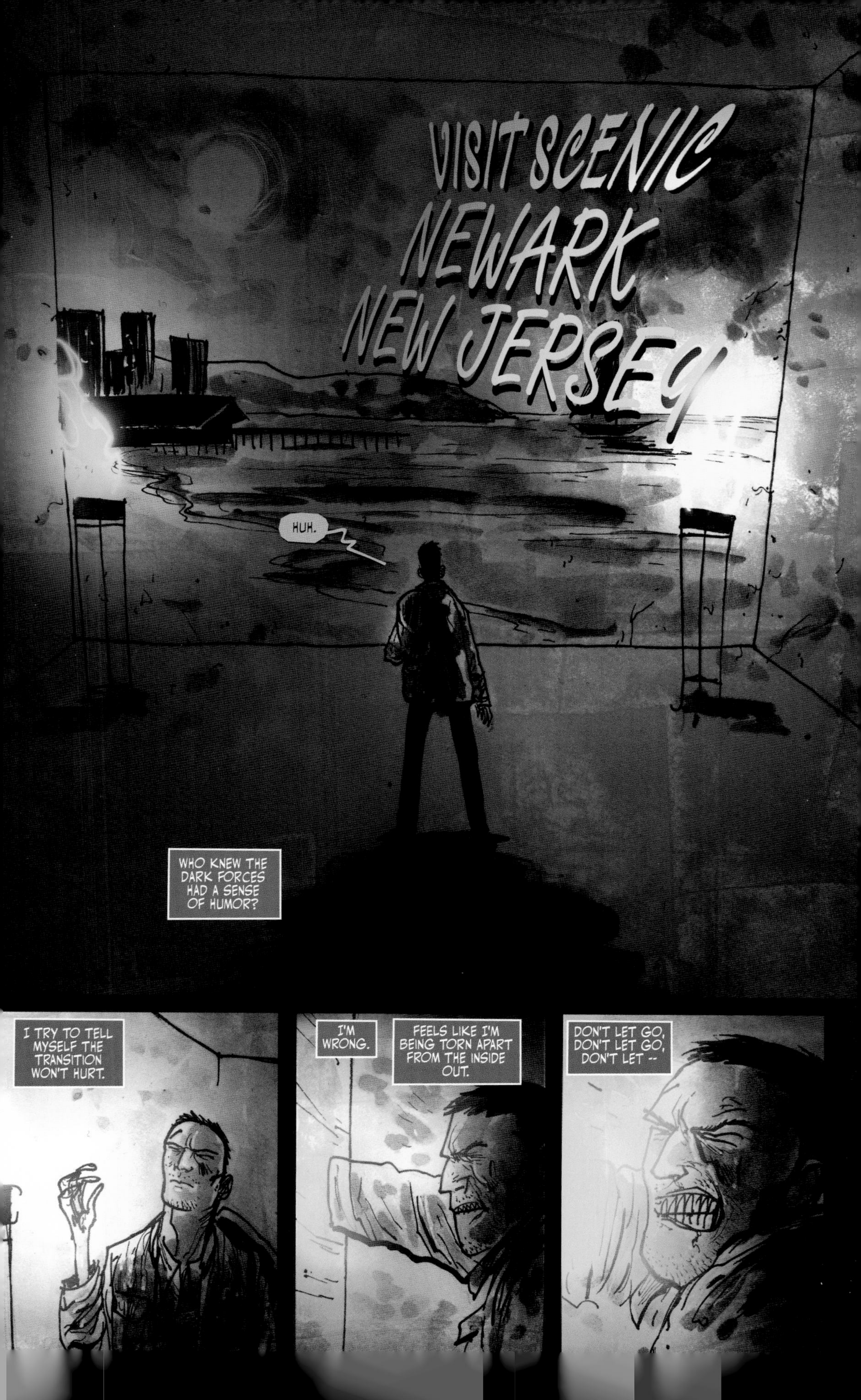
VISIT SCENIC
NEWARK
NEW JERSEY
HUH.
WHO KNEW THE DARK FORCES HAD A SENSE OF HUMOR?
I TRY TO TELL MYSELF THE TRANSITION WON'T HURT.
I'M WRONG.
FEELS LIKE I'M BEING TORN APART FROM THE INSIDE OUT.
DON'T LET GO, DON'T LET GO, DON'T LET --

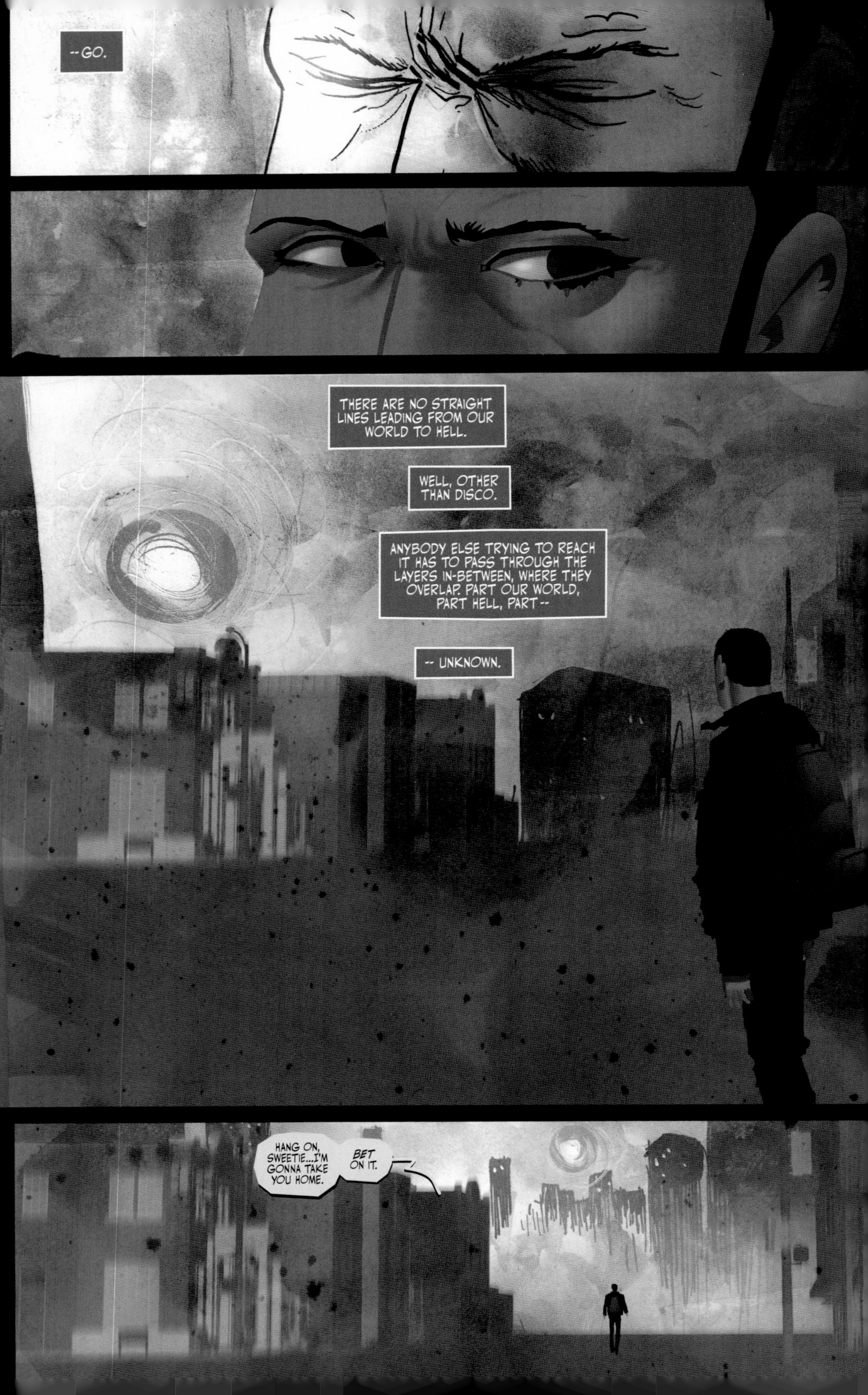
--GO.
THERE ARE NO STRAIGHT LINES LEADING FROM OUR WORLD TO HELL.
WELL, OTHER THAN DISCO.
ANYBODY ELSE TRYING TO REACH IT HAS TO PASS THROUGH THE LAYERS IN-BETWEEN, WHERE THEY OVERLAP. PART OUR WORLD, PART HELL, PART--
-- UNKNOWN.
HANG ON, SWEETIE...I'M GONNA TAKE YOU HOME.
BET ON IT.

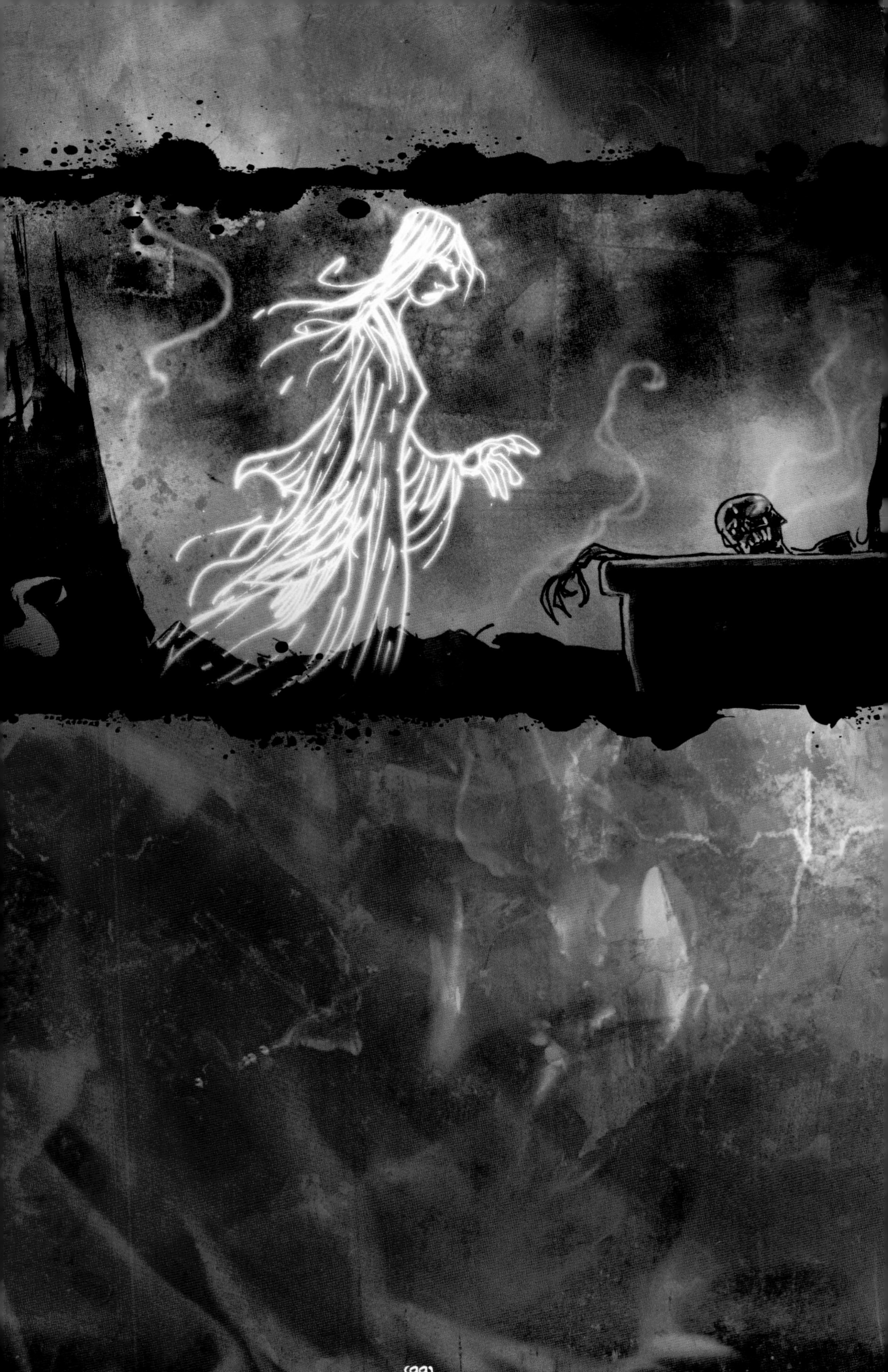

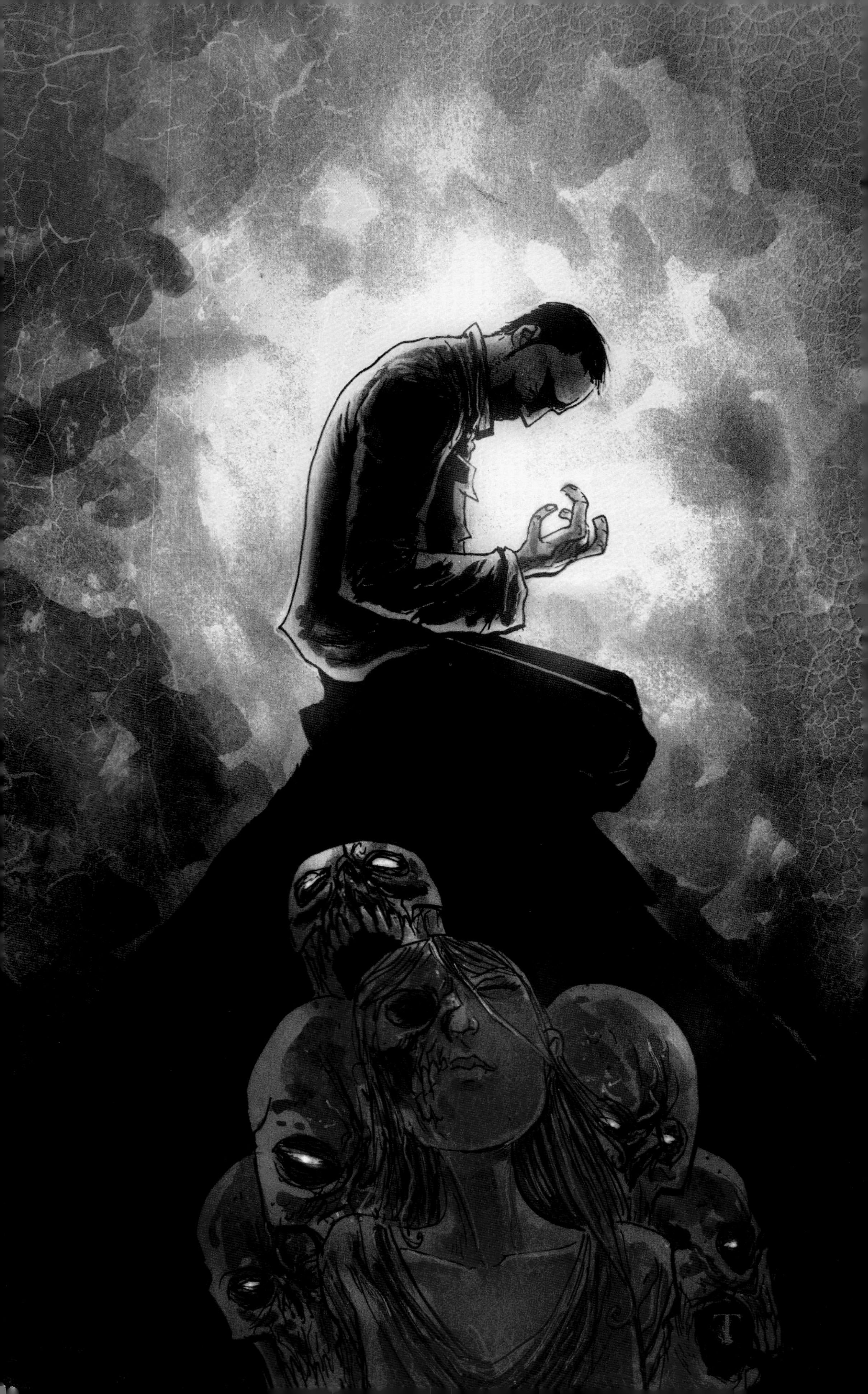

THE MUSLIMS CALL IT *BARZAKH*, THE PLACE BETWEEN LIFE AND AFTERLIFE, WHERE THE SPIRITS OF THE DEAD -- AND SOMETIMES THE LIVING -- END UP WHEN THEY'RE NOT GOOD ENOUGH TO GO UP OR BAD ENOUGH TO GO DOWN.

*POINT* IS, NO MATTER WHERE YOU GO, *EVERY* RELIGION HAS A NAME FOR THE PLACE IN-BETWEEN. BRACKETED BY *LIFE* AND *DEATH*, *DAMNATION* AND *GRACE*, AND WHICHEVER OF THE *POWERS* ARE IN CHARGE THAT DAY.

THEY SPEND *VEDAS* AND *CHAPTERS* AND *SCROLLS* AND *EPISTLES* DESCRIBING THE *RULES* AND THE *LOCATION* AND THE SORT OF ASSHOLES WHO GET *STUCK* THERE.

THE JEWS CALL IT *SHEOL*. TIBETANS CALL IT *BARDO*. CATHOLICS CALL IT *PURGATORY*. INDIAN BUDDHISTS HAVE A NAME FOR IT THAT I CAN'T PRONOUNCE SO I'M NOT EVEN GONNA TRY.

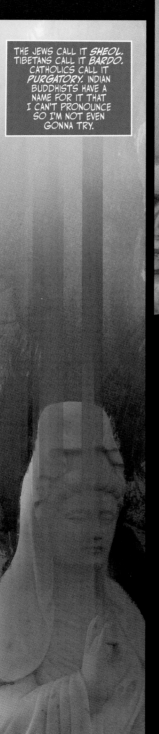

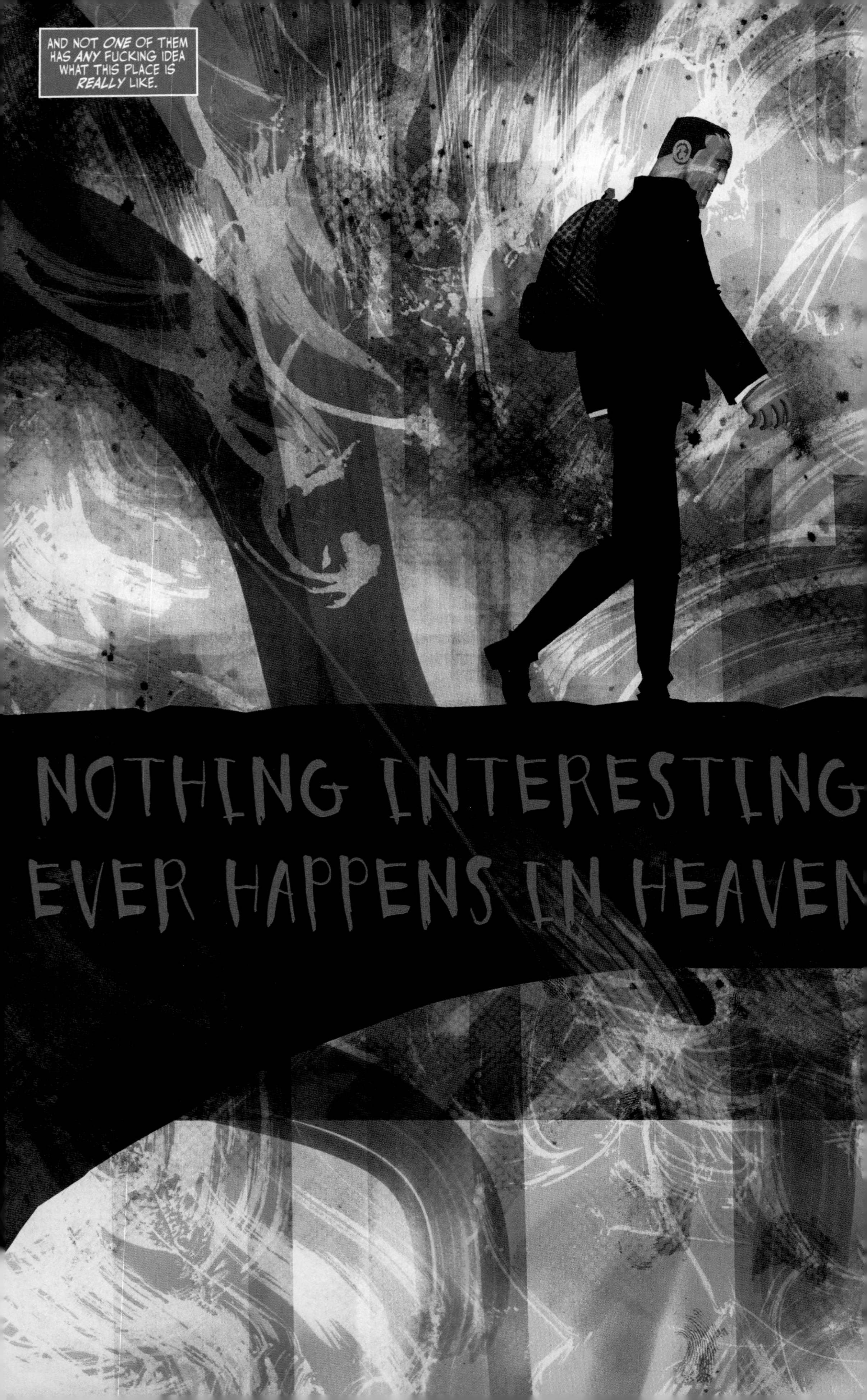
AND NOT *ONE* OF THEM HAS *ANY* FUCKING IDEA WHAT THIS PLACE IS *REALLY* LIKE.
NOTHING INTERESTING EVER HAPPENS IN HEAVEN

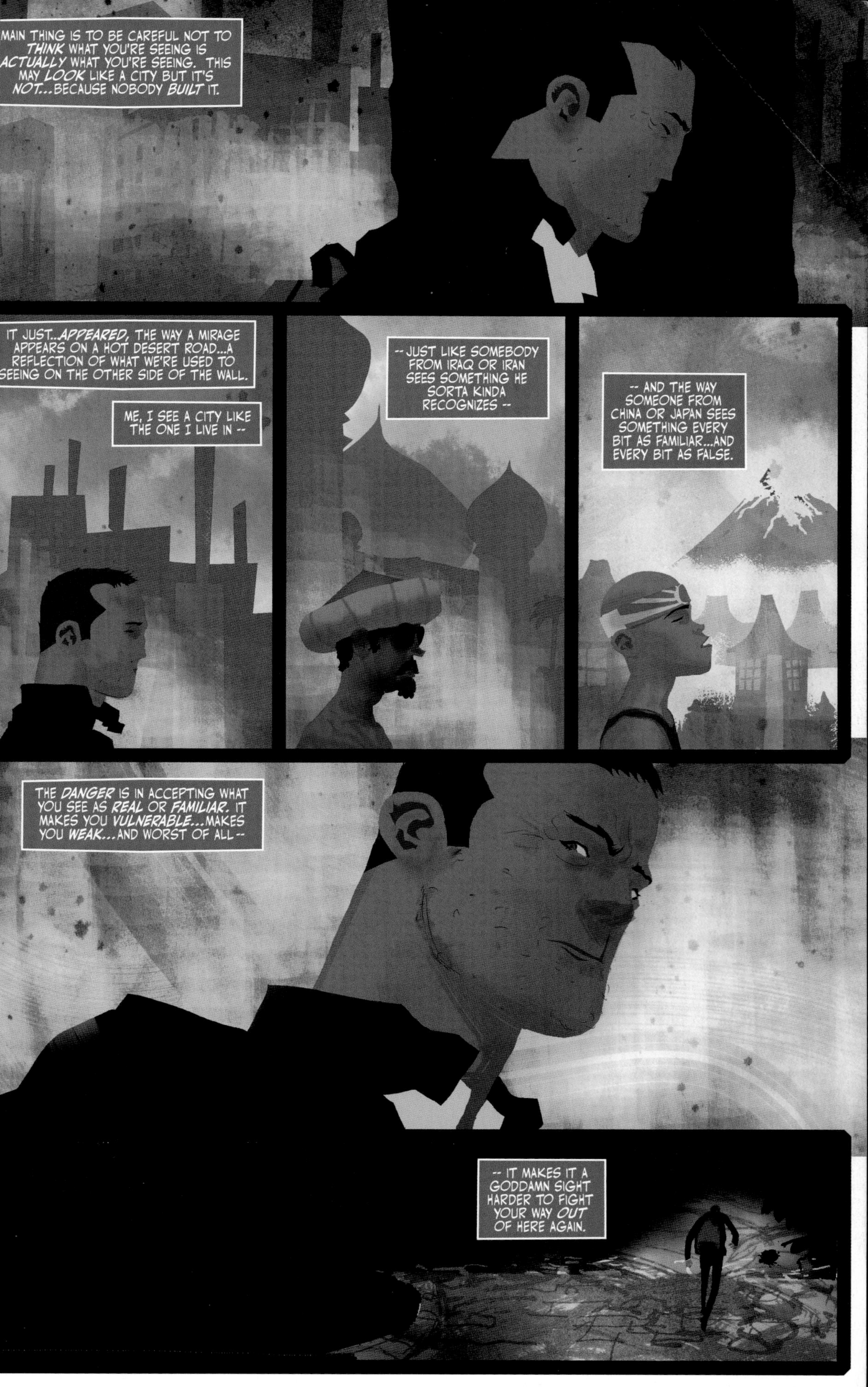
MAIN THING IS TO BE CAREFUL NOT TO THINK WHAT YOU'RE SEEING IS ACTUALLY WHAT YOU'RE SEEING. THIS MAY LOOK LIKE A CITY BUT IT'S NOT...BECAUSE NOBODY BUILT IT.
IT JUST...APPEARED, THE WAY A MIRAGE APPEARS ON A HOT DESERT ROAD...A REFLECTION OF WHAT WE'RE USED TO SEEING ON THE OTHER SIDE OF THE WALL.
ME, I SEE A CITY LIKE THE ONE I LIVE IN --
-- JUST LIKE SOMEBODY FROM IRAQ OR IRAN SEES SOMETHING HE SORTA KINDA RECOGNIZES --
-- AND THE WAY SOMEONE FROM CHINA OR JAPAN SEES SOMETHING EVERY BIT AS FAMILIAR...AND EVERY BIT AS FALSE.
THE DANGER IS IN ACCEPTING WHAT YOU SEE AS REAL OR FAMILIAR. IT MAKES YOU VULNERABLE...MAKES YOU WEAK...AND WORST OF ALL --
-- IT MAKES IT A GODDAMN SIGHT HARDER TO FIGHT YOUR WAY OUT OF HERE AGAIN.

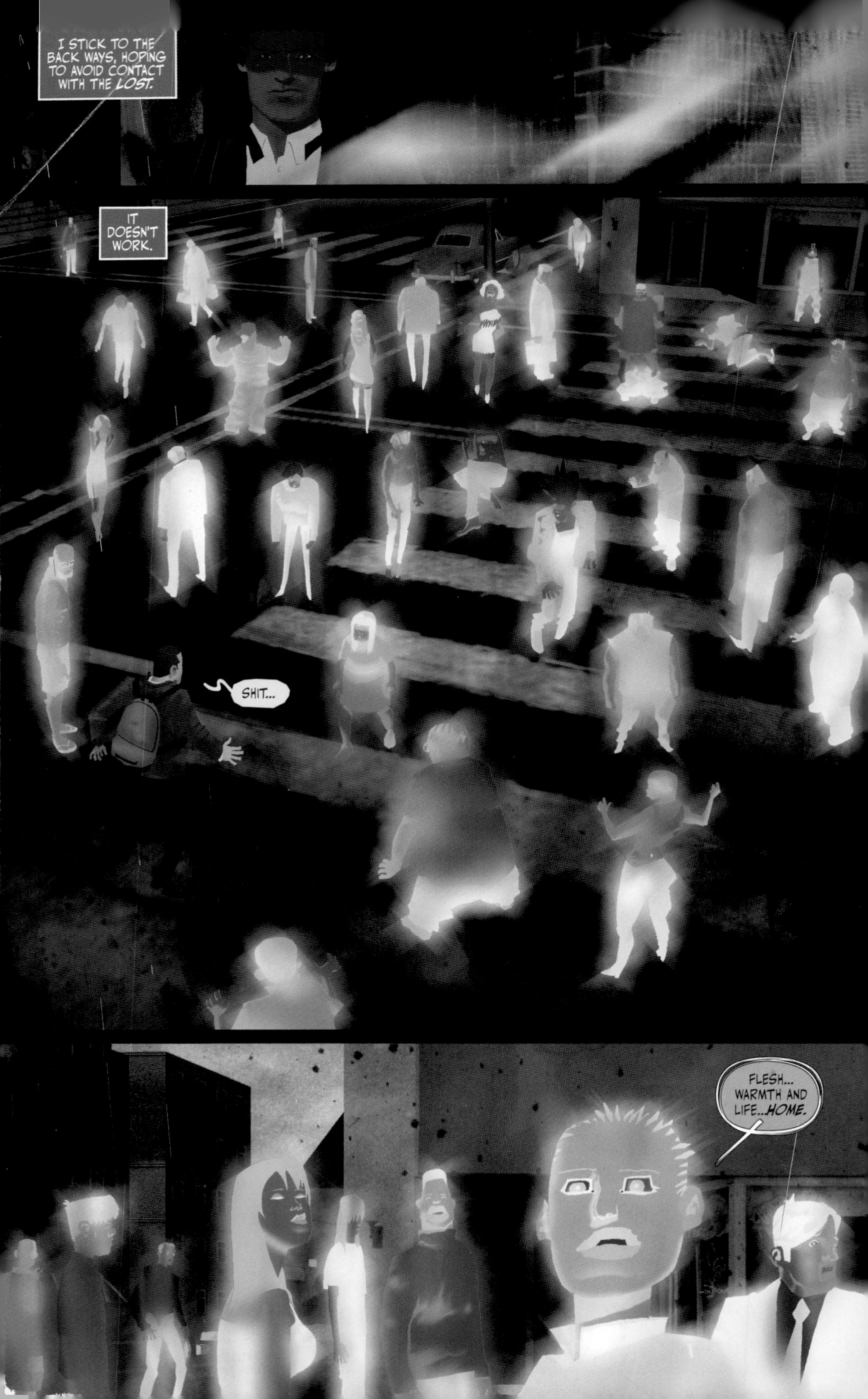
I STICK TO THE BACK WAYS, HOPING TO AVOID CONTACT WITH THE LOST.
IT DOESN'T WORK.
SHIT...
FLESH... WARMTH AND LIFE...HOME.

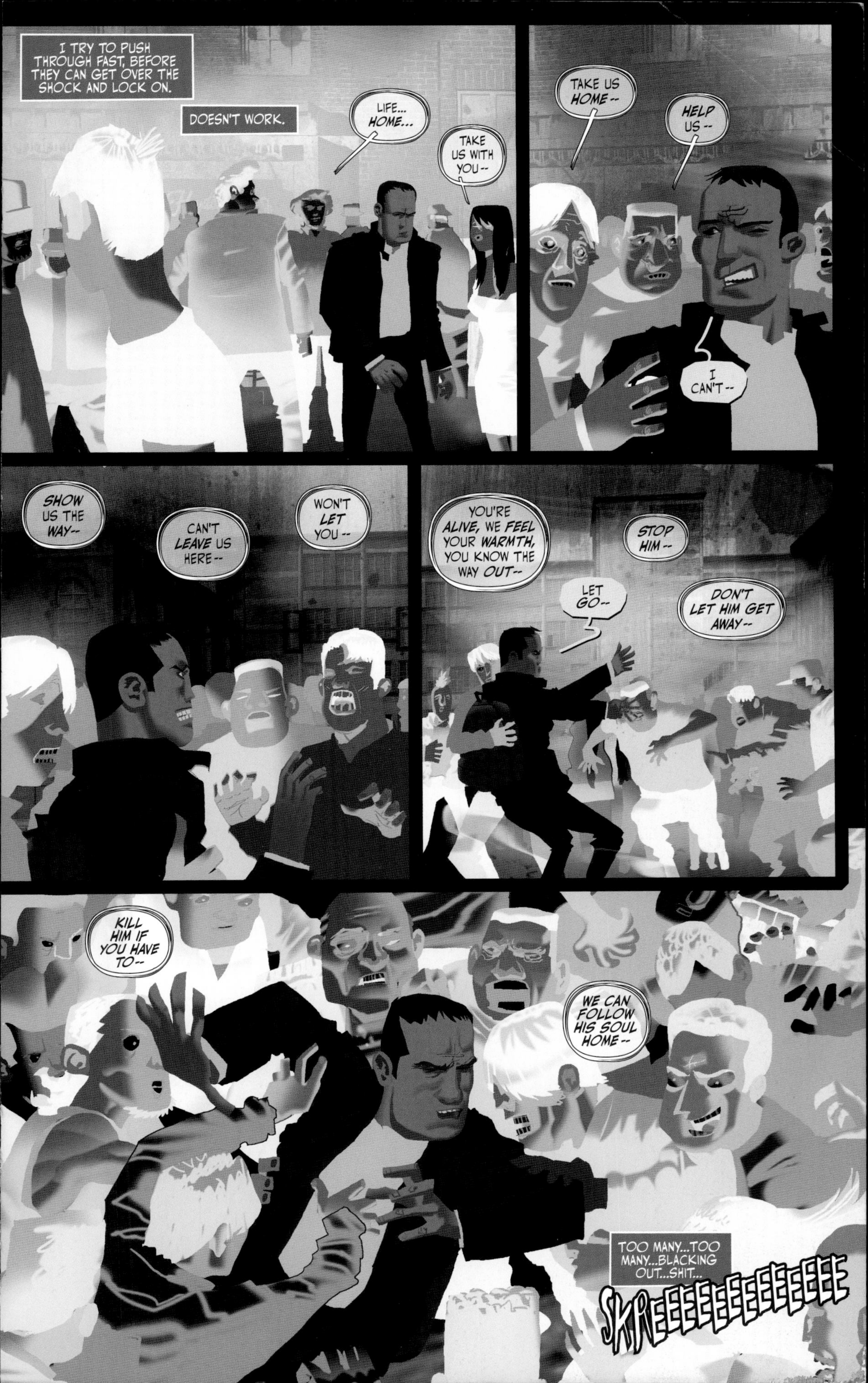

I TRY TO PUSH THROUGH FAST, BEFORE THEY CAN GET OVER THE SHOCK AND LOCK ON.
DOESN'T WORK.
LIFE... HOME...
TAKE US WITH YOU --
TAKE US HOME --
HELP US --
I CAN'T --
SHOW US THE WAY--
CAN'T LEAVE US HERE --
WON'T LET YOU --
YOU'RE ALIVE, WE FEEL YOUR WARMTH, YOU KNOW THE WAY OUT--
STOP HIM --
LET GO--
DON'T LET HIM GET AWAY--
KILL HIM IF YOU HAVE TO--
WE CAN FOLLOW HIS SOUL HOME --
TOO MANY...TOO MANY...BLACKING OUT...SHIT...
SKREEEEEEEEEEEEEE

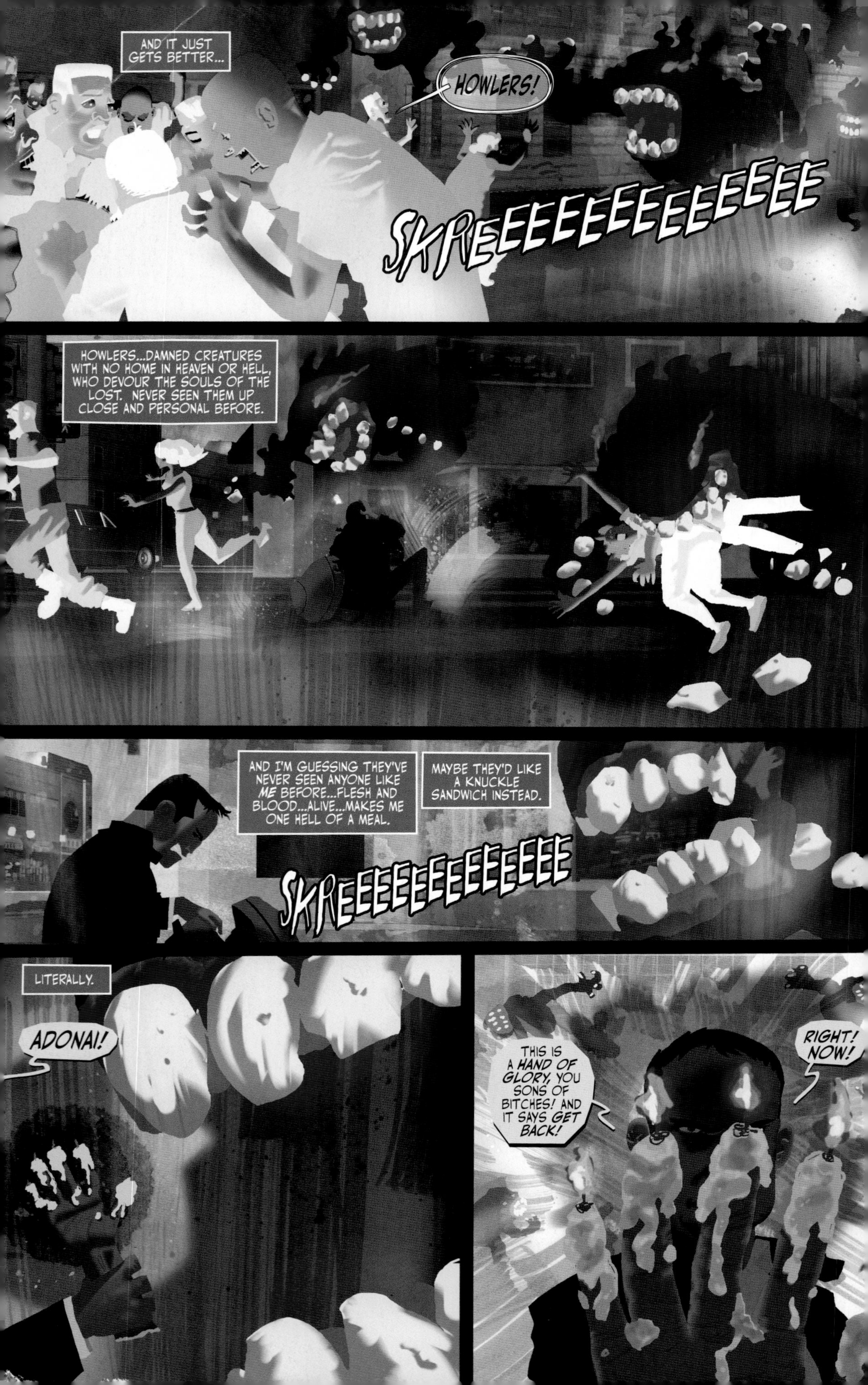
AND IT JUST GETS BETTER...
HOWLERS!
SKREEEEEEEEEEEEEE
HOWLERS...DAMNED CREATURES WITH NO HOME IN HEAVEN OR HELL, WHO DEVOUR THE SOULS OF THE LOST. NEVER SEEN THEM UP CLOSE AND PERSONAL BEFORE.
AND I'M GUESSING THEY'VE NEVER SEEN ANYONE LIKE ME BEFORE...FLESH AND BLOOD...ALIVE...MAKES ME ONE HELL OF A MEAL.
MAYBE THEY'D LIKE A KNUCKLE SANDWICH INSTEAD.
SKREEEEEEEEEEEE
LITERALLY.
ADONAI!
THIS IS A HAND OF GLORY, YOU SONS OF BITCHES! AND IT SAYS GET BACK!
RIGHT! NOW!

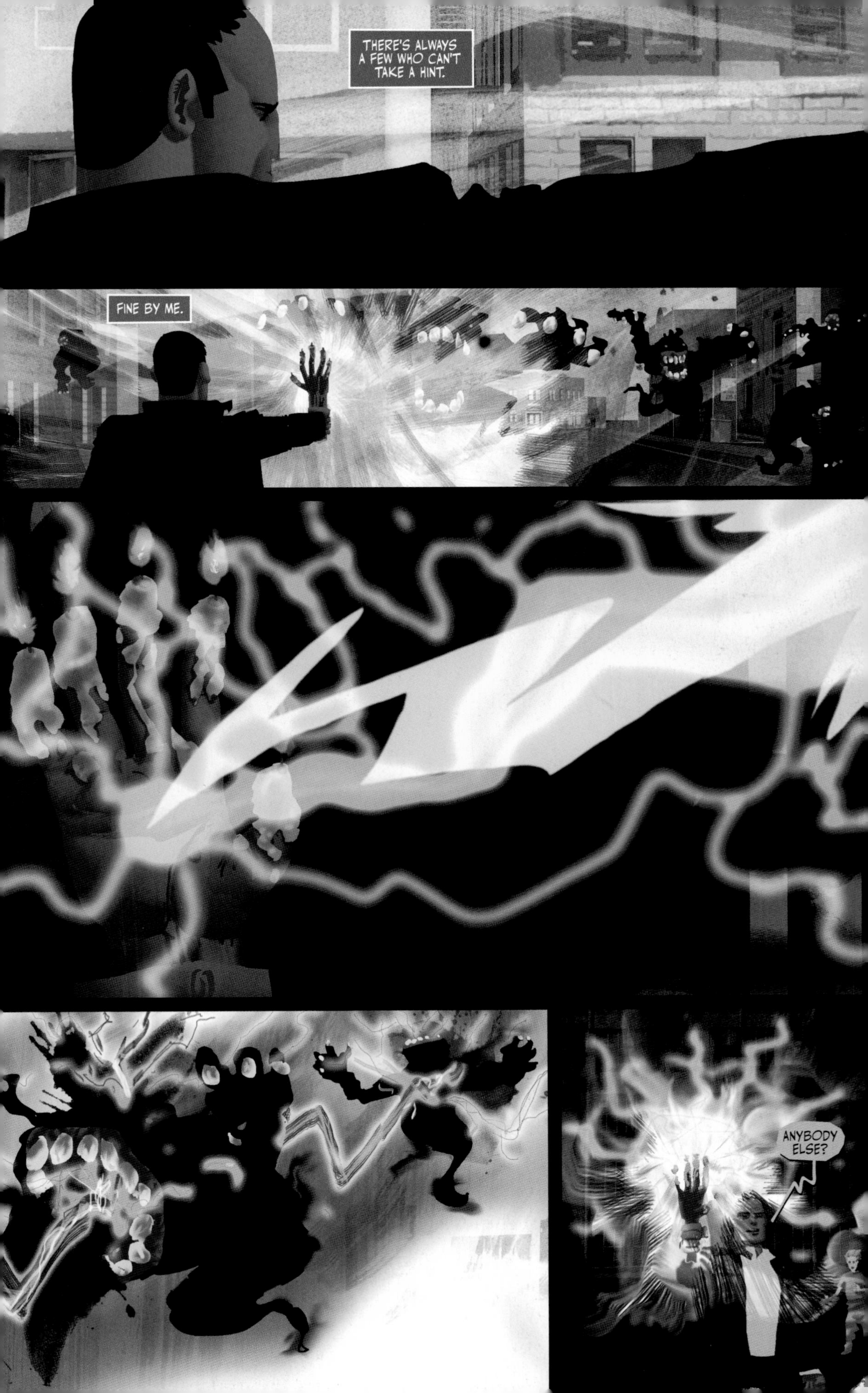
THERE'S ALWAYS A FEW WHO CAN'T TAKE A HINT.
FINE BY ME.
ANYBODY ELSE?

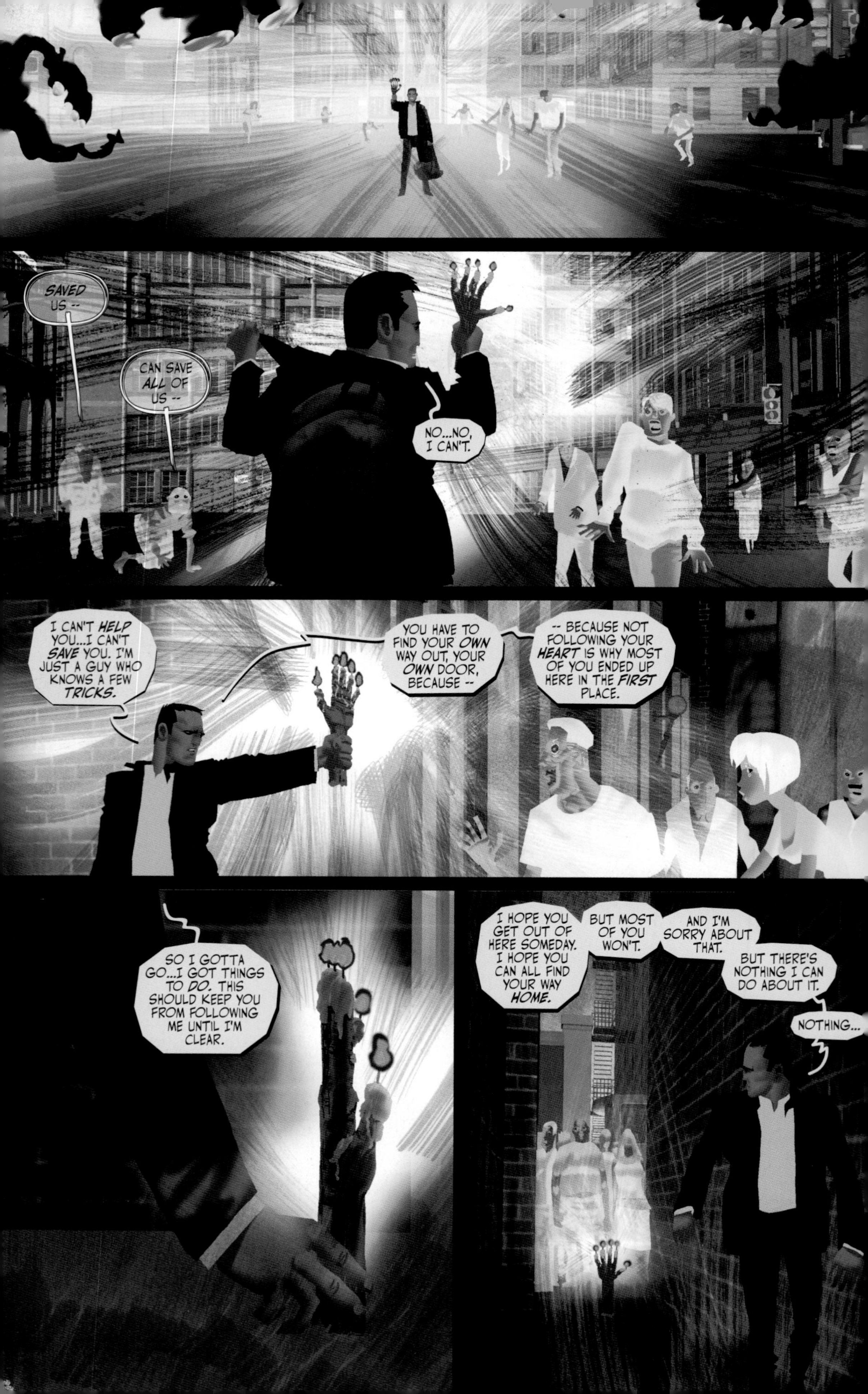
SAVED US --
CAN SAVE ALL OF US --
NO...NO, I CAN'T.
I CAN'T HELP YOU...I CAN'T SAVE YOU. I'M JUST A GUY WHO KNOWS A FEW TRICKS.
YOU HAVE TO FIND YOUR OWN WAY OUT, YOUR OWN DOOR, BECAUSE --
-- BECAUSE NOT FOLLOWING YOUR HEART IS WHY MOST OF YOU ENDED UP HERE IN THE FIRST PLACE.
SO I GOTTA GO...I GOT THINGS TO DO. THIS SHOULD KEEP YOU FROM FOLLOWING ME UNTIL I'M CLEAR.
I HOPE YOU GET OUT OF HERE SOMEDAY. I HOPE YOU CAN ALL FIND YOUR WAY HOME.
BUT MOST OF YOU WON'T.
AND I'M SORRY ABOUT THAT.
BUT THERE'S NOTHING I CAN DO ABOUT IT.
NOTHING...

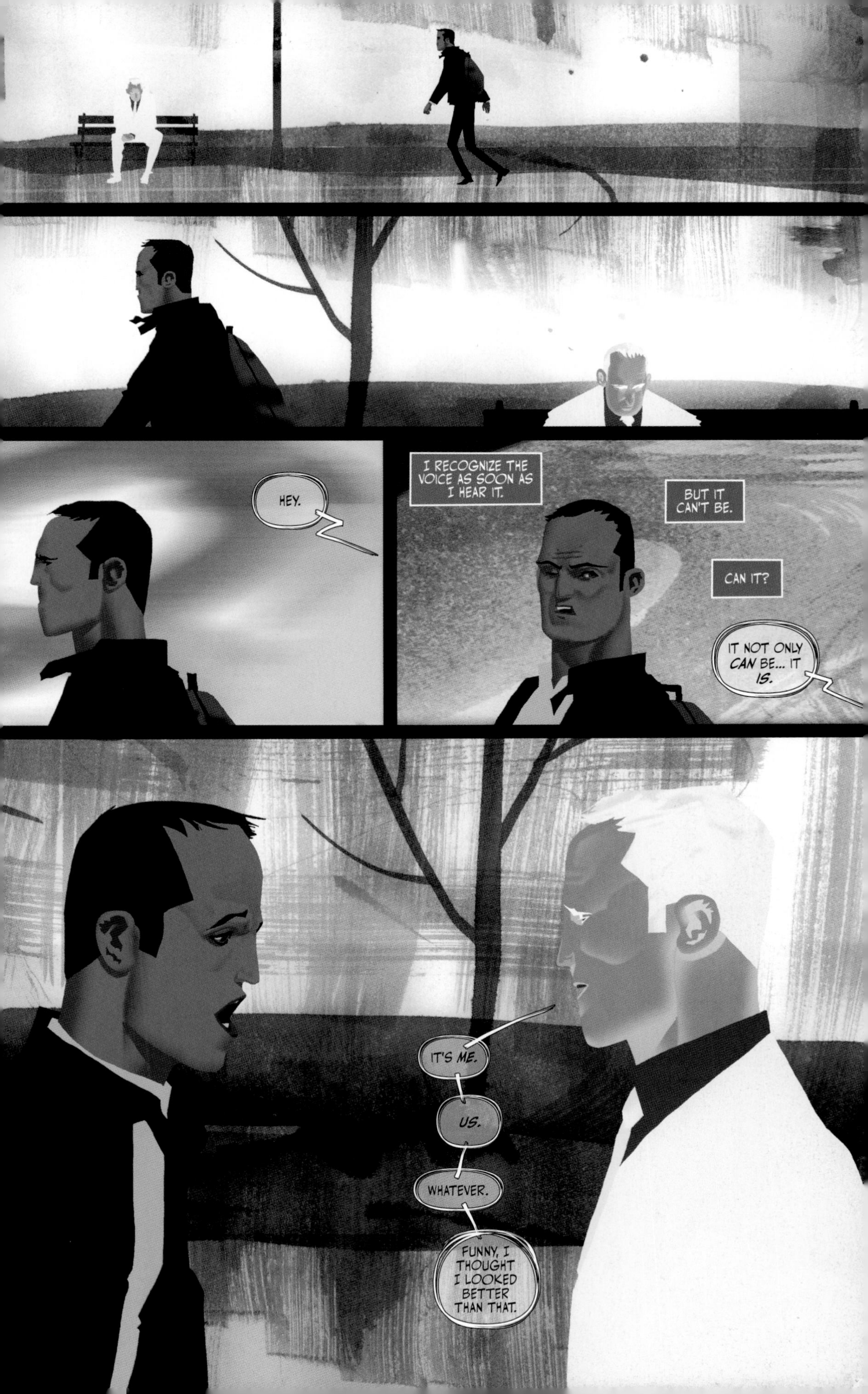
HEY.
I RECOGNIZE THE VOICE AS SOON AS I HEAR IT.
BUT IT CAN'T BE.
CAN IT?
IT NOT ONLY CAN BE... IT IS.
IT'S ME.
US.
WHATEVER.
FUNNY, I THOUGHT I LOOKED BETTER THAN THAT.

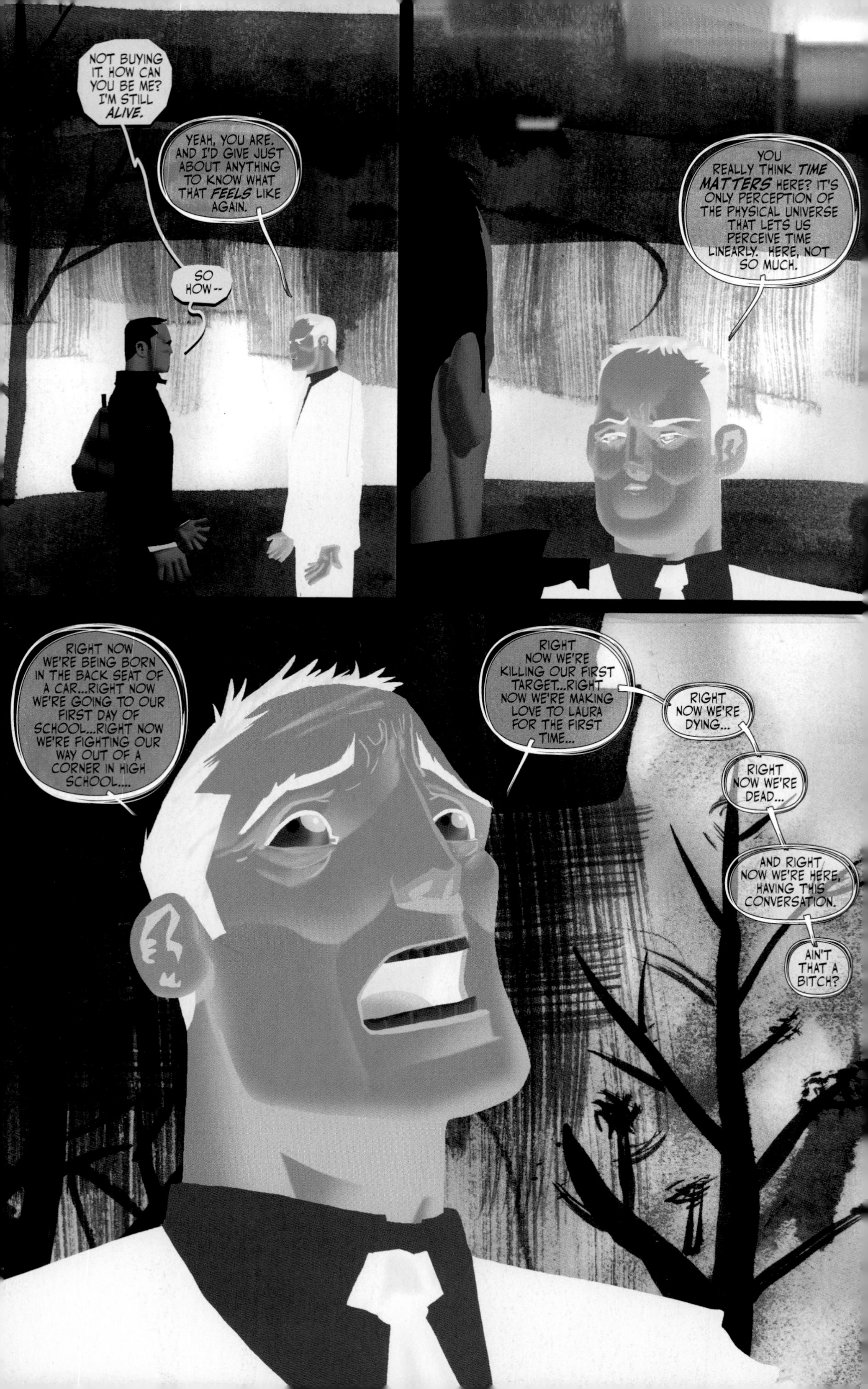
NOT BUYING IT. HOW CAN YOU BE ME? I'M STILL *ALIVE.*
YEAH, YOU ARE. AND I'D GIVE JUST ABOUT ANYTHING TO KNOW WHAT THAT *FEELS* LIKE AGAIN.
SO HOW--
YOU REALLY THINK *TIME MATTERS* HERE? IT'S ONLY PERCEPTION OF THE PHYSICAL UNIVERSE THAT LETS US PERCEIVE TIME LINEARLY. HERE, NOT SO MUCH.
RIGHT NOW WE'RE BEING BORN IN THE BACK SEAT OF A CAR...RIGHT NOW WE'RE GOING TO OUR FIRST DAY OF SCHOOL...RIGHT NOW WE'RE FIGHTING OUR WAY OUT OF A CORNER IN HIGH SCHOOL....
RIGHT NOW WE'RE KILLING OUR FIRST TARGET...RIGHT NOW WE'RE MAKING LOVE TO LAURA FOR THE FIRST TIME...
RIGHT NOW WE'RE DYING...
RIGHT NOW WE'RE DEAD...
AND RIGHT NOW WE'RE HERE, HAVING THIS CONVERSATION.
AIN'T THAT A BITCH?

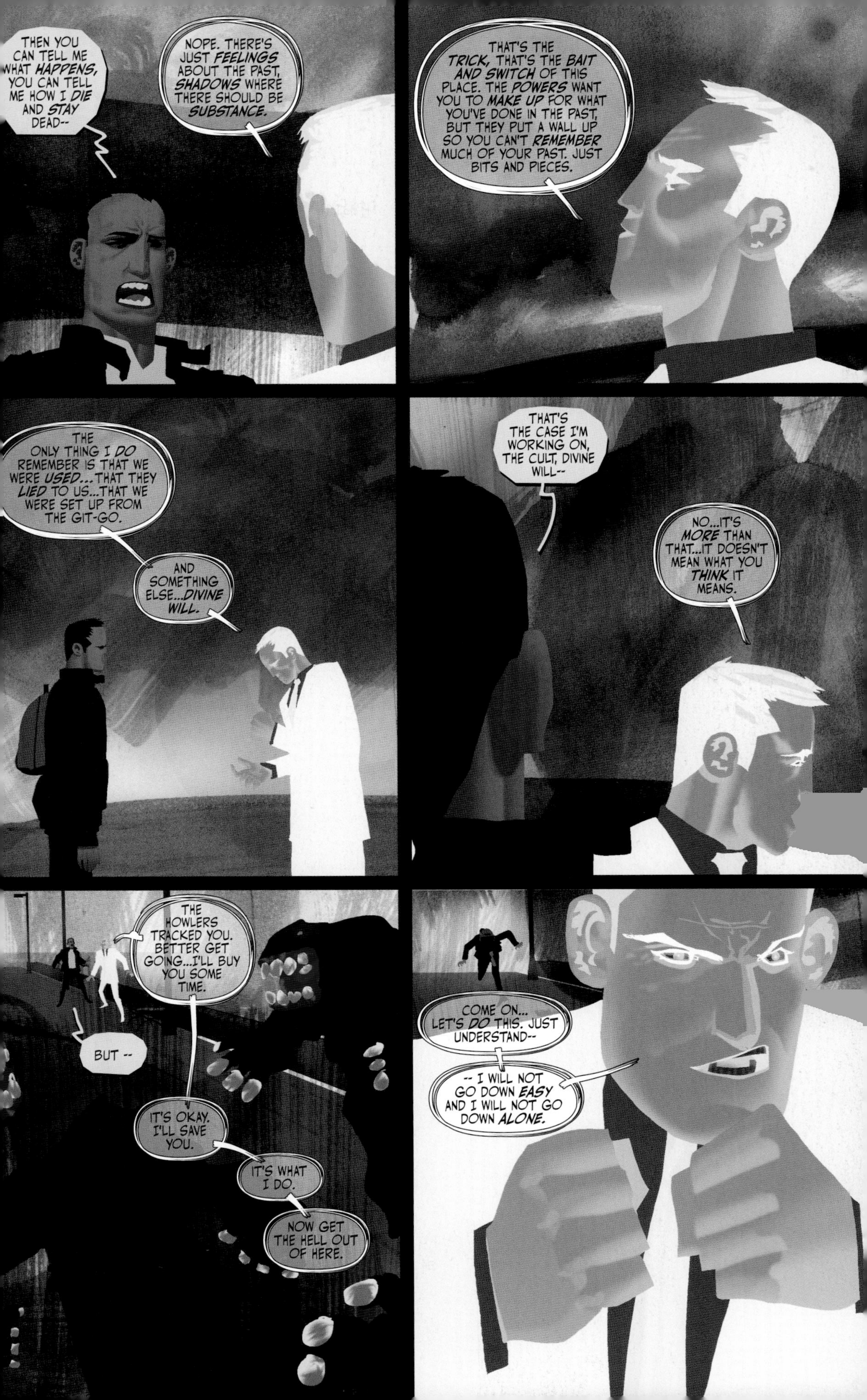
THEN YOU CAN TELL ME WHAT HAPPENS, YOU CAN TELL ME HOW I DIE AND STAY DEAD--
NOPE. THERE'S JUST FEELINGS ABOUT THE PAST, SHADOWS WHERE THERE SHOULD BE SUBSTANCE.
THAT'S THE TRICK, THAT'S THE BAIT AND SWITCH OF THIS PLACE. THE POWERS WANT YOU TO MAKE UP FOR WHAT YOU'VE DONE IN THE PAST, BUT THEY PUT A WALL UP SO YOU CAN'T REMEMBER MUCH OF YOUR PAST. JUST BITS AND PIECES.
THE ONLY THING I DO REMEMBER IS THAT WE WERE USED...THAT THEY LIED TO US...THAT WE WERE SET UP FROM THE GIT-GO.
AND SOMETHING ELSE...DIVINE WILL.
THAT'S THE CASE I'M WORKING ON, THE CULT, DIVINE WILL--
NO...IT'S MORE THAN THAT...IT DOESN'T MEAN WHAT YOU THINK IT MEANS.
THE HOWLERS TRACKED YOU. BETTER GET GOING...I'LL BUY YOU SOME TIME.
BUT --
IT'S OKAY. I'LL SAVE YOU.
IT'S WHAT I DO.
NOW GET THE HELL OUT OF HERE.
COME ON... LET'S DO THIS. JUST UNDERSTAND--
-- I WILL NOT GO DOWN EASY AND I WILL NOT GO DOWN ALONE.

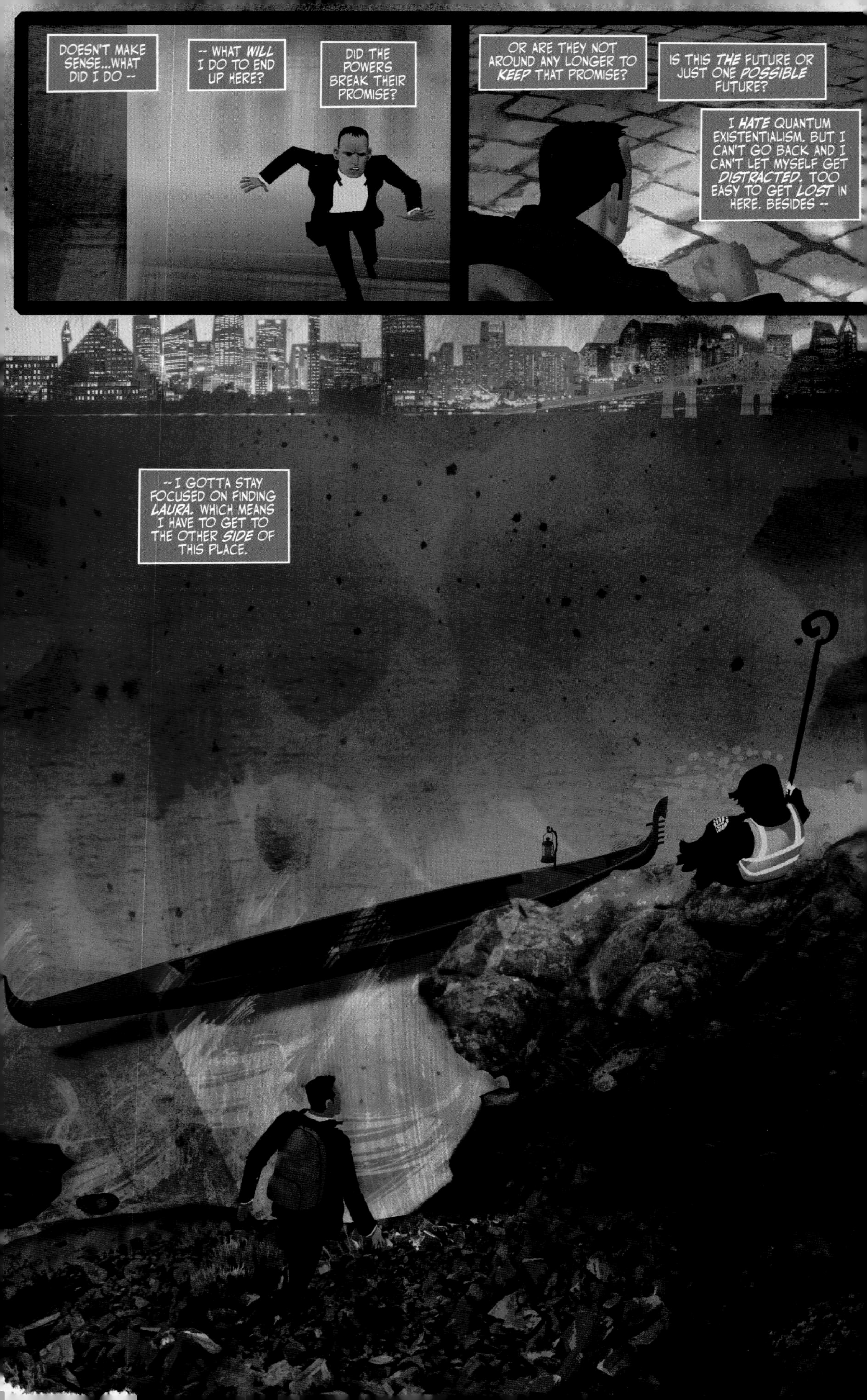
DOESN'T MAKE SENSE...WHAT DID I DO --
-- WHAT *WILL* I DO TO END UP HERE?
DID THE POWERS BREAK THEIR PROMISE?
OR ARE THEY NOT AROUND ANY LONGER TO *KEEP* THAT PROMISE?
IS THIS *THE* FUTURE OR JUST ONE *POSSIBLE* FUTURE?
I *HATE* QUANTUM EXISTENTIALISM. BUT I CAN'T GO BACK AND I CAN'T LET MYSELF GET *DISTRACTED.* TOO EASY TO GET *LOST* IN HERE. BESIDES --
-- I GOTTA STAY FOCUSED ON FINDING *LAURA.* WHICH MEANS I HAVE TO GET TO THE OTHER *SIDE* OF THIS PLACE.

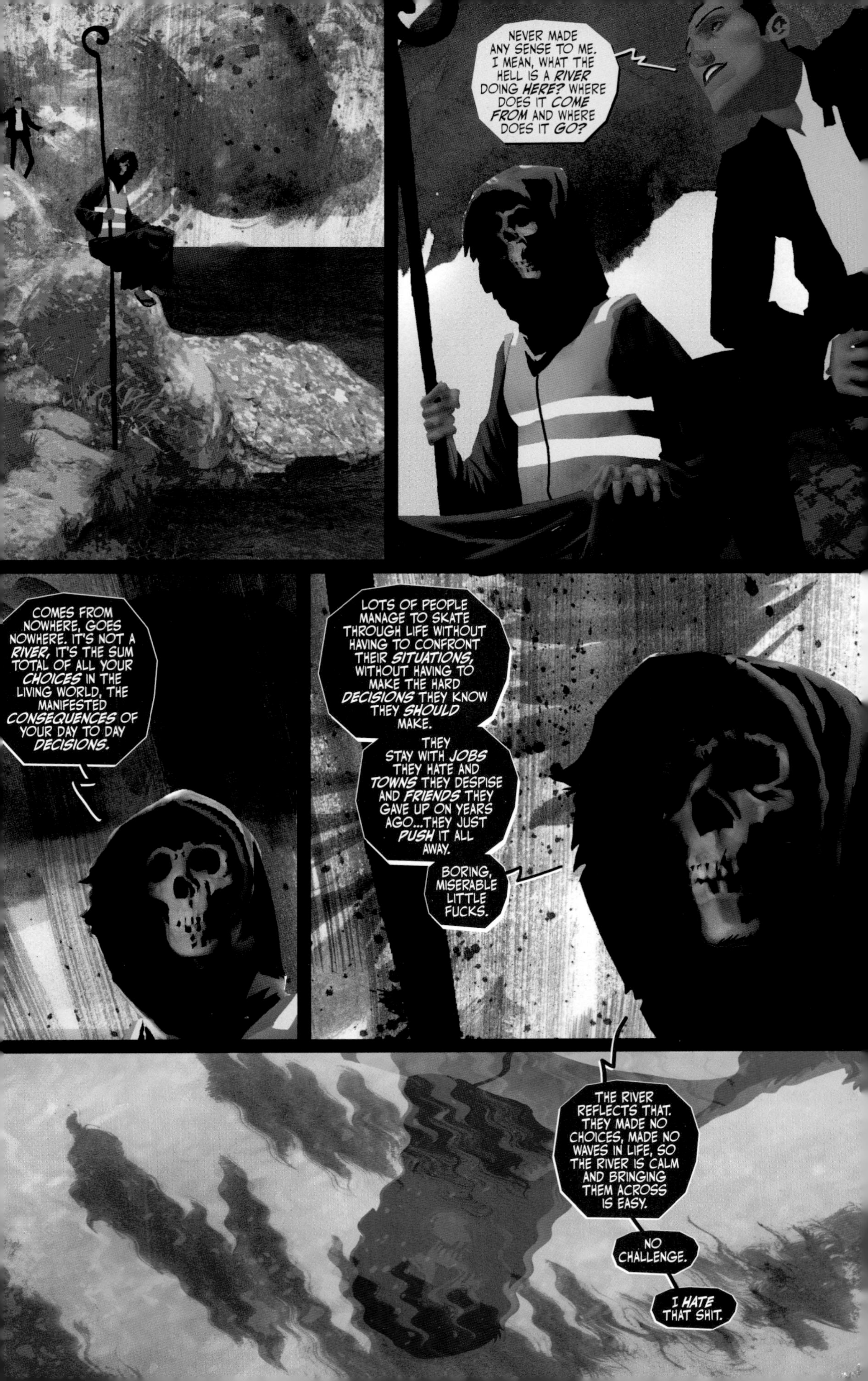
NEVER MADE ANY SENSE TO ME. I MEAN, WHAT THE HELL IS A RIVER DOING HERE? WHERE DOES IT COME FROM AND WHERE DOES IT GO?
COMES FROM NOWHERE, GOES NOWHERE. IT'S NOT A RIVER, IT'S THE SUM TOTAL OF ALL YOUR CHOICES IN THE LIVING WORLD, THE MANIFESTED CONSEQUENCES OF YOUR DAY TO DAY DECISIONS.
LOTS OF PEOPLE MANAGE TO SKATE THROUGH LIFE WITHOUT HAVING TO CONFRONT THEIR SITUATIONS, WITHOUT HAVING TO MAKE THE HARD DECISIONS THEY KNOW THEY SHOULD MAKE.
THEY STAY WITH JOBS THEY HATE AND TOWNS THEY DESPISE AND FRIENDS THEY GAVE UP ON YEARS AGO...THEY JUST PUSH IT ALL AWAY.
BORING, MISERABLE LITTLE FUCKS.
THE RIVER REFLECTS THAT. THEY MADE NO CHOICES, MADE NO WAVES IN LIFE, SO THE RIVER IS CALM AND BRINGING THEM ACROSS IS EASY.
NO CHALLENGE.
I HATE THAT SHIT.

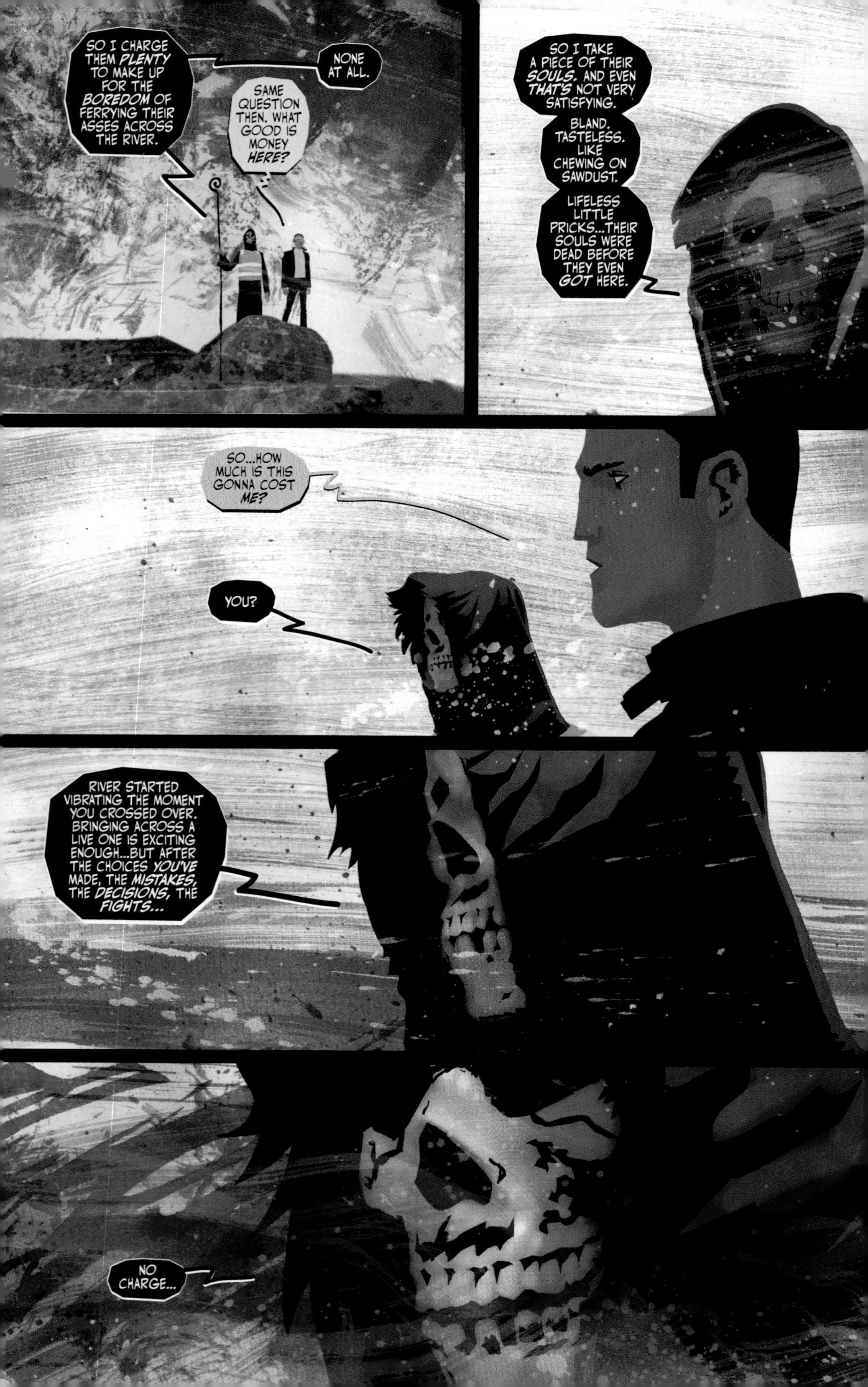
SO I CHARGE THEM *PLENTY* TO MAKE UP FOR THE *BOREDOM* OF FERRYING THEIR ASSES ACROSS THE RIVER.
NONE AT ALL.
SAME QUESTION THEN. WHAT GOOD IS MONEY *HERE?*
SO I TAKE A PIECE OF THEIR *SOULS.* AND EVEN *THAT'S* NOT VERY SATISFYING.
BLAND. TASTELESS. LIKE CHEWING ON SAWDUST.
LIFELESS LITTLE PRICKS...THEIR SOULS WERE DEAD BEFORE THEY EVEN *GOT* HERE.
SO...HOW MUCH IS THIS GONNA COST *ME?*
YOU?
RIVER STARTED VIBRATING THE MOMENT YOU CROSSED OVER. BRINGING ACROSS A LIVE ONE IS EXCITING ENOUGH...BUT AFTER THE CHOICES *YOU'VE* MADE, THE *MISTAKES,* THE *DECISIONS,* THE *FIGHTS...*
NO CHARGE...

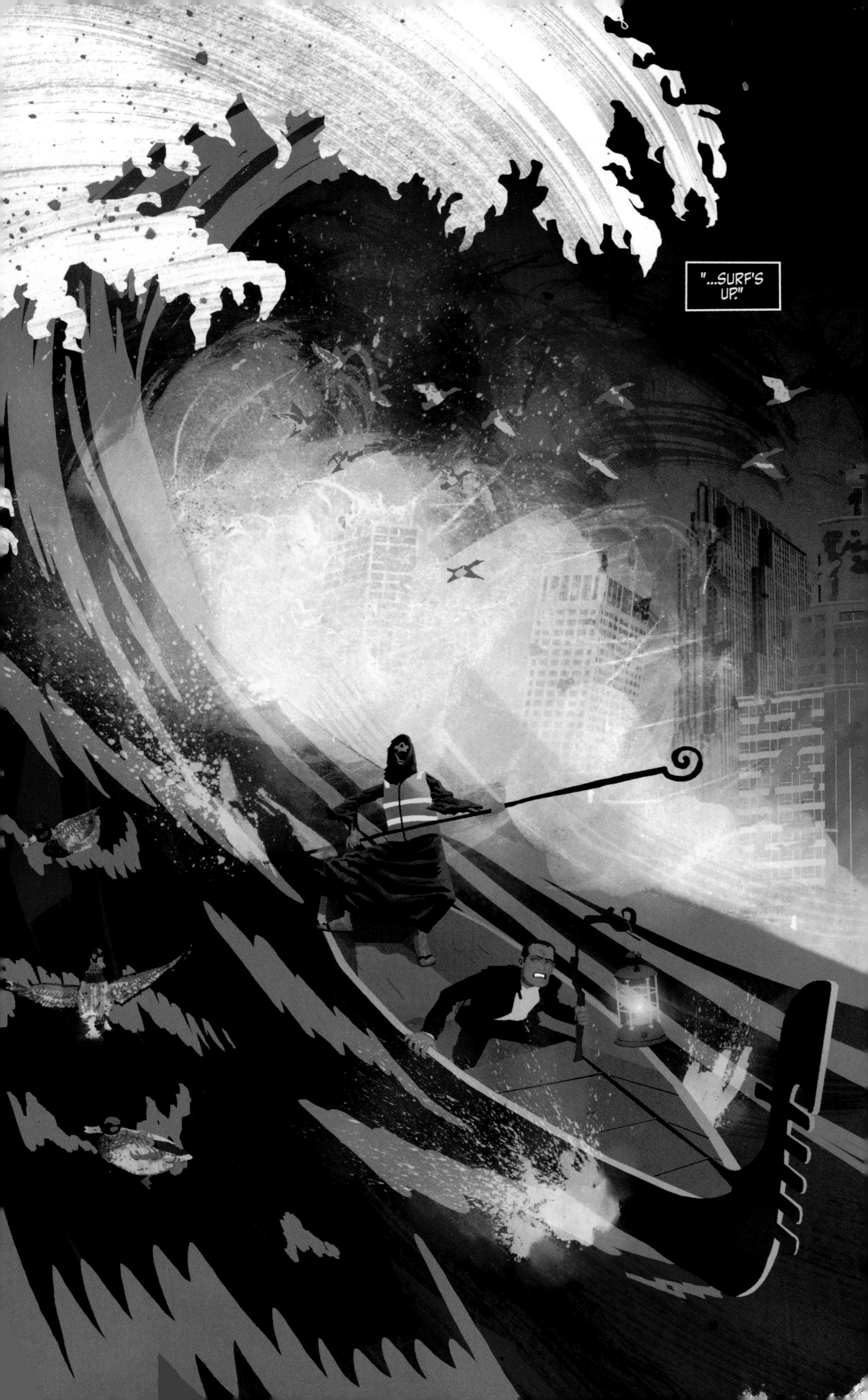
"...SURF'S UP!"

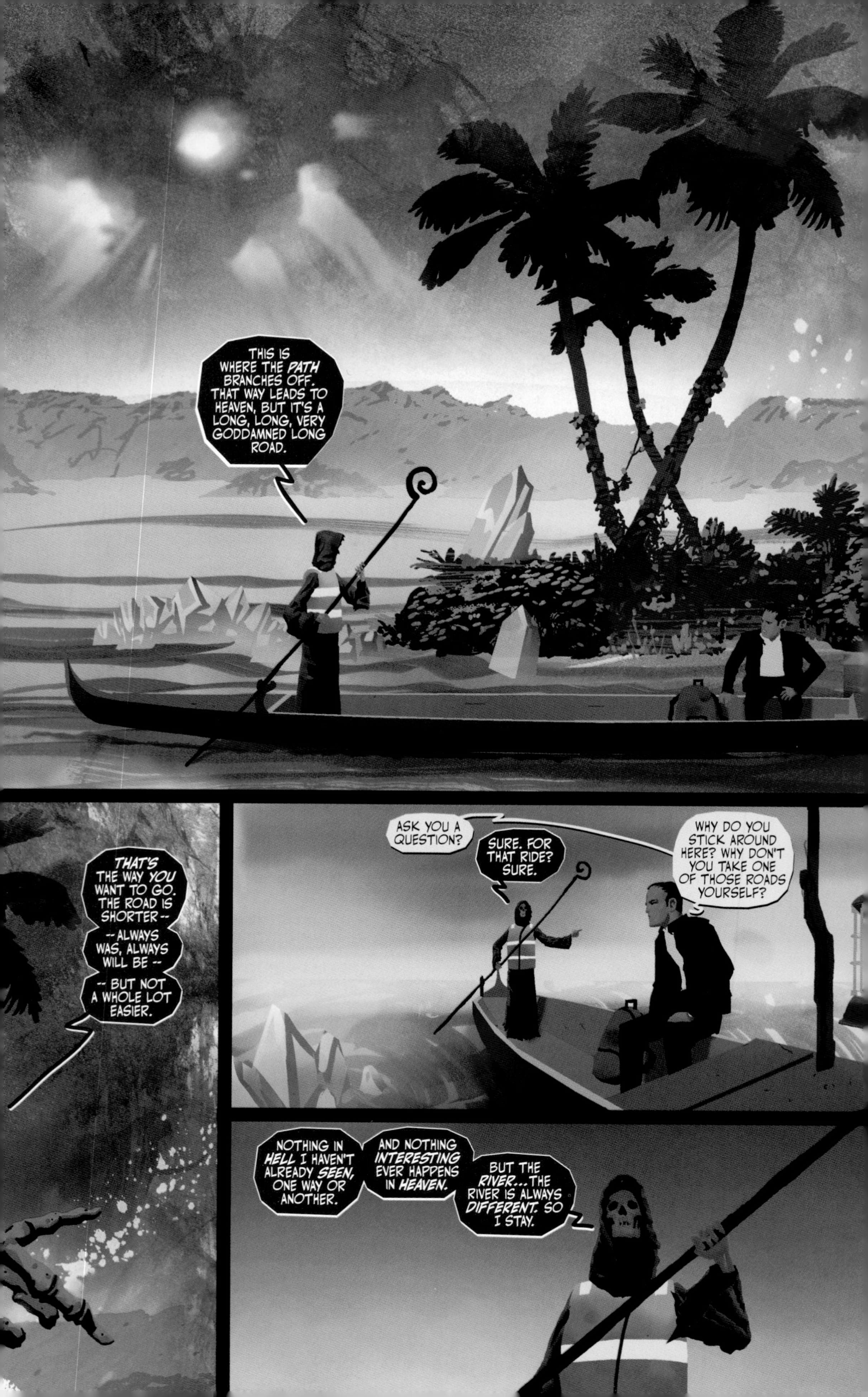
THIS IS WHERE THE *PATH* BRANCHES OFF. THAT WAY LEADS TO HEAVEN, BUT IT'S A LONG, LONG, VERY GODDAMNED LONG ROAD.
*THAT'S* THE WAY *YOU* WANT TO GO. THE ROAD IS SHORTER--
--ALWAYS WAS, ALWAYS WILL BE--
--BUT NOT A WHOLE LOT EASIER.
ASK YOU A QUESTION?
SURE. FOR THAT RIDE? SURE.
WHY DO YOU STICK AROUND HERE? WHY DON'T YOU TAKE ONE OF THOSE ROADS YOURSELF?
NOTHING IN *HELL* I HAVEN'T ALREADY *SEEN,* ONE WAY OR ANOTHER.
AND NOTHING *INTERESTING* EVER HAPPENS IN *HEAVEN.*
BUT THE *RIVER*... THE RIVER IS ALWAYS *DIFFERENT.* SO I STAY.

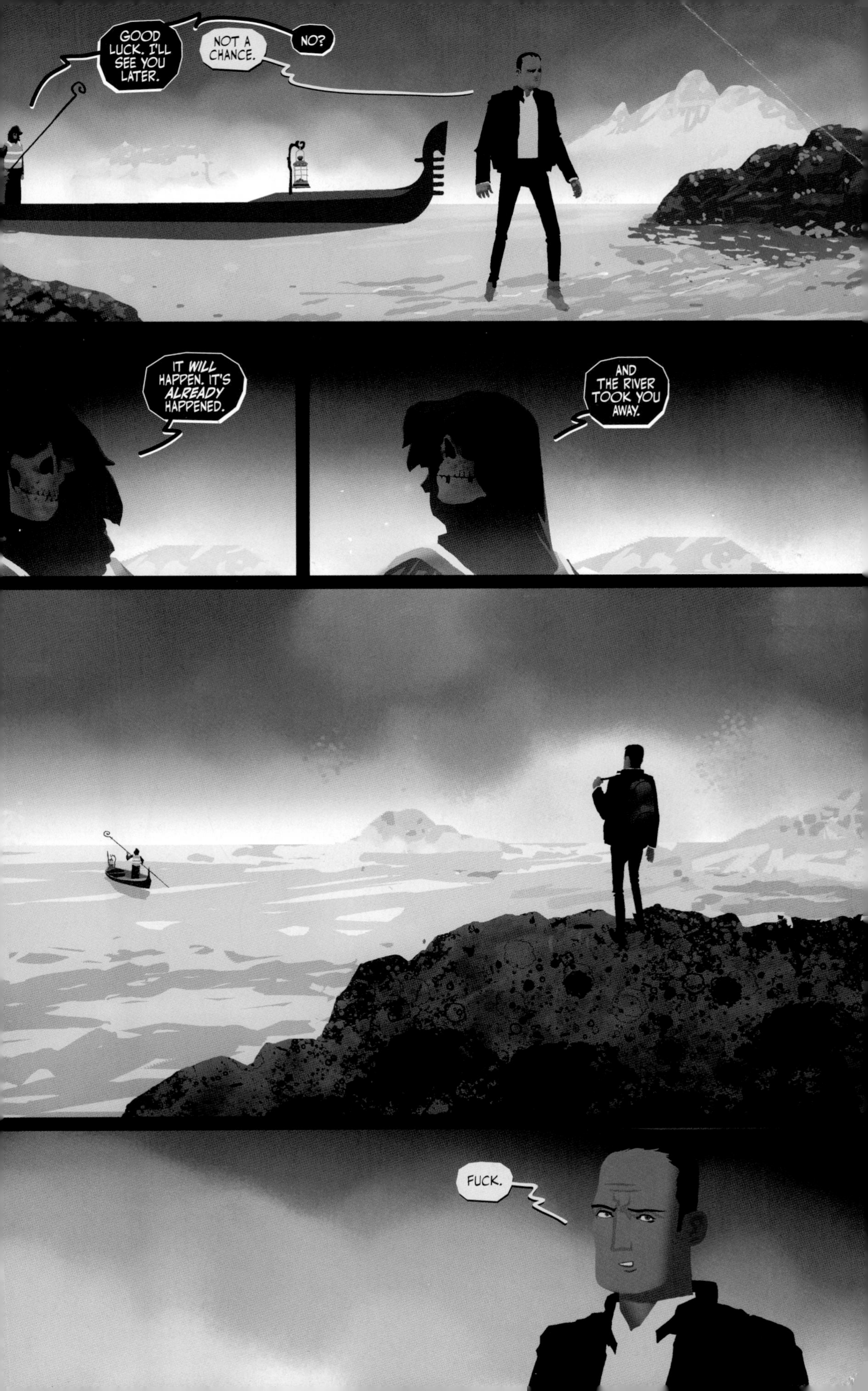
GOOD LUCK. I'LL SEE YOU LATER.
NOT A CHANCE.
NO?
IT WILL HAPPEN. IT'S ALREADY HAPPENED.
AND THE RIVER TOOK YOU AWAY.
FUCK.

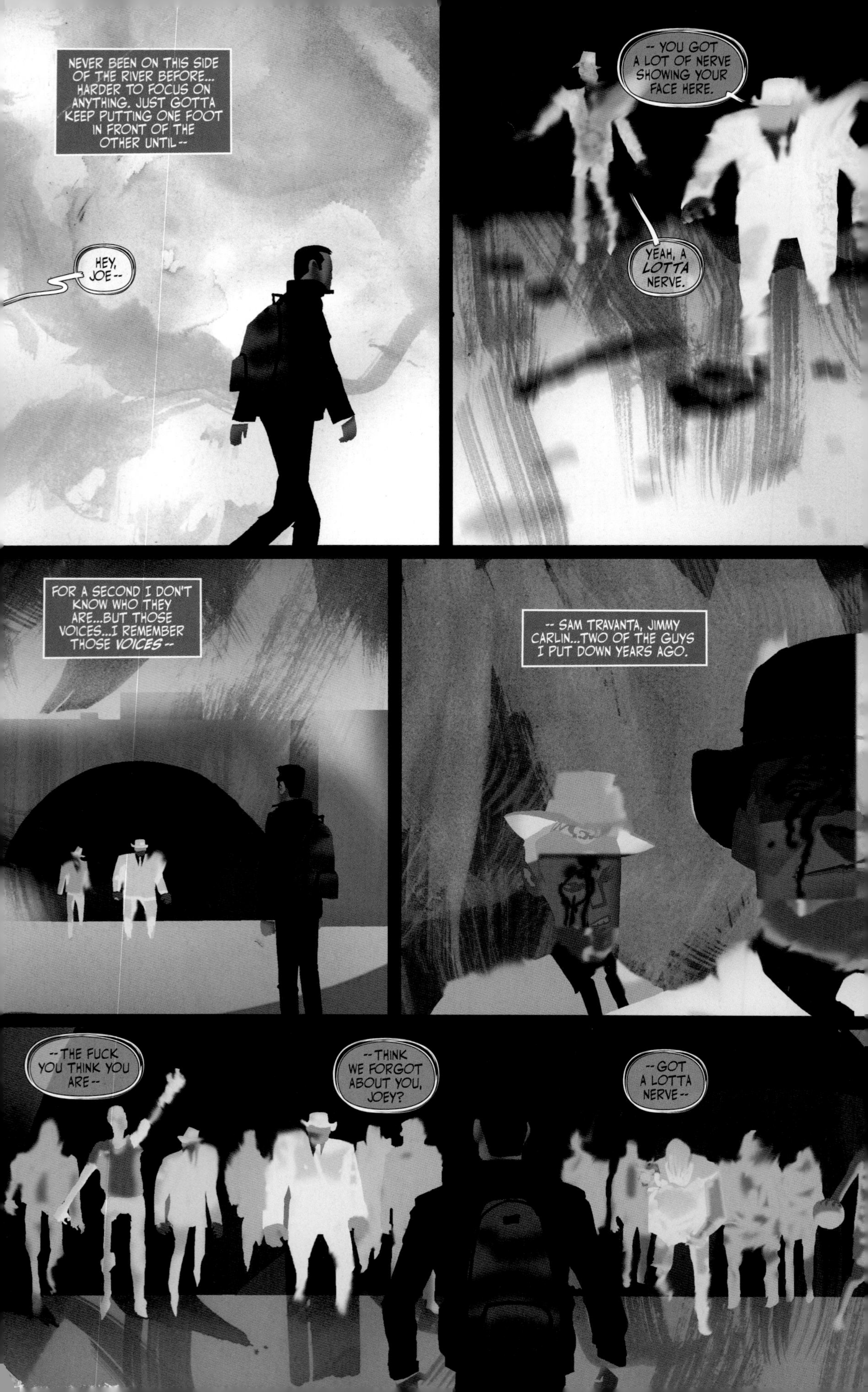
NEVER BEEN ON THIS SIDE OF THE RIVER BEFORE... HARDER TO FOCUS ON ANYTHING. JUST GOTTA KEEP PUTTING ONE FOOT IN FRONT OF THE OTHER UNTIL--
HEY, JOE--
-- YOU GOT A LOT OF NERVE SHOWING YOUR FACE HERE.
YEAH, A *LOTTA* NERVE.
FOR A SECOND I DON'T KNOW WHO THEY ARE...BUT THOSE VOICES...I REMEMBER THOSE *VOICES*--
-- SAM TRAVANTA, JIMMY CARLIN...TWO OF THE GUYS I PUT DOWN YEARS AGO.
-- THE FUCK YOU THINK YOU ARE--
-- THINK WE FORGOT ABOUT YOU, JOEY?
-- GOT A LOTTA NERVE--

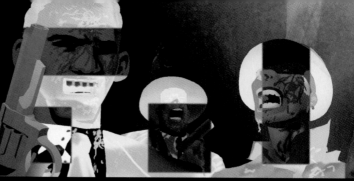

THOSE AREN'T GUNS...JUST *ECHOES* OF GUNS...THEIR *MEMORIES* OF GUNS, BECAUSE THEY CAN'T LET GO OF THE PAST, CAN'T MOVE ON...THE GUNS ARE REAL TO THEM BUT--

NNNGGGGHH!

-- SHIT...REAL ENOUGH FOR ME TOO....

FINE. LET'S DO THIS.

GOTTA GET LOW, FIND COVER...

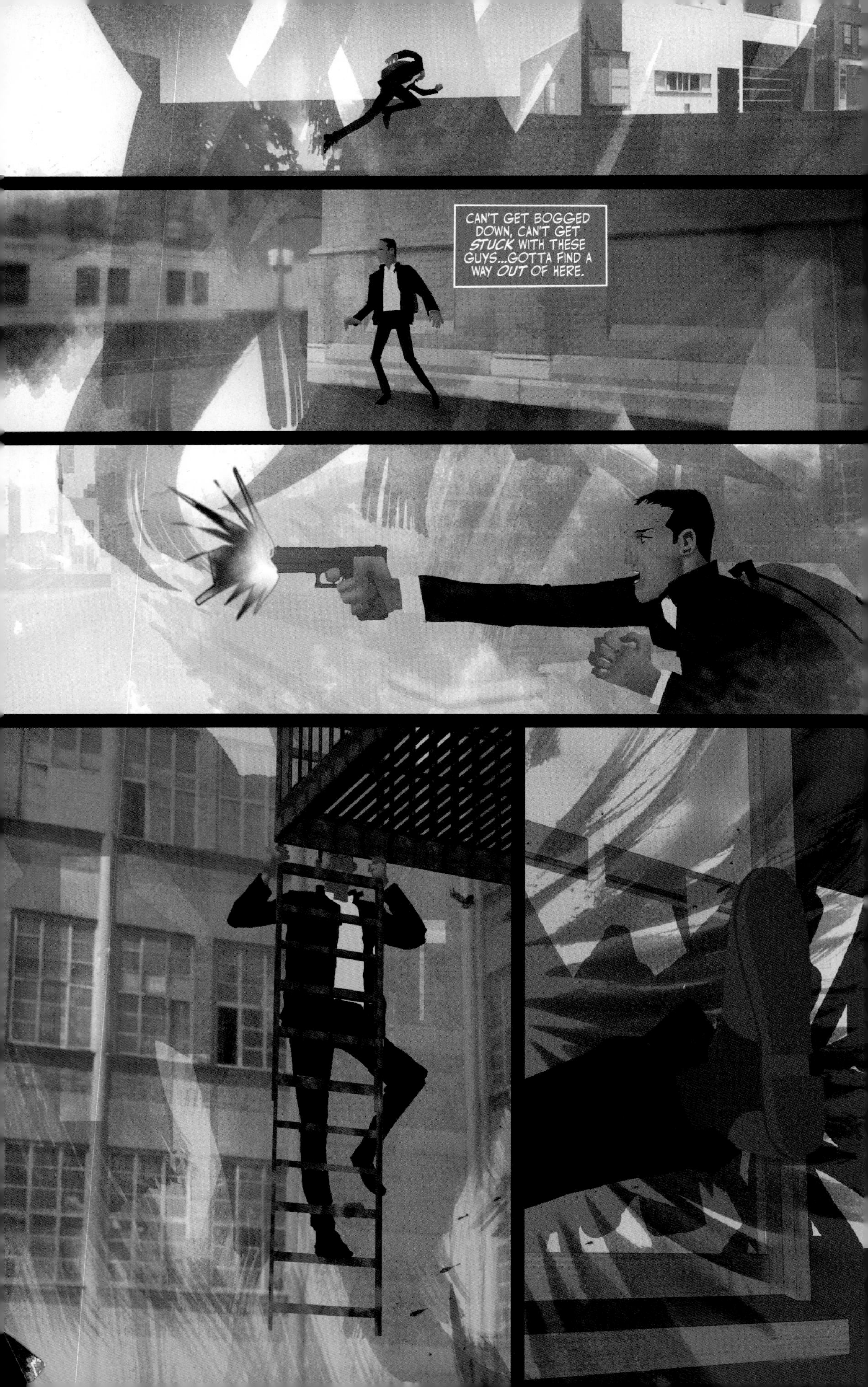
CAN'T GET BOGGED DOWN, CAN'T GET STUCK WITH THESE GUYS...GOTTA FIND A WAY OUT OF HERE.

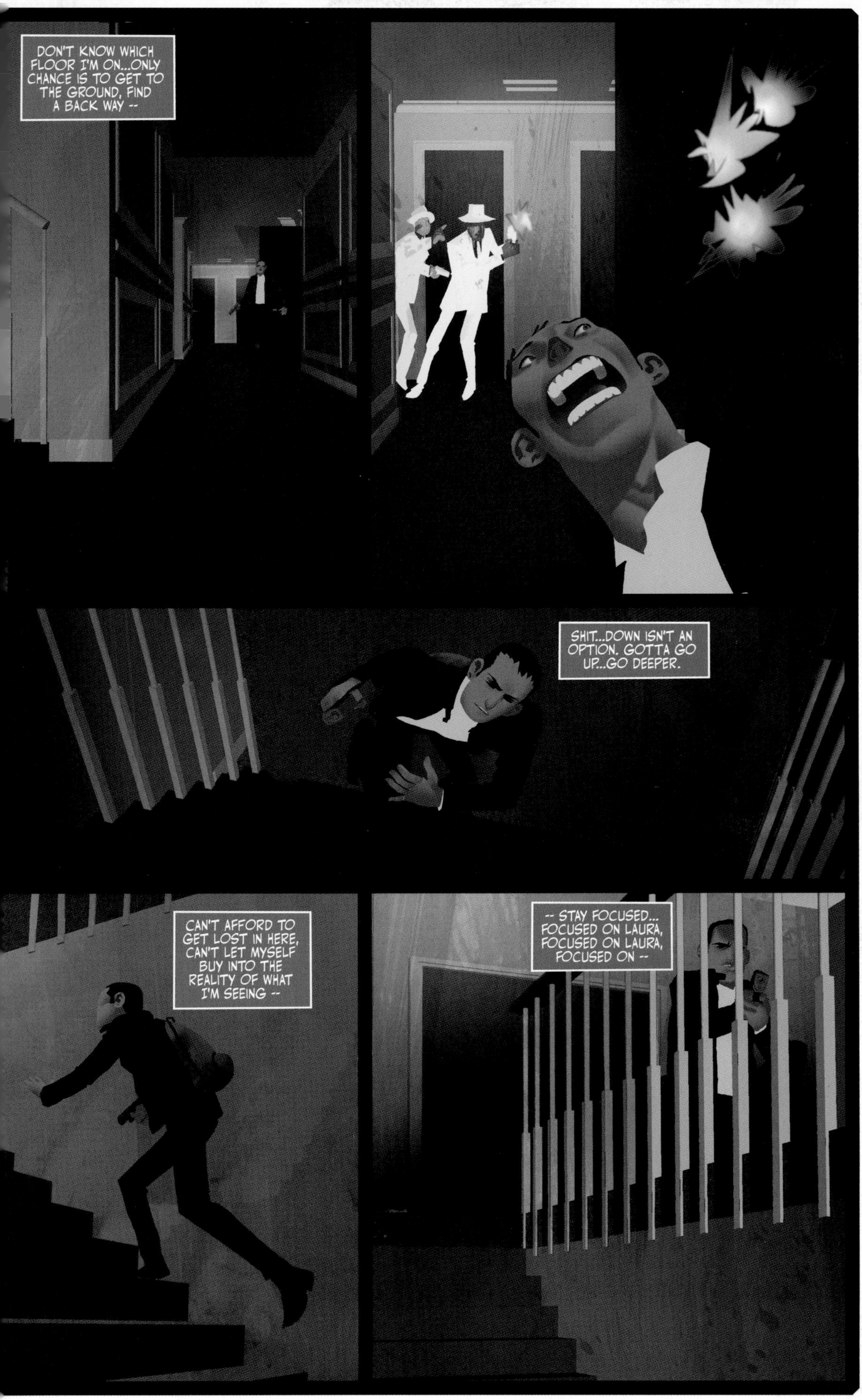
DON'T KNOW WHICH FLOOR I'M ON...ONLY CHANCE IS TO GET TO THE GROUND, FIND A BACK WAY --
SHIT...DOWN ISN'T AN OPTION. GOTTA GO UP...GO DEEPER.
CAN'T AFFORD TO GET LOST IN HERE, CAN'T LET MYSELF BUY INTO THE REALITY OF WHAT I'M SEEING --
-- STAY FOCUSED... FOCUSED ON LAURA, FOCUSED ON LAURA, FOCUSED ON --

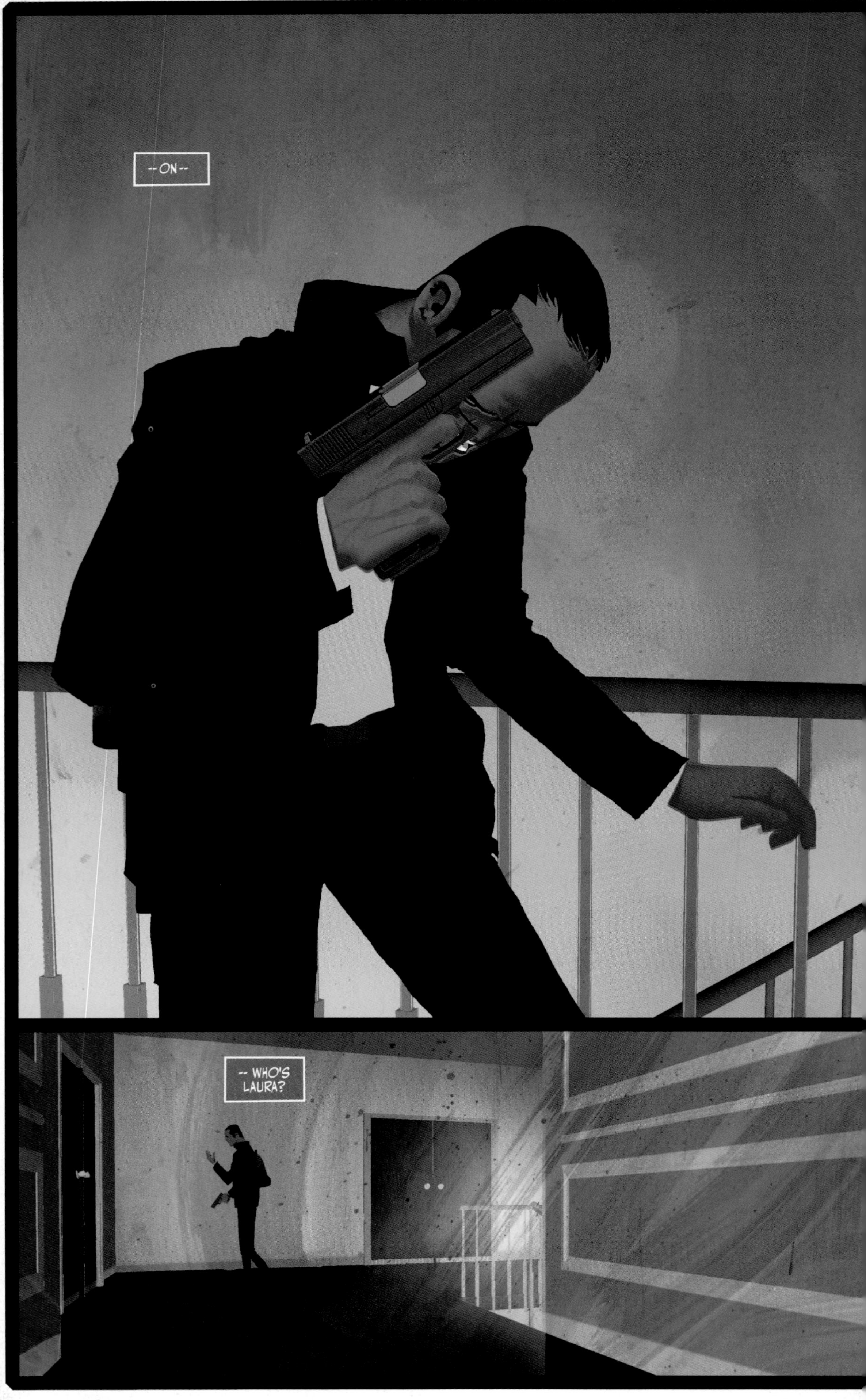
--ON--
-- WHO'S LAURA?

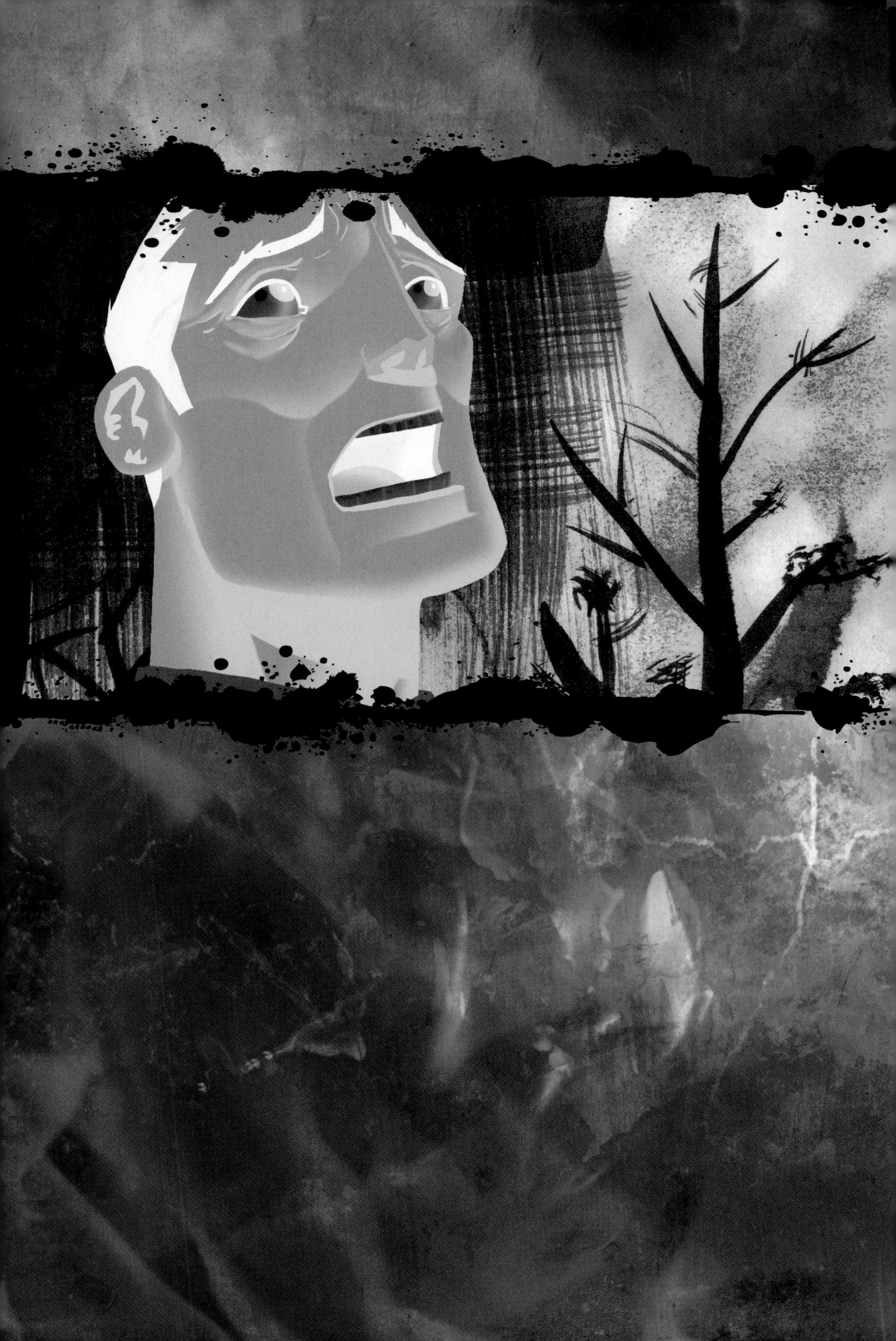

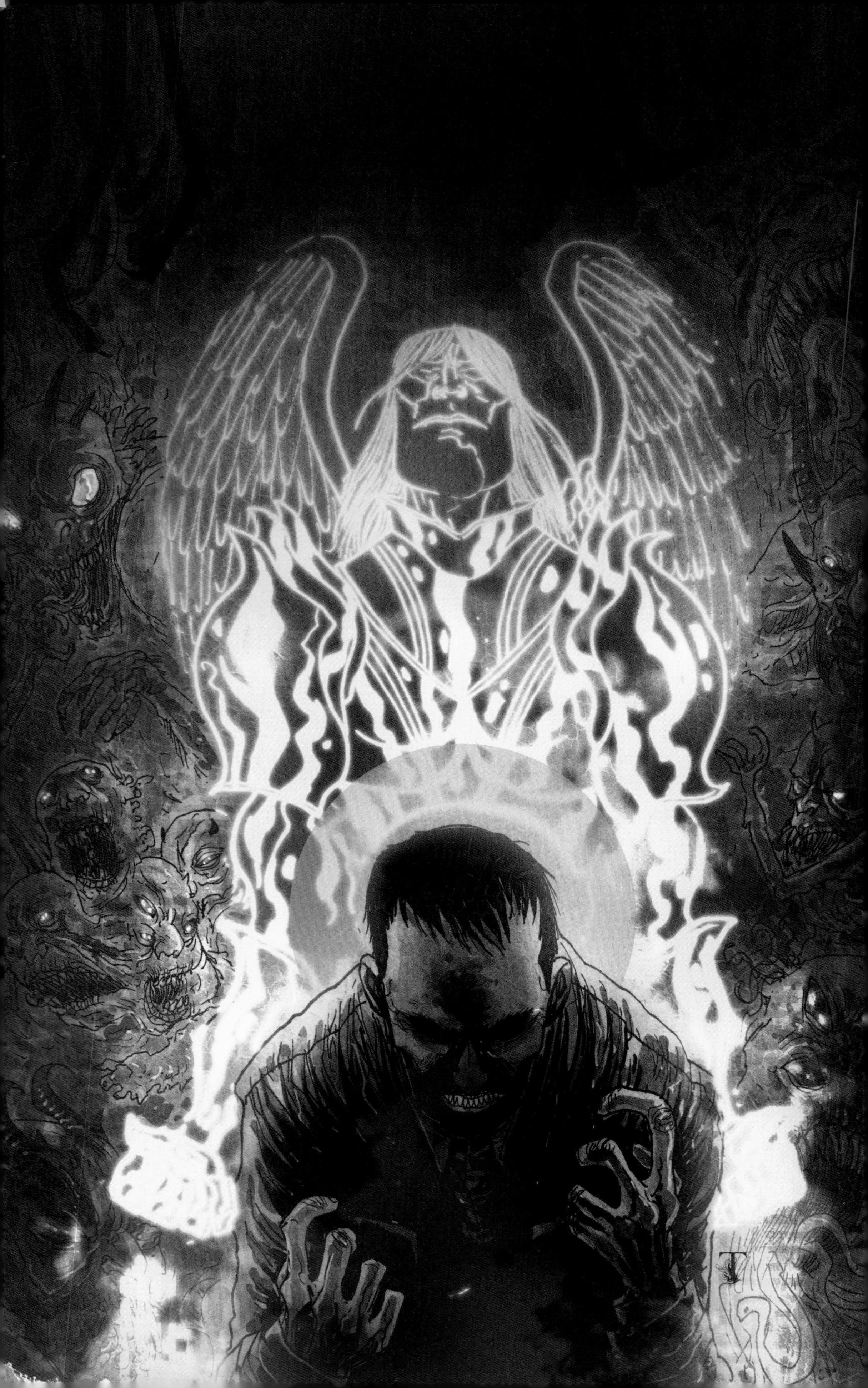

-- THEY *WANTED* THE JOB, *WANTED* THE BONUS FOR PUTTING DOWN TWO OF MR. ANTONIO'S ENEMIES. TWO-FERS ARE *TOUGH* BUT PAY *GREAT.*

CRAP... LOCKED....

NEVER SHOULD'VE TAKEN THIS JOB. SHOULD'VE LET MR. ANTONIO SEND ONE OF THE OTHER GUYS...SOLLY OR MACK --

CHECK UPSTAIRS, HE'S GOTTA BE HERE!

BUT *NO,* I HAD TO TAKE THE JOB OUT OF SOME MISGUIDED SENSE OF *LOYALTY.* NOW TRAVANTA AND CARLIN'S GOONS ARE GONNA CUT ME INTO SMALL PIECES AND FEED ME TO THEIR GOLDFISH.

WORSE STILL, FOR THE LIFE OF ME --

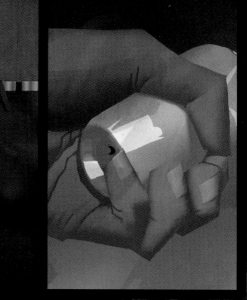

-- I CAN'T REMEMBER HOW THE HELL I GOT *INTO* THIS PLACE...OR HOW I'M SUPPOSED TO GET *OUT* AGAIN.

# SEE ME

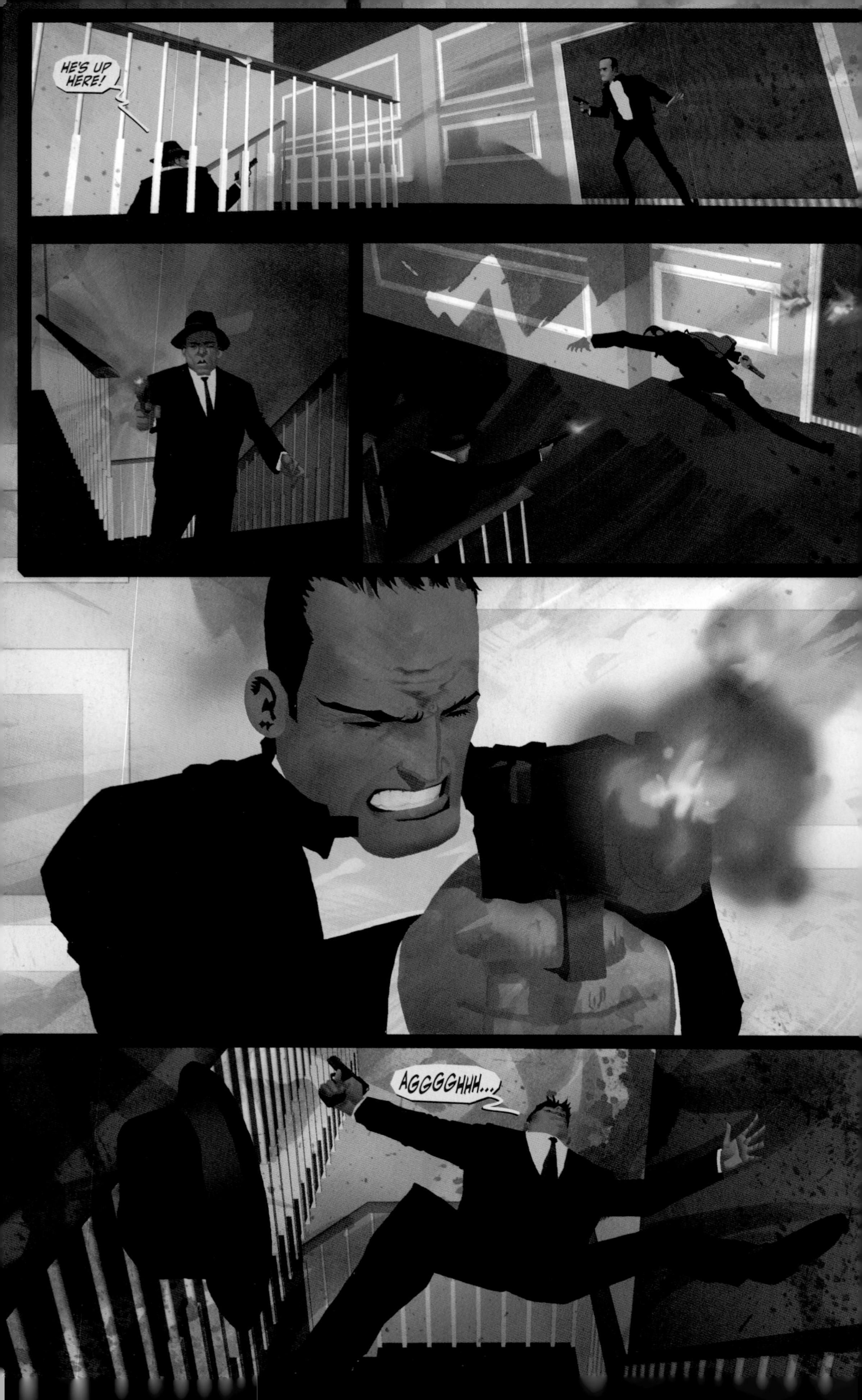
HE'S UP HERE!
AGGGGHHH...!

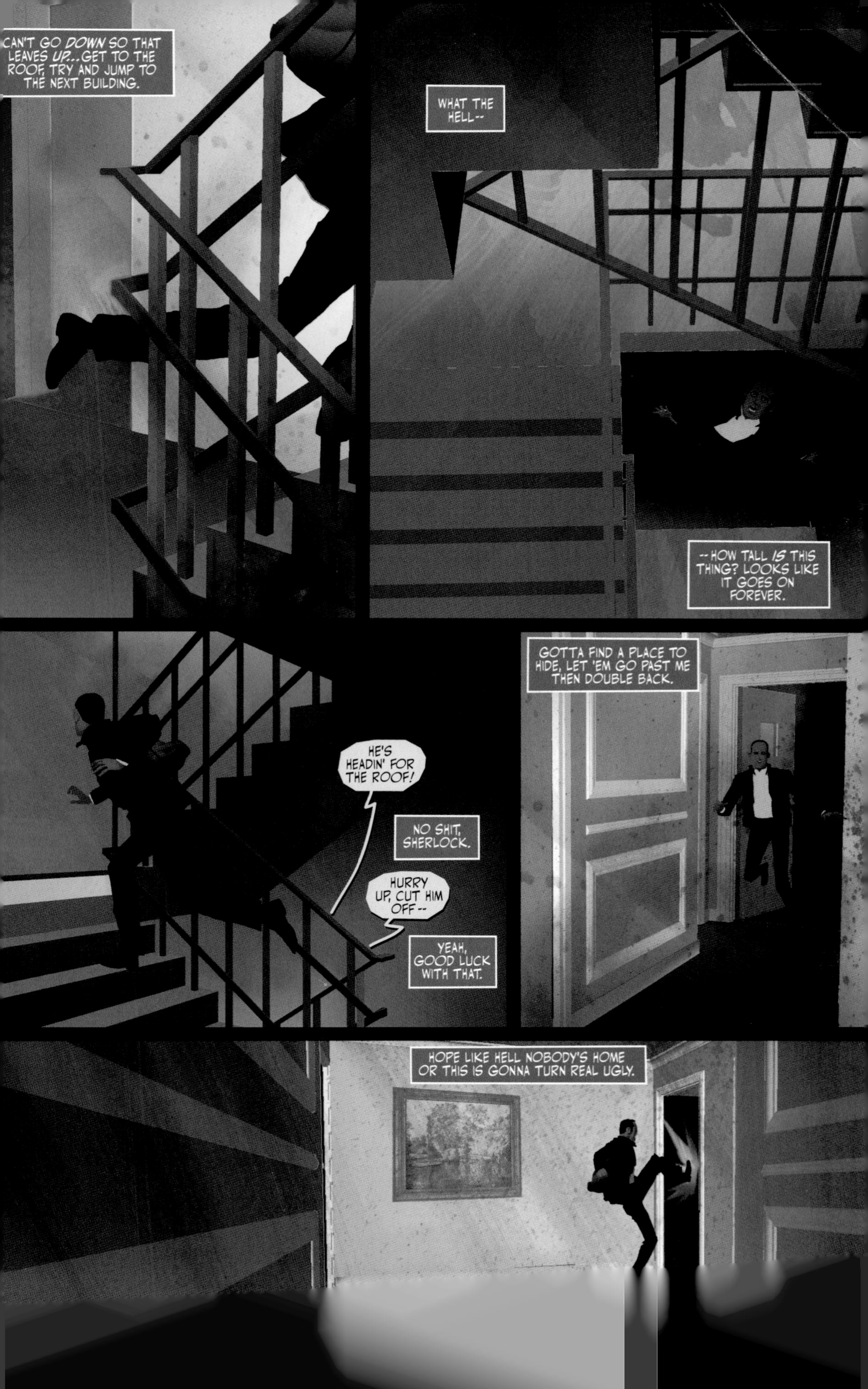
CAN'T GO DOWN SO THAT LEAVES UP...GET TO THE ROOF, TRY AND JUMP TO THE NEXT BUILDING.
WHAT THE HELL--
--HOW TALL IS THIS THING? LOOKS LIKE IT GOES ON FOREVER.
HE'S HEADIN' FOR THE ROOF!
NO SHIT, SHERLOCK.
HURRY UP, CUT HIM OFF--
YEAH, GOOD LUCK WITH THAT.
GOTTA FIND A PLACE TO HIDE, LET 'EM GO PAST ME THEN DOUBLE BACK.
HOPE LIKE HELL NOBODY'S HOME OR THIS IS GONNA TURN REAL UGLY.

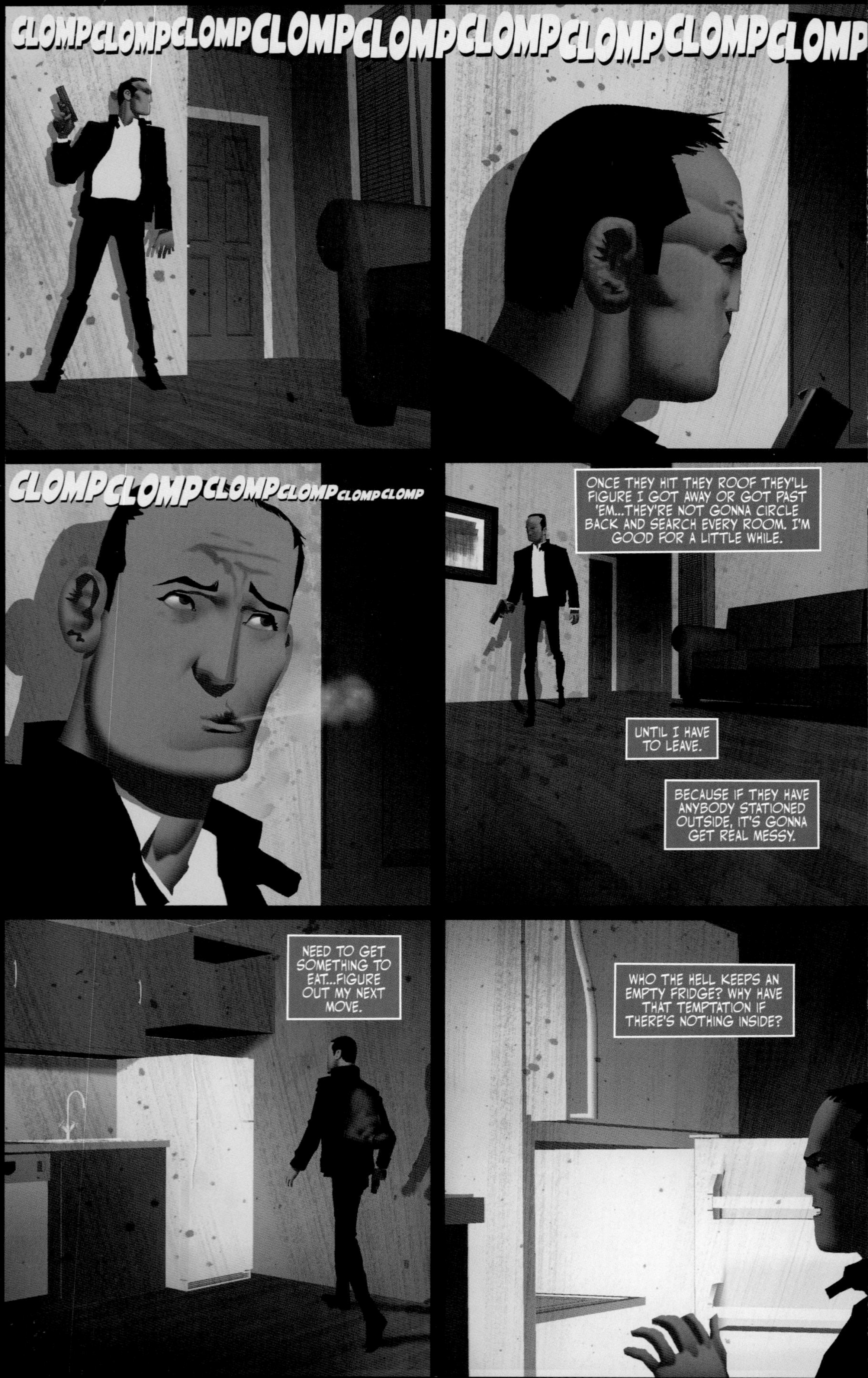
CLOMP CLOMP CLOMP CLOMP CLOMP CLOMP CLOMP CLOMP CLOMP
CLOMP CLOMP CLOMP CLOMP CLOMP CLOMP
ONCE THEY HIT THEY ROOF THEY'LL FIGURE I GOT AWAY OR GOT PAST 'EM...THEY'RE NOT GONNA CIRCLE BACK AND SEARCH EVERY ROOM. I'M GOOD FOR A LITTLE WHILE.
UNTIL I HAVE TO LEAVE.
BECAUSE IF THEY HAVE ANYBODY STATIONED OUTSIDE, IT'S GONNA GET REAL MESSY.
NEED TO GET SOMETHING TO EAT...FIGURE OUT MY NEXT MOVE.
WHO THE HELL KEEPS AN EMPTY FRIDGE? WHY HAVE THAT TEMPTATION IF THERE'S NOTHING INSIDE?

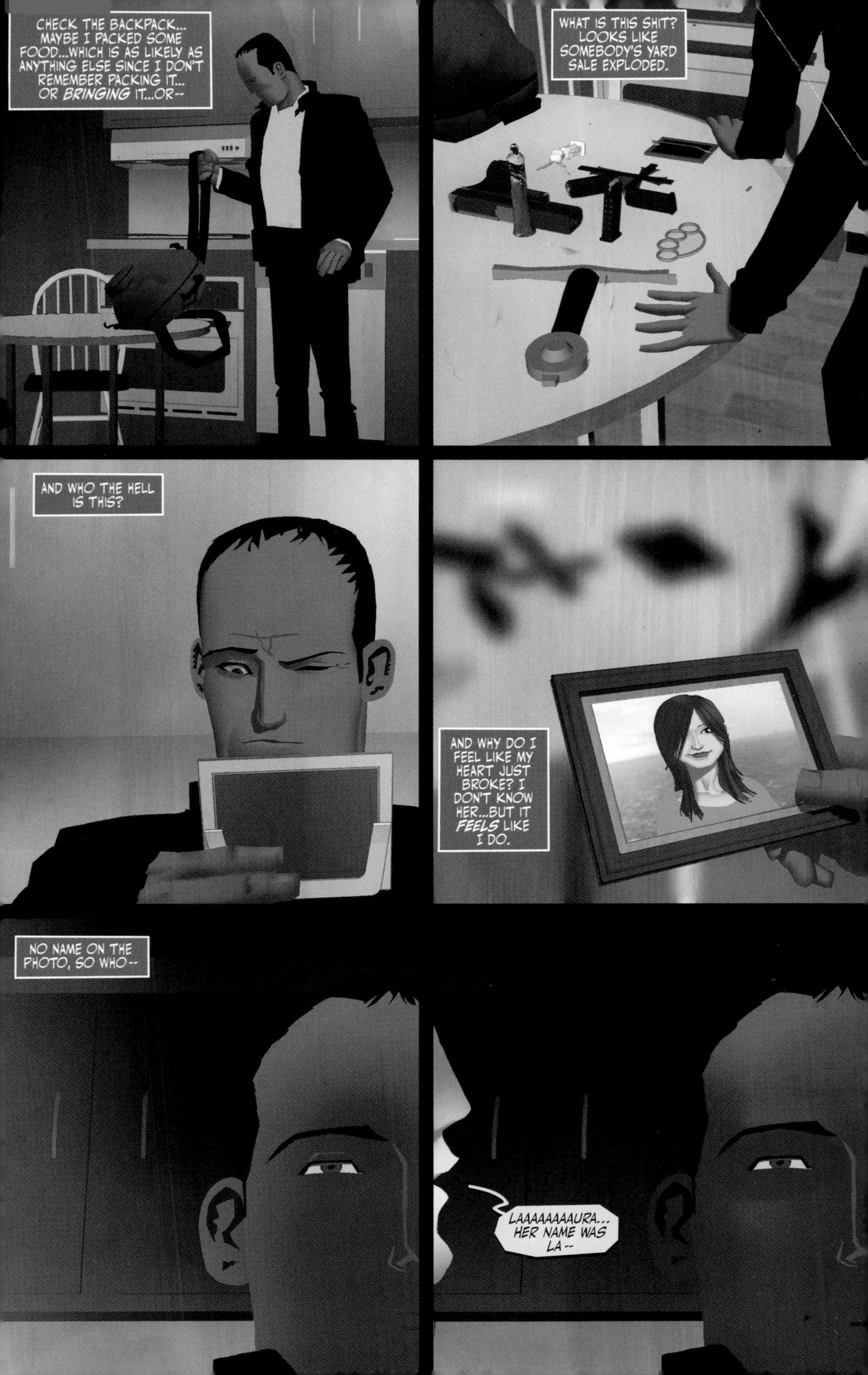
CHECK THE BACKPACK... MAYBE I PACKED SOME FOOD...WHICH IS AS LIKELY AS ANYTHING ELSE SINCE I DON'T REMEMBER PACKING IT... OR *BRINGING* IT...OR--
WHAT IS THIS SHIT? LOOKS LIKE SOMEBODY'S YARD SALE EXPLODED.
AND WHO THE HELL IS THIS?
AND WHY DO I FEEL LIKE MY HEART JUST BROKE? I DON'T KNOW HER...BUT IT *FEELS* LIKE I DO.
NO NAME ON THE PHOTO, SO WHO--
LAAAAAAAAURA... HER NAME WAS LA--

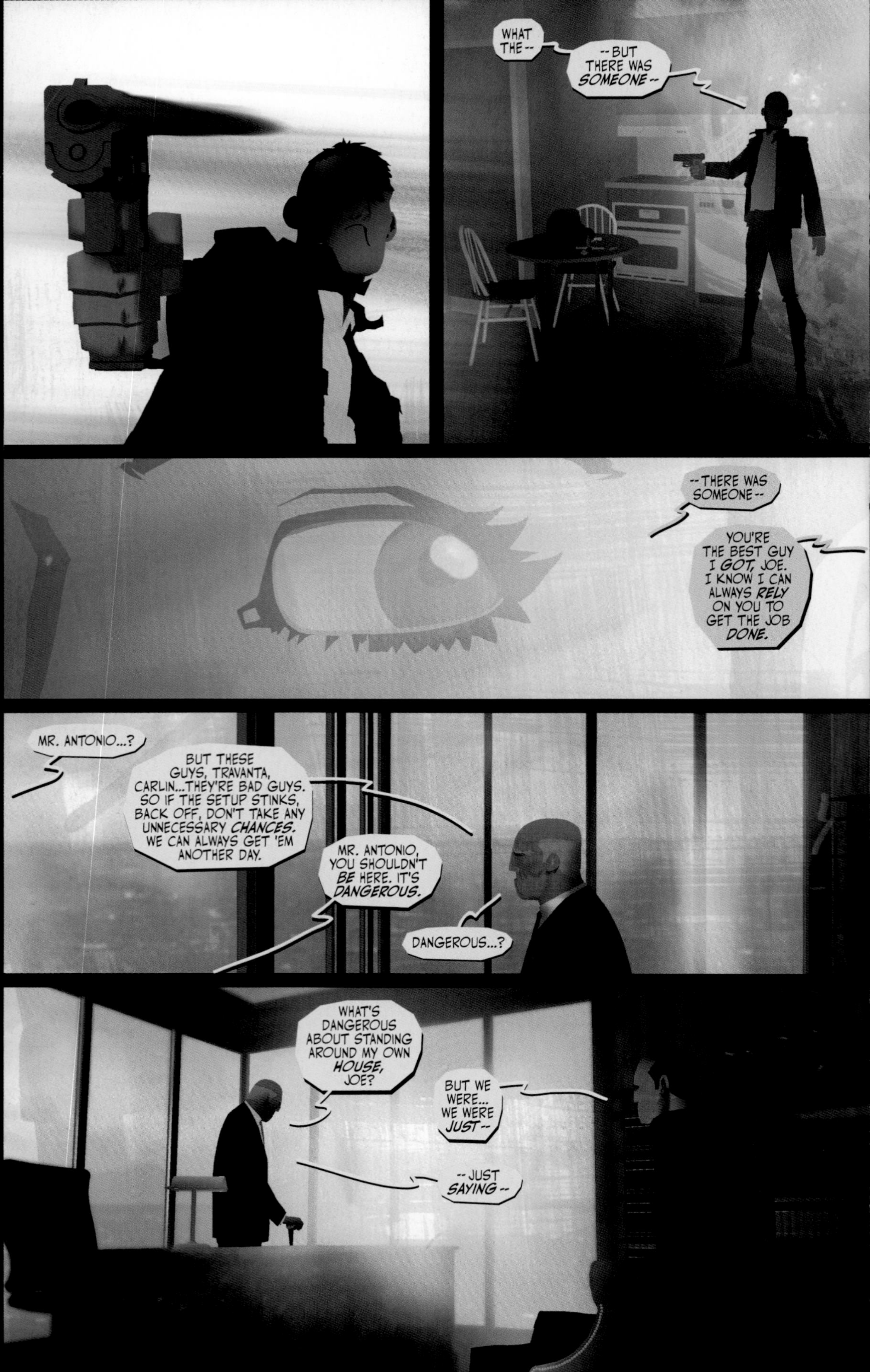
WHAT THE --
-- BUT THERE WAS SOMEONE --
-- THERE WAS SOMEONE --
YOU'RE THE BEST GUY I GOT, JOE. I KNOW I CAN ALWAYS RELY ON YOU TO GET THE JOB DONE.
MR. ANTONIO...?
BUT THESE GUYS, TRAVANTA, CARLIN...THEY'RE BAD GUYS. SO IF THE SETUP STINKS, BACK OFF, DON'T TAKE ANY UNNECESSARY CHANCES. WE CAN ALWAYS GET 'EM ANOTHER DAY.
MR. ANTONIO, YOU SHOULDN'T BE HERE. IT'S DANGEROUS.
DANGEROUS...?
WHAT'S DANGEROUS ABOUT STANDING AROUND MY OWN HOUSE, JOE?
BUT WE WERE... WE WERE JUST --
-- JUST SAYING --

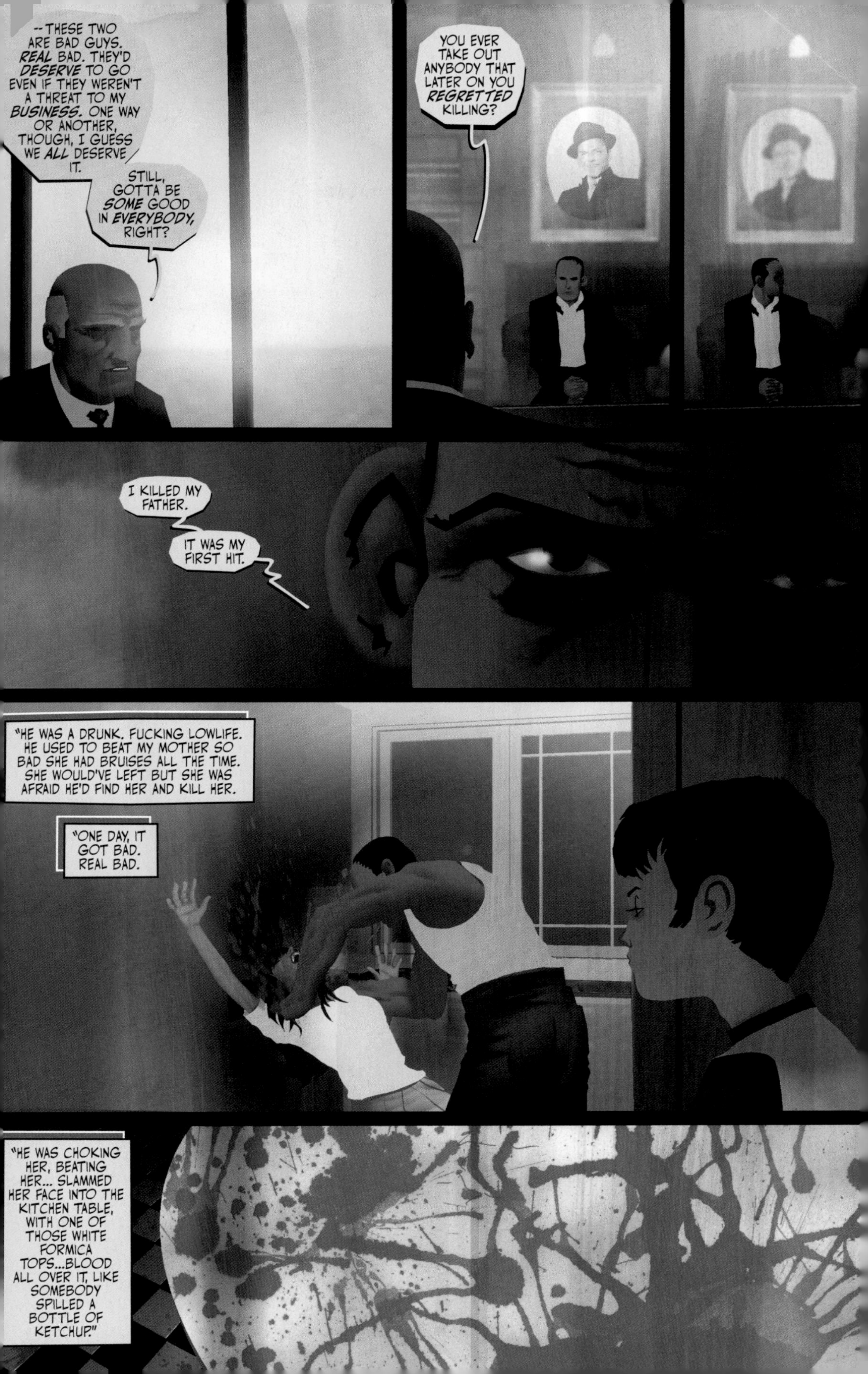
--THESE TWO ARE BAD GUYS. REAL BAD. THEY'D DESERVE TO GO EVEN IF THEY WEREN'T A THREAT TO MY BUSINESS. ONE WAY OR ANOTHER, THOUGH, I GUESS WE ALL DESERVE IT.
STILL, GOTTA BE SOME GOOD IN EVERYBODY, RIGHT?
YOU EVER TAKE OUT ANYBODY THAT LATER ON YOU REGRETTED KILLING?
I KILLED MY FATHER.
IT WAS MY FIRST HIT.
"HE WAS A DRUNK. FUCKING LOWLIFE. HE USED TO BEAT MY MOTHER SO BAD SHE HAD BRUISES ALL THE TIME. SHE WOULD'VE LEFT BUT SHE WAS AFRAID HE'D FIND HER AND KILL HER.
"ONE DAY, IT GOT BAD. REAL BAD.
"HE WAS CHOKING HER, BEATING HER... SLAMMED HER FACE INTO THE KITCHEN TABLE, WITH ONE OF THOSE WHITE FORMICA TOPS...BLOOD ALL OVER IT, LIKE SOMEBODY SPILLED A BOTTLE OF KETCHUP."

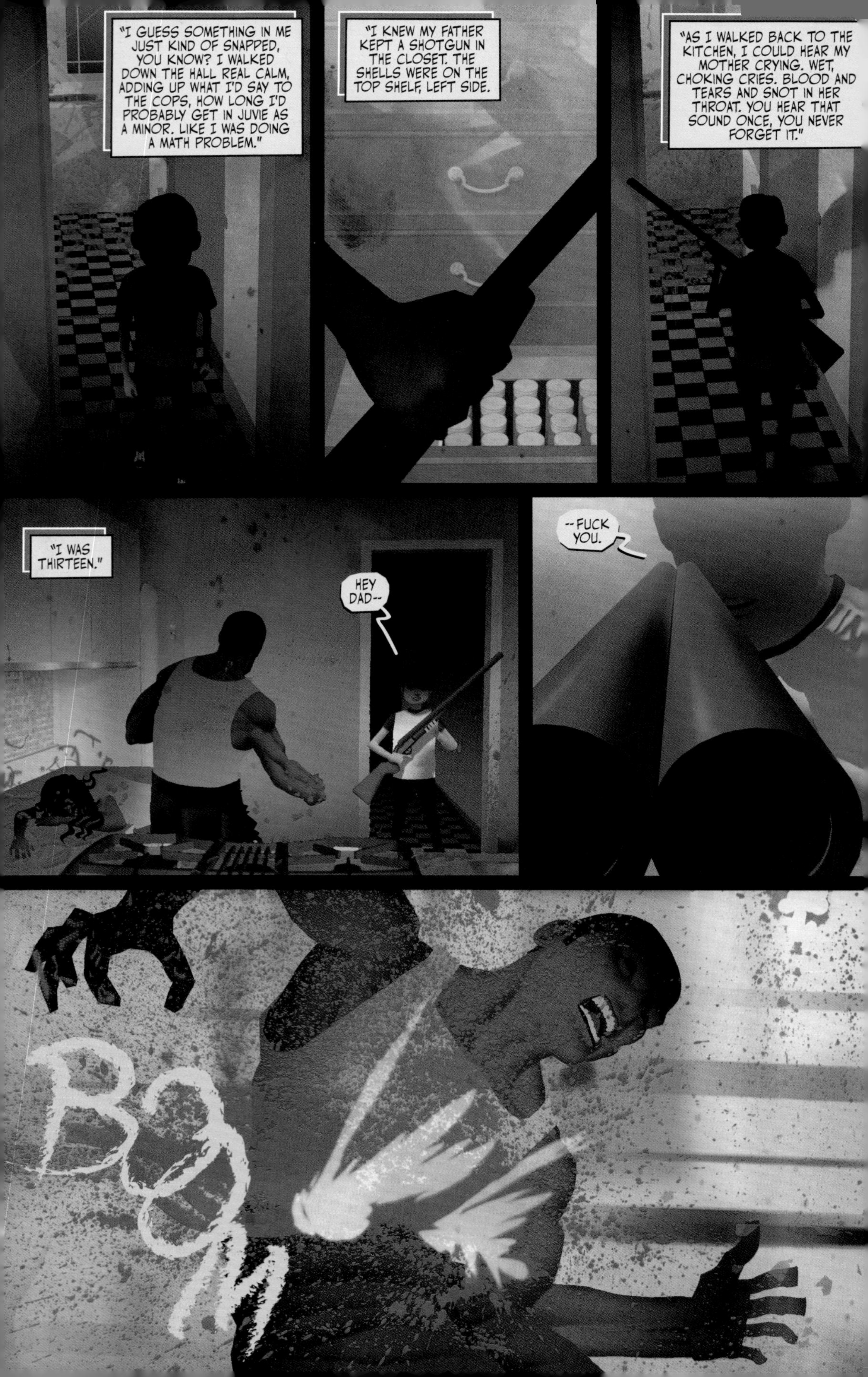
"I GUESS SOMETHING IN ME JUST KIND OF SNAPPED, YOU KNOW? I WALKED DOWN THE HALL REAL CALM, ADDING UP WHAT I'D SAY TO THE COPS, HOW LONG I'D PROBABLY GET IN JUVIE AS A MINOR. LIKE I WAS DOING A MATH PROBLEM."
"I KNEW MY FATHER KEPT A SHOTGUN IN THE CLOSET. THE SHELLS WERE ON THE TOP SHELF, LEFT SIDE.
"AS I WALKED BACK TO THE KITCHEN, I COULD HEAR MY MOTHER CRYING. WET, CHOKING CRIES. BLOOD AND TEARS AND SNOT IN HER THROAT. YOU HEAR THAT SOUND ONCE, YOU NEVER FORGET IT."
"I WAS THIRTEEN."
HEY DAD--
--FUCK YOU.
Boom

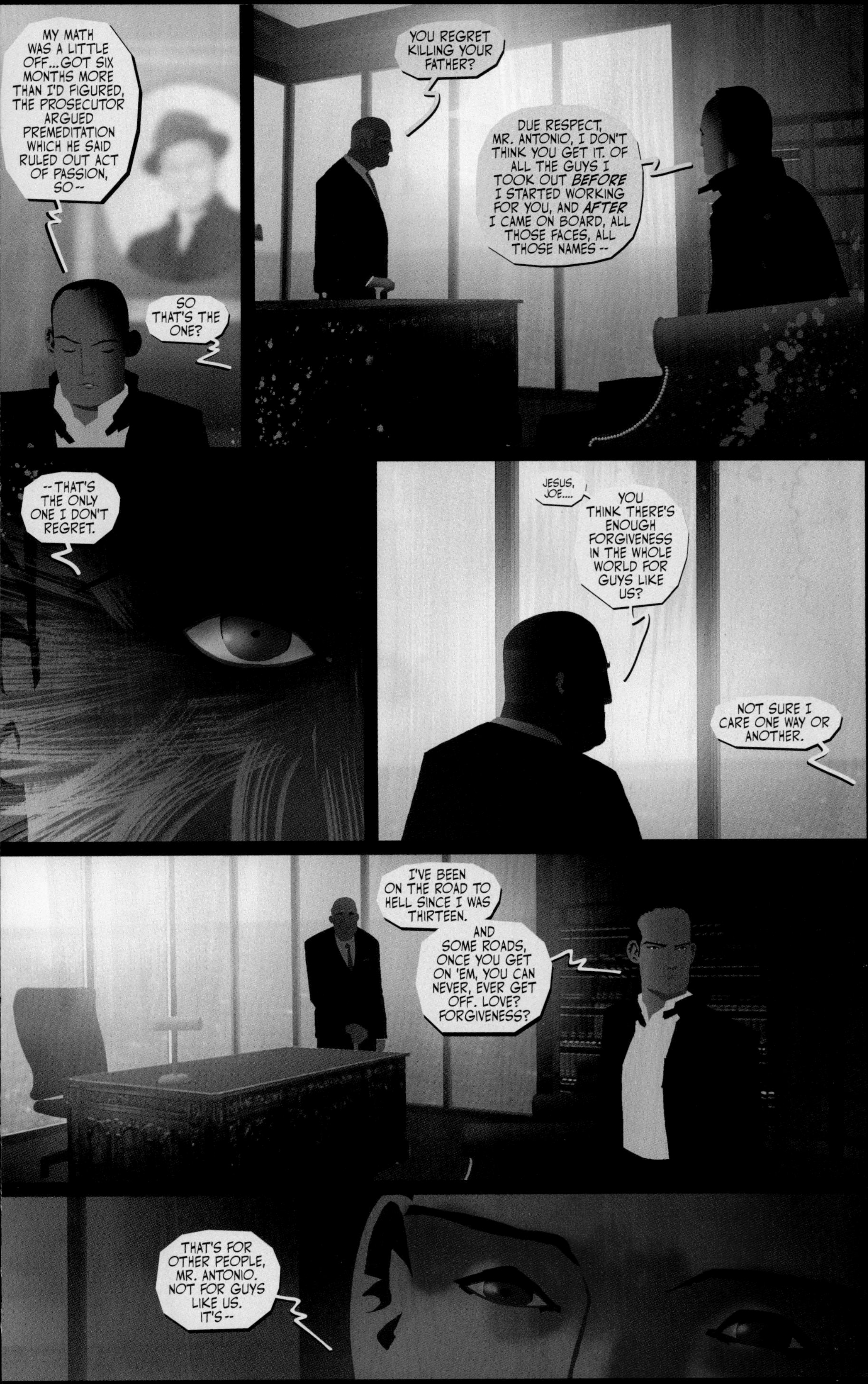
MY MATH WAS A LITTLE OFF...GOT SIX MONTHS MORE THAN I'D FIGURED, THE PROSECUTOR ARGUED PREMEDITATION WHICH HE SAID RULED OUT ACT OF PASSION, SO--
SO THAT'S THE ONE?
YOU REGRET KILLING YOUR FATHER?
DUE RESPECT, MR. ANTONIO, I DON'T THINK YOU GET IT. OF ALL THE GUYS I TOOK OUT BEFORE I STARTED WORKING FOR YOU, AND AFTER I CAME ON BOARD, ALL THOSE FACES, ALL THOSE NAMES --
--THAT'S THE ONLY ONE I DON'T REGRET.
JESUS, JOE....
YOU THINK THERE'S ENOUGH FORGIVENESS IN THE WHOLE WORLD FOR GUYS LIKE US?
NOT SURE I CARE ONE WAY OR ANOTHER.
I'VE BEEN ON THE ROAD TO HELL SINCE I WAS THIRTEEN.
AND SOME ROADS, ONCE YOU GET ON 'EM, YOU CAN NEVER, EVER GET OFF. LOVE? FORGIVENESS?
THAT'S FOR OTHER PEOPLE, MR. ANTONIO. NOT FOR GUYS LIKE US. IT'S--

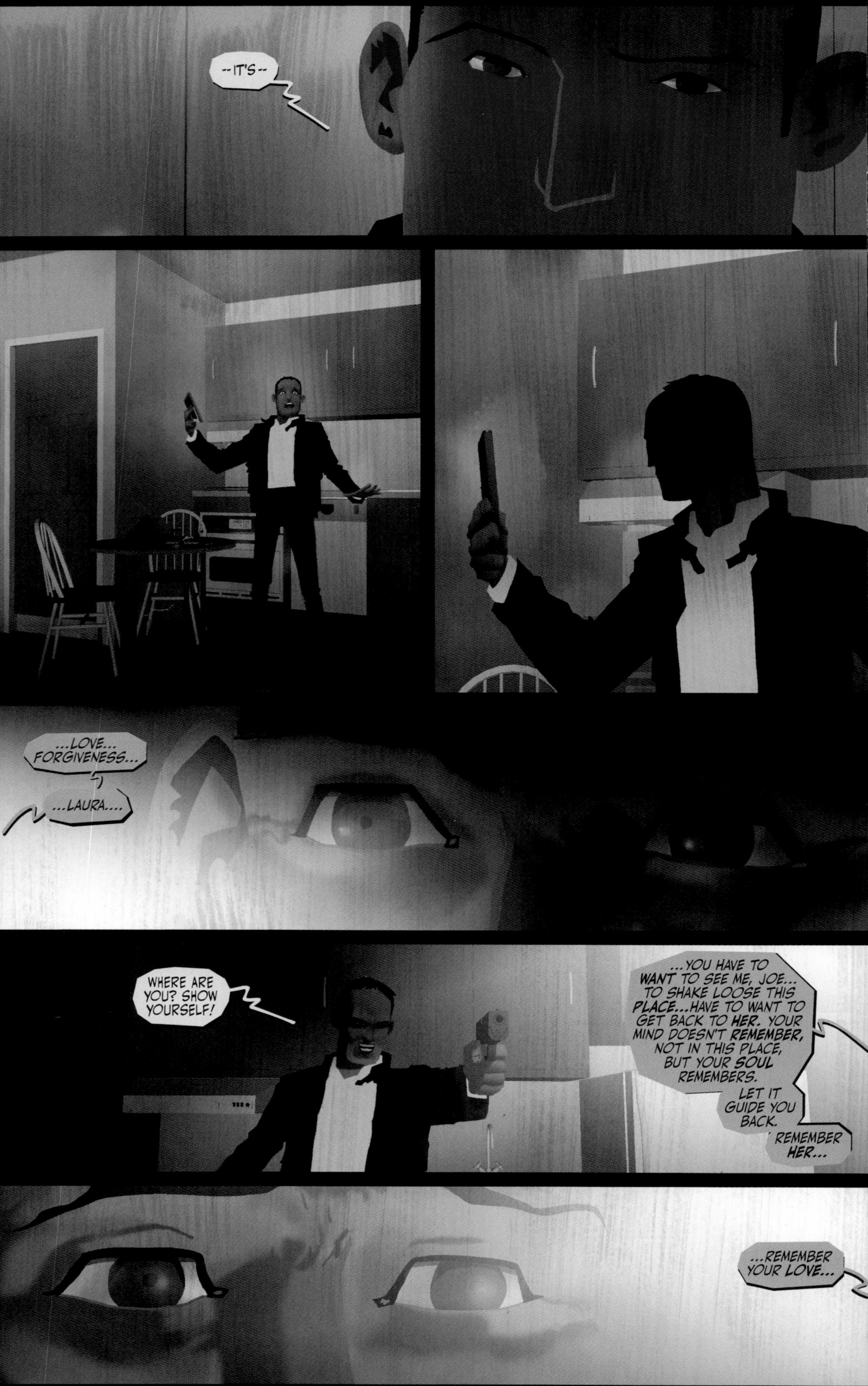
--IT'S--
...LOVE... FORGIVENESS...
...LAURA....
WHERE ARE YOU? SHOW YOURSELF!
...YOU HAVE TO WANT TO SEE ME, JOE... TO SHAKE LOOSE THIS PLACE...HAVE TO WANT TO GET BACK TO HER. YOUR MIND DOESN'T REMEMBER, NOT IN THIS PLACE, BUT YOUR SOUL REMEMBERS.
LET IT GUIDE YOU BACK.
REMEMBER HER...
...REMEMBER YOUR LOVE...

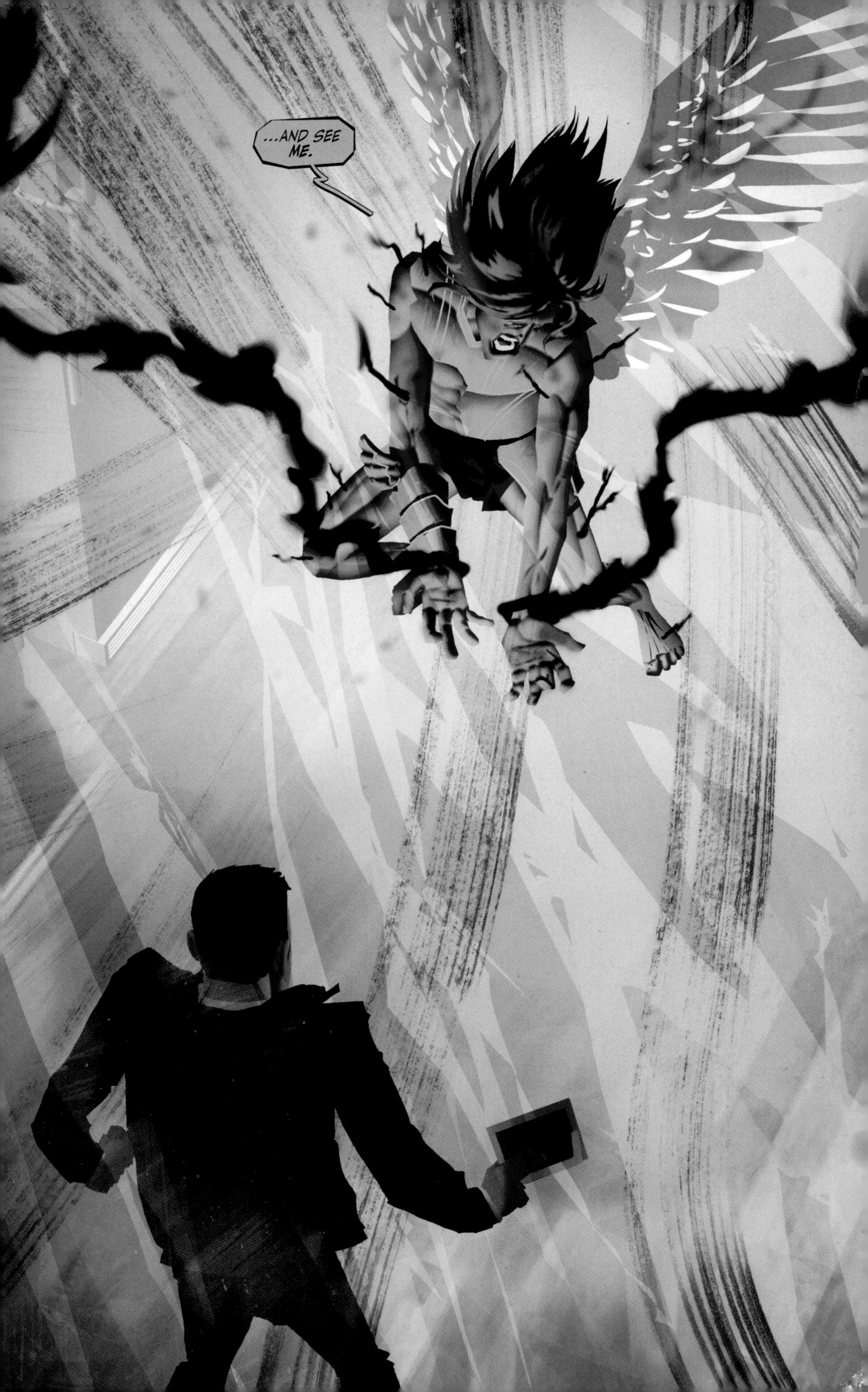
...AND SEE ME.

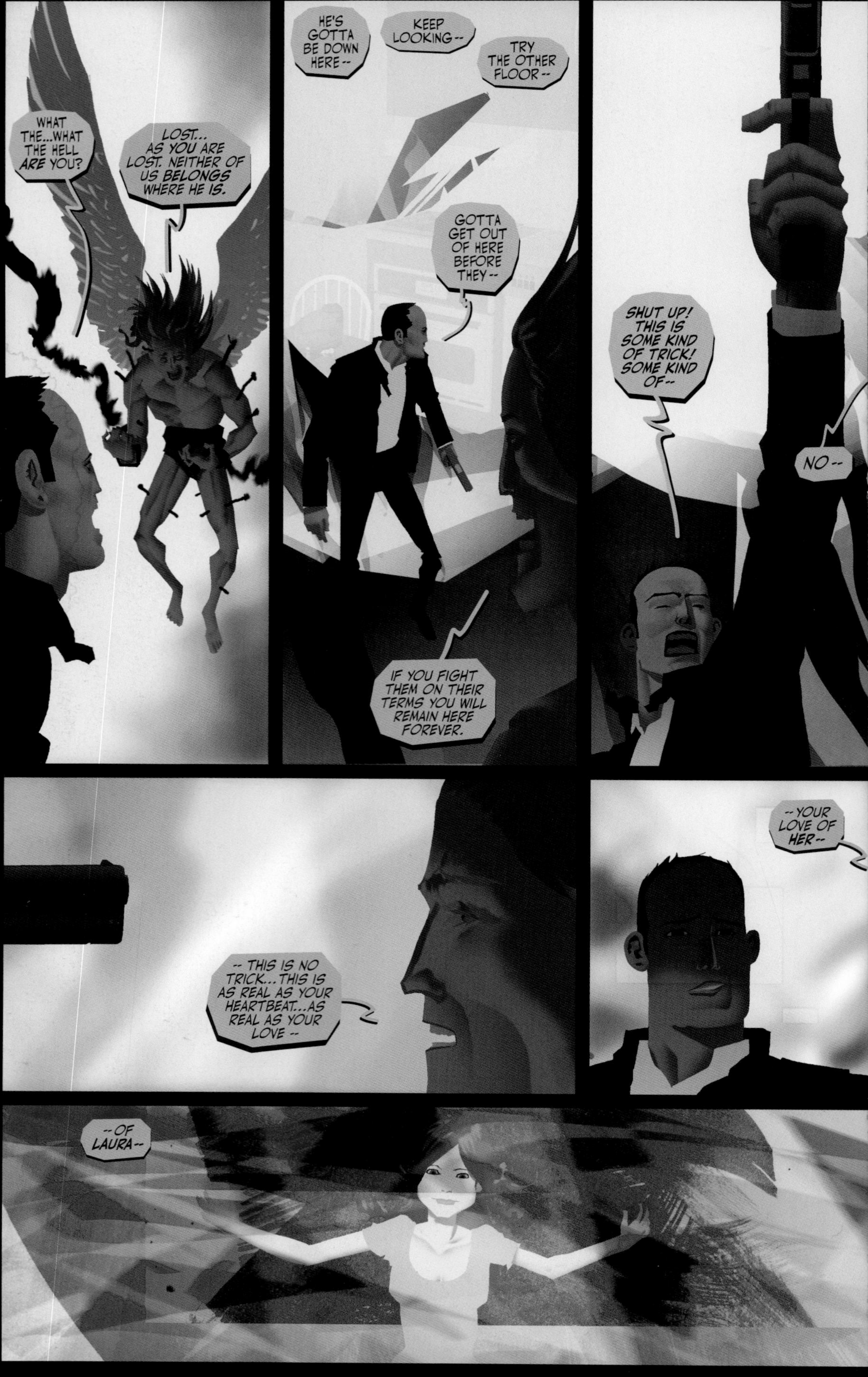
WHAT THE...WHAT THE HELL ARE YOU?
LOST... AS YOU ARE LOST. NEITHER OF US BELONGS WHERE HE IS.
HE'S GOTTA BE DOWN HERE--
KEEP LOOKING--
TRY THE OTHER FLOOR--
GOTTA GET OUT OF HERE BEFORE THEY--
IF YOU FIGHT THEM ON THEIR TERMS YOU WILL REMAIN HERE FOREVER.
SHUT UP! THIS IS SOME KIND OF TRICK! SOME KIND OF--
NO--
-- THIS IS NO TRICK...THIS IS AS REAL AS YOUR HEARTBEAT...AS REAL AS YOUR LOVE --
--YOUR LOVE OF HER--
--OF LAURA--

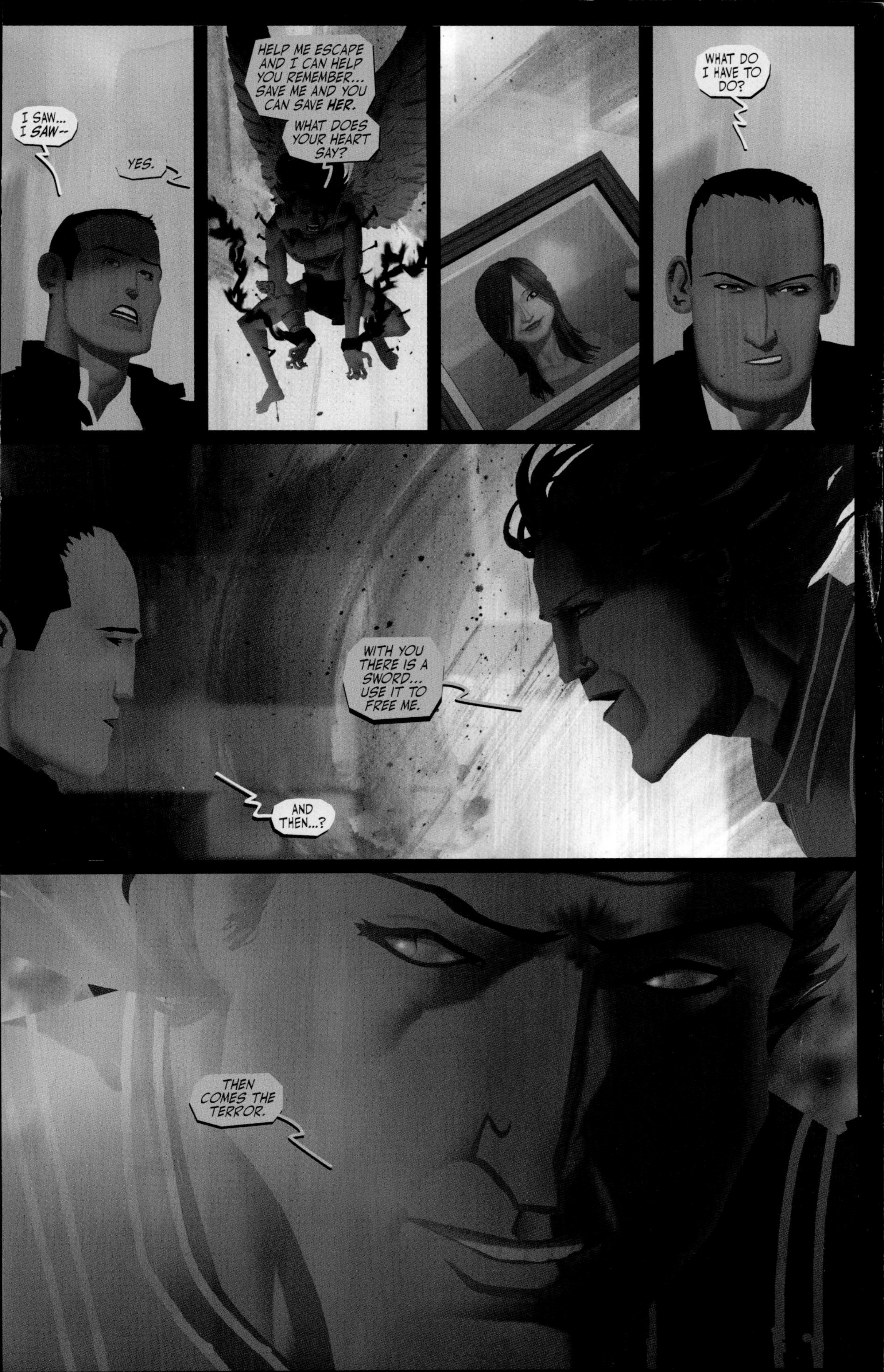
I SAW... I SAW--
YES.
HELP ME ESCAPE AND I CAN HELP YOU REMEMBER... SAVE ME AND YOU CAN SAVE HER.
WHAT DOES YOUR HEART SAY?
WHAT DO I HAVE TO DO?
WITH YOU THERE IS A SWORD... USE IT TO FREE ME.
AND THEN...?
THEN COMES THE TERROR.

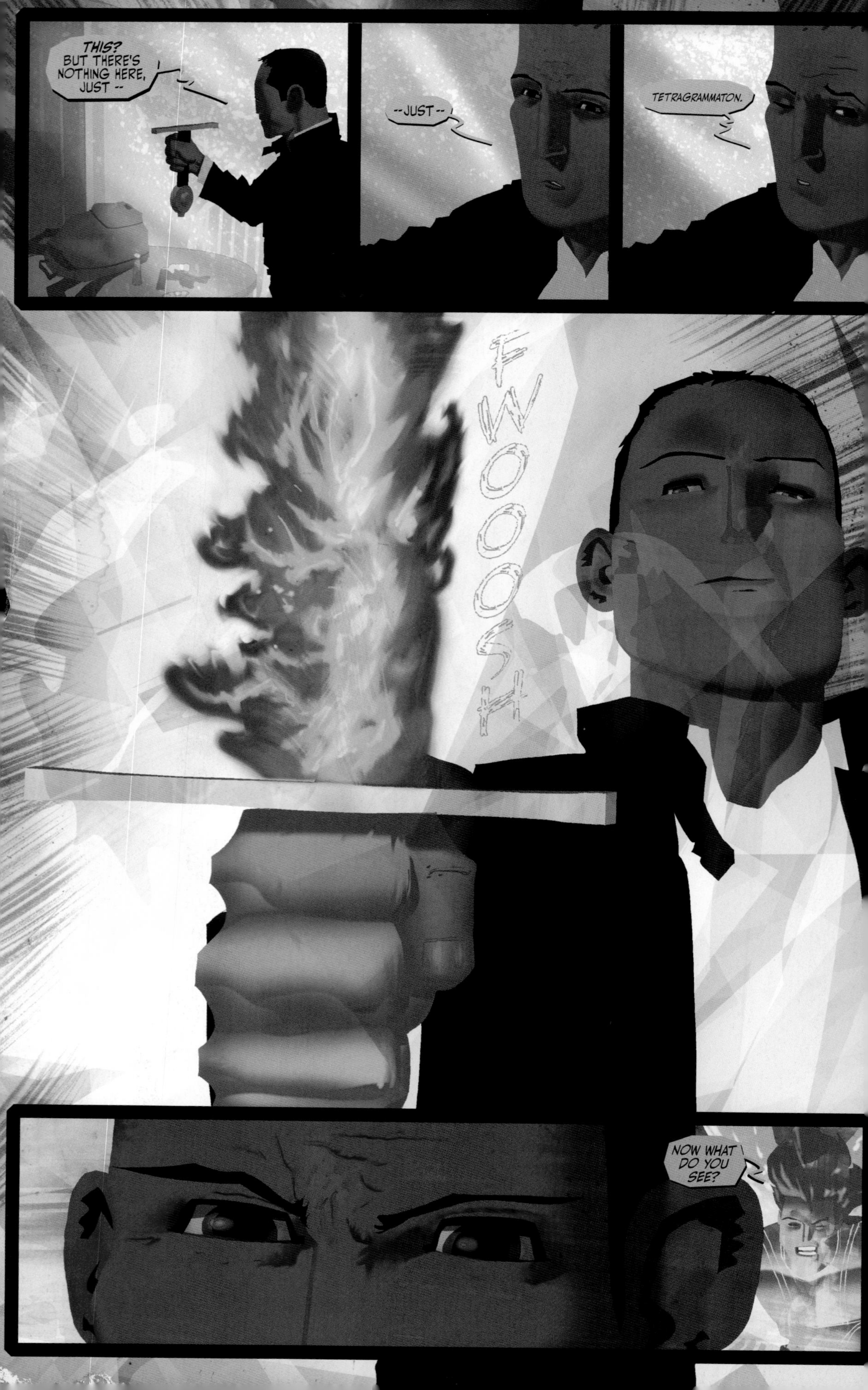
THIS? BUT THERE'S NOTHING HERE, JUST --
--JUST--
TETRAGRAMMATON.
FWOOOSH
NOW WHAT DO YOU SEE?

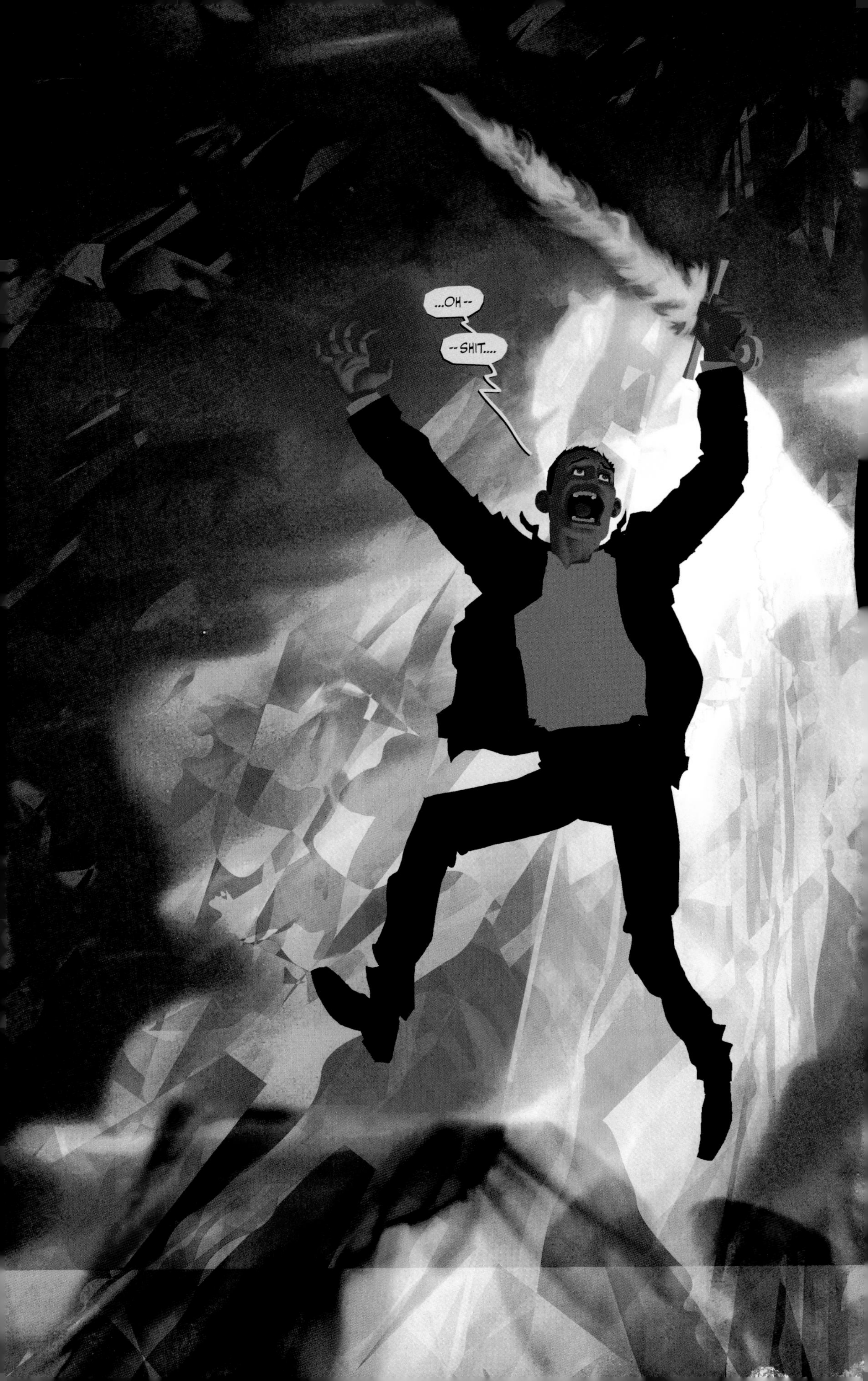
...OH --
-- SHIT....

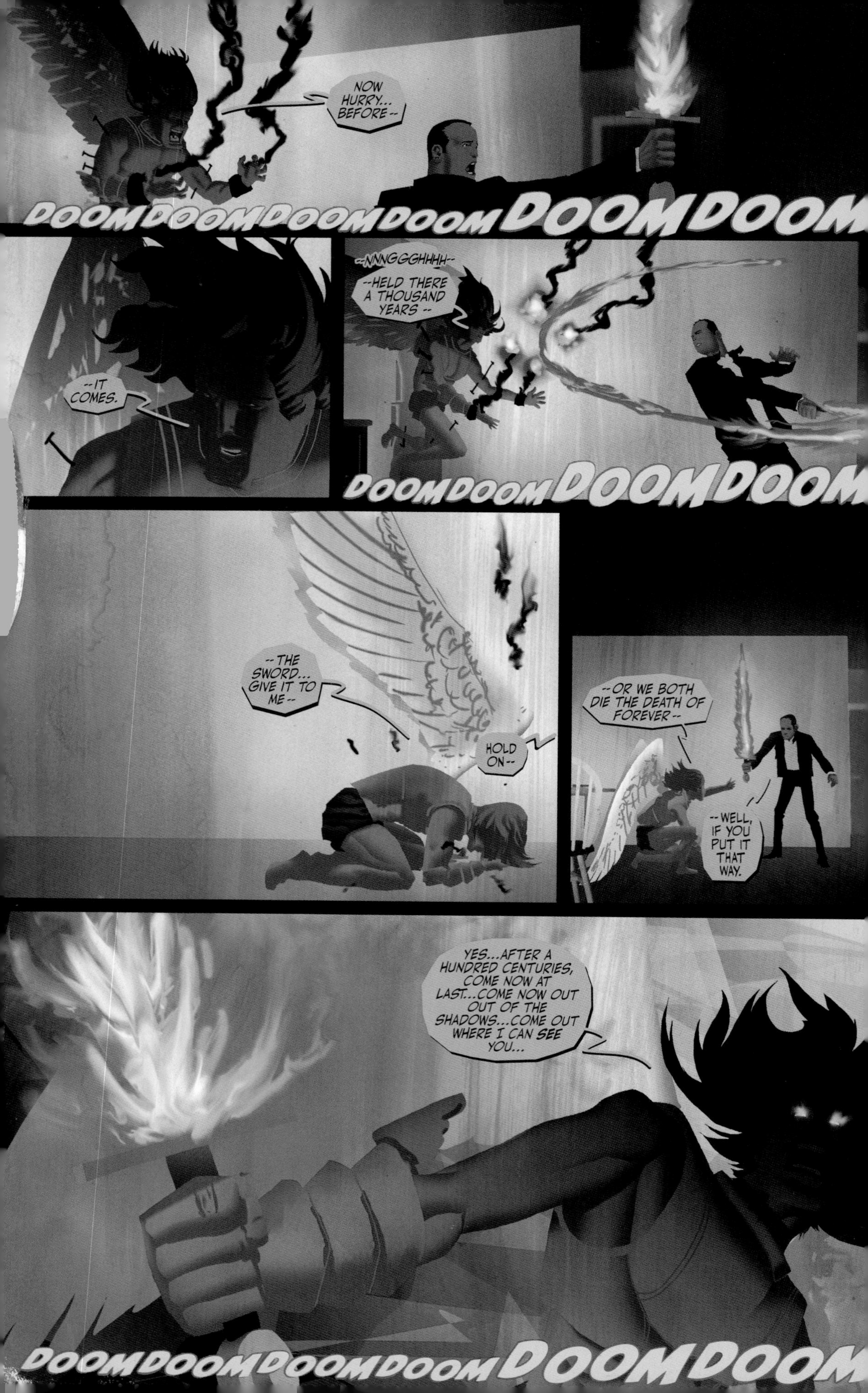
NOW HURRY... BEFORE--
DOOMDOOMDOOMDOOMDOOMDOOM
--IT COMES.
--NNNGGHHHH--
--HELD THERE A THOUSAND YEARS --
DOOMDOOMDOOMDOOM
--THE SWORD... GIVE IT TO ME--
HOLD ON--
--OR WE BOTH DIE THE DEATH OF FOREVER--
--WELL, IF YOU PUT IT THAT WAY.
YES...AFTER A HUNDRED CENTURIES, COME NOW AT LAST...COME NOW OUT OUT OF THE SHADOWS...COME OUT WHERE I CAN SEE YOU...
DOOMDOOMDOOMDOOMDOOMDOOM

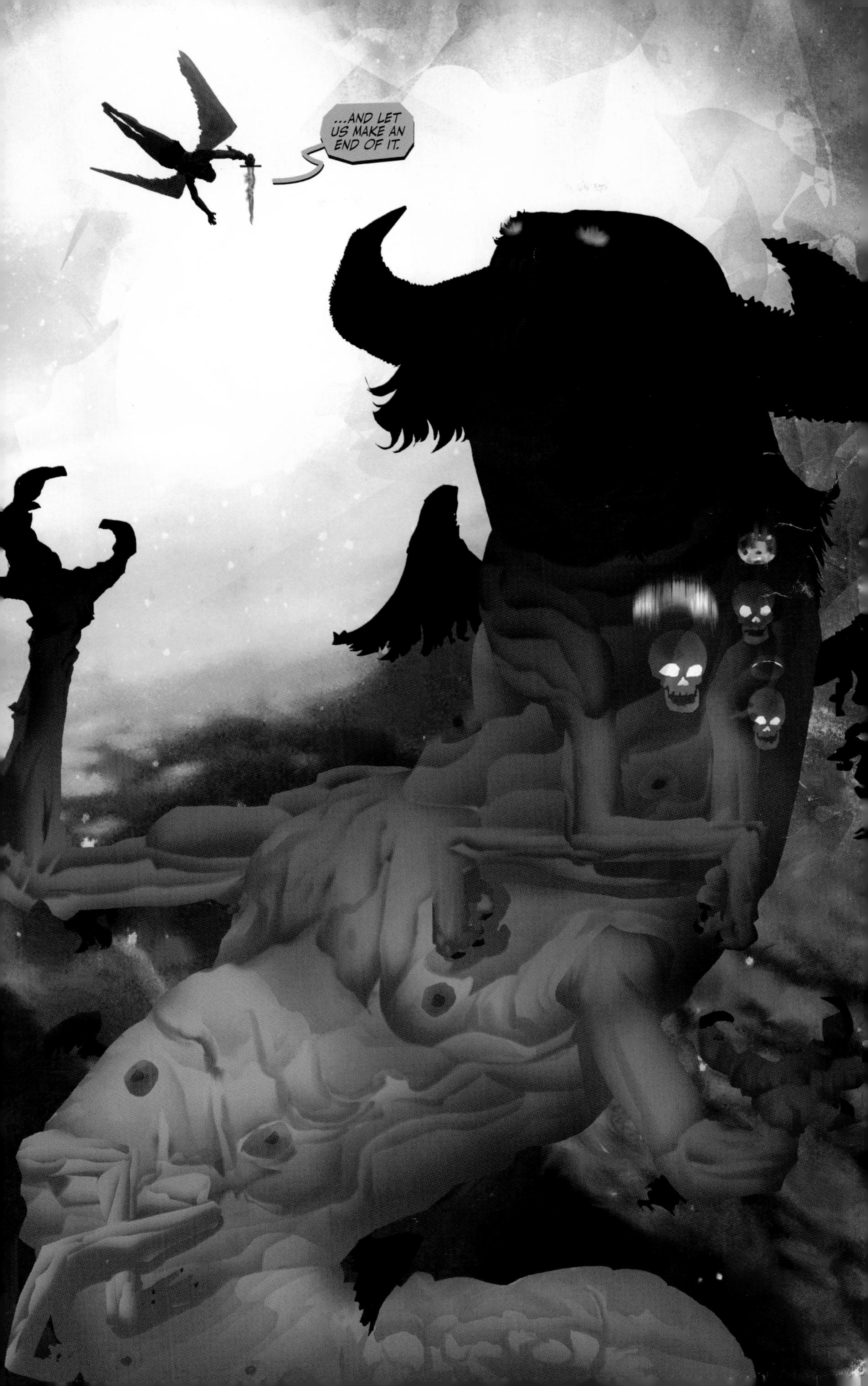
...AND LET US MAKE AN END OF IT.

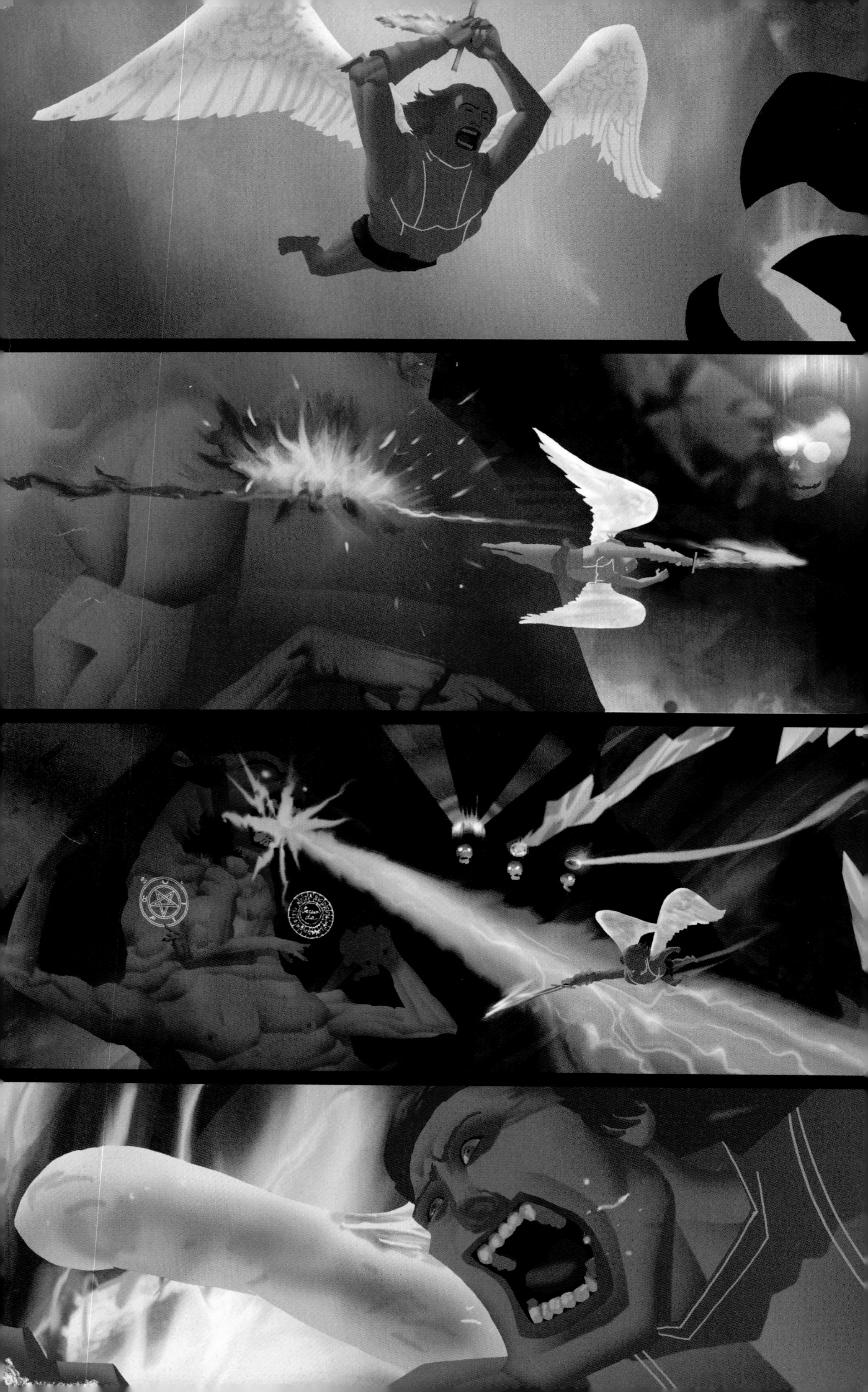

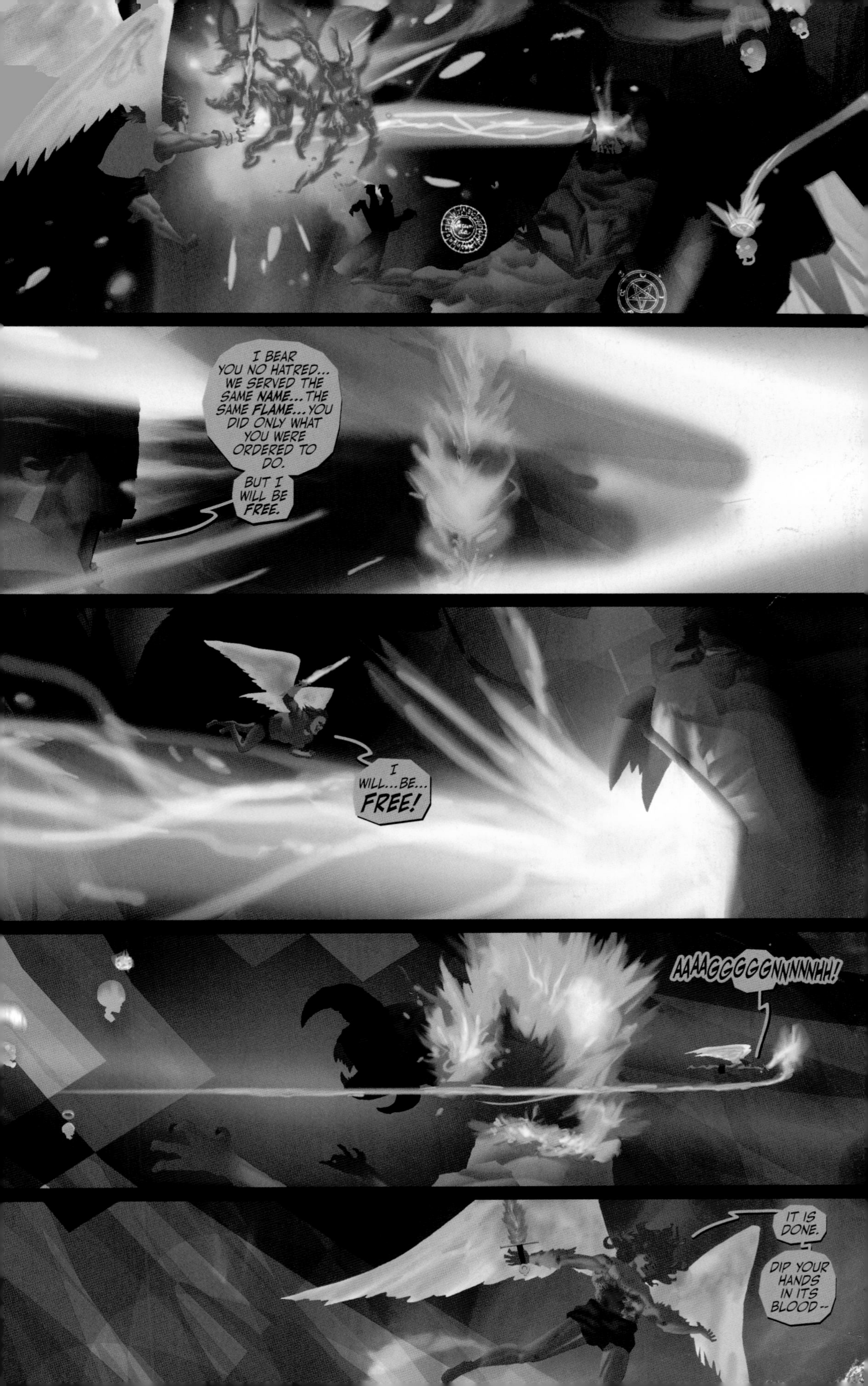
I BEAR YOU NO HATRED... WE SERVED THE SAME NAME... THE SAME FLAME... YOU DID ONLY WHAT YOU WERE ORDERED TO DO.
BUT I WILL BE FREE.
I WILL... BE... FREE!
AAAAGGGGGNNNNNHH!
IT IS DONE.
DIP YOUR HANDS IN ITS BLOOD--

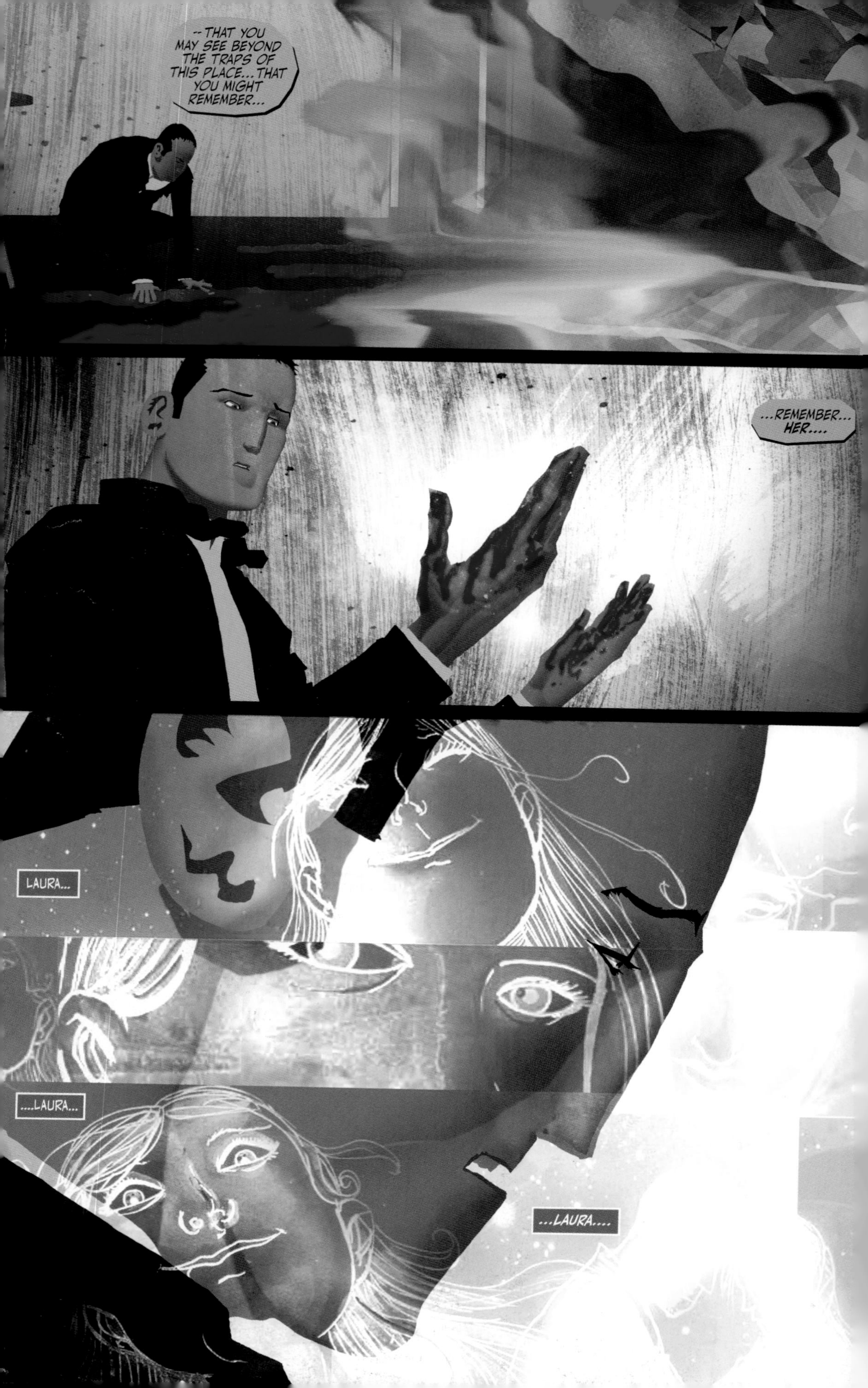

--THAT YOU MAY SEE BEYOND THE TRAPS OF THIS PLACE...THAT YOU MIGHT REMEMBER...
...REMEMBER... HER....
LAURA...
....LAURA...
...LAURA....

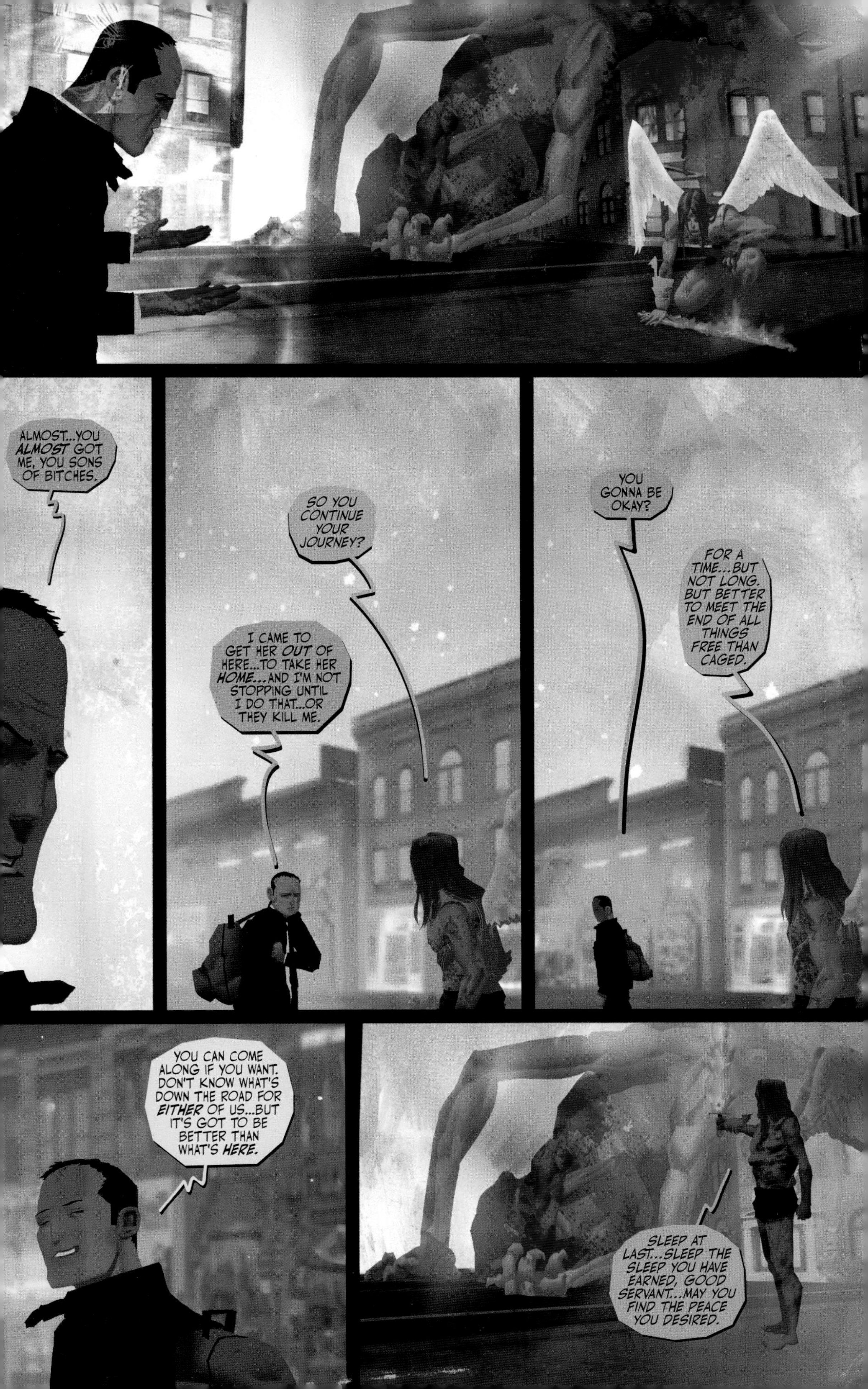
ALMOST...YOU ALMOST GOT ME, YOU SONS OF BITCHES.
SO YOU CONTINUE YOUR JOURNEY?
I CAME TO GET HER OUT OF HERE...TO TAKE HER HOME...AND I'M NOT STOPPING UNTIL I DO THAT...OR THEY KILL ME.
YOU GONNA BE OKAY?
FOR A TIME...BUT NOT LONG. BUT BETTER TO MEET THE END OF ALL THINGS FREE THAN CAGED.
YOU CAN COME ALONG IF YOU WANT. DON'T KNOW WHAT'S DOWN THE ROAD FOR EITHER OF US...BUT IT'S GOT TO BE BETTER THAN WHAT'S HERE.
SLEEP AT LAST...SLEEP THE SLEEP YOU HAVE EARNED, GOOD SERVANT...MAY YOU FIND THE PEACE YOU DESIRED.

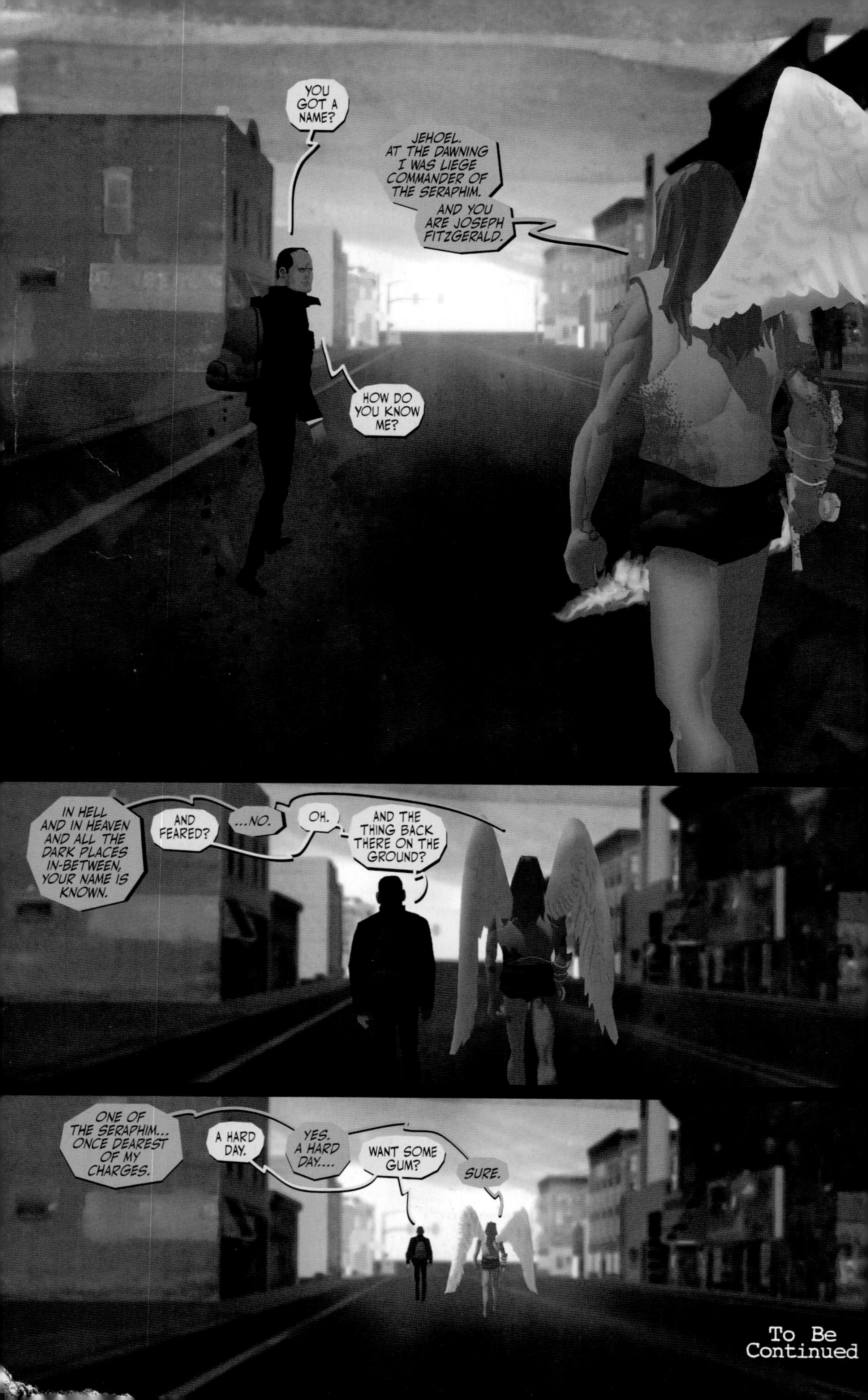
YOU GOT A NAME?
JEHOEL. AT THE DAWNING I WAS LIEGE COMMANDER OF THE SERAPHIM.
AND YOU ARE JOSEPH FITZGERALD.
HOW DO YOU KNOW ME?
IN HELL AND IN HEAVEN AND ALL THE DARK PLACES IN-BETWEEN, YOUR NAME IS KNOWN.
AND FEARED?
...NO.
OH.
AND THE THING BACK THERE ON THE GROUND?
ONE OF THE SERAPHIM... ONCE DEAREST OF MY CHARGES.
A HARD DAY.
YES. A HARD DAY....
WANT SOME GUM?
SURE.
To Be Continued

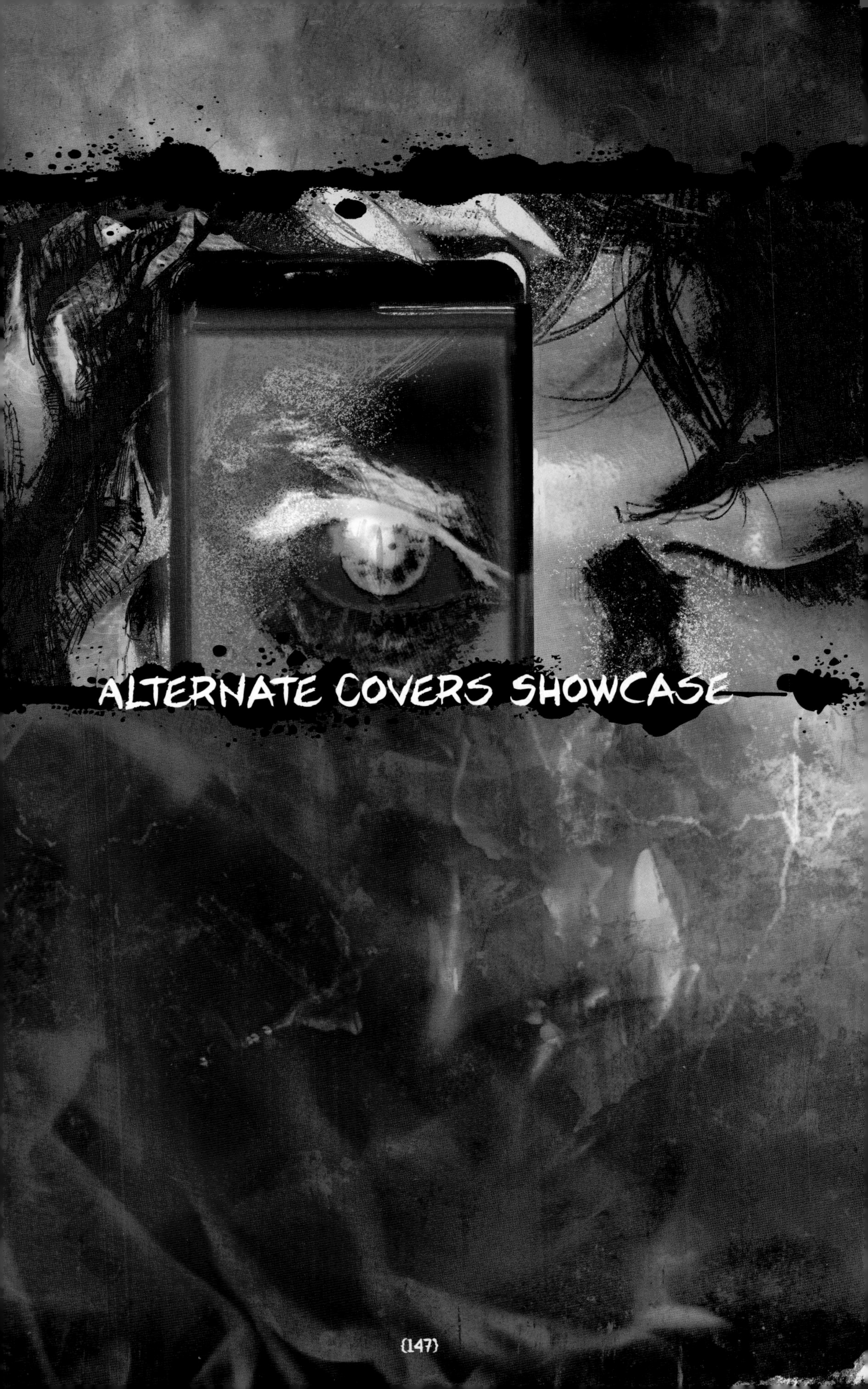

# ALTERNATE COVERS SHOWCASE

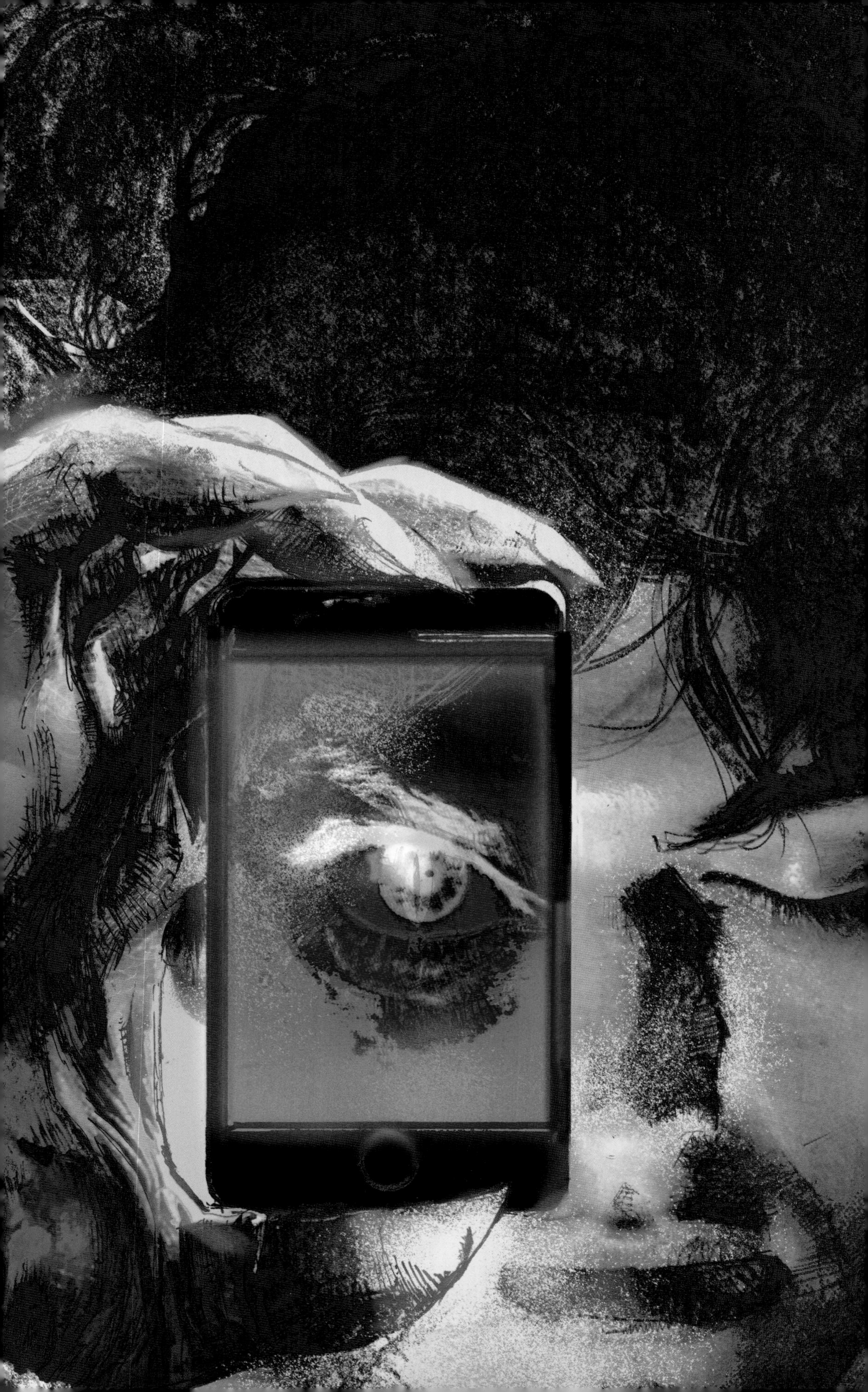

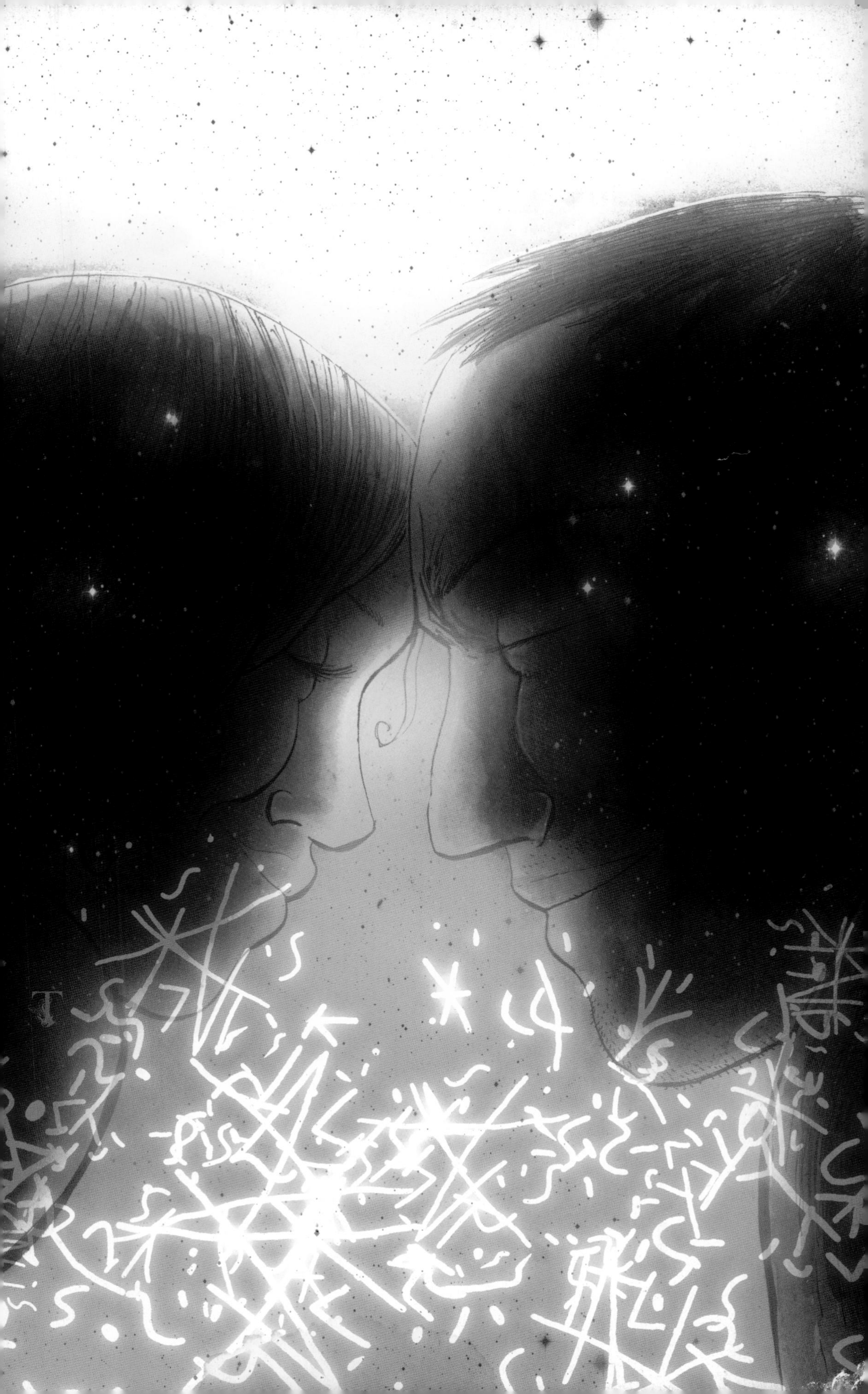

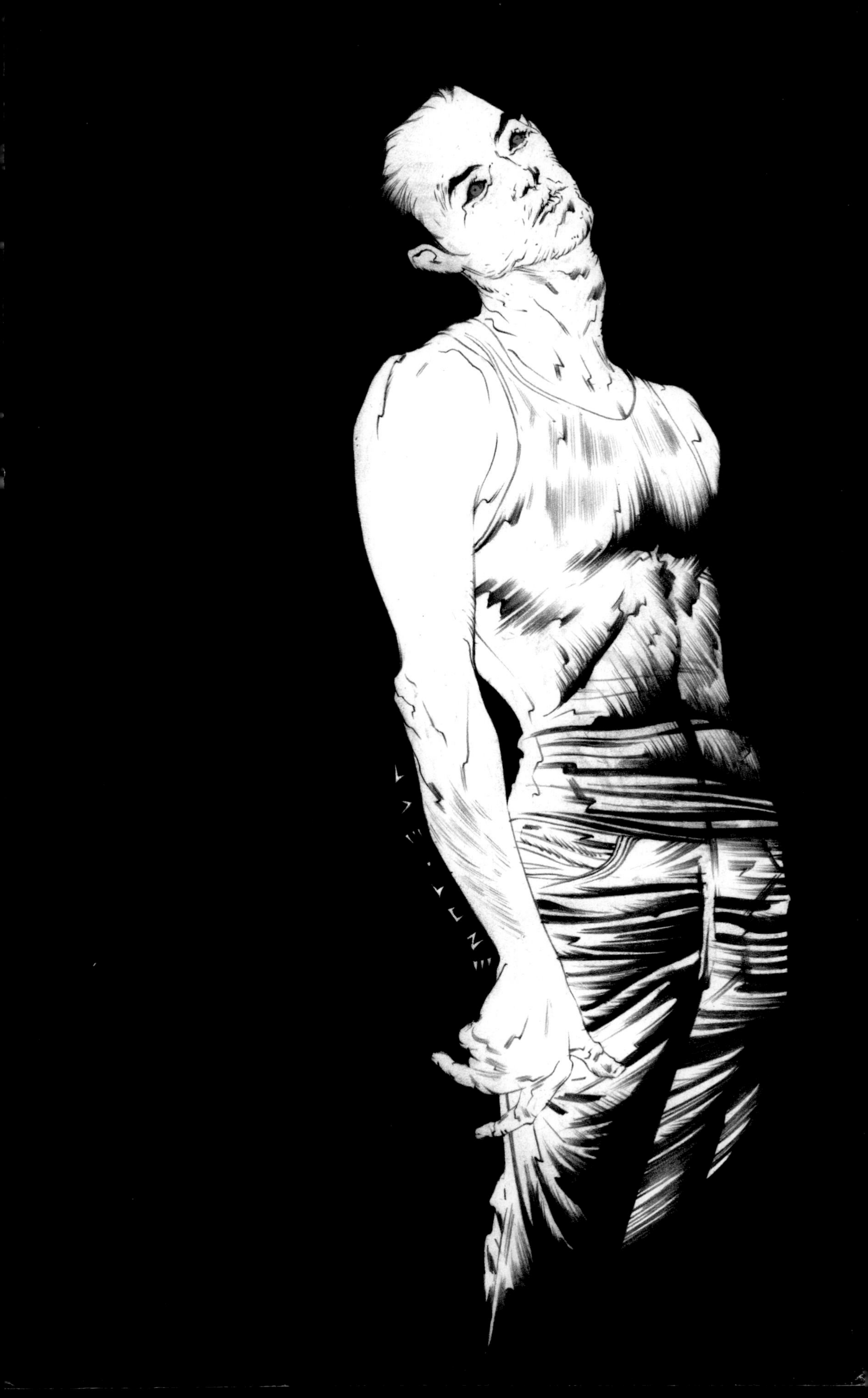

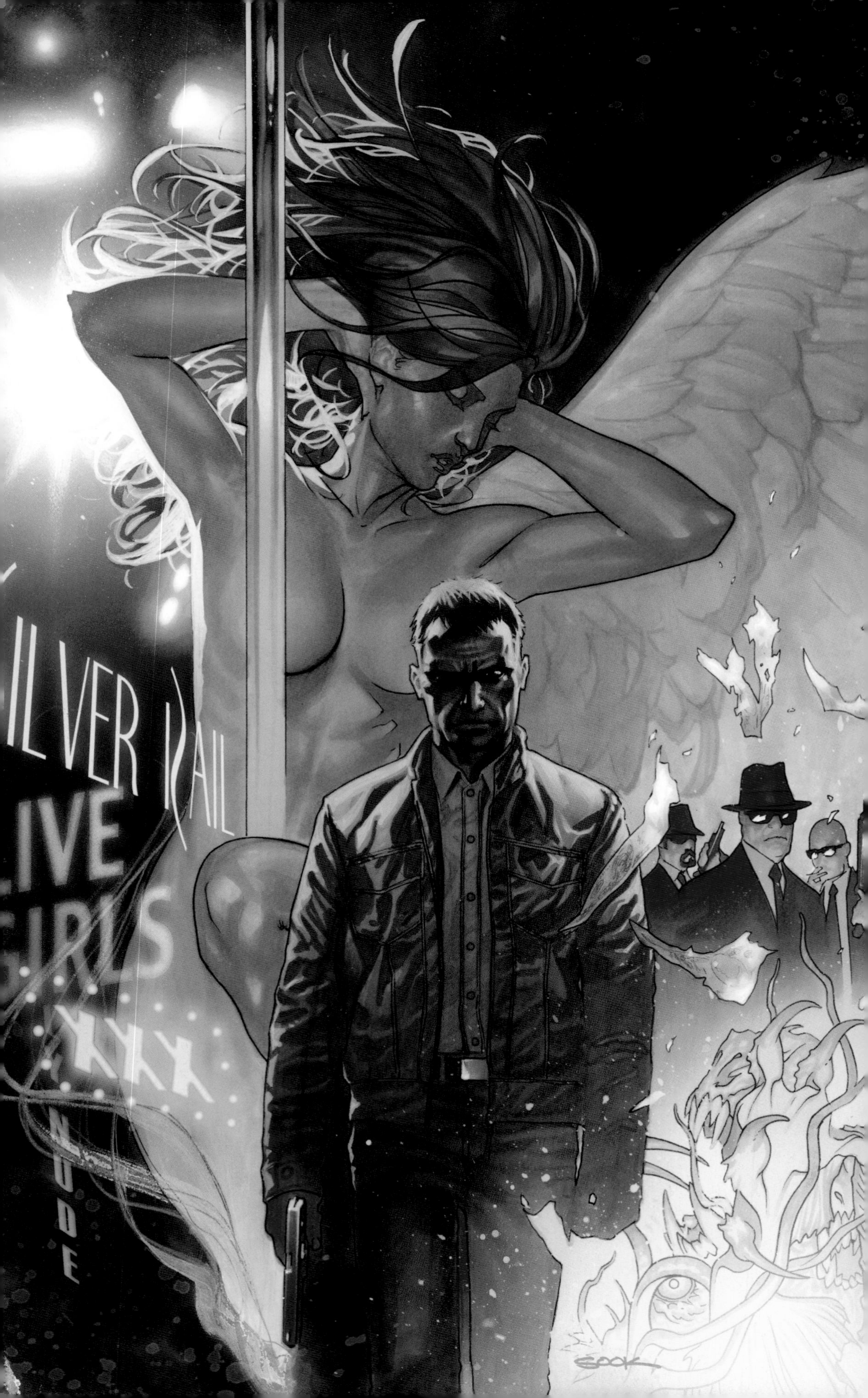
ILVER RAIL
IVE
IRLS
XXX
NUDE
SOOK

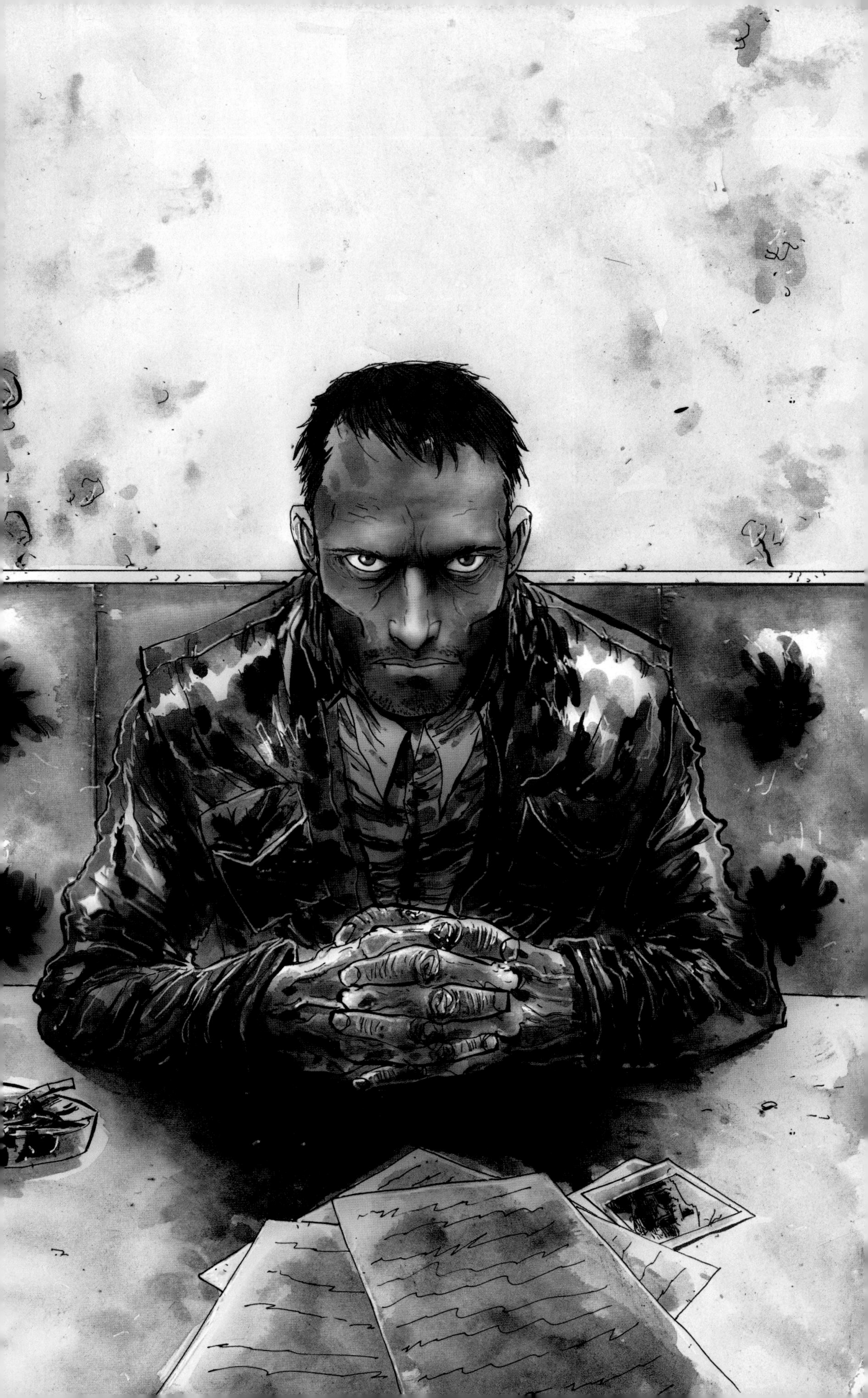

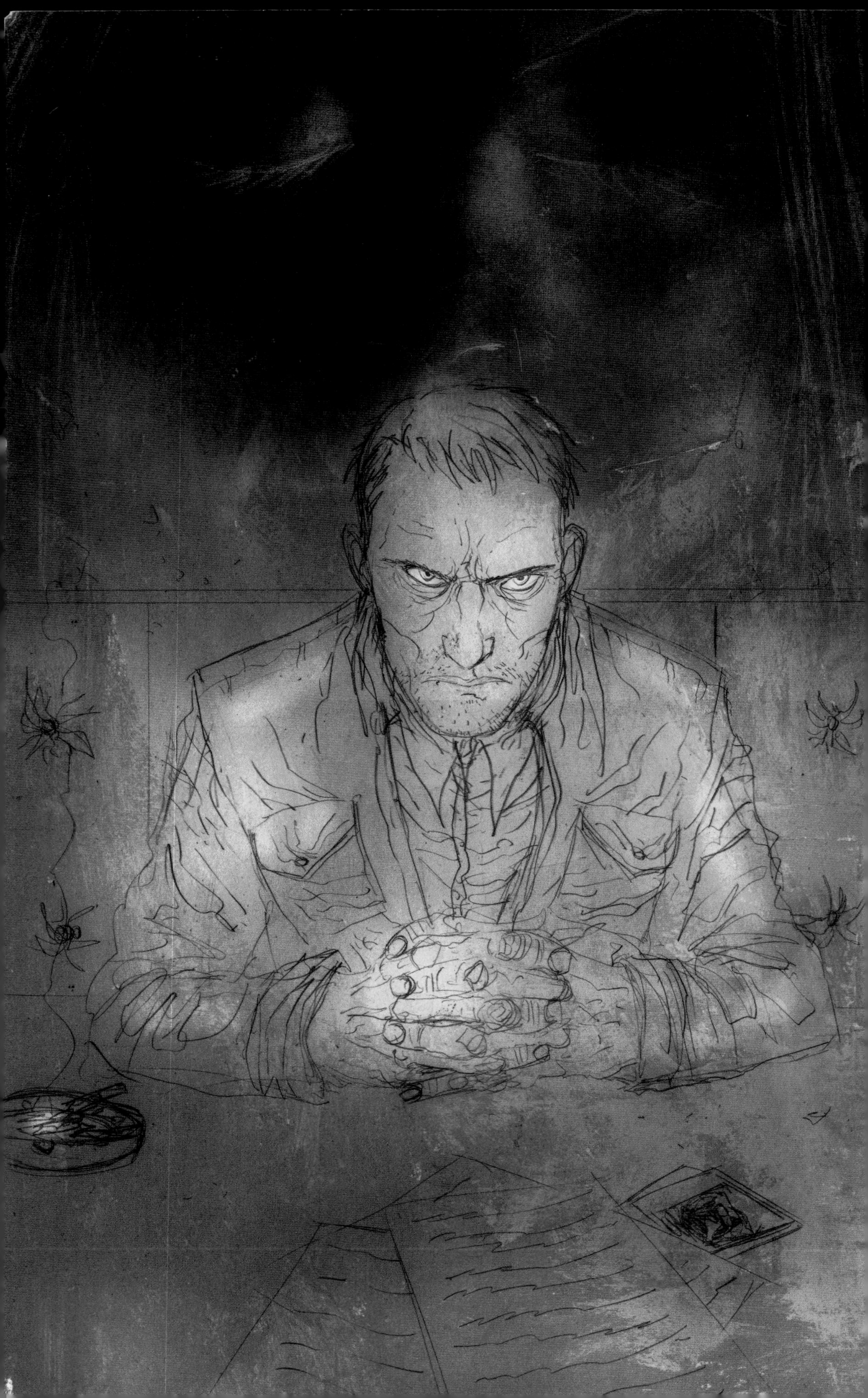

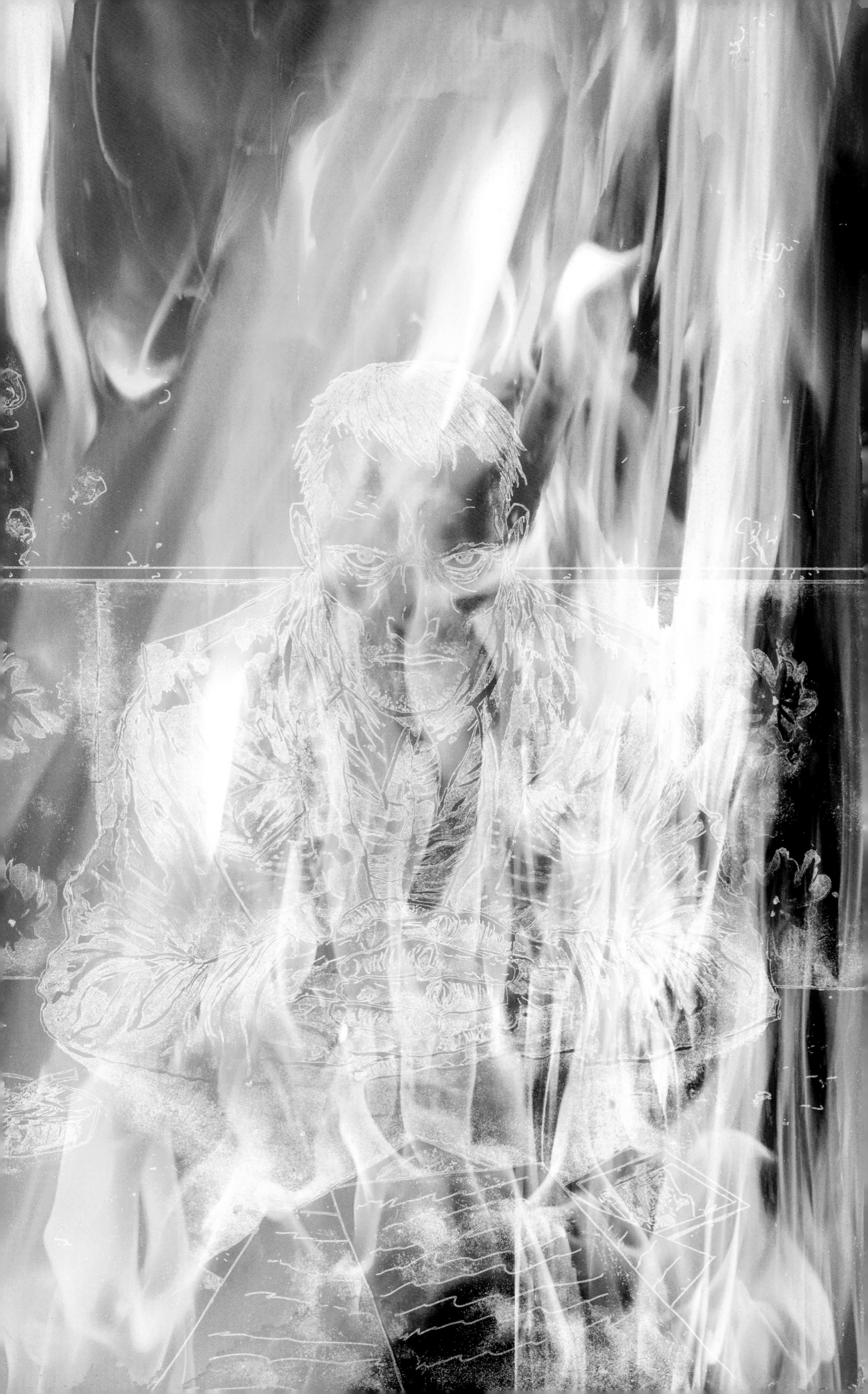

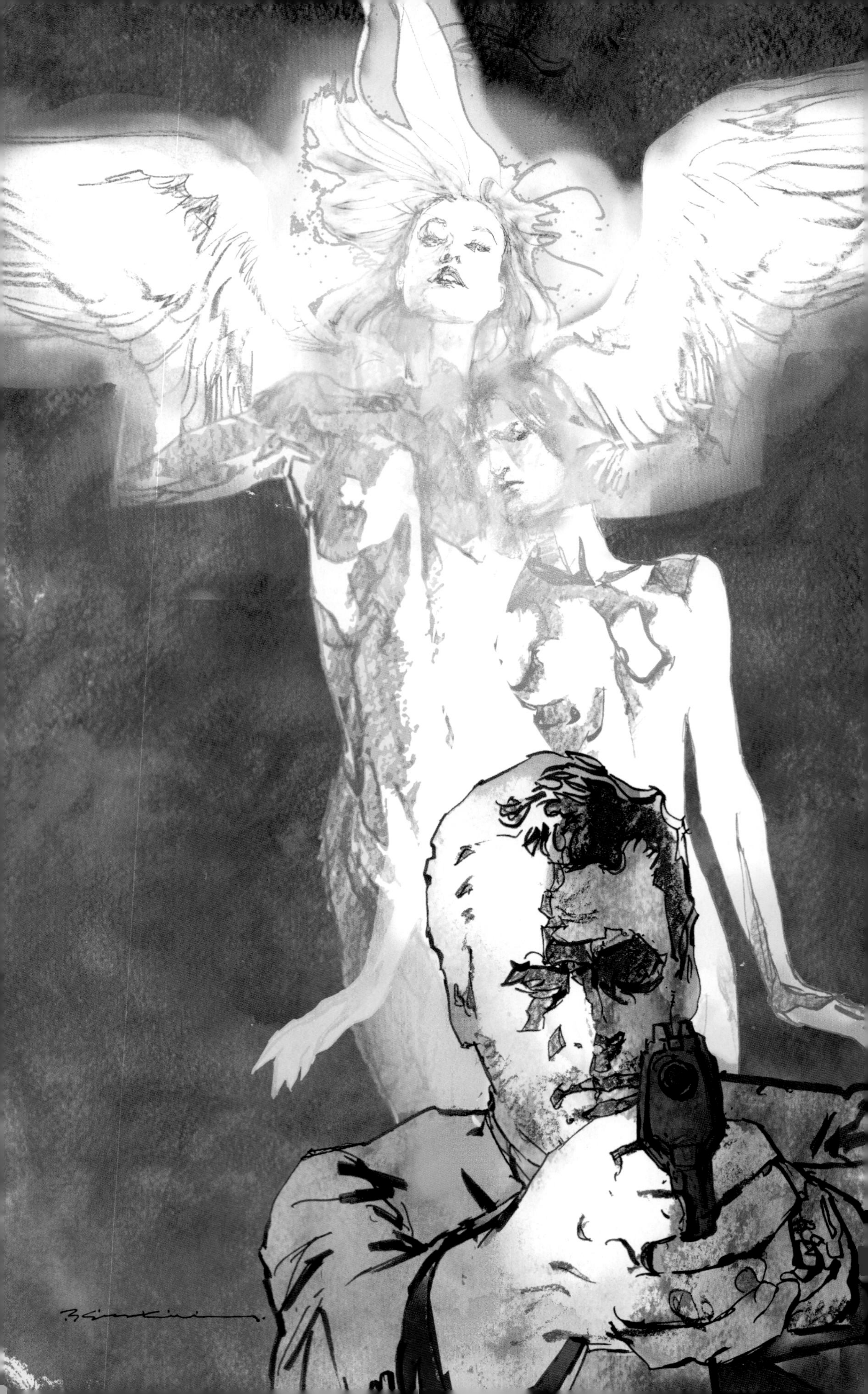

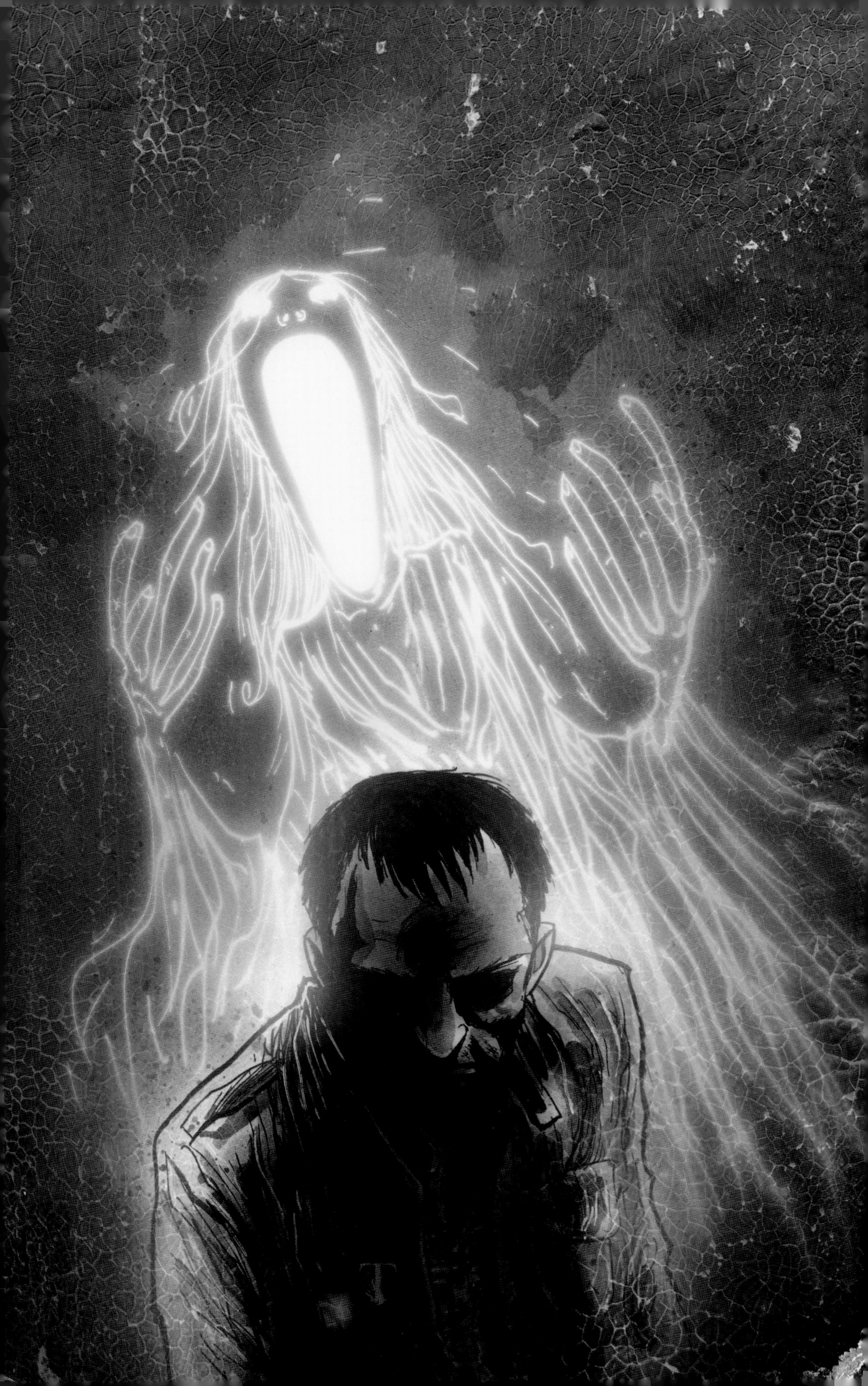

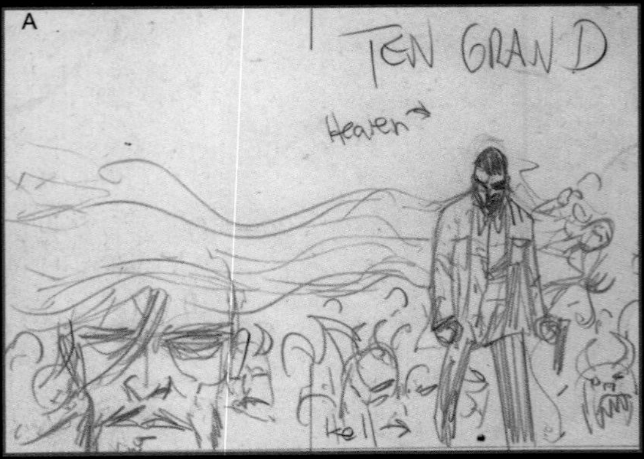
A
TEN GRAND
Heaven
Hell

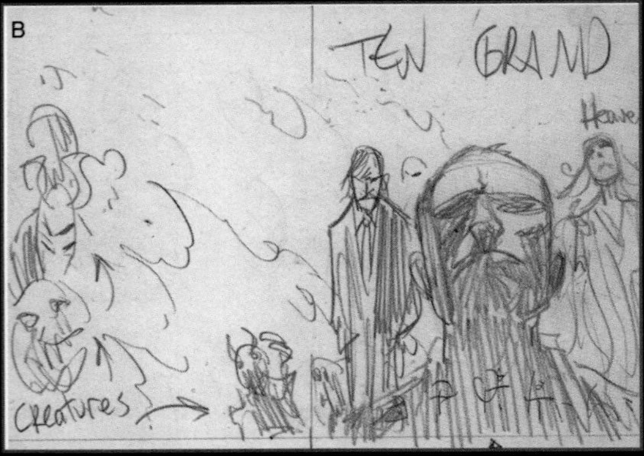
B
TEN GRAND
Creatures

# EVOLUTION OF THE COVER

AT RIGHT AND ABOVE, THUMBNAILS

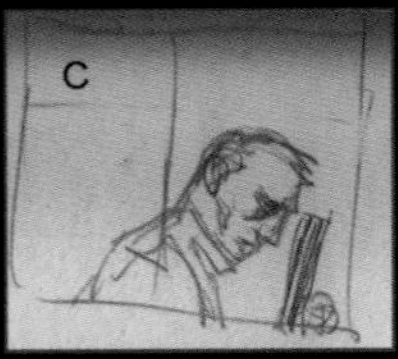
C

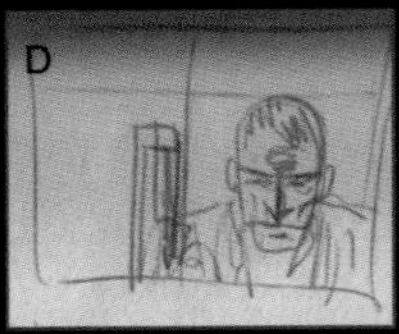
D

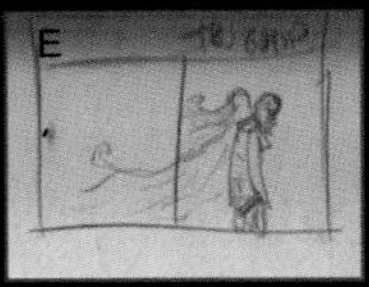
E

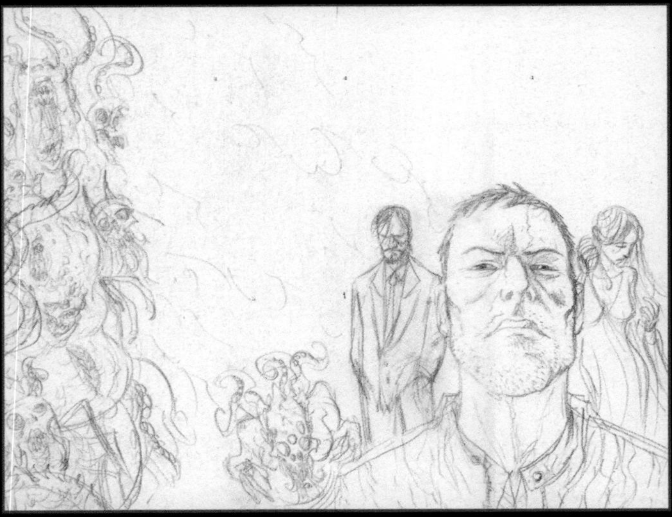

PENCILS

INKS

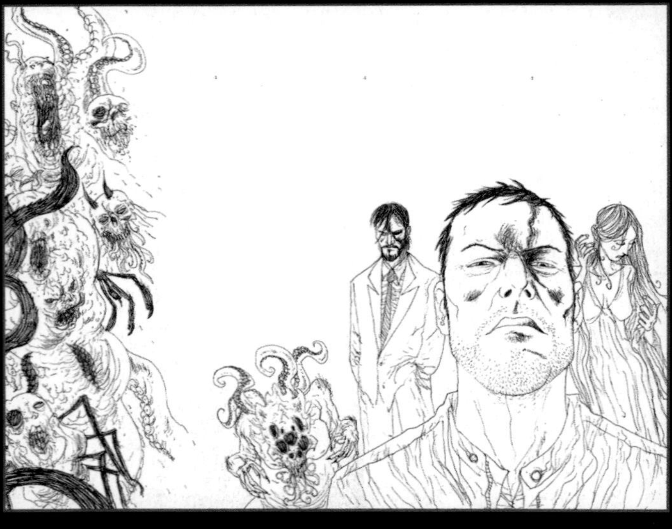

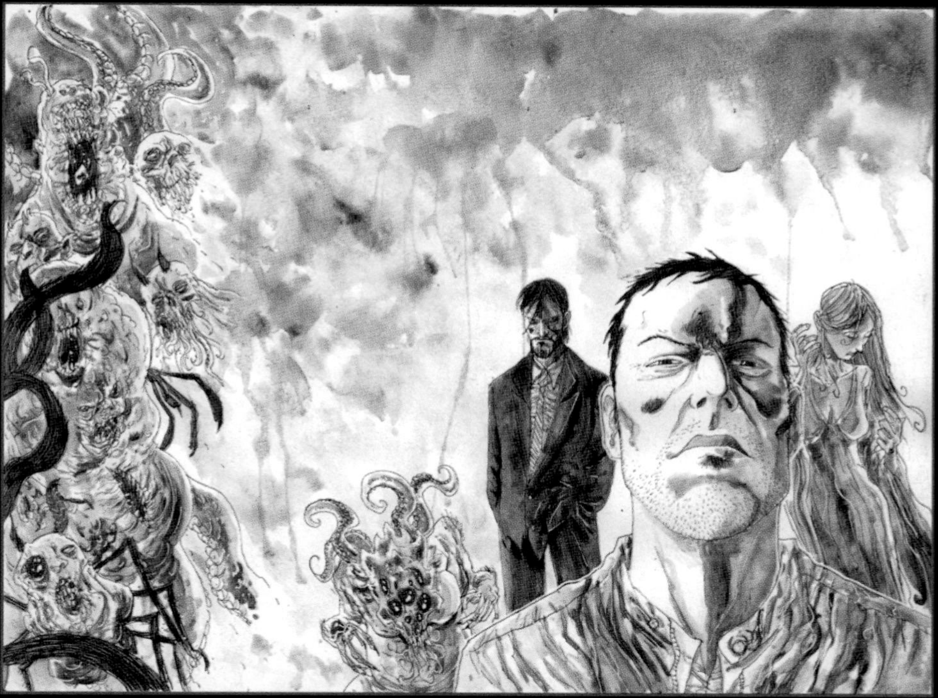

TONES

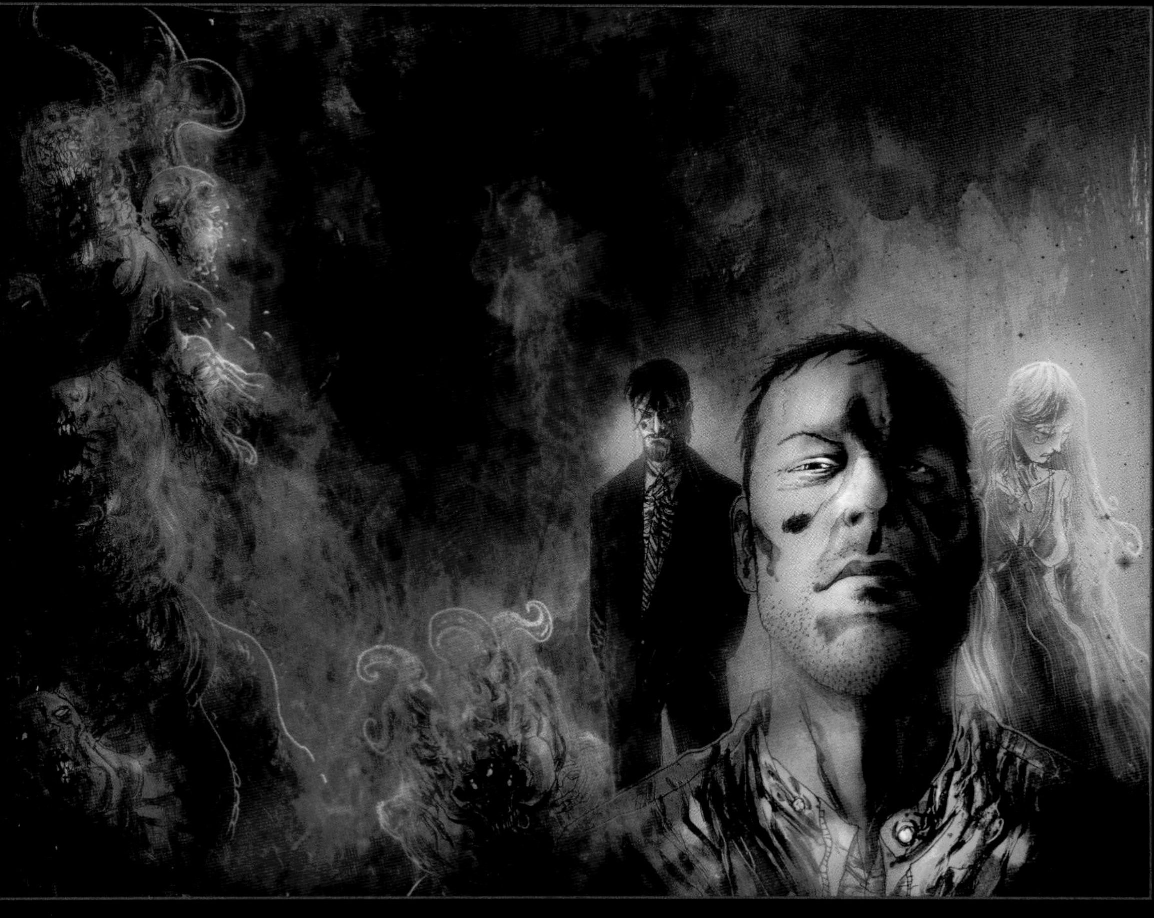

FINAL